Butterflies
of the World

H. L. Lewis

Butterflies of the World

Foreword by J. M. Chalmers-Hunt F.R.E.S.
President of The British Entomological and Natural History Society

CRESCENT BOOKS
New York

Dedicated to my wife, family and friends
who have assisted me in collecting butterflies
all over the world

Acknowledgments

This book could not possibly have been produced without
the kindness, patience and ever-helpful expertise of the
Keeper of Entomology at the British Museum (Natural
History) and his staff, to all of whom I owe an immense
debt of gratitude. Every butterfly illustrated is taken from
the wonderful treasure-house of the national collection,
which additionally contains a number of beautiful species
mentioned here only by name and not figured. Access to
this marvellous collection has indeed been a great
privilege for my helpers and myself, and we have done our
best to use it worthily.

To the team of helpers, too, I offer my thanks. Their
cheerful and careful collaboration over many months was
always an inspiration. The great skill of the photographers
and printers is self-evident. The goodwill and support of
the publisher was a constant encouragement to all of us.
It would be tedious—if indeed it were possible—to list all
those authors to whose works, great and small, I have
referred over the years in building up a personal check-list
of world butterflies, which is now embodied in this
volume. It is my hope that readers will get as much pleasure
out of consulting it as I have experienced in compiling it.

H. L. LEWIS
Hampton, Middlesex, 1973

First published in 1974 by George G. Harrap & Co.
Limited.

Published 1985 by Crescent Books, distributed by Crown
Publishers, Inc.

Library of Congress Cataloging in Publication Data:
Lewis, H. L. 1907–1978
Butterflies of the world.
Includes index.
1. Butterflies – Identification. 2. Butterflies – Pictorial
works. 3. Insects – Identification. 4. Insects – Pictorial
works. I. Title.
QL543.L4 1985   595.78'9 85-10927
ISBN 0-517-481650

Text © the estate of H. L. Lewis, 1973
Illustrations and the collective work
© Lionel Leventhal Limited, 1973

This book was designed and produced by Lionel
Leventhal Limited, 2–6 Hampstead High Street, London
NW3 1QQ. Photography by Michael Dyer Associates
Limited, London. Color origination by Drukkerij de Lange/
van Leer B.V., Deventer.

Printed in Yugoslavia

Contents

Foreword

by J. M. Chalmers-Hunt F.R.E.S.
President of The British Entomological and Natural History Society

An entirely new work on the world's butterflies has long been a desideratum and, with the availability of increased travel facilities, one urgently needed. What has been particularly required until now is not an exhaustive account of cumbersome proportions, but a guide to identification of convenient size which students and others interested in the butterflies of any country could easily use. 'Butterflies of the World' is such a book and, as far as I am aware, the first of its kind to be published.

In order to ensure the utmost accuracy in colour and detail, great care and painstaking skill have gone into each plate, so that these reproductions are among the most realistic in existence.

A feature of special interest too is the authenticity of the material figured: every specimen illustrated is in the renowned collection of the Department of Entomology at the British Museum (Natural History). The author, the photographer and the publisher are all to be congratulated on this book which, I feel sure, will prove invaluable to both the amateur and professional entomologist. I hope it will also stimulate fresh interest and bring delight to butterfly enthusiasts everywhere.

J. M. Chalmers-Hunt

Introduction

Butterflies are among nature's most beautiful gifts to mankind. They have been admired and studied for centuries ; every art form has used their colour and design as an embellishment ; and every man, woman and child has seen them.

It is nevertheless true to say that few people notice more than a very small percentage of the butterfly species that surround them ; fewer still can identify more than a dozen or so, and when folk leave their own country hardly anyone can recognize and name a butterfly in a foreign land.

This is remarkable. In a period when man is conscious as perhaps never before of his environment, he remains all but oblivious of one of its greatest charms. The aim of *Butterflies of the World* is to supply a pleasurable remedy, a fascinating, comprehensive, informed and superlatively beautiful remedy for this lacuna in our general knowledge.

It is possible to buy well-produced books devoted to butterflies, but even the best of them are invariably limited in their scope. They may show only the butterflies of a particular country or area which the author knows well, or they may be too deeply scientific or specialized for the intelligent general public, or insufficiently illustrated ; again, they may deal only with the larger butterflies, and virtually ignore the much more numerous and equally beautiful smaller species ; or the illustrations may be inadequate. Even if an enthusiast were to buy and carry around with him dozens of different volumes, he would still be far from achieving what *Butterflies of the World* enables him to do, for nowhere else will he find many of the illustrations and identifications given here.

The object of this book is therefore easily stated. *Butterflies of the World*, with nearly 7,000 photographic reproductions in colour of actual butterflies, seeks to present all those butterflies, large or small, for all regions of the world, which any ordinary mortal is likely to encounter. Virtually all genera (groups of species) are represented, and some 90 per cent of all but the most elusive species can be identified from the plates, text and index. The pages of this book portray more species than any but the most exhaustive museum collections can show.

The small and medium-sized butterflies are pictured life-size, for to reduce their scale would diminish unduly a full appreciation of their delicate markings. In order to keep the work to manageable proportions, however, certain families of larger butterflies are shown at various reduced scales, their larger natural sizes permitting this scaling down without significant loss of detail. This fact must be borne in mind when identifying specimens either captured or on the wing, and when applying the keys given in the text.

There are more than 10,000 species of butterfly known to science. To illustrate all these many thousands would be impracticable, and only of marginal use. It is impossible to distinguish visually between many of the formal species ; for exact identification they have to be dissected and minute physical variations studied. The differences between some species are often less obvious than those between sexes or subspecies ; and the differences between genera are often slight. Frequently the pattern and colouring of the female is quite different from that of the male, and many species have sub-species which do not closely resemble them. These subspecies may have developed through being established on, for example, different groups of islands, and over many hundreds of years have come to vary in size, shade of colour and so on from the original type, though still from certain character-istics recognizably the same basic species. Many species are, moreover, exceedingly rare, very local, or inhabit inaccessible regions and are not likely therefore to be observed by any but the most intrepid collectors or natural historians.

To illustrate all these species, with their females and subspecies, would require more than 20,000 colour photographs, and a voluminous text and index. The problem has been to keep illustrations and text within practical limits of size and cost without encroaching unacceptably on the purpose of the book.

Because this book is intended to assist in identifying all species, not just to illustrate particularly beautiful or interesting ones, much care and thought has been given not only to the selection of species for illustration but also to whether male or female should be illustrated, whether upper-side or under-side, or possibly all of these features, as well as whether additional notes should be given in the text. Where the under-side has been considered to offer the readiest means of identification, then this has been illustrated. Sometimes the under-side pattern of one species aids the recognition of other species of the same genus, whose upper-side may not be particularly distinctive ; or it may help determine the females of a species or genus which may not otherwise be recognizable as such. In the same way, the illustration of one or two females of a genus may indicate the broad pattern of coloration in many other species of that same genus. But in the interests of economy — both of space and of cost — where illustrations of both the upper-side and of the under-side or of male and female of similar species are desirable for certainty of identification, recourse has sometimes been made to reproducing, for example, the whole upper-side of a butterfly with only half of the under-side alongside it, the whole being the left hand of the picture and the under-side represented by the right-hand half.

Sometimes several visually similar species are individually named in the index without each being illustrated on the plates, a brief statement of the differences being included in the text. Where very similar species are found in geographically separate areas, it has in general been thought sufficient to indicate broadly the area in which a given species flies, and not to specify any minor differences. Nevertheless, by careful study of the illustrations and text, many more butterflies can be identified than can possibly be illustrated ; and it may well be that this study will add an interest and satisfaction that mere visual identification would not give.

Some additional aids to identification that will emerge from study may include such general observations that, as might be expected, the body of the female tends to be stouter than that of the male, and the wings larger, because the female has to carry the eggs. The female's wings (a nice feminine touch) are often rounder, less pointed. Among the Nymphalidae the females are usually more sombrely coloured than the males (they seem in life to have a retiring disposition and are not often seen flaunting, disporting and quarrelling as the males do). In the Satyridae, Amathusidae and Danaidae the female is often lighter in colour, and the male may have a dark sex-brand on the upper-side forewing. As for the Pieridae, the female is in general more heavily marked, usually with black, than the male. Black borders tend to be wider, the wings have additional black spots or patches, and the whole colour scheme is duller and less vivid. The female Hesperid, on the contrary, tends to be less heavily marked than the male and to have additional, or larger, light-coloured spots or patches. Among the Lycaenidae and Nemeobiidae the male is usually the brighter coloured, the female sometimes being uniformly dark brown on the upper-side, with only its under-side giving a clue to its real identity.

The Colour Plates
These provide the basic means of identification, and are reproductions of actual butterflies. Highly accurate though they are, it must not be supposed that there will be no differences apparent between the plate and a specimen waiting to be named. The insects figured have been selected as the norm of a species, but there are inevitably small variations from specimen to specimen, just as there are between human beings. On the other hand, many species closely resemble other species, so that in such cases very careful study of the wing patterns, size and shape and location of markings is essential for correct identification. Sometimes, even with the utmost care, a firm identification will not prove possible, but the genus should always be clear, and the species too, within narrow margins.

As has been explained, the illustrations of certain whole families have been reduced in size. Whole families have been so treated rather than individual large butterflies, because it is necessary in the text to specify, for example, 'larger than similar species', and this would not make sense unless all the species in a genus, and often similar genera, were not equally reduced. Such a reduction in size necessarily decreases the grandeur of certain species. This is sad, but the first object of the book is identification, which this reduction does not impede.

The arrangement of Plates, Text and Index
In order to make the initial identification of the butterflies easier, the plates are grouped,into the following geographical areas :
1. Europe, including Africa north of the Sahara
2. North America
3. South and Central America
4. Africa south of the Sahara
5. Asia south of the Himalayas and Australasia (called here the Indo-Australasian region.)
6. Asia north of the Himalayas, including China and Japan
(Note that sections 1 and 6 cover the Palearctic region.)

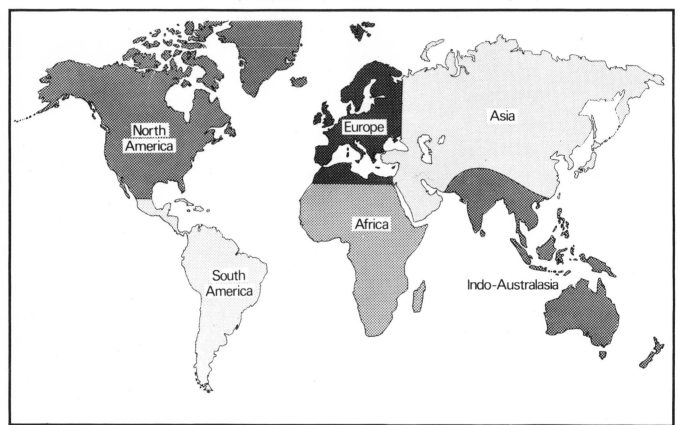

For each of these areas the relevant plates are arranged in similar sequence, all the butterflies of a family being grouped together, the genera alphabetically within the family, and the species alphabetically within genera. The text follows the pages of plates and is arranged and numbered to correspond.

This geographical grouping is chosen because the natural barriers represented by the Sahara, the Himalayas, the oceans and the isthmus of Panama have caused rather specialized development of species within these large but isolated areas, so that not many species overlap from one area into another. Thus the collector of a butterfly in, say, Sri Lanka will turn to section 5 of the plates in the first place. If his butterfly is not figured there, he will then try section 6. It is geographically unlikely that his butterfly will appear in the other sections. There are, however, a very few butterflies of world-wide distribution whose illustrations might be found in sections 1, 5 and 6.

The Text
The text has been kept to a minimum. The generic and specific names of the butterfly and its author are given, and the country or locality where it is most

frequently seen. Butterflies do not need passports to cross frontiers, so their areas of travel do not have precise limits, and frequently overlap those of similar species. Nevertheless, a knowledge of where certain butterflies are likely to be met will certainly aid identification.

Where a type of terrain — for example, mountain, desert, forest or other conditions — provides the 'normal' habitat of a species, a note is included to this effect. Similarly, the food plant is mentioned if this is known, for it may help in locating a species. Small items of particular interest, such as 'dependence on ants', or popular names, are inserted where appropriate.

The text describing any species also includes, as previously indicated, a short list of similar species or subspecies, with a brief list of points of difference ; where the female is notably different from the male of the same species the differences are mentioned. Often a genus, or genera, or many species share similar habits, coloration, appearance or some other characteristic ; general notes to this effect are prefixed to the text under the heading 'General Identification Notes'.

In order to avoid repetition of headings, the information in the text follows a set pattern for each species :

Scientific name and author thereof
Common name
Areas of distribution
Terrain normally inhabited
Larval food plants (Lfp)
Resemblances and differences between sexes
Additional information
Varieties and subspecies (S/S)
Similar species

In every case the first two items will be found in the text, and in many cases they will be the only entries.

Technical terms have been avoided as far as possible in descriptions. 'Costas', 'interspaces', 'cells', 'dorsum' and so on, are not used because they imply the presence of a degree of descriptive detail which is incompatible with the broad imagery of this book. Simple English has been sufficient for the immediate purpose.

The following terms and abbreviations are used in the book :

Species.	Butterflies that interbreed and produce offspring similar to themselves ; different species cannot interbreed, subspecies may.
Genus.	A number of similar species which are given the same generic name.
Family	A number of related genera.
Name.	A butterfly's scientific name is compounded of the generic name (spelt with a capital initial) a specific name (no capital letter and often a subspecific name. For instance, the common small cabbage-white is Pieris rapae ; the very similar subspecies from Hong Kong is Pieris rapae crucivora.
N,E,S,W,C.	Points of the compass, and 'Central'.
♂ ♀	Male and female, the signs of Mars and Venus respectively.
UP, UN.▽△	Upper-side, under-side.
UPF, UPH.	Upper-side forewing, upper-side hindwing.
UNF, UNH.	Under-side forewing, under-side hindwing.
WSF, DSF.	Wet season form, dry season form (which may vary widely in areas where the rainy season is a concentrated one).

The Index
The index entry gives reference only to plate number and the insect's number on the plate. Plate numbers and insect numbers are also shown throughout the text, so that the index serves text as well as plates. Species indexed in italics are not illustrated, but the textual and plate reference given for each should enable the specimen to be identified pictorially. This covers those few inquiries where the name of a butterfly is known but its appearance is not.

A number of species are neither illustrated nor described, but this is very small in proportion to the whole. Those species omitted entirely are generally extremely rare or inhabit inaccessible territory, and are thus unlikely to be encountered by most collectors ; or else they so much resemble other species that pictorial differentiation is impossible, and only dissection and examination can provide precise evidence of identity.

Nomenclature

Entomology is a living study. New species and subspecies are constantly being discovered, and often modern examination of insects previously thought to be of the same species has shown that this is not the case. In the same way, previously accepted species are sometimes found not to be true species, but only subspecies. Clearly, such butterflies have to be renamed. In some cases very large groups of butterflies have not yet been fully studied, or the conclusions reached about them by a researcher have not yet become universally accepted. The genus Thecla and its species in South America is an example.

It is not therefore claimed that the names and classifications given in this book are universally acceptable. Finality in nomenclature may well lie a century or more in the future. But the names given in the book are those commonly in use, and to be found in the latest works of scholarship, and will be recognized by any competent entomologist.

This book, accurate and scientific within its limits, cannot possibly be wholly comprehensive. For many countries of the world there are far more detailed accounts of the butterflies of particular areas available ; but for many other areas there exist either no publications at all, or very poor ones, or productions written in a foreign language only ; and illustrations, where any are included, may often be more confusing than helpful, because so many are reproduced in monochrome only.

Butterflies of the World, whilst intended primarily as a scientific book, is also designed to give pleasure to the general reader, and can be used profitably by anyone anywhere in the world for both enjoyment and reference.

Key to life sizes

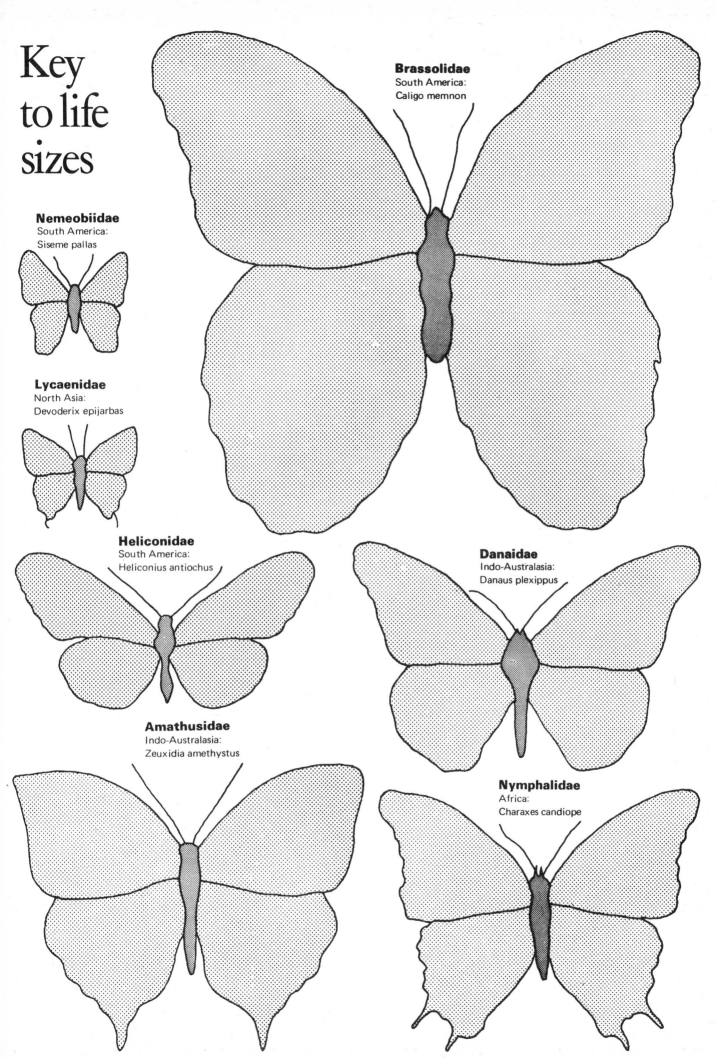

Brassolidae
South America:
Caligo memnon

Nemeobiidae
South America:
Siseme pallas

Lycaenidae
North Asia:
Devoderix epijarbas

Heliconidae
South America:
Heliconius antiochus

Danaidae
Indo-Australasia:
Danaus plexippus

Amathusidae
Indo-Australasia:
Zeuxidia amethystus

Nymphalidae
Africa:
Charaxes candiope

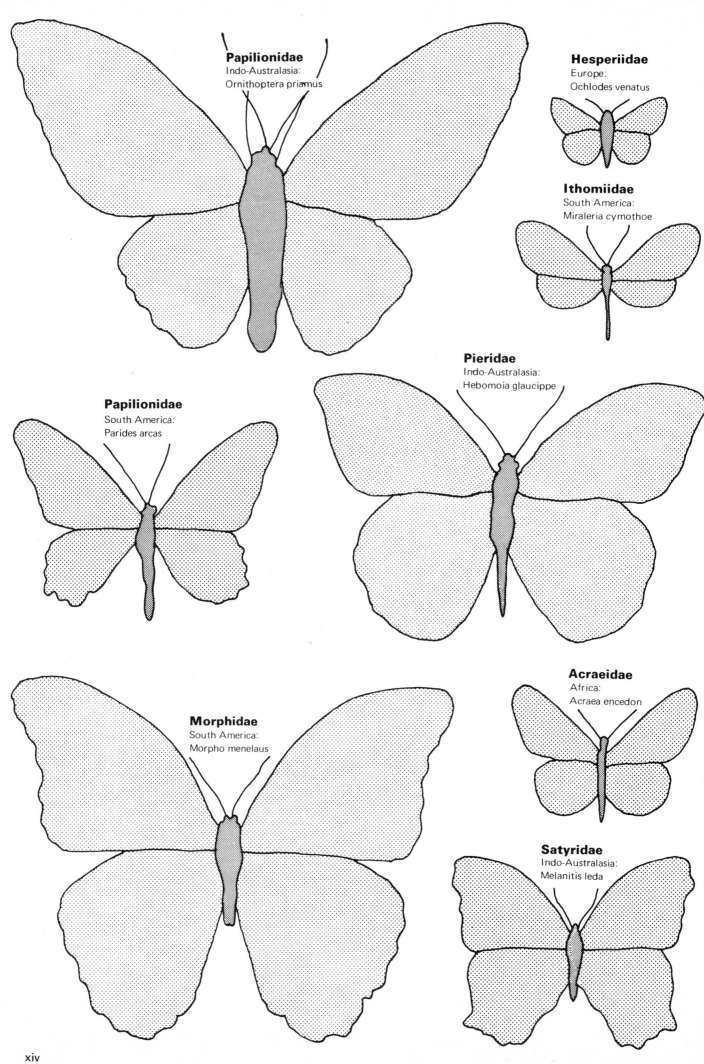

Papilionidae
Indo-Australasia:
Ornithoptera priamus

Hesperiidae
Europe:
Ochlodes venatus

Ithomiidae
South America:
Miraleria cymothoe

Papilionidae
South America:
Parides arcas

Pieridae
Indo-Australasia:
Hebomoia glaucippe

Acraeidae
Africa:
Acraea encedon

Morphidae
South America:
Morpho menelaus

Satyridae
Indo-Australasia:
Melanitis leda

xiv

General Identification Notes

ACRAEA
In this genus the females are often paler than the males or have white bars or patches on UPF or UNF. The UN of the sexes is similar, and the actual number and spacing of the spots on the wings is a major help to identification.

AGRIAS
Of this magnificent genus hardly two specimens have the same colouring and marking. Of all the species there are many forms and subspecies.

ANTHENE
The females frequently are very different from the male UP, often being black with a greater or lesser white area. Known as 'Hairtails' in South Africa.

BEBEARIA
Although the females are usually larger than the males and frequently differ in colour or marking, the undersides are similarly marked and provide a ready means of identification. The females often have dark wing tips spotted or banded with white, or with yellowish transverse bands on the UPF.

BEMATISTES (formerly Planema)
The females differ from the males in the bands and patches often being whitish instead of yellow to orange brown. The number and spacing of the spots on the hindwing is a great help in separating closely allied species.

BIBASIS
The genus is crepuscular, flying in twilight at dusk and dawn, when the click of their wings can be heard as they turn in flight even though they themselves cannot be seen in the darkness.

CANDALIDES
A large genus with many similar species distributed among the islands near New Guinea. Practically every island has its own form, differing slightly from the form on neighbouring islands.

CATONEPHELE
With one exception the species of Catonephele, both male and female, greatly resemble each other. Therefore only a few species are figured.

CATOPSILIA
This genus is commonly known as the 'Migrants'.

CHARAXES
Male sometimes with no tail, or one tail less than female. They feed on sap and rotting fruit.

COLIAS
In this genus the females generally have more dark markings on the forewing than the males. They are commonly called 'Sulphurs'.

COLOTIS
Tend to develop wet and dry season forms. The wet (summer) season forms usually have stronger black markings on UP, which in the dry season may disappear entirely. They are commonly called 'Orange Tips'.

CYMOTHOE
Male and female often quite different in colouring. Females usually dark, often with white vertical bands on each wing, sometimes very broad; in other cases they have the same colouring but with broad dark borders to the wings.

DANAUS
This genus is commonly known as the 'Tigers'.

DELIAS
In this genus the females often have the upper wings, especially the forewing, darkened or with black markings broader than in the males. LFP is often mistletoe. Commonly known as 'Jezebels'.

DEUDORIX
The females often dark, blackish brown UP, but UN similar to male UN.

DIAETHRIA
The species is remarkably uniform on the UN, which is characterised by 'figure of eight' markings. Many species are also very similar on UP; only a selection are therefore illustrated.

EPITOLA
Most are rare, the females are often not known and when they are known differ from the males, often by a whitish band UPF.

ERYNNIS
A large and similar genus of butterflies, where often the male genitalia or dissection are the only means of identification. For this reason only a selection is illustrated.

EUPHAEDRA
Shade loving forest butterflies.

EUPLOEA
This genus is commonly known as the 'Crows'.

EUPTYCHIA
The common name in the U.S.A. is 'Satyrs'; they occur mostly in woods.

EUREMA
This genus is commonly known as the 'Grass Yellows'.

EURYPHENE
Male and female almost always dissimilar. The males usually dark, iridescent, faintly patterned, the females frequently with a transverse white or yellow band on the forewing. Both sexes usually with a dark dot in UNH cell.

HAMADRYAS
These butterflies make a loud clicking or rattling sound when they fly, but settle on tree trunks with head down and wings spread flat, so that they resemble the lichen on the bark.

HASORA
This genus is commonly known as the 'Awls'.

HELICONIUS
This is a most remarkable genus, confined entirely to tropical America, whose markings are mimicked by many other genera, although basically the pattern of the markings varies but little. This makes identifications very difficult indeed, and on the wing in life impossible.

HESPERIDAE
In the Family of Hesperidae there are many genera within which the species are most difficult to distinguish; sometimes elaborate

dissection is required. This situation is particularly prevalent in the South American Hesperidae, so that in many cases one or two illustrations have to suffice to cover perhaps fifteen species. In such cases the aim has been to enable identification of the genus rather than the species.

HYPOCHRYSOPS
This genus is commonly known in Australia as the 'Jewels'. A species in which the male UP is usually blue with a black border, the females with lighter blue or white patches on their wings. UN similar.

HYPOLYCAENA
This genus is commonly known as the 'Tits'.

IOLAUS
This genus is commonly known in South Africa as 'Sapphires'. LFP is often mistletoe on Mimosa trees.

JALMENUS
Another genus of Lycaenids, attended by ants. There are several such Lycaenid genera.

JAMIDES
This genus is commonly known as the 'Ceruleans'.

JEMADIA
Another genus where it is very difficult to separate the species.

KEDESTES
This genus is commonly known in South Africa as 'Rangers'.

LETHE
The females often have a white diagonal band on the forewings. The larvae generally feed on bamboo, which is where the butterflies are usually found.

LIPHYRA
The larvae feed on the ant larvae in the arboreal nests of the Green Tree-Ant.

METISELLA
This genus is commonly known in South Africa as 'Sylphs'.

MIMERESIA
The females tend to have more extensive colour on the UPF.

MYCALESIS
This genus is commonly known as 'Bush Browns'.

NACADUBA
A large genus of small blue butterflies all very similar in appearance, variable, and the species only distinguishable by very slight differences. Several species are therefore not illustrated.

NARATHURA
This genus is commonly known as the 'Oak Blues'. A large genus, the males in general a shining blue or green UP, the females being usually duller and with wider black borders. The surest way of identification is by the UN, and even this is often very difficult and resort has to be had to dissection. Only a selection of the more striking species therefore is illustrated.

NEMEOBIIDAE
The American common name for the species

of this family in North America is 'Metalmarks'. It is a large family and the genera are difficult to separate out and identify.

NEPTIS
A very large genus with many species hard to identify. They commonly are black with yellow or white barred wings in a great variety of similar combinations.

OENEIS
Commonly known as the 'Arctics', extremely hairy to withstand cold. The larvae feed on lichens and grasses and hibernate as larvae.

OGYRIS
This is an Australian genus, only otherwise found in New Guinea. The larvae feed on Loranthus.

ORNITHOPTERA
This genus is commonly known as 'Birdwings'.

OSMODES
From West African primeval tropical forests. The females UP differs from the males.

PARATHYMA
Like neptis, black and white or black and orange, and like them in many very similar combinations which make identification difficult.

PARNARA, PELOPIDAS AND BORBO
Three similar genera commonly known as 'Swifts'.

PEDALIODES
A large genus of mostly high-altitude butterflies from the Cordillera of Colombia and Bolivia. Owing to their similarities only a few representative species are illustrated.

PHASIS
This genus is commonly known in South Africa as 'Coppers'.

PHILIRIS
This genus is commonly known as the 'Moonbeams'.

PHYCIODES (in North America)
A numerous genus of small orange brown butterflies, some species being only possible to identify by dissection. The winter brood is darker than the summer one.

PIERIDAE
The females are commonly darker than males on the upper side, have broader black borders or more dark markings.

PLATYLESCHES
This genus is commonly known in South Africa as 'Hoppers'.

PRECIS
Very marked seasonal dimorphism is common in this genus. This affects markings and wing shape. Generally the dry season forms are larger, the wings are more falcate (so that when closed they resemble a leaf), the under surface is dull and almost unmarked except for a median band that looks like the stalk of a leaf, and very often dark blue or brown tones replace the white markings on the upper surface.

PYRRHOPYGE
A numerous genus of extremely similar species, many of which are scarcely separable as distinct species. A selection of

the more readily distinguishable is illustrated.

SARANGESA
A large number of species, all very alike. The species illustrated give a good cross-section of their appearance.

SPIALIA
A group of small butterflies very difficult to separate into species. A few typical Spialia are illustrated; there are several others scarcely to be separated by illustration and therefore omitted. Commonly called 'Sandmen' in South Africa.

TARACTROCERA
This genus is commonly known as 'Grass Darts'.

TELICOTA
This genus contains a large number of very similar species; a selection only is illustrated.

THYSONOTIS
A number of very similar species from the New Guinea area, the males of a bright blue colour and the females of dark brown to black colouring.

PAPILIONIDAE (1:2)

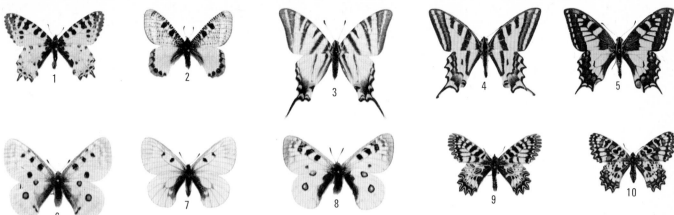

NYMPHALIDAE (3:4)

1. Allancastria cerisyi
2. Archon apollinus
3. Iphiclides podalirius
4. Papilio alexanor
5. Papilio machaon
6. Parnassius apollo
7. Parnassius mnemosyne
8. Parnassius phoebus
9. Zerinthia polyxena
10. Zerinthia rumina ♀

11. Aglais urticae
12. Apatura ilia
13. Limenitis reducta
14. Araschnia levana
15. Argynnis paphia
16. Araschnia levana
17. Boloria pales ▽
18. Argynnis paphia ♀ ▽ △
19. Argyronome laodice ▽ △
20. Brenthis daphne ♀ ▽ △

21. Brenthis hecate ♀ ▽ △
22. Charaxes jasius
23. Boloria pales △
24. Brenthis ino ▽ △
25. Clossiana chariclea ▽ △
26. Clossiana euphrosyne
27. Clossiana frigga ▽ △
28. Clossiana dia ▽ △

1

1. Clossiana polaris ▽△
2. Clossiana selene △
3. Clossiana selene ▽
4. Clossiana thore ▽△
5. Clossiana titania ▽△
6. Euphydryas aurinia
7. Euphydryas aurinia ♀ ▽△
8. Euphydryas cynthia
9. Euphydryas desfontainii
10. Euphydryas iduna ▽△
11. Euphydryas maturna ▽△
12. Fabriciana adippe
13. Fabriciana adippe ▽△
14. Fabriciana adippe
15. Fabriciana elisa ▽△
16. Fabriciana niobe ▽
17. Inachis io ♀
18. Fabriciana niobe △
19. Issoria lathonia △
20. Issoria lathonia ▽
21. Apatura iris
22. Limenitis populi
23. Ladoga camilla
24. Neptis sappho
25. Nymphalis antiopa
26. Nymphalis polychloros
27. Nymphalis xanthomelas ♀
28. Melitaea cinxia ▽△

PIERIDAE (1:1)

1. Melitaea diamina
2. Melitaea didyma ♀ △
3. Melitaea didyma
4. Melitaea phoebe △
5. Melitaea trivia
6. Mellicta asteria
7. Mellicta athalia △
8. Mellicta athalia ▽
9. Mellicta aurelia △
10. Mellicta aurelia ▽
11. Mellicta deione ▽△
12. Mellicta parthenoides ▽△
13. Mesoacidalia aglaja ▽
14. Mesoacidalia aglaja △
15. Polygonia c-album
16. Pologonia egea
17. Pandoriana pandora ♀ ▽△
18. Vanessa atalanta
19. Vanessa cardui
20. Anthocharis belia ▽△
21. Anthocharis cardamines ▽△
22. Anthocharis cardamines ♀ ▽
23. Anthocharis damone ▽△
24. Anthocharis gruneri ▽△
25. Aporia crataegi
26. Colias chrysotheme ♂♀
27. Colias crocea ♂
28. Colias crocea ♀

3

1. Colias erate ♀
2. Colias erate ♂
3. Colias hecla ♂ ♀
4. Colias hyale ♂ ▽△
5. Colias hyale ♀
6. Colias nastes

7. Colias palaeno ♂ ♀
8. Colias phicomone ♂ △
9. Colotis daira
10. Elphinstonia charlonia ▽△
11. Euchloe belemia ▽△
12. Euchloe pechi ▽△

13. Pieris mannii
14. Gonepteryx cleopatra
15. Gonepteryx rhamni
16. Pieris brassicae
17. Euchloe tagis ▽△
18. Leptidea sinapis

4

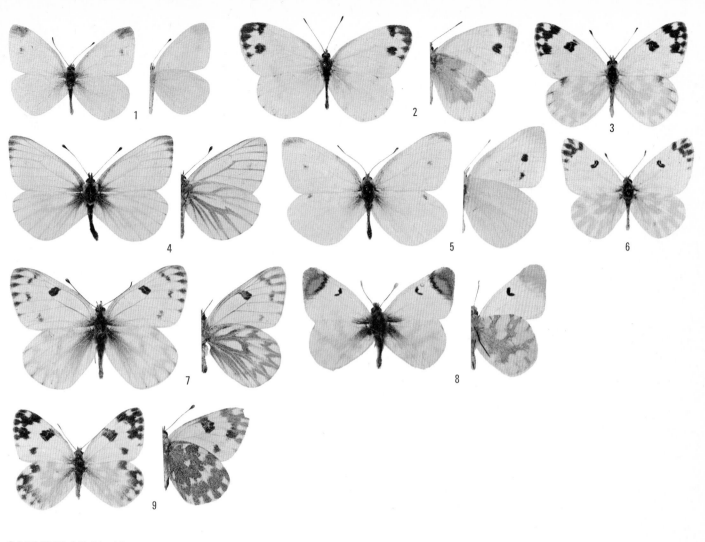

SATYRIDAE (1:1)

1. Pieris ergane ▽△
2. Pieris krueperi ▽△
3. Pontia daplidice
4. Pieris napi ▽△
5. Pieris rapae ▽△
6. Pontia chloridice

7. Synchloe callidice ▽△
8. Zegris eupheme ▽△
9. Pontia daplidice ♀ ▽△
10. Aphantopus hyperantus ▽△
11. Arethusana arethusa ▽△
12. Coenonympha arcanioides

13. Berberia abdelkader ♀ ▽△
14. Brintesia circe ▽△
15. Coenonympha arcania △▽
16. Coenonympha corinna
17. Coenonympha dorus ▽△
18. Coenonympha glycerion △

5

1. Coenonympha hero ▽△
2. Coenonympha iphiodes
3. Coenonympha leander
4. Coenonympha oedippus ▽△
5. Coenonympha pamphilus
6. Coenonympha tullia ▽△
7. Chazara briseis ▽△
8. Chazara prieuri

9. Erebia aethiops ▽△
10. Erebia disa ▽△
11. Erebia epiphron ▽△
12. Erebia epistygne ▽△
13. Erebia gorgone ▽△
14. Erebia ligea ▽△
15. Erebia melas ▽△
16. Erebia mnestra ▽△

17. Erebia oeme ▽△
18. Erebia pronoe
19. Erebia phegea ▽△
20. Erebia tyndarus ▽
21. Erebia tyndarus △
22. Erebia zapateri
23. Hipparchia alcyone

1. Hipparchia hansii ▽△
2. Hipparchia semele △
3. Hipparchia semele ♀ ▽
4. Hipparchia statilinus ▽△
5. Hyponephele lupinus
6. Hyponephele lycaon ♂

7. Hyponephele lycaon ♀
8. Lasiommata megera ▽△
9. Kirinia roxelana
10. Lasiommata maera
11. Lopinga achine ▽△
12. Maniola jurtina ♂

13. Maniola jurtina ♀
14. Melanargia galathea
15. Melanargia ines
16. Melanargia larissa ▽△

7

1. Melanargia occitanica ▽△
2. Melanargia russiae ▽△
3. Pyronia cecilia
4. Minois dryas △
5. Oeneis glacialis ♀▽♂△
6. Pseudochazara geyeri

7. Oeneis jutta ▽△
8. Oeneis norna ♂▽♀△
9. Pyronia bathseba ▽△
10. Pararge aegeria ▽△
11. Pyronia janiroides ♂♀
12. Pyronia tithonus ♀

13. Pseudochazara hippolyte
14. Satyrus actaea △
15. Satyrus actaea ▽
16. Pseudochazara mamurra ▽△
17. Pyronia tithonus ♂
18. Pseudotergumia fidia ▽△

LYCAENIDAE (1:1)

1. Agriades pyrenaicus
2. Agrodiaetus admetus ▽△
3. Agrodiaetus damon
4. Agrodiaetus damon
5. Agrodiaetus dolus
6. Albulina orbitulus △
7. Albulina orbitulus ▽
8. Aricia agestis △▽
9. Aricia anteros
10. Aricia nicias ♀ ▽△
11. Callophrys avis
12. Callophrys rubi △
13. Celastrina argiolus ▽△
14. Celastrina argiolus ♀

15. Cigaritis zohra ▽
16. Cigaritis zohra △
17. Cyaniris semiargus △
18. Everes argiades △
19. Eumedonia eumedon ▽△
20. Everes argiades ▽
21. Glaucopsyche alexis △
22. Freyeria trochylus △
23. Glaucopsyche melanops ▽△
24. Heodes alciphron
25. Heodes tityrus ▽
26. Heodes tityrus △
27. Heodes virgaurae
28. Heodes virgaurae ♀ ▽△

29. Cyclirius webbianus
30. Iolana iolas △
31. Iolana iolas ▽
32. Kretania psylorita
33. Laeosopis roboris
34. Lampides boeticus △
35. Lycaeides argyrognomon ▽△
36. Lycaena dispar
37. Lycaena helle
38. Lycaena dispar ♀ △▽
39. Lycaena phlaeas △
40. Lycaena phlaeas ▽
41. Lysandra albicans

1. Lysandra bellargus ♀ ▽ △
2. Lysandra bellargus
3. Lysandra coridon
4. Maculinea arion
5. Maculinea teleius ▽ △
6. Meleageria daphnis
7. Meleageria daphnis ♀
8. Nordmannia ilicis △
9. Palaeochrysophanus hippothoe
10. Palaeochrysophanus hippothoe ♀
11. Philotes abencerragus

12. Philotes baton ▽
13. Philotes baton △
14. Philotes bavius ♀ △
15. Plebicula amanda ♂ ▽ △
16. Plebicula dorylas ▽ △
17. Plebicula escheri
18. Plebicula escheri ♀ △ ▽
19. Plebicula amanda
20. Plebejus pylaon ♀ ▽ △
21. Plebejus argus ▽ △
22. Plebejus pylaon

23. Polyommatus eros
24. Polyommatus icarus ♀ △
25. Polyommatus icarus
26. Quercusia quercus ♂ ▽ △
27. Quercusia quercus ♀
28. Scolitantides orion ▽
29. Scolitantides orion △
30. Strymonidia pruni ▽ △
31. Strymonidia spini △
32. Strymonidia spini ▽
33. Tarucus theophrastus △

NEMEOBIIDAE
(1 : 1)

HESPERIIDAE (1 : 1)

<table>
<tr><td>1. Thecla betulae ♀</td><td>13. Carterocephalus silvicolus</td><td>25. Pyrgus centaureae ▽△</td></tr>
<tr><td>2. Thecla betulae △</td><td>14. Erynnis marloyi</td><td>26. Pyrgus fritillarius △</td></tr>
<tr><td>3. Thersamonia thersamon ▽△</td><td>15. Erynnis tages</td><td>27. Pyrgus malvae</td></tr>
<tr><td>4. Thersamonia thetis</td><td>16. Gegenes nostrodamus ▽△</td><td>28. Pyrgus onopordi</td></tr>
<tr><td>5. Tomares ballus</td><td>17. Gegenes nostrodamus ♀</td><td>29. Pyrgus serratulae △</td></tr>
<tr><td>6. Tomares ballus ▽△</td><td>18. Hesperia comma ▽</td><td>30. Spialia phlomidis ▽△</td></tr>
<tr><td>7. Vacciniina optilete ▽△</td><td>19. Hesperia comma △</td><td>31. Spialia sertorius ▽</td></tr>
<tr><td>8. Zizeeria knysna</td><td>20. Heteropterus morpheus △</td><td>32. Spialia sertorius △</td></tr>
<tr><td>9. Zizeeria lysimon △</td><td>21. Muschampia cribrellum ▽△</td><td>33. Thymelicus acteon</td></tr>
<tr><td>10. Hamearis lucina</td><td>22. Muschampia proto △▽</td><td>34. Thymelicus sylvestris</td></tr>
<tr><td>11. Carcharodus alceae</td><td>23. Ochlodes venatus ▽△</td><td></td></tr>
<tr><td>12. Carterocephalus palaemon △▽</td><td>24. Pyrgus alveus ▽△</td><td></td></tr>
</table>

PAPILIONIDAE (1 : 2)

HELICONIIDAE (1 : 2)

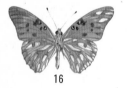

LIBYTHEIDAE (1 : 1)

DANAIDAE (1 : 2)

1. Battus philenor △	8. Papilio eurymedon	15. Parnassius clodius
2. Battus polydamas	9. Papilio glaucus ♀	16. Dione vanillae △
3. Eurytides marcellus	10. Papilio glaucus ♂	17. Libytheana carinenta
4. Papilio aristodemus	11. Papilio polyxenes	18. Danaus eresimus
5. Papilio cresphontes	12. Papilio palamedes	19. Danaus gilippus
6. Papilio daunus	13. Papilio troilus	20. Danaus plexippus
7. Papilio indra	14. Papilio zelicaon	

NYMPHALIDAE (3 : 4)

1. Anaea aidea
2. Anaea andria
3. Anartia amathea
4. Anartia fatima
5. Anartia jatrophae
6. Asterocampa celtis
7. Asterocampa clyton ♂ ▽
8. Asterocampa clyton ♀ △
9. Chlosyne acastus ▽△
10. Chlosyne gabbii △
11. Chlosyne harrisii ▽△

12. Chlosyne hoffmanni
13. Chlosyne janais
14. Chlosyne lacinia △
15. Chlosyne nycteis ▽
16. Chlosyne nycteis △
17. Clossiana alberta
18. Clossiana astarte △
19. Clossiana bellona ▽△
20. Clossiana improba △
21. Euptoieta claudia
22. Euptoieta hegesia △

23. Euphydryas anicia
24. Euphydryas augusta ♀
25. Euphydryas chalcedon △
26. Euphydryas macglashani △▽
27. Euphydryas nubigena
28. Euphydryas phaeton
29. Euphydryas rubicunda
30. Eunica tatila
31. Junonia lavinia
32. Limenitis archippus

13

1. Limenitis astyanax
2. Limenitis arthemis
3. Limenitis californica
4. Limenitis bredowi ♀ △
5. Limenitis lorquini
6. Limenitis weidemeyeri △
7. Mestra amymone
8. Metamorpha stelenes
9. Phyciodes picta
10. Phyciodes phaon △

11. Marpesia petreus
12. Nymphalis milberti
13. Phyciodes camillus
14. Phyciodes frisia
15. Phyciodes montana
16. Phyciodes texana
17. Phyciodes mylitta ▽△
18. Phyciodes tharos ▽△
19. Phyciodes vesta
20. Poladryas minuta ▽△

21. Polygonia comma
22. Polygonia faunus △
23. Polygonia interrogationis
24. Polygonia j-album △
25. Polygonia orcas
26. Polygonia progne △
27. Polygonia satyrus
28. Polygonia zephyrus

1. Phyciodes leanira
2. Polygonia faunus ▽
3. Pyrameis tammeamea
4. Speyeria adiante
5. Speyeria aphrodite ▽
6. Speyeria aphrodite △
7. Speyeria atlantis
8. Speyeria atossa
9. Speyeria bremneri
10. Speyeria calgariana
11. Speyeria callippe
12. Speyeria clio △
13. Speyeria coronis ♀ ♂ ▽ △
14. Speyeria cybele ♂ △
15. Speyeria diana ♂
16. Speyeria diana ♀
17. Speyeria cybele ♀
18. Speyeria eurynome
19. Speyeria edwardsii ▽ △
20. Speyeria halcyone ▽ △
21. Speyeria hippolyta △

1. Speyeria hesperis ▽△
2. Speyeria idalia
3. Speyeria lais ▽
4. Speyeria mormonia ▽△
5. Speyeria macaria
6. Speyeria nevadensis ▽△

7. Speyeria nitocris
8. Speyeria nokomis ♀
9. Speyeria zerene ▽
10. Speyeria semiramis ♀ ▽△
11. Speyeria zerene △
12. Texola perse △

13. Thessalia wrightii △
14. Thessalia cyneas ♀△
15. Thessalia wrightii ▽
16. Vanessa virginiensis ♀△
17. Vanessa carye
18. Thessalia alma

PIERIDAE (3 : 4)

1. Anteos maerula
2. Ascia josephina
3. Anthocharis cethura
4. Anthocharis sara
5. Anthocharis lanceolota △
6. Anthocharis limonea
7. Colias alexandra ♀
8. Colias boothii
9. Colias philodice
10. Colias elis
11. Colias cesonia
12. Colias christina ♂♀
13. Colias eurydice
14. Colias therapis

15. Colias gigantea △
16. Colias eurytheme △
17. Colias hageni ♀ ▽
18. Colias interior
19. Colias pelidne ♀
20. Euchloe ausonides
21. Euchloe olympia
22. Euchloe pima
23. Euchloe sara ♀ ♂ ▽△
24. Eurema daira ♀
25. Eurema boisduvaliana
26. Nathalis iole
27. Eurema daira ♂
28. Eurema nicippe

29. Eurema salome
30. Colias scudderi
31. Neophasia menapia
32. Neophasia terlooii ♀
33. Eurema lisa
34. Paramidea genutia
35. Phoebis agarithe
36. Pieris cruciferarum
37. Eurema mexicana
38. Pontieuchloia beckeri
39. Pontieuchloia protodice ♂
40. Pontieuchloia protodice ♀

1. Cercyonis meadii △
2. Cercyonis paulus △
3. Cercyonis pegala ▽△
4. Cercyonis sthenele △
5. Coenonympha california ♀
6. Coenonympha elko
7. Coenonympha inornata △
8. Gyrocheilus patrobas △▽
9. Erebia episodea
10. Erebia rossii △
11. Erebia theano
12. Euptychia areolatus △
13. Oenis bore △▽
14. Coenonympha haydeni △
15. Gnodia portlandia △
16. Euptychia cymele
17. Euptychia gemma △
18. Hermeuptychia hermes △
19. Euptychia mitchelli △
20. Euptychia henshawi
21. Euptychia rubricata
22. Neominois ridingsii
23. Oeneis chryxus
24. Oeneis brucei

LYCAENIDAE (3 : 4)

1. Oeneis ivallda
2. Oeneis macounii
3. Oeneis melissa △
4. Oeneis nevadensis
5. Oeneis uhleri △
6. Satyrodes eurydice
7. Paramecera xicaque
8. Agriades podarce △▽
9. Atlides halesus
10. Callipsyche behrii
11. Cyaniris pseudargiolus
12. Everes amyntula
13. Everes comyntas
14. Erora laeta ▽
15. Eumaeus atala

16. Feniseca tarquinius
17. Brephidium exilis △
18. Erora laeta △
19. Glaucopsyche antiacis
20. Glaucopsyche lygdamus △
21. Glaucopsyche xerces △
22. Hemiargus ammon
23. Hemiargus ceraunus ♀ △
24. Hypaurotis crysalus
25. Hemiargus isola ♂ △
26. Hemiargus isola ♀ ▽
27. Hemiargus thomasi △
28. Incisalia augustinus
29. Incisalia irus △
30. Incisalia niphon ♀ △

31. Incisalia polios
32. Icaricia lycea △
33. Icaricia pheres
34. Leptotes cassius
35. Lycaeides melissa ♂ △
36. Lycaeides melissa ♀ ▽
37. Lycaeides shasta ▽△
38. Lycaeides aster △
39. Lycaena epixanthe △
40. Lycaena arota △
41. Lycaena gorgon
42. Lycaena helloides
43. Lycaena heteronea △
44. Lycaena mariposa ▽
45. Lycaena mariposa △

NEMEOBIIDAE (1 : 1)

1. Lycaena rubidus	17. Plebejus aquila △	33. Strymon ontario
2. Lycaena snowi ♀	18. Plebejus saepiolus ♀ ▽ △	34. Strymon titus △
3. Lycaena thoe ♂	19. Plebejus saepiolus △	35. Thecla adenostomatis
4. Lycaena thoe ♀	20. Satyrium fuliginosa △	36. Thecla dryope △
5. Lycaena xanthoides △	21. Strymon acis △	37. Thecla grunus ♀
6. Mitoura grunus	22. Strymon falacer △	38. Thecla loki △
7. Mitoura gryneus △	23. Strymon avalona	39. Apodemia mormo
8. Mitoura nelsoni ♀	24. Strymon cecrops △	40. Apodemia walkeri
9. Mitoura saepium	25. Strymon columella	41. Emesis ares
10. Mitoura spinctorum	26. Strymon edwardsi ♀ △	42. Emesis muticum △
11. Mitoura xami ▽ △	27. Strymon favonius △	43. Emesis nemesis ♀
12. Phaedrotus sagittigera △	28. Strymon leda	44. Lasaia sessilis
13. Philotes battoides ♀ △	29. Strymon liparops △	45. Lephelisca virginiensis
14. Philotes enoptes	30. Strymon m-album ♀ △	46. Lephelisca wrighti
15. Philotes sonorensis	31. Strymon martialis	47. Lymnas cephise
16. Plebejus acmon	32. Strymon melinus ▽ △	

HESPERIIDAE (1 : 1)

1. Achalarus lyciades △
2. Amblyscirtes aenus △
3. Amblyscirtes belli
4. Amblyscirtes carolina
5. Amblyscirtes cassus
6. Amblyscirtes fimbriata
7. Amblyscirtes eos △
8. Amblyscirtes oslari △
9. Ancyloxipha numitor
10. Amblyscirtes nysa △
11. Amblyscirtes vialis △
12. Amblyscirtes textor △
13. Amblyscirtes exoteria

14. Atalopedes campestris
15. Atrytone arogos ♀
16. Atrytone aspa
17. Atrytone conspicua
18. Atrytone dion △
19. Atrytonopsis deva △
20. Atrytonopsis hianna △
21. Atrytone logan
22. Atrytone pilatka ♀
23. Autochton cellus
24. Calpodes ethlius
25. Chioides albofasciatus △
26. Celotes nesses

27. Codactractus alcaeus △
28. Cogia hippalus △
29. Copaeodes aurantiaca ♀ △
30. Copaeodes minima
31. Ephyriades brunnea
32. Epargyreus clarus △
33. Erynnis albomarginatus
34. Erynnis funeralis ♀
35. Erynnis horatius ♀
36. Erynnis icelus
37. Erynnis martialis
38. Erynnis persius
39. Heliopetes ericetorum ♀

21

1. Hesperia attalus ♀ △
2. Hesperia laurentina △
3. Hesperia leonardus △
4. Hesperia metea △
5. Hesperia pawnee
6. Lerodea eufala
7. Hylephila phylaeus
8. Hesperia ruricola △
9. Hesperia sassacus
10. Hesperia uncas ♀ △
11. Ochlodes snowi
12. Oarisma garita
13. Megathymus cofaqui ♀
14. Megathymus smithi
15. Megathymus streckeri ♀
16. Lerema accius ♀ △

17. Megathymus yuccae
18. Oarisma powesheik △
19. Ochlodes sylvanoides
20. Oligoria maculata
21. Panoquina panoquin △
22. Panoquina ocola
23. Pholisora aepheus
24. Pholisora hayhurstii
25. Pholisora mejicanus
26. Plestia dorus △
27. Poanes aaroni
28. Poanes hobomok △
29. Poanes massasoit △
30. Poanes viator
31. Polites baracoa
32. Polites manataaqua

33. Polites mystic
34. Polites peckius △
35. Polites sabuleti △
36. Polites themistocles ♀
37. Polites verna ♀
38. Polites vibex △
39. Problema byssus
40. Pyrgus communis
41. Pyrgus ruralis △
42. Pyrgus scriptura
43. Pyrgus syrichtus △
44. Systasea zampa
45. Thorybes pylades △
46. Thorybes bathyllus
47. Wallengrenia otho

22

PAPILIONIDAE (1 : 2)

1. Battus belus ▽△
2. Battus crassus
3. Battus madyas
4. Battus polystictus
5. Battus zetes
6. Baronia brevicornis ♀
7. Euryades duponchelli
8. Euryades corethrus ♀
9. Eurytides agesilaus
10. Eurytides ariarathes
11. Eurytides asius
12. Eurytides belesis
13. Eurytides dolicaon
14. Eurytides telesilaus
15. Eurytides epidaus
16. Eurytides euryleon
17. Eurytides iphitas
18. Eurytides lacandones
19. Eurytides leucaspis
20. Eurytides lysithous
21. Eurytides marchandi
22. Eurytides microdamas
23. Eurytides pausanias
24. Eurytides orabilis

1. Eurytides phaon
2. Eurytides philolaus
3. Eurytides protesilaus
4. Eurytides protodamas
5. Eurytides salvini
6. Eurytides stenodesmus
7. Troides rhadamantus
8. Papilio aglaope

9. Papilio anchisiades
10. Papilio andraemon
11. Papilio androgeus ♀
12. Papilio androgeus ♂
13. Papilio bachus
14. Papilio birchalli
15. Papilio cacicus △
16. Papilio caiguanabus ♀

17. Papilio chiansiades
18. Papilio cleotas
19. Papilio epenetus ♀
20. Papilio garamas
21. Papilio erostratus
22. Papilio euterpinus

1. Papilio hectorides ♀
2. Papilio hectorides ♂
3. Papilio homerus ♀
4. Papilio hellanichus
5. Papilio hyppason
6. Papilio lycophron
7. Papilio oxynius
8. Papilio machaonides
9. Papilio pelaus
10. Papilio pharnaces
11. Papilio thersites
12. Papilio torquatus ♂
13. Papilio torquatus ♀
14. Papilio victorinus
15. Papilio warscewiczi △
16. Papilio xanthopleura
17. Papilio zagreus
18. Parides aeneas
19. Parides agavus
20. Parides anchises

25

1. Parides arcas ♀
2. Parides ascanius
3. Parides chabrias
4. Parides childrenae
5. Parides columbus
6. Parides coelus ♀
7. Parides cutorina ♀
8. Parides erithalion ♀
9. Parides erlaces
10. Parides gundlachianus
11. Parides iphidamas ♂
12. Parides iphidamas ♀ △
13. Parides lycimenes
14. Parides lysander
15. Parides montezuma
16. Parides neophilus
17. Parides nephalion ♀
18. Parides orellana
19. Parides phalaecus
20. Parides phosphorus
21. Parides photinus
22. Parides polyzelus
23. Parides sesostris ♀
24. Parides timias ♀
25. Parides triopas
26. Parides tros
27. Parides vertumnus ♀
28. Parides zacynthus

MORPHIDAE (1 : 2)

1. Morpho achilles
2. Morpho aega ♂
3. Morpho anaxibia △
4. Morpho catenarius
5. Morpho aega ♀
6. Morpho cypris ♀
7. Morpho deidamia
8. Morpho didius
9. Morpho granadensis △
10. Morpho hercules
11. Morpho menelaus ♀
12. Morpho menelaus ♂
13. Morpho laertes △
14. Morpho portis
15. Morpho patroclus

BRASSOLIDAE (1 : 2)

1. Morpho peleides ▽
2. Morpho peleides △
3. Morpho perseus
4. Morpho polyphemus

5. Morpho rhetenor ♂
6. Morpho rhetenor ♀
7. Caligo beltrao
8. Brassolis sophorae ♀

9. Caligo atreus
10. Caligo martia
11. Caligo idomeneus
12. Caligo memnon ♂ ▽

1. Caligo memnon ♀ △
2. Eryphanis aesacus ♀
3. Caligo teucer
4. Catoblepia xanthus
5. Dasyopthalma creusa ▽
6. Dasyopthalma creusa △
7. Dynastor darius
8. Eryphanis polyxena △
9. Eryphanis reevesi
10. Narope cyllabarus
11. Narope cyllastros ▽△
12. Opoptera aorsa
13. Opoptera sulcius
14. Opsiphanes batea
15. Opsiphanes berecynthia ♂ ▽
16. Opsiphanes berecynthia ♀ △
17. Opsiphanes boisduvalii
18. Opsiphanes cassiae
19. Opsiphanes quiteria
20. Opsiphanes tamarindi
21. Penetes pamphanis
22. Selenophanes cassiope

1. Adelpha abia
2. Adelpha alala
3. Adelpha arete
4. Adelpha boreas
5. Adelpha celerio
6. Adelpha cocala
7. Adelpha cytherea
8. Adelpha demialba
9. Adelpha epione ▽△
10. Adelpha erotia
11. Adelpha felderi △
12. Adelpha iphicla △
13. Adelpha irmina
14. Adelpha isis
15. Adelpha lara
16. Adelpha leuceria
17. Adelpha melona
18. Adelpha nea △
19. Adelpha olynthia
20. Adelpha plesaure
21. Adelpha plylaca ▽△
22. Adelpha serpa △
23. Adelpha serpa ▽

1. Adelpha syma ▽△
2. Adelpha thoas
3. Adelpha tracta
4. Adelpha zalmona △
5. Adelpha zea △
6. Agrias aedon
7. Agrias amydon △

8. Agrias claudia
9. Agrias hewitsonius
10. Agrias narcissus ♀
11. Agrias phalcidon
12. Agrias sardanapalus
13. Anaea artacaena
14. Anaea appias

15. Anaea ates △
16. Anaea aureola
17. Anaea callidryas
18. Anaea chaeronea
19. Anaea chrysophana
20. Anaea echemus ▽△

31

1. Anaea cyanea
2. Anaea electra
3. Anaea panariste ♀
4. Anaea glycerium
5. Anaea lineata
6. Anaea octavius
7. Anaea onophis
8. Anaea morvus
9. Anaea nessus
10. Anaea eribotes
11. Anaea glauce
12. Anaea panariste
13. Anaea tyrianthina
14. Anaea polyxo △
15. Anaea vicinia ♀
16. Anaea sosippus
17. Anaea xenocles △
18. Anaea pasibula

1. Anaea zelica ♀
2. Anartia lytrea
3. Atlantea perezi
4. Antillea pelops
5. Bolboneura sylphis △
6. Anaeomorpha splendida
7. Batesia hypochlora △
8. Baeotus japetus △

9. Baeotus baeotus
10. Callicore aegina △
11. Callicore atacama △
12. Callicore brome
13. Callicore clymena △
14. Callicore codomannus
15. Callicore excelsior
16. Callithea leprieuri

17. Callicore faustina
18. Callicore hydaspes △
19. Callicore maimuna
20. Callidula pyramus
21. Callicore pitheas △
22. Callicore sorana △
23. Callicore texa ▽△

1. Callicore patelina
2. Callicore zelphanta ▽△
3. Callithea adamsi △
4. Callizona acesta
5. Callithea batesii ♀
6. Callithea markii
7. Chlosyne narva
8. Callithea sapphira

9. Callithea sonkai
10. Catagramma aphidna
11. Catonephele antinoe
12. Catonephele numilia ♀
13. Catonephele numilia ♂
14. Catonephele nyctimus ♂
15. Catonephele nyctimus ♀
16. Chlosyne erodyle △

17. Myscelia antholia
18. Chlosyne ehrenbergii △
19. Chlosyne lacinia
20. Chlosyne eumeda
21. Chlosyne marina
22. Chlosyne melanarge

1. Coea acheronta
2. Coenophlebia archidona △
3. Colobura dirce △
4. Consul hippona
5. Cybdelis mnasylus
6. Cyclogramma bachis
7. Diaethria astala
8. Diaethria candrena
9. Diaethria clymena ▽

10. Diaethria eupepla
11. Cyclogramma pandama ▽△
12. Diaethria clymena △
13. Diaethria metiscus ▽△
14. Diaethria neglecta ▽△
15. Didonis biblis
16. Doxocopa agathina
17. Doxocopa callianira △
18. Doxocopa cherubina

19. Doxocopa clothilda
20. Doxocopa cyane
21. Doxocopa felderi
22. Doxocopa griseldis △
23. Doxocopa lavinia ♀
24. Doxocopa pavonii
25. Doxocopa laure
26. Doxocopa zalmunna

35

1. Doxocopa zunilda ♂ △
2. Doxocopa zunilda ♀
3. Dynamine agacles ▽
4. Dynamine agacles △
5. Dynamine arene △
6. Dynamine anubis
7. Dynamine artemisia ♀
8. Dynamine chryseis
9. Dynamine dyonis
10. Dynamine erchia
11. Dynamine geta

12. Dynamine gisella
13. Dynamine glauce △
14. Dynamine mylitta ♂▽△
15. Dynamine mylitta ♀
16. Dynamine myrrhina ▽
17. Dynamine myrrhina △
18. Dynamine racidula
19. Dynamine salpensa △
20. Dynamine thalassina
21. Dynamine tithia ♀ ♂
22. Dynamine zenobia

23. Ectima liria △
24. Epiphile adrasta
25. Epiphile dilecta
26. Epiphile epicaste
27. Epiphile eriopis
28. Epiphile plusios ♀
29. Epiphile orea
30. Epiphile lampethusa ▽△
31. Eunica alcmena
32. Eunica anna ▽△

1. Eunica augusta ♂
2. Eunica augusta ♀
3. Eunica bechina △
4. Eunica caelina ♀ △
5. Eunica caresa ♂ ♀
6. Eunica careta ♀
7. Eunica chlorochroa △

8. Eunica clytia ▽△
9. Eunica elegans △
10. Eunica margarita
11. Eunica mygdonia ▽△
12. Eunica norica
13. Eunica macris
14. Eunica orphise

15. Eunica venusia ▽
16. Eunica venusia △
17. Gnathotriche exclamationis ▽△
18. Hamadryas amphinome ♂▽▽
19. Hamadryas arethusa ♂♀▽△

1. Hamadryas atlantis
2. Hamadryas chloe
3. Hypna clytemnestra
4. Hamadryas februa △
5. Hamadryas feronia
6. Hypanartia dione

7. Hypanartia kefersteinii
8. Hamadryas fornax △
9. Hypanartia godmanii
10. Historis orion
11. Hypanartia lethe △
12. Libythina cuvieri

13. Issoria inca △
14. Issoria cytheris ▽△
15. Lucinia sida △
16. Marpesia chiron ▽△
17. Marpesia coresia △
18. Marpesia harmonia

1. Marpesia iole ♀
2. Marpesia livius △
3. Marpesia marcella ♂
4. Marpesia marcella ♀
5. Marpesia merops
6. Marpesia crethon
7. Metamorpha epaphus
8. Metamorpha sulpitia △
9. Microtia elva
10. Mestra teleboas △
11. Mestra hypermnestra
12. Myscelia ethusa
13. Myscelia orsis ♂
14. Myscelia orsis ♀
15. Napeocles jucunda
16. Nica flavilla △
17. Nessaea batesii
18. Nessaea obvinus ♀
19. Nessaea obvinus ♂
20. Nessaea regina △
21. Panacea divalis
22. Panacea procilla
23. Panacea prola

39

1. Panacea regina △
2. Peria lamis ▽
3. Perisama bonplandii ▽△
4. Perisama cabirnia
5. Perisama calamis △
6. Perisama cecidas
7. Perisama chaseba
8. Perisama cloelia ▽
9. Perisama cloelia △
10. Perisama humboldtii △
11. Perisama lebasii △
12. Perisama nyctimene △
13. Perisama patara
14. Perisama priene
15. Perisama vaninka
16. Phyciodes acralina
17. Phyciodes actinote
18. Phyciodes aequatorialis
19. Phyciodes alsina
20. Phyciodes angusta
21. Phyciodes annita
22. Phyciodes callonia
23. Phyciodes castilla ♀
24. Phyciodes castilla ♂
25. Phyciodes catula
26. Phyciodes clio ▽
27. Phyciodes clio △
28. Phyciodes corybassa
29. Phyciodes drusilla
30. Phyciodes elaphiaea
31. Phyciodes emerantia
32. Phyciodes eranites △
33. Phyciodes etia
34. Phyciodes eunice
35. Phyciodes eutropia
36. Phyciodes fulviplaga ▽△
37. Phyciodes geminia
38. Phyciodes ianthe ▽△
39. Phyciodes ildica

1. Phyciodes ithomoides ♀
2. Phyciodes lansdorfi
3. Phyciodes ptolyca
4. Prepona demophon
5. Phyciodes levina
6. Phyciodes margaretha
7. Phyciodes murena
8. Phyciodes nussia
9. Phyciodes orthia
10. Phyciodes otanes △
11. Phyciodes letitia
12. Phyciodes quintilla
13. Phyciodes saladillensis ♀ ▽ △
14. Phyciodes sestia ♀
15. Phyciodes teletusa
16. Phyciodes verena ♀
17. Polygonia zephyrus
18. Polygrapha cyanea
19. Prepona antimache △
20. Prepona laertes △
21. Zaretis isidora ♂
22. Zaretis isidora ♀
23. Prepona buckleyana
24. Phyciodes leucodesma
25. Phyciodes liriope
26. Phyciodes nigrella
27. Phyciodes northbrundii

41

1. Prepona chromus ♀
2. Prepona deiphile
3. Pyrameis myrinna
4. Prepona meander △
5. Prepona neoterpe
6. Pyrrhogyra edocla

7. Pyrrhogyra neaerea △
8. Prepona pheridamas
9. Prepona pylene △
10. Siderone nemesis
11. Prepona xenagoras △
12. Pycina zamba △

13. Smyrna blomfildia △
14. Temenis laothoe
15. Temenis pulchra
16. Texola elada
17. Vila azeca ▽△

ACRAEIDAE (1 : 2)

HELICONIIDAE (1 : 2)

1. Actinote alalia
2. Actinote alcione
3. Actinote anteas
4. Actinote callianthe △
5. Actinote demonica
6. Actinote dicaeus
7. Actinote equatoria
8. Actinote eresia
9. Altinote erinome
10. Actinote guatemalena
11. Actinote hylonome
12. Actinote laverna
13. Actinote leucomelas

14. Actinote mamita ♀
15. Altinote neleus
16. Actinote ozomene
17. Actinote parapheles
18. Actinote pellenea △
19. Actinote stratonice
20. Actinote terpsinoe
21. Altinote radiata
22. Anetia cubana
23. Anetia insignis
24. Anetia numidia △
25. Dione juno △
26. Dione moneta

27. Dryadula phaelusa △
28. Dryas julia
29. Eueides cleobaea
30. Eueides isabella
31. Eueides lineatus
32. Eueides lybia
33. Eueides pavana
34. Heliconius aliphera
35. Heliconius amaryllis
36. Heliconius anderida △
37. Heliconius antiochus
38. Heliconius aoede

43

1. Heliconius aristiona
2. Heliconius atthis △
3. Heliconius burneyi
4. Heliconius charitonia
5. Heliconius cydno
6. Heliconius cyrbia
7. Heliconius doris
8. Heliconius eanes
9. Heliconius edias
10. Heliconius erato
11. Heliconius ethra
12. Heliconius hecale
13. Heliconius hermathena
14. Heliconius heurippa
15. Heliconius hortense
16. Heliconius ismenius
17. Ituna lamirus
18. Heliconius melpomene
19. Heliconius metharme
20. Heliconius nanna
21. Heliconius narcaea
22. Heliconius novartus △
23. Heliconius numata
24. Heliconius pardalinus
25. Heliconius petiverana
26. Heliconius phyllis
27. Heliconius quitalena
28. Heliconius vicini
29. Heliconius sapho
30. Heliconius sara
31. Heliconius silvana
32. Heliconius tales
33. Heliconius telesiphe

44

1.	Heliconius vetustus	15.	Ceratinia dorilla ♀	29.	Dygoris dircenna
2.	Heliconius vibilia	16.	Ceratinia jolaia	30.	Elzunia humboldti △
3.	Heliconius vulcanus	17.	Ceratinia nise ♀	31.	Episcada salvinia
4.	Heliconius wallacei	18.	Ceratinia nise ♂	32.	Episcada sylpha
5.	Heliconius xanthocles	19.	Corbulis cymo △	33.	Epithomia alpho
6.	Heliconius xenoclea	20.	Corbulis ocalea	34.	Epithomia methonella △
7.	Philaethria dido	21.	Corbulis oreas	35.	Eutresis hypereia
8.	Podotricha euchroia △	22.	Corbulis orolina	36.	Forbestra truncata
9.	Aeria eurimedia △	23.	Corbulis virginia	37.	Garsaurites xanthostola
10.	Athesis dercyllidas △	24.	Dircenna dero	38.	Godyris crinippa
11.	Athyrtis mechanitis	25.	Dircenna klugi ♀	39.	Godyris duillia
12.	Callithomia hezia	26.	Dircenna vandona	40.	Godyris gonussa ♀
13.	Callithomia schulzi △	27.	Dircenna varina	41.	Godyris hewitsoni
14.	Callithomia villula	28.	Dircenna visina		

1. Godyris zavaletta
2. Heterosais giulia ♀
3. Heterosais nephele
4. Hyalenna perasippa
5. Hyalenna teresita
6. Hyaliris fenestella △
7. Hyaliris vallonia
8. Hypoleria albinotata
9. Hypoleria andromica
10. Hypoleria libethris
11. Hypoleria morgane
12. Hypoleria ortygia
13. Hypoleria oto
14. Hyposcada abida
15. Hyposcada adelphina
16. Hyposcada fallax
17. Hyposcada kezia

18. Hyposcada sinilia ♀
19. Hypothiris angelina
20. Hypothiris antea
21. Hypothiris antonia
22. Hypothiris callispila
23. Hypothiris catilla
24. Hypothiris honesta
25. Hypothiris lycaste
26. Hypothiris mergelena
27. Hypothiris metella ♂ ♀
28. Hypothiris ninonia
29. Hypothiris ocna
30. Hypothiris oulita
31. Hypothiris philetaera
32. Hypothiris thea
33. Hypothiris tricolor ♀
34. Ithomia agnosia

35. Ithomia celemia
36. Ithomia derasa
37. Ithomia diasia
38. Ithomia ellara △
39. Ithomia epona
40. Ithomia lagusa
41. Ithomia oenanthe △
42. Ithomia patilla △
43. McClungia salonina △
44. Mechanitis doryssus ♀
45. Mechanitis lycidice
46. Mechanitis lysimnia
47. Mechanitis macrinus
48. Mechanitis mantineus
49. Mechanitis messenoides
50. Mechanitis nesaea

46

1. Mechanitis polymnia
2. Melinaea idae
3. Melinaea lilis
4. Melinaea mediatrix
5. Melinaea messatis △
6. Melinaea messenina
7. Melinaea satevis
8. Melinaea scylax
9. Melinaea zaneka
10. Miraleria cymothoe
11. Napeogenes corena
12. Napeogenes duessa ♂
13. Napeogenes duessa ♀
14. Napeogenes cranto
15. Napeogenes flossina
16. Napeogenes inachia

17. Napeogenes larina
18. Napeogenes peridia
19. Napeogenes pharo
20. Napeogenes stella
21. Napeogenes sulphurina △
22. Oleria aegle
23. Oleria astraea
24. Oleria deronda
25. Oleria estella
26. Oleria ida
27. Oleria makrena △
28. Oleria orestilla △
29. Oleria priscilla
30. Oleria susiana △
31. Oleria tigella
32. Oleria zelica

33. Olyras montagui
34. Olyras praestans
35. Pseudoscada aureola
36. Pseudoscada florula
37. Pseudoscada seba ♀
38. Pteronymia apuleia
39. Pteronymia latilla
40. Pteronymia laura
41. Pteronymia lilla
42. Pteronymia picta ♀
43. Pteronymia tigranes △
44. Pteronymia veia
45. Pteronymia zerlina △
46. Rhodussa viola
47. Sais zitella
48. Scada gazoria ♀

DANAIDAE (1 : 2)

PIERIDAE (3 : 4)

1. Scada kusa
2. Scada zemira
3. Thyridia confusa
4. Tithorea hermias
5. Tithorea pinthias
6. Tithorea tarricina
7. Velamysta torquatilla
8. Xanthocleis aedesia

9. Xanthocleis menophilus
10. Lycorea ceres
11. Lycorea cleobaea
12. Danaus cleophile
13. Anteos clorinde
14. Appias drusilla ♀
15. Anteos menippe
16. Ascia buniae

17. Ascia monuste
18. Catasticta bithys △
19. Catasticta colla △
20. Catasticta pharnakia
21. Ascia sincera △
22. Catasticta flisa ▽△
23. Catasticta chrysolopha
24. Catasticta uricaecheae

48

1. Catasticta nimbice ▽△
2. Catasticta notha
3. Catasticta froujadei
4. Catasticta semiramis △
5. Catasticta sisamnus
6. Catasticta straminea △
7. Catasticta teutile ♀△
8. Catasticta tomyris ▽△
9. Catasticta troezenides △
10. Charonias eurytele
11. Charonias theano
12. Colias antarctica ♂♀▽△
13. Colias cynops ♀△
14. Colias dimera ▽
15. Colias dinora ♀♂▽△
16. Colias dimera △
17. Colias flaveola
18. Colias lesbia ♂♀
19. Colias vautieri
20. Dismorphia amphione
21. Dismorphia erythroe
22. Dismorphia cornelia
23. Dismorphia cretacea
24. Dismorphia cubana
25. Dismorphia cordillera
26. Dismorphia foedora ♀▽△
27. Dismorphia ithomia
28. Dismorphia leonora
29. Dismorphia lua △
30. Dismorphia medora
31. Dismorphia lysis

1. Dismorphia melia ♀ ♂
2. Dismorphia mirandola
3. Dismorphia nemesis ▽ △
4. Dismorphia orise
5. Dismorphia rhetes
6. Dismorphia spio
7. Dismorphia theonoe
8. Dismorphia theucharila
9. Dismorphia theugenis
10. Eroessa chilensis

11. Eucheira socialis
12. Eurema albula
13. Eurema arbela
14. Eurema atinas
15. Eurema deva
16. Hesperocharis agasicles
17. Dismorphia fortunata ▽ △
18. Dismorphia sororna ♂
19. Dismorphia sororna ♀
20. Eurema gratiosa

21. Eurema messalina
22. Eurema elathea
23. Eurema limbia
24. Eurema hyona
25. Eurema proterpia
26. Eurema neda △
27. Eurema phiale
28. Eurema reticulata △
29. Eurema sybaris △

1. Eurema thymetus △
2. Eurema westwoodi ♀
3. Eurema westwoodi ♂
4. Hesperocharis anguitia △
5. Hesperocharis aureomaculata △
6. Hesperocharis graphites
7. Haballia demophile ♀
8. Haballia locusta
9. Haballia mandela △
10. Haballia pandosia
11. Haballia pisonis △
12. Haballia tithoreides ♀ ♂
13. Leptophobia eleone
14. Kricogonia lyside
15. Leptophobia caesia ▽
16. Leptophobia caesia △
17. Leptophobia eleusis
18. Leptophobia euthemia
19. Leptophobia subargentea △
20. Leodonta dysoni △
21. Leptophobia nephthis
22. Leptophobia olympia
23. Leptophobia pinara
24. Leucidia brephos
25. Leucidia exigua
26. Nathalis planta
27. Melete florinda △
28. Melete lycimnia
29. Melete peruviana ♀
30. Melete polyhymnia

1. Melete salacia △
2. Pereute autodyca
3. Hesperocharis hirlanda △
4. Hesperocharis idiotica △
5. Hesperocharis marchali
6. Hesperocharis nera ▽
7. Hesperocharis nera △
8. Hesperocharis nereina

9. Pereute charops △
10. Pereute leucodrosine
11. Pereute swainsoni ♀ △
12. Phoebis orbis ♀
13. Pereute telthusa
14. Perrhybris lypera △
15. Perrhybris pyrrha ♂ ▽
16. Perrhybris pyrrha ♀ △

17. Phoebis cipris
18. Phoebis eubule
19. Phoebis avellaneda
20. Phoebis orbis ♂
21. Phoebis editha ♀
22. Phulia illimani ♀ △
23. Phulia nympha

1. Phoebis philea ♂
2. Phoebis philea ♀
3. Phoebis rurina
4. Phoebis sennae ♀
5. Phoebis statira
6. Pieris pylotis
7. Pieris viardi ♂
8. Pieris viardi ♀
9. Pierocolias huanaco
10. Theochila itatiayae

11. Pseudopieris nehemia △▽
12. Tatochila blanchardii ♀ △
13. Tatochila mercedis ♀
14. Tatochila theodice ♀
15. Tatochila vauvolxemii
16. Pierocolias nysias ♂ △
17. Pierocolias nysias ♀ ▽
18. Dismorphia deione ♀
19. Dismorphia hippotas
20. Archonias bellona ♀

21. Catasticta marcapita
22. Archonias tereas
23. Dismorphia methymna △
24. Dismorphia teresa
25. Catasticta teutanis
26. Catasticta manco ▽
27. Catasticta manco △
28. Catasticta modesta

53

1. Altopedaliodes tena
2. Argyreuptychia penelope △
3. Amphidecta pignerator
4. Antirrhaea archaea ♀

5. Antirrhaea avernus
6. Antirrhaea geryon ♀
7. Antirrhaea miltiades ♀
8. Antirrhaea phasiane ♀

9. Antopedaliodes antonia
10. Archeuptychia cluena ▽△
11: Argyreuptychia ocypete △

1. Auca coctei ▽△
2. Argyrophorus argenteus ▽△
3. Caeruleuptychia coelestis
4. Bia actorion
5. Caerois chorinaeus
6. Caeruleuptychia lobelia
7. Caeruleuptychia coelica △

8. Caerois gerdrudtus
9. Calisto pulchella △
10. Calisto zangis
11. Cepheuptychia angelica ♀△
12. Cepheuptychia cephus ♀
13. Cepheuptychia glaucina
14. Cheimas opalinus

15. Chilanella stelligera △
16. Chloreuptychia agatha △
17. Chloreuptychia agaya
18. Chloreuptychia arnaea
19. Chloreuptychia tolumnia
20. Cithaerias aurorina

55

1. Cithaerias esmeralda
2. Cithaerias menander
3. Cithaerias philis
4. Corades argentata △
5. Corades cybele △
6. Corades cistene △
7. Corades enyo ♀
8. Corderopedaliodes pandates
9. Corades pannonia △
10. Corades iduna
11. Corades ulema ▽△

56

1. Daedalma dinias △
2. Dioriste cothonides △
3. Dioriste leucospilos ♀ △
4. Dioriste tauropolis
5. Eretris calisto △

6. Drucina championi
7. Drucina leonata
8. Drucina venerata
9. Dulcedo polita
10. Elina lefebvrei

11. Eretris apuleja △
12. Erichthodes erichtho △
13. Erichthodes julia △
14. Eteona tisiphone ♂
15. Eteona tisiphone ♀

57

1. Euptychia ambigua
2. Euptychia gera
3. Euptychia mermeria △
4. Euptychia philodice ▽△
5. Euptychia innocentia △
6. Euptychia polyphemus △
7. Etcheverinus chilensis △
8. Euptychia grimon △

9. Euptychia harmonia △
10. Euptychia maepius △
11. Euptychia mollina
12. Euptychia ocelloides △
13. Euptychia paeon △
14. Euptychia phares
15. Euptychia picea
16. Euptychia salvini △

17. Euptychia terrestris △
18. Euptychoides saturnus △
19. Faunula patagonica △
20. Godartiana byses △
21. Haetera piera
22. Junea doraete △

1. Junea dorinde
2. Lymanopoda labda △
3. Lymanopoda nivea
4. Junea whitelyi △
5. Lasiophila circe
6. Lymanopoda obsoleta △
7. Lasiophila cirta
8. Lasiophila phalaesia △
9. Lasiophila prosymna
10. Lymanopoda albomaculata △
11. Lymanopoda acraeida ▽△
12. Lymanopoda ciuna
13. Magneuptychia batesii ▽
14. Lymanopoda panacea ▽△
15. Lymanopoda samius
16. Magneuptychia cluena

1. Magneuptychia lea ▽△
2. Magneuptychia libye
3. Magneuptychia nortia △
4. Magneuptychia ocnus ▽
5. Magneuptychia ocnus △
6. Magneuptychia tricolor
7. Manerebia cyclopina △

8. Manataria hercyna
9. Maniola limonias
10. Megeuptychia antonoe
11. Neomaenas edmondsii △
12. Neomaenas haknii ♀ ♂ ↘ △
13. Mygona irmina
14. Mygona paeania

15. Neomaenas poliozona △
16. Neomaenas servilia ♂ △
17. Mygona prochyta △
18. Mygona thammi
19. Neomaenas servilia ♀

1. Oressinoma typhla
2. Oxeoschistus pronax
3. Oxeoschistus protagenia ♀ △
4. Oxeoschistus puerta △
5. Oxeoschistus simplex △
6. Pampasatyrus quies △

7. Panarche callipolis △
8. Parataygetis lineata △
9. Pareuptychia hesione △
10. Paryphthimoides poltys
11. Pedaliodes albonotata
12. Pedaliodes empusa △

13. Pedaliodes piletha △
14. Pedaliodes praxithea
15. Pedaliodes jeptha △
16. Pedaliodes juba

1. Pedaliodes pactyes
2. Pedaliodes pammenes
3. Pedaliodes paneis △
4. Pedaliodes pelinna
5. Pedaliodes pelinaea

6. Pedaliodes perperna △
7. Pedaliodes peucestas
8. Pedaliodes phaeaca
9. Pedaliodes phaedra
10. Pedaliodes pheres △

11. Pedaliodes phrasiclea △
12. Pedaliodes physcoa
13. Pedaliodes pisonia △
14. Pedaliodes plotina
15. Pedaliodes polusca

1. Pedaliodes porcia △
2. Pedaliodes poesia △
3. Pedaliodes tena
4. Penrosada lena
5. Pierella helvina

6. Pherepedaliodes pheretiades △
7. Pharneuptychia phares △
8. Pierella hortona
9. Pierella hyceta
10. Pierella lena

11. Pierella nereis
12. Pierella astyoche
13. Pindis pellonia

1. Pierella rhea
2. Posttaygetis penelea △
3. Praefaunula armilla △
4. Praepedaliodes phanias △
5. Pronophila cordillera ▽
6. Punargentus lamna
7. Proboscis orsedice
8. Pronophila orcus △
9. Quilaphoetosus monachus ♀ △
10. Pronophila rosenbergi △
11. Pronophila timanthes
12. Spinantenna tristis △
13. Pseudomaniola gerlinda △
14. Pseudomaniola phaselis △
15. Splendeuptychia ashna △
16. Satyrotaygetis satyrina △

1. Pronophila thelebe
2. Splendeuptychia cosmophila △
3. Steroma bega ▽△
4. Splendeuptychia furina
5. Taygetis albinotata
6. Taygetis andromeda △
7. Taygetis celia △
8. Taygetis chrysogone
9. Vareuptychia usitata △
10. Ypthimoides celmis
11. Vareuptychia themis △
12. Taygetis sylvia △
13. Taygetis rectifascia △
14. Ypthimoides renata △

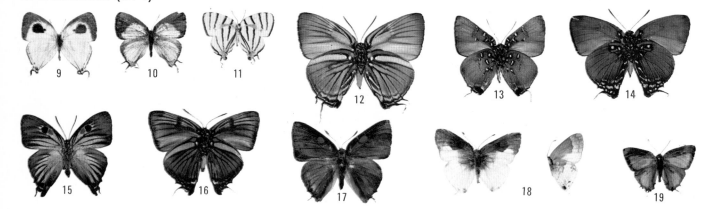

LYCAENIDAE (3 : 4)

1. Taygetis virgilia	8. Neila memyrioides △	15. Atlides polybe
2. Taygetis xenana △	9. Arawacus linus	16. Atlides scamander △
3. Ypthimoides poltys	10. Arawacus phaea	17. Bithys phoenissa ♂ ▽
4. Ypthimoides modesta △	11. Arawacus sito △	18. Callicista albata ▽ △
5. Taygetis ypthima △	12. Atlides bacis ♀ △	19. Callicista angelia
6. Tetraphlebia glaucope △	13. Atlides getus △	
7. Thiemeia phoronea △	14. Atlides carpasia △	

1. Callicista bubastus △
2. Callicista ligia
3. Callicista yojoa ♀ △
4. Calycopis atrius ▽ △
5. Calycopis badaca △
6. Calycopis beon ♀
7. Calycopis beon ♂
8. Calycopis cinniana △
9. Calycopis cleon △
10. Calycopis demonassa △
11. Callipsyche dindymus
12. Calycopis hesperitis ▽
13. Calycopis hesperitis △
14. Calycopis orcidia △
15. Calycopis phrutus
16. Calycopis vesulus ▽△
17. Eumaeus debora
18. Hemiargus hanno △

19. Lamprospilus genius △
20. Oenomaus ortygnus △
21. Oenomaus rustan
22. Panthiades pelion △
23. Parachilades speciosa △
24. Polyniphes dumenilii
25. Pseudolucia chilensis
26. Pseudolucia faga △
27. Strymon azia
28. Strymon bazochii ▽△
29. Strymon pastor ♀ △
30. Strymon simaethis △
31. Strymon telea ♀ △
32. Siderus tephraeus
33. Theclopsis eryx △
34. Theclopsis eryx
35. Thecla aegides
36. Thecla agricolor △

37. Thecla americensis △
38. Thecla aphaca △
39. Thecla atesa △
40. Thecla auda
41. Thecla bagrada △
42. Thecla barajo △
43. Thecla bassania △
44. Thecla bitias ▽△
45. Thecla brescia ▽
46. Thecla busa
47. Thecla cadmus
48. Thecla caesaries ♀ △
49. Thecla calesia △
50. Thecla calus △
51. Thecla comae △
52. Thecla celida △
53. Thecla commodus △
54. Thecla conchylium

1. Thecla crines △
2. Thecla critola
3. Thecla cupentus
4. Thecla draudti
5. Thecla emendatus △
6. Thecla doryasa
7. Thecla elongata
8. Thecla ducalis △
9. Thecla emessa
10. Thecla endymion ▽△
11. Thecla erema
12. Thecla ericusa ♀△
13. Thecla eunus △
14. Thecla falerina
15. Thecla fusius △
16. Thecla gibberosa
17. Thecla gabatha
18. Thecla galliena

19. Thecla crambusa △
20. Thecla badeta △
21. Thecla halciones △
22. Thecla hemon ♂♀△△
23. Thecla herodotus ▽
24. Thecla herodotus △
25. Thecla hesperitis
26. Thecla jada ▽△
27. Thecla janias △
28. Thecla jebus △
29. Thecla laudonia
30. Thecla lausus ♀△
31. Thecla lenitas △
32. Thecla lisus △
33. Thecla literatus
34. Thecla longula
35. Thecla loxurina ▽
36. Thecla loxurina △

37. Thecla lycabas △
38. Thecla malvina △▽
39. Thecla marsyas △
40. Thecla mavors △
41. Thecla megacles △
42. Thecla minyia △
43. Thecla monica ♀△
44. Thecla meton △
45. Thecla mirma
46. Thecla mycon ♀△
47. Thecla mantica △
48. Thecla myrtillus △
49. Thecla myrtusa △
50. Thecla ocrisia ▽△
51. Thecla ophelia
52. Thecla orcynia △
53. Thecla oreala △

1. Thecla orgia ♂ △
2. Thecla orgia ♀ ▽
3. Thecla orobia △
4. Thecla pedusa △
5. Thecla phaleros ▽△
6. Thecla velina △
7. Thecla pholeus
8. Thecla platyptera
9. Thecla palegon ▽△
10. Thecla polibetes ▽△
11. Thecla parthenia △
12. Thecla sala △
13. Thecla satyroides ♀△▽
14. Thecla seudiga △
15. Thecla serapio
16. Thecla strephon △▽
17. Thecla spurius △▽
18. Thecla talayra △

19. Thecla tagyra △
20. Thecla tamos △
21. Thecla tarama △
22. Thecla telemus ♂
23. Thecla telemus ♀
24. Thecla terentia △
25. Thecla teresina ♀△
26. Thecla teucria ♀△
27. Thecla thabena
28. Thecla thales ▽
29. Thecla thales △
30. Thecla thargelia
31. Thecla theocritus
32. Thecla thespia △
33. Thecla tiasa ♂△
34. Thecla tiasa ♀△
35. Thecla timaeus
36. Thecla tolmides △

37. Thecla trebula △
38. Thecla una ▽△
39. Thecla undulata ♀△
40. Thecla valentina ♀△
41. Thecla verania △
42. Theorema eumenia ♂▽
43. Theorema eumenia ♀△
44. Theritas cypria △
45. Theritas coronata ▽△
46. Theritas imperialis △▽
47. Tmolus basalides ▽
48. Tmolus basalides △
49. Tmolus cydrara △
50. Tmolus celmus △
51. Zizula tulliola △
52. Tmolus echion ▽△

69

1. Alesa amesis ♀
2. Amarynthis meneria ♀
3. Amphiselenis chama
4. Ancyluris aulestes ♀
5. Ancyluris formosa
6. Ancyluris colubra ♂ ♀
7. Ancyluris formosissima △
8. Ancyluris huascar
9. Ancyluris inca
10. Ancyluris jurgensenii ♀
11. Ancyluris meliboeus ♂ △
12. Ancyluris meliboeus ♀ △
13. Anteros acheus △

14. Anteros allectus ♀ ▽
15. Anteros allectus ♀ △
16. Anteros bracteata
17. Anteros carausius ♀ ♂ △▽
18. Anteros formosus
19. Apodemia carteri
20. Apodemia nais ▽△
21. Argyrogramma holosticta
22. Argyrogramma saphirina ♀
23. Argyrogramma sulphurea
24. Argyrogramma trochilia ♂
25. Argyrogramma trochilia ♀
26. Astraeodes areuta

27. Argyrogramma venilia
28. Audre epulus ♀ △
29. Audre albinus
30. Audre dovina
31. Audre aurinia ♀ △
32. Audre chilensis
33. Audre erostratus ▽
34. Audre erostratus △
35. Baeotis melanis
36. Baeotis nesaea
37. Baeotis zonata
38. Barbicornis acroleuca

1. Barbicornis melanops
2. Brachyglenis esthema
3. Calliona argenissa
4. Calliona irene
5. Callistium cleadas
6. Calociasma lilina
7. Calydna cabira ♂ △
8. Calydna cabira ♀ ▽
9. Calydna calyce ♀
10. Calydna catana
11. Calydna cea
12. Calydna charila
13. Calydna punctata
14. Calydna thersanda ♂ ♀
15. Caria chrysame

16. Caria domitianus
17. Caria lampeto
18. Caria stillaticia △
19. Cariomothis erotylus
20. Cariomothis erythromelas △
21. Cartea vitula
22. Chalodeta epijessa △
23. Catocyclotis aemulius
24. Chalodeta chaonitis
25. Chamaelimnas briola
26. Chamaelimnas joviana
27. Chamaelimnas splendens
28. Chamaelimnas villagomes
29. Charis anius
30. Charis anius △

31. Charis cadytis
32. Charis chrysus △
33. Charis gyas △
34. Charis gynea
35. Charis thedora
36. Chimastrum argentea
37. Chorinea faunus
38. Calydna caieta
39. Colaciticus johnstoni
40. Calydna calamisa ♂ ♀
41. Comphotis irrorata
42. Corrachia leucoplaga
43. Cremna actoris
44. Crocozona coecias

71

1. Cyrenia martia
2. Dinoptotis orphana △
3. Echenais bolena
4. Diopthalma telegone ▽
5. Diopthalma telegone △
6. Dysmathia portia
7. Echenais leucophaea ♀
8. Echenais micator
9. Echenais penthea ♀
10. Echenais aminias
11. Echenais leucocyana ▽△
12. Echenais zerna

13. Ematurgina bifasciata
14. Emesis progne
15. Echenais pulcherrima
16. Echenais senta
17. Emesis brimo △
18. Emesis cypria
19. Emesis lucinda ♀△
20. Emesis lucinda ♂▽△
21. Emesis mandana
22. Emesis tenedia ♀△▽
23. Emesis velutina △
24. Emesis zela ♀

25. Esthemopsis clonia
26. Esthemopsis jessi
27. Esthemopsis sericina
28. Esthemopsis thyatira
29. Eunogyra satyrus
30. Eurybia latifasciata
31. Eurybia leucolopha
32. Eurybia carolina
33. Eurybia halimede
34. Eurybia juturna

1. Eurybia lycisca
2. Eurybia nicaeus △
3. Eurybia patrona
4. Euselasia aurantia
5. Euselasia chrysippe
6. Euselasia amphidecta △
7. Euselasia angulata △
8. Euselasia argentia △
9. Euselasia authe
10. Euselasia cafusa △
11. Euselasia corduena
12. Euselasia erythraea

13. Euselasia euboea
14. Euselasia eucrates ♀ ♂
15. Euselasia eugeon △
16. Euselasia euoras
17. Euselasia euphaes
18. Euselasia euriteus ▽ △
19. Euselasia euryone ▽ △
20. Euselasia eusepus △
21. Euselasia gelanor △
22. Euselasia gelon
23. Euselasia gyda
24. Euselasia hieronymi

25. Euselasia labdacus △
26. Euselasia lisias △
27. Euselasia melaphaea
28. Euselasia arbas △
29. Euselasia orfita △
30. Euselasia pellonia ♀ △
31. Euselasia subargentea △
32. Euselasia thucydides
33. Euselasia uzita ♂
34. Euselasia uzita ♀

1. Hades hecamede
2. Hades noctula △
3. Helicopis acis
4. Helicopis cupido △
5. Hyphilaria nicias
6. Hyphilaria anophthalma ♀ ▽△
7. Hyphilaria parthenis ♀
8. Imelda glaucosmia
9. Hermathena candidata ♀
10. Ithomeis astrea
11. Ithomeis eulema

12. Ithomiola callixena
13. Ithomiola cascella
14. Lasaia meris ▽
15. Lasaia meris △
16. Lasaia oileus △
17. Juditha lamis ♀ △
18. Juditha lamis ♂ ▽
19. Lemonias agave ♀ △
20. Lemonias glaphyra
21. Lemonias thara
22. Lemonias zygia △

23. Lepricornis melanchroia
24. Leucochimona philemon
25. Lucillella camissa
26. Lymnas aegates
27. Lymnas ambryllis
28. Lymnas pulcherrima
29. Lymnas cinaron
30. Lymnas iarbas
31. Lymnas pixe
32. Lymnas xarifa

1. Lyropteryx apollonia △
2. Lyropteryx lyra ♀ ♂
3. Melanis agyrtus
4. Menander coruscans
5. Mesene croceella
6. Mesene epaphus ♂ ♀
7. Menander hebrus ♂
8. Menander hebrus ♀
9. Menander menander △
10. Mesene hya
11. Mesene margaretta
12. Mesene nepticula
13. Mesene phareus

14. Mesene silaris
15. Mesenopsis bryaxis
16. Mesopthalma idotea
17. Mesosemia calypso
18. Mesosemia ephyne
19. Mesosemia eumene ♀
20. Mesosemia gaudiolum
21. Mesosemia loruhama ♀
22. Mesosemia ibycus
23. Mesosemia machaera △
24. Mesosemia macrina
25. Mesosemia melpia ♀
26. Mesosemia messeis

27. Mesosemia metuana ♀ ♂
28. Mesosemia mevania
29. Mesosemia minos
30. Mesosemia odice
31. Mesosemia ahava
32. Mesosemia orbona
33. Mesosemia philocles
34. Mesosemia sifia
35. Mesosemia ulrica
36. Mesosemia zanoa
37. Mesosemia zorea

1. Metacharis lucius
2. Metacharis ptolomaeus △
3. Methonella cecilia
4. Mimocastina rothschildi ♀ △
5. Necyria bellona
6. Nahida coenoides
7. Napaea beltiana
8. Napaea eucharila
9. Monethe albertus
10. Napaea nepos
11. Napaea theages

12. Napaea umbra △
13. Necyria manco
14. Necyria zaneta △
15. Nelone cadmeis △
16. Nelone hypochalybe ▽
17. Nelone hypochalybe △
18. Nymphidium mantus
19. Notheme eumeus
20. Nymphidium azanoides △
21. Nymphidium cachrus
22. Nymphidium lisimon

23. Nymphidium caricae
24. Nymphidium ninias
25. Nymphidium onaeum
26. Nymula agle
27. Nymula calyce
28. Nymula chaonia
29. Nymula mycone △
30. Nymula nymphidioides
31. Nymula orestes ♀

1. Nymula phliasus ♀
2. Nymula phylleus
3. Nymula tytia ♂ ▽
4. Nymula tytia ♀ △
5. Orimba alemaeon
6. Orimba cruentata
7. Orimba epitus ♀
8. Orimba epitus ♂ △▽
9. Orimba jansoni
10. Orimba tapaja ♂
11. Orimba terias △
12. Orimba tapaja ♀
13. Orimba tutana ♀ △
14. Ourochnemis archytes △
15. Pachythone gigas
16. Pachythone palades
17. Pachythone lateritia
18. Panara phereclus △
19. Pandemos pasiphae
20. Parcella amarynthina
21. Parnes nycteis △
22. Peropthalma tullius
23. Periplacis glaucoma
24. Phaenochitonia bocchoris
25. Phaenochitonia cingulus
26. Phaenochitonia sophistes △
27. Polystichtis apotheta
28. Phaenochitonia phoenicura
29. Pheles heliconides
30. Polystichtis argenissa
31. Polystichtis emylius
32. Polystichtis florus
33. Polystichtis laobotas ♀ △
34. Polystichtis latona
35. Polystichtis lasthenes ♀ ♂

77

1. Polystichtis lucianus
2. Polystichtis porthaon
3. Polystichtis rhodope
4. Polystichtis thara
5. Polystichtis zeanger
6. Polystichtis siaka
7. Pseudopeplia grande
8. Rhetus arcius
9. Pretus preta
10. Symmachia hippea
11. Symmachia leopardina
12. Rhetus dysonii

13. Riodina lycisca
14. Riodina lysippus
15. Riodina lysistratus
16. Rodinia calpharnia
17. Roeberella calvus
18. Stichelia dukinfieldia
19. Semomesia croesus
20. Setabis gelasine △▽
21. Stichelia sagaris
22. Symmachia asclepia
23. Setabis pythia
24. Siseme alectryo △

25. Siseme aristoteles △
26. Siseme luculenta
27. Siseme pallas
28. Siseme peculiaris
29. Stalachtis calliope
30. Stalachtis euterpe
31. Symmachia jugurtha
32. Stalachtis phlegia
33. Styx infernalis
34. Symmachia cleonyma △
35. Stalachtis phaedusa

1. Symmachia menetas
2. Symmachia praxila
3. Symmachia probator
4. Symmachia threissa
5. Symmachia triangularis
6. Symmachia tricolor
7. Teratophthalma axilla
8. Teratophthalma marsena
9. Syrmatia dorilas
10. Themone pais
11. Theope eudocia
12. Theope barea
13. Tharops trotschi

14. Theope basilea
15. Theope foliorum
16. Theope lycaenina
17. Theope matuta
18. Theope pieridoides
19. Theope pedias ▽△
20. Theope publius △
21. Theope virgilius
22. Theope simplicia
23. Theope syngenes △
24. Theope theritas
25. Theope thestias △
26. Theope thootes

27. Thisbe irenea ♂ ▽
28. Thisbe molela
29. Thisbe irenea ♀ △
30. Thisbe lycorias
31. Voltinia theata ♀ △
32. Uraneis hyalina
33. Zabuella tenella △
34. Thysanota galena △
35. Xenandra helius
36. Xinias cynosema
37. Uraneis zamuro ♀
38. Xenandra prasinata
39. Zelotaea phasma

1. Atarnes sallei
2. Atrytonopsis zaovinia ▽
3. Astraptes fulgerator
4. Astraptes hopferi
5. Astraptes naxos
6. Astraptes pheres
7. Astraptes talus
8. Augiades crinisus ▽
9. Bolla cupreiceps
10. Bungalotis midas
11. Burca braco
12. Burca undulatus △
13. Butleria elwesi
14. Butleria facetus △
15. Butleria fruticolens △
16. Buzyges idothea
17. Cabares paterculus △
18. Cabares potrillo △

19. Cabirus procas ♂
20. Cabirus procas ♀
21. Calliades phrynicus
22. Callimormus alsimo △
23. Callimormus corades △
24. Camptopleura theramenes
25. Carrhenes canescens
26. Carrhenes unifasciata
27. Carystoides basochis
28. Carystoides maroma △
29. Carystus jolus △
30. Carystus phorcus △
31. Charidia lucaria
32. Cecropterus aunus
33. Cecropterus neis
34. Celaenorrhinus eligius
35. Charidia empolaeus
36. Celaenorrhinus shema △

37. Chiomara asychis
38. Chioides catillus △
39. Chioides jethira
40. Chiomara mithrax
41. Chloeria psittacina △
42. Choranthus radians △
43. Choranthus vitellius
44. Chrysoplectrum perniciosus
45. Chrysoplectrum pervivax △
46. Clito bibulus
47. Clito clito
48. Cobalus calvina
49. Cobalus virbius
50. Codactractus imalena
51. Cogia abdul △
52. Cogia calchas △
53. Cogia eluina
54. Conga zela △

81

1. Conognathus platon
2. Corticea epiberus
3. Cumbre cumbre
4. Croniades machaon
5. Cycloglypha thrasybulus
6. Cyclosemia anastomosis △
7. Cymaenes tripunctus
8. Cynea cynea
9. Cynea irma ♀ △
10. Dalla agathocles
11. Dalla caenides
12. Dalla caicus △
13. Dalla cyprius
14. Dalla cypselus
15. Dalla dimidiatus △
16. Dalla dognini
17. Dalla eryonas △
18. Dalla epiphaneus ▽
19. Dalla hesperioides
20. Dalla ibhara △

21. Dalla jelskyi △
22. Dalla semiargentea
23. Damas clavus △
24. Dardarina daridaeus △
25. Dardarina dardaris
26. Decinea percosius
27. Diaeus lacaena
28. Dion carmenta ♀ △
29. Dion rubrinota △
30. Drephalys alcmon
31. Drephalys oriander ♀ △
32. Drephalys phoenicoides △
33. Dyscophellus euribates
34. Ectomis cythna
35. Dyscophellus porcius
36. Dyscophellus ramusis
37. Dubiella fiscella △
38. Ebrietas osyris △
39. Ebusus ebusus △
40. Elbella polyzona

41. Elbella scylla
42. Enosis immaculata
43. Enosis misera △
44. Entheus lemna
45. Entheus priassus ♂
46. Entheus priassus ♀
47. Epargyreus barisses △
48. Epargyreus exadeus
49. Ephyriades arcas ♀
50. Ephyriades zephodes
51. Eprius veleda
52. Eracon bufonia △
53. Eracon clinias △
54. Erynnis gesta ♀
55. Erynnis heteroptera
56. Euphyes derasa △
57. Euphyes peneia ♀ △
58. Eutychide complana
59. Eutychide olympia

1. Eutychide physcella △
2. Falga jeconia
3. Gindanes brebisson △
4. Gindanes brontinus
5. Gorgopas viridiceps
6. Gorgythion begga △
7. Grais stigmaticus
8. Haemactis sanguinalis
9. Halotus angellus △
10. Helias phalaenoides ♀
11. Heliopetes arsalte
12. Heliopetes domicella
13. Heliopetes laviana
14. Heliopetes macaira △
15. Heliopetes omrina
16. Hyalothyrus neleus
17. Hylephila boulleti △
18. Hylephila ignorans
19. Justinia justinianus △
20. Lamponia lamponia
21. Lento lento
22. Lerema lineosa
23. Levina levina △

24. Lerodea edata △
25. Librita librita
26. Lucida lucia △
27. Ludens ludens ♀ △
28. Lycas argenteus △
29. Lychnuchus celsus
30. Marela tamyroides △
31. Mellana mella
32. Lychnuchoides ozias △
33. Mellana perfida △
34. Mellana villa
35. Metron chysogastra △
36. Metron oropa
37. Microceris variicolor
38. Milanion hemes
39. Milanion filumnus
40. Mimoniades ocyalus △
41. Mimoniades eupheme △
42. Mimoniades nurscia △
43. Mimoniades punctiger
44. Misius misius △
45. Mnasilus penicillatus △
46. Mnasitheus chrysophrys △

47. Mnestheus ittona △
48. Moeris remus △
49. Moeris striga △
50. Moeris moeris △
51. Molo heraea
52. Molo humeralis
53. Monca telata △
54. Morys cerdo
55. Morys etelka △
56. Morvina morvus △
57. Morys lyde
58. Mycteris crispus
59. Mylon melander
60. Mylon pulcherius
61. Myscelus amystis
62. Myscelus assaricus
63. Myscelus draudti △
64. Myscelus illustris
65. Myscelus belti
66. Myscelus phoronis
67. Myscelus rogersi △

84

1. Pellicia zamia △
2. Penicula cocoa
3. Perichares agrippa
4. Perichares butus
5. Perichares lindigiana
6. Perichares lotus ♀
7. Perichares philetes △
8. Phanes abaris △
9. Phanes almoda △
10. Phanus vitreus
11. Pheraeus argynnis △
12. Piruna gyrans
13. Phareas coeleste
14. Phocides batabano
15. Phocides oreides
16. Phocides pialia
17. Phocides polybius
18. Phocides thermus
19. Poanopsis puxillius
20. Phocides urania
21. Polygonus lividus △
22. Polyctor fera
23. Polyctor polyctor
24. Polythrix auginus
25. Polythrix decurtata
26. Polythrix gyges
27. Polythrix metallescens
28. Polythrix roma
29. Pompeius athenion △
30. Pompeius chittara
31. Pompeius dares △
32. Porphyrogenes omphale
33. Porphyrogenes vulpecula ▽
34. Proteides maysii △
35. Proteides mercurius
36. Pseudosarbia phaenicola
37. Psoralis exclamationis △
38. Pyrrhocalles antiqua ♀
39. Pyrrhopyge arax
40. Pynhopyge amyclas
41. Pyrrhopyge bixae △
42. Pyrrhopyge chalybea

1. Pyrrhopyge creona
2. Pyrrhopyge creon
3. Pyrrhopyge decipiens
4. Pyrrhopyge erythrosticta
5. Pyrrhopyge hygieia
6. Pyrrhopyge jonas
7. Pyrrhopyge kelita
8. Pyrrhopyge markena △
9. Pyrrhopyge latifasciata △
10. Pyrrhopyge araxes △
11. Pyrrhopyge pelota
12. Pyrrhopyge rubricollis
13. Pyrrhopyge sergius
14. Pyrrhopyge spatiosa

15. Pyrrhopygopsis agaricon
16. Pyrgus trisignatus △
17. Pyrgus veturius
18. Pyrrhopygopsis socrates △
19. Pyrdalus corbulo ♀
20. Pythonides amaryllis
21. Pythonides assecla
22. Pythonides lusorius △
23. Pythonides proxenus
24. Quadrus cerealis △
25. Quadrus contubernalis
26. Quadrus lugubris
27. Quinta cannae ♀ △
28. Rhinthon chiriquensis

29. Ridens biolleyi △
30. Ridens mephitis △
31. Ridens ridens
32. Sabina sabina
33. Sacrator polites
34. Salatis fulrius
35. Saliana salius △
36. Salatis salatis
37. Saliana placens △
38. Saliana triangularis
39. Saturnus tiberius
40. Sarbia damippe

1. Sarmientoia phaselis
2. Serdis venezuelae
3. Serdis viridicans △
4. Serdis statius
5. Sophista aristoteles
6. Sophista latifasciata
7. Sostrata cronion
8. Sostrata grippa △
9. Sostrata lucullea
10. Sostrata scintillans
11. Spathilepia clonius
12. Spioniades artemides
13. Staphylus mazans
14. Synapte lunata △
15. Synapte syraces △
16. Synole elana △
17. Synole hylaspes △

18. Synapte malitiosa
19. Talides sergestus △
20. Tarsoctenus papias
21. Tarsoctenus corytus ♀
22. Tarsoctenus plutia
23. Tarsoctenus praecia
24. Telemiades amphion
25. Telemiades avitus
26. Telemiades ceramina
27. Telles arcalaus △
28. Thargella fuliginosa ♀ △
29. Theagenes aegides △
30. Thespieus dalman △
31. Thespieus himella △
32. Thespieus macareus
33. Thespieus opigena △
34. Thespieus othna △

35. Thoon modius
36. Thoon taxes
37. Thracides nanea
38. Thracides phidon ▽
39. Thracides phidon △
40. Timochares trifasciata
41. Timochreon satyrus
42. Tirynthia conflua △
43. Tisias quadrata △
44. Tisias lesueur ♀
45. Tromba xanthura △
46. Typhedanus ampyx
47. Typhedanus undulatus △
48. Typhedanus galbula △
49. Urbanus chalco
50. Typhedanus orion

87

1. Turesis lucas
2. Urbanus corydon
3. Urbanus dorantes △
4. Urbanus doryssus
5. Urbanus proteus
6. Urbanus simplicius
7. Udranomia kikkawai
8. Udranomia spitzi
9. Wallengrenia drury
10. Wallengrenia ophites
11. Vacerra egla
12. Vacerra hermesia △
13. Vehilius clavicula
14. Vehilius labdacus
15. Vehilius venosus △
16. Vehilius vetula △
17. Vettius artona △
18. Jemadia gnetus
19. Jemadia hospita
20. Jera tricuspidata
21. Vettius fantasos △
22. Vettius coryna ♀ △
23. Vettius lafrenaye △
24. Vettius marcus ▽
25. Vettius marcus △
26. Vettius phyllus
27. Vlasta extrusus △
28. Vinius arginote △
29. Vinius tryhana
30. Virga cometho △
31. Xeniades orchamus
32. Zariaspes mythecus
33. Xeniades pteras
34. Xenophanes tryxus ♀
35. Zera scybis
36. Zopyrion satyrina △
37. Zenis minos
38. Zera hyacinthinus △

PAPILIONIDAE (1 : 2)

1. Graphium agamedes
2. Graphium almansor
3. Graphium antheus
4. Graphium auriger
5. Graphium hachei
6. Graphium colonna
7. Graphium endochus
8. Graphium cyrnus
9. Graphium evombar
10. Graphium auriger △
11. Graphium illyris
12. Graphium kirbyi
13. Graphium latreillianus
14. Graphium leonidas
15. Graphium levassori
16. Graphium philonoe
17. Graphium policenes
18. Graphium pylades △
19. Graphium ridleyanus
20. Graphium tynderaeus △
21. Papilio antimachus
22. Papilio constantinus
23. Papilio antenor
24. Papilio charopus
25. Papilio cynorta ♀ ▽ ♂ △
26. Papilio bromius ▽

1. Papilio dardanus ♀
2. Papilio dardanus ♂
3. Papilio dardanus ♀
4. Papilio delalande
5. Papilio demodocus
6. Papilio echerioides ♂
7. Papilio echerioides ♀

8. Papilio epiphorbas
9. Papilio gallienus △
10. Papilio hesperus
11. Papilio hornimani △
12. Papilio jacksoni ♀
13. Papilio lormieri
14. Papilio phorcas

15. Papilio mackinnoni
16. Papilio mnestheus △
17. Papilio nireus
18. Papilio nobilis
19. Papilio ophidicephalus
20. Papilio mechowianus

90

1. Papilio rex
2. Papilio zalmoxis ▽△
3. Papilio zenobia

1. Antanartia abyssinica
2. Antanartia delius
3. Antanartia hippomene
4. Antanartia schaeneia △
5. Apaturopsis cleocharis
6. Ariadne enotrea
7. Ariadne pagenstecheri
8. Asterope amulia △

9. Asterope benguelae △
10. Asterope boisduvali
11. Asterope madagascariensis △▽
12. Asterope morantii △
13. Asterope natalensis ♂ △
14. Asterope natalensis ♀ ▽
15. Asterope occidentalium
16. Asterope pechueli

17. Asterope trimeni △
18. Aterica galene ▽△
19. Aterica rabena
20. Bebearia absolon
21. Bebearia arcadius
22. Bebearia barombina
23. Bebearia comus △

1. Bebearia carshena
2. Bebearia cutteri ♀ ▽
3. Bebearia cutteri ♂ △
4. Bebearia iturina
5. Bebearia demetra △
6. Bebearia elpinice △
7. Bebearia laetitia ♂ ▽△

8. Bebearia tentyris △
9. Bebearia laetitia ♀
10. Bebearia mardania ♂ ▽△
11. Bebearia mardania ♀
12. Bebearia nivaria ▽△
13. Bebearia octogramma ♀
14. Bebearia sophus ♀ △

15. Bebearia partita ▽△
16. Bebearia phantasia ♂ ▽△
17. Bebearia phranza ♀
18. Bebearia phantasia ♀
19. Bebearia senegalensis
20. Bebearia staudingeri ♂ ♀

93

1. Bebearia theognis
2. Byblia acheloia
3. Catacroptera cloanthe
4. Catuna crithea
5. Charaxes acraeoides
6. Charaxes ameliae ♂

7. Charaxes achaemenes
8. Charaxes anticlea ♀ △
9. Catuna sikorana
10. Charaxes bebra △
11. Charaxes baumanni
12. Charaxes analava △

13. Charaxes ameliae ♀
14. Charaxes boueti
15. Charaxes bohemanni ♀
16. Charaxes bohemanni ♂ △
17. Charaxes brutus

1. Charaxes candiope
2. Charaxes castor ▽
3. Charaxes castor △
4. Charaxes cithaeron ♂ ▽
5. Charaxes cithaeron ♀ △
6. Charaxes etesippe △
7. Charaxes doubledayi
8. Charaxes druceanus
9. Charaxes etesippe ▽
10. Charaxes cynthia ♀ △
11. Charaxes ethalion ♀
12. Charaxes etheocles ♂

1. Charaxes etheocles ♀
2. Charaxes eudoxus △
3. Charaxes protoclea ♂
4. Charaxes eupale
5. Charaxes guderiana
6. Charaxes protoclea ♀
7. Charaxes hadrianus
8. Charaxes hildebrandti
9. Charaxes jahlusa △
10. Charaxes kahldeni
11. Charaxes laodice
12. Charaxes lichas
13. Charaxes lucretius ♂
14. Charaxes lucretius ♀
15. Charaxes nichetes
16. Charaxes numenes ♂
17. Charaxes nobilis △

1. Charaxes numenes ♀
2. Charaxes paphianus
3. Charaxes pelias
4. Charaxes pollux
5. Charaxes smaragdalis
6. Charaxes tiridates ♂ △

7. Charaxes tiridates ♀ ▽
8. Charaxes violetta ♂ △
9. Charaxes violetta ♀ ▽
10. Charaxes xiphares ♂
11. Charaxes xiphares ♀
12. Charaxes zelica

13. Charaxes zingha ♂ △
14. Charaxes zoolina ♂ ▽
15. Charaxes zoolina ♀ △
16. Charaxes zingha ♀

97

1. Cirrochroa niasica
2. Cymothoe alcimeda
3. Cymothoe anitorgis ♂ △
4. Cymothoe anitorgis ♀ ▽
5. Cymothoe beckeri ♂ △
6. Cymothoe beckeri ♀ ▽

7. Cymothoe caenis ♂
8. Cymothoe caenis ♀
9. Cymothoe capella ♀
10. Cymothoe cloetensi
11. Cymothoe capella ♂△
12. Cymothoe coccinata ♂

13. Cymothoe coccinata ♀
14. Cymothoe elabontas
15. Cymothoe confusa ♀
16. Cymothoe egesta
17. Cymothoe fumosa

1. Cymothoe fumana ♀
2. Cymothoe hesiodotus ♀
3. Cymothoe jodutta ♂
4. Cymothoe hyarbita ♀
5. Cymothoe hypatha ♂
6. Cymothoe hyarbita ♂

7. Cymothoe jodutta ♀
8. Cymothoe lucasi ♂
9. Cymothoe lurida
10. Cymothoe lucasi ♀
11. Cymothoe theobene ♂
12. Cymothoe oemilius

13. Cymothoe pluto ▽△
14. Cymothoe preussi ♂
15. Cymothoe preussi ♀
16. Cymothoe melanjae

100

1. Cymothoe theobene ♀
2. Cymothoe weymeri
3. Cynandra opis ♂ ♀
4. Cyrestis camillus
5. Euphaedra aureola
6. Euphaedra ceres ▽ △
7. Euphaedra cyparissa △
8. Euphaedra edwardsi
9. Euphaedra eleus ♀ △
10. Euphaedra francina
11. Euphaedra eupalus
12. Euphaedra eusemoides
13. Euphaedra gausape △
14. Euphaedra harpalyce △
15. Euphaedra imperialis

1. Euphaedra inanum ♀
2. Euphaedra judith
3. Euphaedra medon ▽
4. Euphaedra medon △
5. Euphaedra neophron
6. Euphaedra perseis
7. Euphaedra preussi △
8. Euphaedra sarita
9. Euphaedra spatiosa
10. Euphaedra themis ♀
11. Euphaedra xypete ♀ ▽
12. Euphaedra xypete ♂ △
13. Euphaedra zampa
14. Euryphene abasa ▽ △
15. Euryphene amaranta △

1. Euryphene ampedusa ♀
2. Euryphene ampedusa ♂
3. Euryphene aridatha ♀
4. Euryphene atossa ♀ △
5. Euryphene atrovirens ♀
6. Euryphene camarensis
7. Euryphene doriclea △
8. Euryphene duseni ♀
9. Euryphene gambiae ♀ ▽ △
10. Euryphene goniogramma ♂
11. Euryphene goniogramma ♀
12. Euryphene karschi
13. Euryphene grosesmithi ▽ △
14. Euryphene iris ♂ ♀
15. Euryphene lysandra △
16. Euryphene mawamba ♀
17. Euryphene milnei
18. Euryphene saphirina ♂ ♀
19. Euryphene simplex ♀
20. Euryphura achlys
21. Euryphura albula ♀
22. Euryphura isuka ♀
23. Euryphura nobilis

1. Euryphura plantilla
2. Euryphura porphyrion
3. Eurytela alinda ▽ △
4. Eurytela dryope
5. Euxanthe wakefieldi
6. Euxanthe eurinome ♀
7. Euxanthe trajanus
8. Eurytela hiarbas
9. Hadrodontes varanes
10. Hamanumida daedalus
11. Hypolimnas antevorta
12. Harmilla elegans
13. Hypolimnas dexithea
14. Hypolimnas deceptor

103

1. Hypolimnas dinarcha
2. Hypolimnas dubia
3. Crenidomimas concordia
4. Hypolimnas mechowi
5. Hypolimnas salmacis
6. Issoria excelsior
7. Issoria hanningtoni ▽ △
8. Hypolimnas usambara
9. Lachnoptera ayresii
10. Kallima rumia ♀
11. Kallima ansorgei
12. Kallima cymodice ♀
13. Kallima jacksoni
14. Kallima rumia ♂
15. Issoria smaragdifera △
16. Lachnoptera iole ♀
17. Neptidopsis ophione
18. Neptidopsis platyptera

1. **Neptis** agatha △
2. **Neptis** exalenca △
3. **Neptis** frobenia
4. **Neptis** incongrua
5. **Neptis** melicerta
6. **Neptis** jamesoni
7. **Neptis** metella △
8. **Neptis** nemetes
9. **Neptis** nicomedes
10. **Neptis** nicoteles

11. **Neptis** paula
12. **Neptis** saclava
13. **Neptis** seeldrayersi
14. **Palla** decius
15. **Phalanta** columbina △
16. **Precis** clelia
17. **Precis** hadrope ♀
18. **Precis** andremiaja
19. **Precis** infracta
20. **Precis** andremi

21. **Precis** antilope
22. **Precis** archesia ▽
23. **Precis** artaxia
24. **Precis** ceryne △
25. **Precis** chorimene △
26. **Precis** coelestina △
27. **Precis** eurodoce
28. **Precis** limnoria ▽
29. **Precis** octavia
30. **Precis** octavia

1. Precis pelarga
2. Precis pelarga
3. Precis rhadama
4. Precis sinuata
5. Precis sophia △
6. Precis westermanni ♀
7. Pseudacraea boisduvali
8. Pseudacraea clarki
9. Precis terea
10. Pseudacraea dolomena
11. Pseudacraea eurytus ♀
12. Pseudacraea glaucina
13. Precis tareta
14. Pseudacraea imitator
15. Pseudacraea kuenowi
16. Pseudacraea lucretia ▽
17. Pseudacraea lucretia △
18. Pseudacraea poggei
19. Pseudacraea simulator
20. Pseudacraea semire
21. Precis westermanni ♂
22. Precis tugela
23. Pseudacraea striata

1. Pseudacraea warburgi
2. Pseudargynnis hegemone
3. Pseudoneptis coenobita
4. Salamis anacardi
5. Salamis anteva ▽△

6. Salamis cacta
7. Vanessula milca
8. Precis natalica
9. Salamis parhassus
10. Salamis temora

11. Salamis cytora
12. Mesoxantha ethosea
13. Palla decius ♀
14. Charaxes monteiri ♀
15. Charaxes thomasius △

ACRAEIDAE (1 : 2)

1. Acraea acerata ▽ △
2. Acraea acrita
3. Acraea admatha
4. Acraea aglaonice
5. Acraea alciope ♂
6. Acraea alciope ♀
7. Acraea alicia △
8. Acraea althoffi ♂
9. Acraea althoffi ♀
10. Acraea amicitiae ♀
11. Acraea anacreon
12. Acraea anemosa △
13. Acraea asboloplintha
14. Acraea aubyni
15. Acraea axina
16. Acraea bonasia △
17. Acraea braesia
18. Acraea butleri
19. Acraea buttneri

20. Acraea cabira △
21. Acraea caecilia
22. Acraea caldarena ♀ △
23. Acraea camaena ♀
24. Acraea cepheus ♀ △
25. Acraea cerasa
26. Acraea chaeribula
27. Acraea chilo
28. Acraea conradti △
29. Acraea dammii
30. Acraea doubledayi
31. Acraea egina ♂ △
32. Acraea egina ♀
33. Acraea equatorialis
34. Acraea encedon
35. Acraea esebria ▽
36. Acraea esebria △
37. Acraea eugenia ♀
38. Acraea excelsior

39. Acraea horta △
40. Acraea hova
41. Acraea igola
42. Acraea insignis
43. Acraea jodutta
44. Acraea johnstoni
45. Acraea kraka
46. Acraea leucopyga
47. Acraea lycoa
48. Acraea mahela
49. Acraea masamba
50. Acraea natalica
51. Acraea mirifica △
52. Acraea neobule
53. Acraea newtoni
54. Acraea niobe
55. Acraea nohara △

1. Acraea mairessei △
2. Acraea obeira
3. Acraea oberthuri △
4. Acraea oncaea ♂ ▽
5. Acraea oncaea ♀ △
6. Acraea oreas
7. Acraea orina
8. Acraea orestia
9. Acraea oscari
10. Acraea parrhasia △
11. Acraea peneleos
12. Acraea penelope
13. Acreae pentapolis
14. Acraea perenna
15. Acraea periphanes
16. Acraea petraea
17. Acraea pharsalus

18. Acraea pseudolycia ♂ △
19. Acraea pseudolycia ♀ ▽
20. Acraea quirina
21. Acraea quirinalis ♀ △
22. Acraea rabbaiae
23. Acraea rahira ♀
24. Acraea ranavalona
25. Acraea safie
26. Acraea satis
27. Acraea semivitrea
28. Acraea sotikensis
29. Acraea servona ▽
30. Acraea servona △
31. Acraea stenobea ♀
32. Acraea terpsichore ♂
33. Acraea terpsichore ♀
34. Acraea uvui

35. Acraea vesperalis
36. Acraea violarum ♀
37. Acraea vogersi
38. Acraea wigginsi
39. Acraea zetes ♀
40. Acraea zetes ♂
41. Acraea zitja △
42. Acraea zonata
43. Bematistes adrasta
44. Bematistes aganice
45. Bematistes consanguinea
46. Bematistes elongata
47. Bematistes epaea ♂
48. Bematistes epaea ♀
49. Bematistes epiprotea ♀
50. Bematistes excisa
51. Bematistes poggei ♀ △

DANAIDAE (1 : 2)

PIERIDAE (3 : 4)

1. Anaphaeis anomala
2. Anaphaeis aurota ♂ ▽
3. Anaphaeis aurota ♀ △
4. Anaphaeis eriphia
5. Appias epaphia ♀ ♂ △▽
6. Appias lasti
7. Appias phaola ♀
8. Appias sylvia
9. Belenois aurota

10. Belenois calypso △
11. Belenois creona ♂
12. Belenois creona ♀
13. Belenois gidica ♀
14. Belenois gidica ♂ △
15. Belenois hedyle
16. Belenois helcida
17. Belenois raffrayi
18. Belenois solilucis

19. Belenois subeida
20. Belenois theora
21. Belenois theuszi △
22. Belenois thysa ♀ ▽
23. Belenois thysa ♂ △
24. Belenois zochalia ♀ △
25. Catopsilia pyranthe ♂ ▽△
26. Colotis agoye
27. Catopsilia pyranthe ♀

111

1. Colotis regina
2. Colotis ducissa
3. Colotis subfasciatus
4. Colotis vesta
5. Colotis pallene ♀
6. Colotis zoe ♂
7. Colotis zoe ♀
8. Dixeia astarte
9. Dixeia doxocharina △▽
10. Dixeia cebron
11. Dixeia capricornus ♀
12. Dixeia liliana ♀
13. Dixeia pigea ♀
14. Dixeia spilleri ♂ ♀
15. Eronia leda
16. Eronia pharis △
17. Eronia cleodora
18. Eronia cleodora △
19. Eurema brigitta ▽
20. Eurema brigitta △
21. Eurema desjardinsi
22. Eurema eximia ♀
23. Eurema hapale △
24. Eurema hecabe ▽
25. Eurema hecabe △
26. Leptosia alcesta
27. Leptosia medusa
28. Mylothris bernice
29. Mylothris agathina ♀ ▽
30. Mylothris agathina ♂ △

113

1. Mylothris chloris △
2. Mylothris mortoni
3. Mylothris ngaziya
4. Mylothris nubila ♀
5. Mylothris poppea ♂
6. Mylothris poppea ♀
7. Mylothris rhodope ♀
8. Mylothris sagala ♂

9. Mylothris sagala ♀
10. Mylothris yulei
11. Mylothris sulphurea
12. Mylothris trimenia
13. Mylothris smithi
14. Nepheronia argia ♀ △
15. Nepheronia argia
16. Nepheronia buqueti △

17. Nepheronia argia ♀ ▽
18. Nepheronia thalassina
19. Pontia helice △
20. Pseudopontia paradoxa
21. Eurema brenda
22. Pieris brassicoides △

SATYRIDAE (1:1)

1. Aphysoneura pigmentaria △
2. Bicyclus auricruda
3. Bicyclus campina △
4. Bicyclus iccius
5. Cassionympha cassius
6. Coenonympha vaucheri
7. Coenura aurantiaca ♀ △

8. Coenyropsis bera
9. Henotesia eliasis
10. Dingana bowkeri
11. Dingana dingana
12. Elymniopsis bammakoo
13. Henotesia ankora
14. Elymniopsis phegea

15. Elymniopsis ugandae
16. Eumenis atlantis
17. Gnophodes parmeno
18. Henotesia antahala △
19. Henotesia ankaratra ♀
20. Henotesia avelona ♀
21. Henotesia masikora

1. Henotesia narcissus
2. Henotesia paradoxa ▽ △
3. Henotesia strigula
4. Henotesia peitho △
5. Henotesia perspicua
6. Henotesia phaea
7. Henotesia simonsi
8. Mycalesis dubia △
9. Heteropsis drepana ♀
10. Lasiommata maderakal
11. Mycalesis anynana ♀ △
12. Leptoneura clytus
13. Melanitis libya
14. Leptoneura swanepoeli △
15. Leptoneura oxylus
16. Meneris tulbaghia
17. Mycalesis aurivillii
18. Mintha mintha
19. Mycalesis ansorgei ♀
20. Mycalesis asochis ♀

1. Mycalesis ena
2. Mycalesis evadne
3. Mycalesis funebris △
4. Mycalesis golo △
5. Mycalesis dorothea ▽△
6. Mycalesis italus ♂ △

7. Mycalesis hewitsoni
8. Mycalesis italus ♀ ▽
9. Mycalesis kenia
10. Mycalesis mandanes △
11. Mycalesis matuta
12. Mycalesis martius △

13. Mycalesis nobilis △
14. Mycalesis phalanthus △
15. Mycalesis obscura △
16. Mycalesis safitza ▽
17. Mycalesis safitza △
18. Mycalesis sandace △

117

1. Mycalesis saussurei
2. Mycalesis sciathis △
3. Mycalesis vulgaris △
4. Neita neita
5. Neocoenyra cooksoni
6. Ypthima albida
7. Neocoenyra durbani △
8. Neocoenyra extensii
9. Neocoenyra gregorii
10. Physcaeneura pione ♀ ♂ ▽ △

11. Physcaeneura leda ♀ △
12. Pseudonympha magus △
13. Physcaeneura panda △
14. Paralethe dendrophilus
15. Pseudonympha hippia
16. Pseudonympha machacha △
17. Pseudonympha magus
18. Ypthima itonia △
19. Ypthima sufferti △
20. Ypthima triopthalma

21. Pseudonympha narycia
22. Pseudonympha trimeni △
23. Ypthima batesi △
24. Ypthima doleta
25. Neocoenyra duplex △
26. Tarsocera cassus △
27. Ypthima zanjuga ♀ △
28. Stygionympha vigilans
29. Tarsocera cassina

LYCAENIDAE (3 : 4)

119

1. Capys alphaeus
2. Capys disjunctus ♂ ▽
3. Capys disjunctus ♀ △
4. Castalius calice
5. Castalius cretosus
6. Castalius isis
7. Castalius hintza
8. Castalius marganitaceus
9. Castalius melaena
10. Catachrysops eleusis
11. Chloroselas pseudozeritis ▽ △
12. Citrinophila erastus
13. Citrinophila tenera
14. Cooksonia trimeni
15. Crudaria leroma ♀ △
16. Cnodontes pallida
17. Cupidopsis cissus ♂ △
18. Cupidopsis cissus ♀ ▽
19. Cupidopsis iobates

20. Deudorix virgata
21. Dapidodigma hymen △
22. Deloneura barca △
23. Deloneura millari
24. Desmolycaena mazoensis △
25. Deudorix antalus ♀
26. Deudorix caerulea
27. Deudorix caliginosa △
28. Deudorix dariares ♀ △
29. Deudorix dinochares ♂ ▽
30. Deudorix dinochares ♂ △
31. Deudorix dinochares ♀ ▽
32. Deudorix diocles
33. Deudorix kafuensis
34. Deudorix odana
35. Deudorix lorisona
36. Deudorix zela ♀ ▽
37. Deudorix zela ♀ △ ·
38. Diopetes angelita ♂

39. Diopetes angelita ♀
40. Diopetes aurivilliusi ♀ △
41. Diopetes catalla △
42. Diopetes violetta
43. Durbania amakoza
44. Durbania limbata △
45. Durbaniella clarki ♀
46. Durbaniella saga △
47. Eicochrysops hippocrates
48. Eicochrysops mahallakoaena
49. Eicochrysops messapus ▽ △
50. Epamera aemulus △
51. Epamera aethria
52. Epamera alienus △
53. Epamera aphneoides △
54. Epamera bellina
55. Epamera fontainei

121

1. Epamera laon △
2. Epamera mimosae △
3. Epamera mermis
4. Epamera nursei △
5. Epamera pollux △
6. Epamera sappirus △
7. Epamera sidus △
8. Epamera silanus
9. Epamera stenogrammica
10. Epitola albomaculata △
11. Epitola badura
12. Epitola batesi ♀ △
13. Epitola carcina ♀ ▽ △
14. Epitola catuna △
15. Epitola ceraunia △
16. Epitola conjuncta

17. Epitola crowleyi ♂ △
18. Epitola crowleyi ♀ ▽
19. Epitola gerina
20. Epitola hewitsoni
21. Epitola honorius
22. Epitola leonina
23. Epitola liana △
24. Epitola nigra
25. Epitola nitida ♀
26. Epitola miranda
27. Epitola posthumus ♂
28. Epitola posthumus ♀
29. Epitola staudingeri
30. Epitola sublustris
31. Epitola uniformis ♀
32. Epitola viridana

33. Epitolina catori ♀ △
34. Epitolina dispar
35. Eresina bilinea △
36. Eresina toroensis
37. Euchrysops abyssinia △
38. Euchrysops albistriata
39. Euchrysops barkeri ♀ ▽ △
40. Euchrysops dolorosa ♀
41. Euchrysops hypopolia
42. Euchrysops kabrosae
43. Euchrysops malathana
44. Euchrysops osiris
45. Euchrysops scintilla ▽
46. Euchrysops scintilla △
47. Euliphyra leucyanea ♀ △

1. Euliphyra mirifica
2. Everes micylus △
3. Everes togara
4. Harpendyreus aequatorialis △
5. Harpendyreus noquasa
6. Harpendyreus tsomo △
7. Hemiolaus ceres
8. Hemiolaus dolores △
9. Hewitsonia similis △
10. Hewitsonia similis ▽
11. Hypokopelates aruma ♂
12. Hypokopelates aruma ♀
13. Hypokopelates eleala ♂ △
14. Hypokopelates eleala ♀ ▽
15. Hypokopelates mera
16. Hypolycaena hatita ♂

17. Hypolycaena hatita ♀
18. Hypolycaena lebona
19. Hypolycaena liara
20. Hypolycaena philippus
21. Hypomyrina nomenia
22. Iolaphilus calisto
23. Iolaphilus laonides △
24. Iolaphilus ismenias ♀
25. Iolaphilus julus ♂ ▽
26. Iolaphilus julus ♀ △
27. Iolaphilus menas
28. Iolaphilus piaggae
29. Iolaus bolissus ▽
30. Iolaus eurisus ♀
31. Iridana nigeriana ▽△
32. Iridana rougeoti ♀ △

33. Lachnocnema bibulus ♂ △
34. Lachnocnema bibulus ♀ ▽
35. Lachnocnema brimo
36. Lachnocnema durbani △
37. Lachnocnema luna ♀ △
38. Lachnocnema magna △
39. Lachnocnema niveus ♀
40. Larinopoda lagyra
41. Larinopoda latimarginata
42. Larinopoda lircaea △
43. Leptomyrina boschi
44. Leptomyrina hirundo
45. Leptomyrina lara
46. Leptomyrina phidias

123

1. Lepidochrysops aethiopia
2. Lepidochrysops ariadne ♀ △
3. Lepidochrysops caffrariae ♂ △
4. Lepidochrysops caffrariae ♀ ▽
5. Lepidochrysops coxii
6. Lepidochrysops delicata ♀
7. Lepidochrysops glauca
8. Lepidochrysops gigantea
9. Lepidochrysops grahami △
10. Lepidochrysops ignota
11. Lepidochrysops lacrimosa △
12. Lepidochrysops letsea
13. Lepidochrysops methymna ▽
14. Lepidochrysops methymna △
15. Lepidochrysops nevillei ♀ △
16. Lepidochrysops ortygia △
17. Lepidochrysops patricia

18. Lepidochrysops parsimon
19. Lepidochrysops peculiaris ♂ ▽
20. Lepidochrysops peculiaris ♀ △
21. Lepidochrysops plebeia △
22. Lepidochrysops polydialecta
23. Lepidochrysops procera △
24. Lepidochrysops tantalus △
25. Lepidochrysops victoriae
26. Lipaphnaeus aderna
27. Lipaphnaeus ella
28. Liptena campimus △
29. Liptena catalina
30. Liptena despecta △
31. Liptena eukrines ▽ △
32. Liptena fatima
33. Liptena ferrymani △
34. Liptena helena ▽ △

35. Liptena hollandi △
36. Liptena homeyeri
37. Liptena ideoides
38. Liptena ilma △
39. Liptena libyssa ♀ △
40. Liptena lybia △
41. Liptena nubifera △
42. Liptena opaca
43. Liptena o-rubrum ♂ △
44. Liptena o-rubrum ♀ ▽
45. Liptena perobscura
46. Liptena praestans △
47. Liptena otlauga ♀
48. Liptena turbata
49. Liptena similis △

124

1. Liptena subvariegata ♂ △
2. Liptena subvariegata ♂ ▽
3. Liptena subvariegata ♀ △
4. Liptena undina △
5. Liptena undularis
6. Liptena xanthostola
7. Lipaphnaeus leonina △
8. Lycaena abboti
9. Lycaena orus
10. Megalopalpus metaleucus
11. Megalopalpus zymna △
12. Micropentila adelgitha △
13. Micropentila alberta △
14. Mimacraea apicalis
15. Micropentila gabunica
16. Micropentila brunnea
17. Micropentila mpigi △
18. Mimacraea eltringhami
19. Mimacraea fulvaria

20. Mimacraea heurata
21. Mimacraea krausei
22. Mimacraea landbecki △
23. Mimacraea marshalli △
24. Mimacraea neokoton
25. Mimacraea skoptoles
26. Mimeresia cellularis ♂
27. Mimeresia debora △
28. Mimeresia dinora △
29. Mimeresia neavei
30. Mimeresia libentina
31. Mimeresia semirufa
32. Myrina dermaptera ▽△
33. Myrina silenus
34. Neaveia lamborni
35. Neoepitola barombiensis △
36. Oboronia güssfeldti
37. Oboronia punctatus
38. Ornipholidotos kirbyi

39. Oxylides faunus ♂ △
40. Oxylides faunus ♀ ▽
41. Syrmoptera melanomitra △
42. Oxylides amasa
43. Oraidium barberae △
44. Phlyana stactalla △
45. Phlyaria cyara
46. Phlyaria heritsia
47. Ornipholidotos peucetia
48. Ornipholidotos muhata
49. Ornipholidotos paradoxa
50. Pentila abraxas
51. Pentila aspasia
52. Pentila auga
53. Pentila bitje
54. Pentila hewitsoni
55. Pentila laura

125

1. Pentila mombasae
2. Pentila occidentalium △
3. Pentila pauli △
4. Pentila petreia △
5. Pentila phidia
6. Pentila preussi
7. Pentila rotha
8. Pentila torrida
9. Pentila tropicalis △
10. Phasis argyraspis △
11. Phasis lycegenes ♀ △
12. Phasis malagrida
13. Phasis sardonyx ▽
14. Phasis sardonyx △
15. Phasis felthami
16. Phasis thero △
17. Phasis wallengreni ♀ △
18. Phytala elais

19. Phytala hyettina
20. Phytala hyettoides
21. Phytala intermixta ♀
22. Phytala vansomereni △
23. Pilodeudorix diyllus
24. Poecilmitis chrysaor
25. Poecilmitis palmus △
26. Poecilmitis thysbe
27. Poecilmitis zeuxo △
28. Powellana cottoni ♂ △
29. Powellana cottoni ♀ ▽
30. Pseudaletis agrippina
31. Pseudaletis batesi
32. Pseudaletis clymenus
33. Pseudaletis leonis
34. Pseudaletis mazanguli
35. Pseudonacaduba aethiops
36. Pseudonacaduba sichela △

37. Scolitantides notoba △
38. Spalgis lemolea
39. Spindasis crustaria △
40. Spindasis ella
41. Spindasis homeyeri △
42. Spindasis mozambica
43. Spindasis namaqua △
44. Spindasis natalensis ▽ △
45. Spindasis phanes ♀
46. Spindasis somalina △
47. Spindasis subaureus
48. Spindasis tavetensis △
49. Spindasis trimeni △
50. Spindasis waggae ♀
51. Stugeta bowkeri
52. Stugeta marmorea ♀

NEMEOBIIDAE (1 : 1)

33

34

35

36

LIBYTHEIDAE (1 : 1)

37

38

39

1. Tanuetheira timon
2. Tarucus thespis ▽
3. Tarucus bowkeri ♀
4. Tarucus sybaris
5. Tarucus thespis △
6. Telipna acraea ♀
7. Telipna carnuta
8. Telipna bimacula
9. Telipna erica △
10. Telipna transverstigma △
11. Teratoneura isabellae △
12. Teriomima puellaris
13. Teriomima subpunctata △

14. Thermoniphas plurilimbata
15. Thestor basuta ♀
16. Thestor brachyara △
17. Thestor protumnus
18. Thestor obscurus
19. Thestor strutti
20. Toxochitona gerda
21. Uranothauma poggei ♀ ▽
22. Trichiolaus mermeros △
23. Uranothauma antinorii
24. Uranothauma crawshayi △
25. Uranothauma falkensteini
26. Uranothauma nubifer

27. Zizina antanossa △
28. Uranothauma poggei ♂ ▽△
29. Virachola bimaculata △
30. Virachola livia
31. Zeritis neriene
32. Zeritis sorhageni △
33. Abisara gerontes
34. Abisara rogersi ♀
35. Abisara rutherfordi ♂ ▽
36. Abisara rutherfordi ♀ △
37. Abisara talantus
38. Libythea labdaca
39. Saribia tepahi △

127

1. Abantis bicolor
2. Abantis bismarcki
3. Abantis leucogaster
4. Abantis paradisea
5. Abantis zambesiaca
6. Abantis tettensis △
7. Abantis venosa
8. Acada annulifer
9. Acada biseriatus
10. Acleros mackenii ▽
11. Acleros mackenii △
12. Acleros placidus △
13. Alenia sandaster △
14. Andronymus neander
15. Andronymus philander △
16. Artitropa comus ♀ △
17. Artitropa erinnys △

18. Artitropa shelleyi
19. Astictopterus anomaeus △
20. Astictopterus inornatus
21. Astictopterus stellatus △
22. Borbo borbonica △
23. Borbo detecta △
24. Borbo fallax
25. Borbo fatuellus △
26. Borbo gemella △
27. Borbo holtzii ♀ △
28. Borbo lugens △
29. Borbo micans △
30. Borbo perobscura
31. Borbo ratek
32. Brusa saxicola
33. Caenides benga
34. Caenides dacena ♀ △

35. Caenides hidarioides
36. Caenides soritia △
37. Calleagris hollandi △
38. Calleagris jamesoni
39. Calleagris kobela
40. Calleagris lacteus
41. Caprona pillaana
42. Celaenorrhinus atratus
43. Celaenorrhinus bettoni △
44. Celaenorrhinus chrysoglossa
45. Celaenorrhinus galenus
46. Celaenorrhinus humbloti
47. Celaenorrhinus illustris
48. Celaenorrhinus meditrina
49. Celaenorrhinus mokeezi
50. Celaenorrhinus proxima
51. Celaenorrhinus rutilans

52. Ceratricia aurea
53. Ceratricia flava ♀
54. Ceratricia nothus △
55. Ceratricia phocion
56. Chondrolepis niveicorni
57. Coliades anchises
58. Coliades aeschylus
59. Coliades chalybe
60. Coliades fervida
61. Coliades forestan △
62. Coliades keithloa △
63. Coliades libeon
64. Coliades pisistratus △
65. Coliades ramanatek

128

129

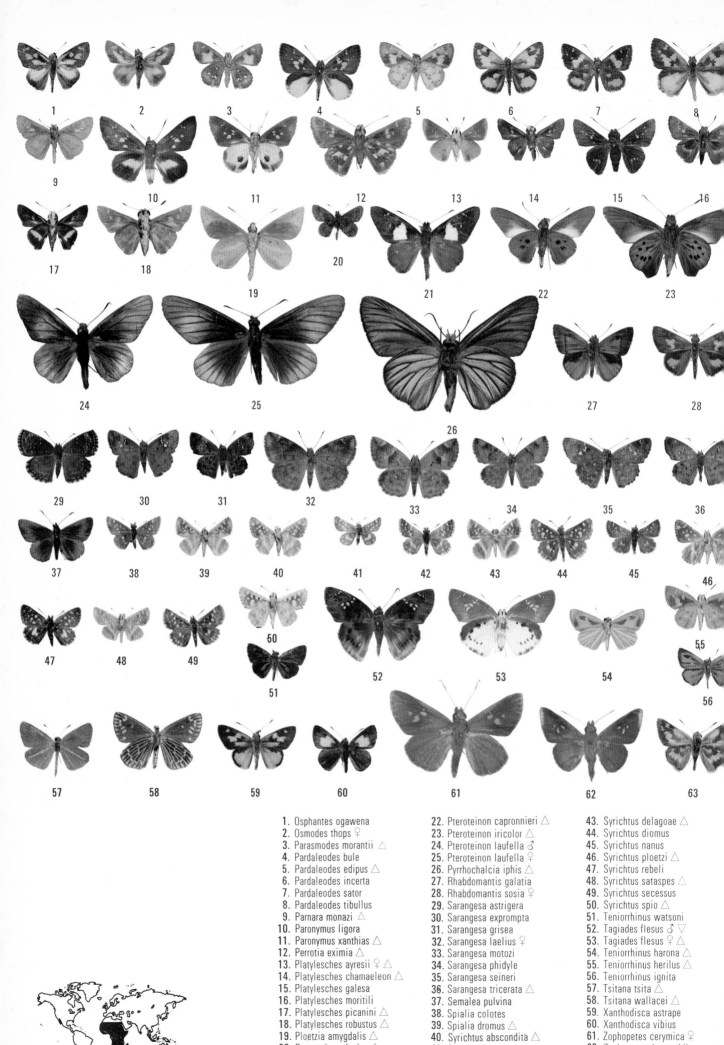

1. Osphantes ogawena
2. Osmodes thops ♀
3. Parasmodes morantii △
4. Pardaleodes bule
5. Pardaleodes edipus △
6. Pardaleodes incerta
7. Pardaleodes sator
8. Pardaleodes tibullus
9. Parnara monazi △
10. Paronymus ligora
11. Paronymus xanthias △
12. Perrotia eximia △
13. Platylesches ayresii ♀ △
14. Platylesches chamaeleon △
15. Platylesches galesa
16. Platylesches moritili
17. Platylesches picanini △
18. Platylesches robustus △
19. Ploetzia amygdalis △
20. Prosopalpus duplex △
21. Pteroteinon caenira

22. Pteroteinon capronnieri △
23. Pteroteinon iricolor △
24. Pteroteinon laufella ♂
25. Pteroteinon laufella ♀
26. Pyrrhochalcia iphis △
27. Rhabdomantis galatia
28. Rhabdomantis sosia ♀
29. Sarangesa astrigera
30. Sarangesa exprompta
31. Sarangesa grisea
32. Sarangesa laelius ♀
33. Sarangesa motozi
34. Sarangesa phidyle
35. Sarangesa seineri
36. Sarangesa tricerata △
37. Semalea pulvina
38. Spialia colotes
39. Spialia dromus △
40. Syrichtus abscondita △
41. Syrichtus agylla
42. Syrichtus asterodia

43. Syrichtus delagoae △
44. Syrichtus diomus
45. Syrichtus nanus
46. Syrichtus ploetzi △
47. Syrichtus rebeli
48. Syrichtus sataspes △
49. Syrichtus secessus
50. Syrichtus spio △
51. Teniorrhinus watsoni
52. Tagiades flesus ♂ ▽
53. Tagiades flesus ♀ △
54. Teniorrhinus harona △
55. Teniorrhinus herilus △
56. Teniorrhinus ignita
57. Tsitana tsita △
58. Tsitana wallacei △
59. Xanthodisca astrape
60. Xanthodisca vibius
61. Zophopetes cerymica ♀
62. Zophopetes dysmephila
63. Zenonia zeno

PAPILIONIDAE (1 : 2)

1. Chilasa paradoxa
2. Chilasa paradoxa
3. Chilasa slateri
4. Graphium empedovana
5. Chilasa veiovis
6. Graphium agetes
7. Dabasa gyas ♀
8. Dabasa payeni

9. Graphium androcles
10. Graphium agamemnon
11. Cressida cressida
12. Graphium antiphates ▽
13. Graphium aristeus
14. Graphium arycles ▽
15. Graphium bathycles ▽
16. Graphium cloanthus

17. Graphium delesserti ♀
18. Graphium deucalion
19. Graphium doson ▽
20. Graphium evemon △
21. Graphium macareus
22. Graphium macleayanus
23. Graphium nomius
24. Graphium ramaceus

131

1. Graphium thule
2. Graphium wallacei
3. Graphium weiski
4. Graphium xenocles
5. Lamproptera meges

6. Ornithoptera chimaera
7. Pachlioptera aristolochiae △
8. Ornithoptera croesus
9. Ornithoptera priamus
10. Ornithoptera goliath

11. Pachlioptera atropos
12. Pachlioptera jophon
13. Ornithoptera paradisea ♀
14. Pachlioptera liris
15. Ornithoptera paradisea ♂

1. Ornithoptera victoriae ♀
2. Ornithoptera urvillianus ♀
3. Ornithoptera urvillianus ♂
4. Papilio deiphobus
5. Papilio aegeus ♂
6. Papilio aegeus ♀ △

7. Papilio deiphobus ♂ △
8. Papilio ascalaphus △
9. Papilio deiphobus ♀
10. Pachlioptera polydorus
11. Papilio crino
12. Papilio anactus

13. Papilio canopus
14. Papilio castor
15. Papilio ambrax
16. Papilio demolion

133

1. Ornithoptera victoriae ♂
2. Papilio lorquinianus
3. Papilio gambrisius ♀
4. Papilio elephenor △
5. Papilio euchenor
6. Papilio iswara △

7. Papilio godeffroyi
8. Papilio hoppo
9. Papilio ilioneus ♀ △
10. Papilio fuscus
11. Papilio krishna
12. Papilio laglaizei ▽

13. Papilio laglaizei △
14. Papilio dravidarum
15. Papilio memnon ♂
16. Papilio memnon ♀ △
17. Papilio memnon ♀

1. Papilio nephelus
2. Papilio palinurus
3. Papilio peranthus
4. Papilio polymnestor
5. Parides hageni
6. Papilio phestus
7. Parides nox
8. Papilio hector
9. Papilio woodfordi
10. Parides latreillei
11. Parides neptunus
12. Papilio ulysses ▽
13. Papilio toboroi △
14. Parides philoxenus
15. Parides varuna
16. Parides priapus ♀
17. Papilio ulysses △
18. Parnassius simo
19. Trogonoptera brookiana ♂

135

1. Parides coon
2. Papilio rumanzovia △
3. Trogonoptera brookiana ♀
4. Troides helena ♂
5. Troides helena ♀
6. Troides haliphron
7. Troides hypolitus
8. Troides haliphron
9. Teinopalpus imperialis ♂
10. Eurytides xanticles
11. Troides mirandus
12. Teinopalpus imperialis ♀
13. Troides mirandus

AMATHUSIIDAE (1 : 2)

1. Aemona amathusia ♀
2. Aemona lena ♀
3. Amathusia binghami △
4. Amathusia masina
5. Amathusia perakana ♀ △
6. Amathusia phidippus △
7. Amathuxidia amythaon ♂ ▽
8. Amathuxidia amythaon ♀ △
9. Discophora bambusae
10. Discophora celinde ♀
11. Faunis arcesilaus
12. Faunis gracilis
13. Discophora necho ♂
14. Discophora necho ♀
15. Discophora timora △
16. Discophora tullia
17. Enispe cycnus
18. Enispe euthymius △
19. Faunis faunula
20. Discophora deo

1. Faunis kirata △
2. Faunis menado △
3. Faunis phaon △
4. Faunis stomphax
5. Hyantis hodeva
6. Morphopsis albertisi
7. Stichopthalma camadeva
8. Stichopthalma louisa
9. Stichopthalma nourmahal ♀ △
10. Tenaris artemis △
11. Tenaris artemis ▽
12. Tenaris bioculatus ♀
13. Tenaris chionides
14. Tenaris diana
15. Tenaris dimona △
16. Tenaris domitilla
17. Tenaris gorgo
18. Tenaris horsfieldi ♀
19. Tenaris myops ♀
20. Tenaris myops ♂
21. Tenaris onolaus
22. Tenaris phorcas ♀

. Tenaris selene △
. Tenaris schonbergi
. Tenaris staudingeri
. Tenaris urania
. Thaumantis diores
. Thaumantis klugius

7. Thaumantis noureddin
8. Thaumantis odana ♀ △
9. Xanthotaenia busiris △
10. Thauria aliris ♂ △
11. Thauria aliris ♀ ▽
12. Zeuxidia amethystus ♂

13. Zeuxidia amethystus ♀
14. Zeuxidia aurelius ♂
15. Zeuxidia aurelius ♀
16. Zeuxidia doubledayi ♀ △

1. Abrota ganga ♀
2. Amnosia decora ♂
3. Amnosia decora ♀
4. Apatura ambica
5. Apatura chevana
6. Apaturina erminia

7. Apatura parisatis ♀
8. Apatura parisatis ♂
9. Argyreus hyperbius ♂ ♀
10. Apatura rhea ♀
11. Ariadne ariadne
12. Ariadne isaeus

13. Ariadne merione
14. Ariadne taeniata
15. Byblia ilithyia
16. Calinaga lhatso
17. Cethosia chrysippe
18. Cethosia cyane ♀

1. Cirrochroa orissa
2. Cirrochroa regina △
3. Cirrochroa tyche ♀
4. Cyrestis lutea
5. Cupha erymanthis
6. Cupha lampetia
7. Cupha maeonides

8. Cyrestis maenalis
9. Cupha prosope
10. Cyrestis achates
11. Cyrestis acilia
12. Cyrestis cocles
13. Cyrestis nivea
14. Cyrestis telamon

15. Cyrestis thyonneus
16. Dichorragia nesimachus
17. Cyrestis themire
18. Dilipa morgiana
19. Doleschallia bisaltide ▽
20. Doleschallia bisaltide △

1. Doleschallia dascon
2. Doleschallia dascylus ♀
3. Doleschallia hexopthalmos
4. Eulaceura osteria ♂
5. Eulaceura osteria ♀
6. Euripus consimilis ♂
7. Euripus consimilis ♀
8. Euripus halitherses ♂
9. Euripus halitherses ♀
10. Euthalia aconthea △
11. Euthalia agnis
12. Euthalia aeetes
13. Euthalia aeropa
14. Euthalia cyanipardus
15. Euthalia aetion
16. Euthalia alpheda
17. Euthalia anosia
18. Euthalia cocytus ♀

143

1. Euthalia nara ♀
2. Euthalia patala
3. Euthalia phemius ♀
4. Euthalia phemius ♂
5. Fabriciana kamala ▽△
6. Euthalia satrapes
7. Euthalia teuta ♂ ♀
8. Herona marathus
9. Herona sumatrana
10. Hestina nama
11. Hypolimnas alimena ♂
12. Hypolimnas alimena ♀
13. Hypolimnas antilope
14. Hypolimnas bolina

145

1. Hypolimnas bolina ♀
2. Hypolimnas deois
3. Hypolimnas misippus ♂ △
4. Hypolimnas misippus ♀ ▽
5. Hypolimnas diomea
6. Hypolimnas octocula △
7. Hypolimnas pandarus
8. Hypolimnas panopion ♀
9. Laringa horsfieldii ♂
10. Laringa horsfieldii ♀
11. Kallima paralekta ♂ ▽
12. Kallima paralekta ♀ △
13. Kallima philarchus
14. Lebadea martha
15. Lebadea alankara
16. Laringa castelnaui
17. Limenitis danava

1. Kallima spiridiva
2. Limenitis daraxa
3. Limenitis dudu
4. Neptis consimilis
5. Neptis duryodana
6. Neptis cyrilla

7. Neptis eblis ♀
8. Limenitis imitata
9. Limenitis lymire
10. Limenitis lysanias
11. Limenitis procris
12. Limenitis zulema

13. Mynes geoffroyi △
14. Mynes geoffroyi ▽
15. Mynes woodfordi △
16. Neptis ananta
17. Neptis anjana
18. Polyura dehaani △

147

1. Neptis columella △
2. Neptis ebusa
3. Neptis heliodore
4. Neptis heliopolis
5. Neptis hordonia △
6. Neptis illigera △
7. Neptis jumbah △
8. Neptis mahendra
9. Neptis manasa △

10. Neptis miah
11. Neptis mysia
12. Neptis nandina
13. Neptis nausicaa
14. Neptis nirvana
15. Neptis nitetis
16. Neptis nycteus
17. Neptis paraka
18. Neptis praslini

19. Neptis sankara
20. Neptis satina
21. Neptis shepherdi ♀
22. Neptis shepherdi ♂
23. Neptis venilia
24. Neptis vikasi △
25. Neptis zaida
26. Neurosigma doubledayi
27. Pandita sinope

1. Pantoporia asura
2. Pantoporia cama ♂ ♀
3. Pantoporia eulimene
4. Pantoporia gordia
5. Pantoporia karwara △
6. Pantoporia kasa △
7. Pantoporia larymna
8. Pantoporia nefte ♀

9. Pantoporia nefte ♂
10. Pantoporia opalina ♀
11. Pantoporia perius △
12. Pantoporia pravara
13. Pantoporia ranga
14. Pantoporia selenophora ♂
15. Pantoporia selenophora ♀
16. Pantoporia speciosa

17. Parthenos sylvia
18. Parthenos tigrina
19. Parathyma reta
20. Pareba vesta
21. Phalanta alcippe
22. Phalanta phalantha

1. Polyura athamas ♀
2. Polyura delphis ▽
3. Polyura eudamippus
4. Polyura jalysus △
5. Polyura moori
6. Precis orithya

7. Polyura pyrrhus
8. Polyura schreiberi ♀
9. Precis almana
10. Precis atlites
11. Precis evigone
12. Precis hedonia

13. Prothoe calydonia ♀ △
14. Prothoe australis ♀
15. Precis villida
16. Precis hierta
17. Precis iphita
18. Prothoe australis △

1. Prothoe calydonia
2. Prothoe franckii
3. Pyrameis dejeani
4. Symbrenthia hippochlus
5. Pyrameis itea
6. Pyrameis gonarilla
7. Pyrameis indica
8. Rhinopalpa polynice
9. Rhinopalpa polynice ♀ △
10. Stibochiona coresia
11. Stibochiona nicea
12. Symbrenthia hippalus △
13. Stibochiona schonbergi ♀
14. Symbrenthia hypselis ♀ ▽ △
15. Symbrenthia hypatia △
16. Symbrenthia niphanda △
17. Tanaecia aruna
18. Tanaecia cibaritis △
19. Tanaecia clathrata
20. Tanaecia julii △

1. Tanaecia lutala ♀
2. Tanaecia munda
3. Tanaecia palguna
4. Tanaecia pelea
5. Terinos atlita △
6. Terinos clarissa

7. Terinos taxiles
8. Terinos terpander
9. Terinos tethys
10. Vagrans egista
11. Vanessa canace
12. Vindula arsinoe ♂

13. Vindula arsinoe ♀
14. Vindula erota
15. Yoma sabina
16. Cirrochroa thais

ACRAEIDAE (1 : 2)

DANAIDAE (1 : 2)

1. Acraea andromacha
2. Acraea violae
3. Miyana moluccana ▽
4. Miyana moluccana △
5. Danaus genutia
6. Danaus melaneus
7. Danaus septentrionis
8. Danaus affinis ♂ ▽
9. Danaus affinis ♀ △

10. Danaus aglea
11. Danaus aspasia
12. Danaus choaspes
13. Danaus eryx
14. Danaus ferruginea
15. Danaus gautama ♀
16. Danaus hamata
17. Danaus ismare
18. Danaus juventa

19. Danaus limniace
20. Danaus lotis
21. Danaus melanippus
22. Danaus melanippus
23. Danaus philene
24. Danaus pumila
25. Danaus schenki ♀

153

1. Danaus sita
2. Danaus similis
3. Euploea alcathoe △
4. Euploea andamanensis
5. Euploea arisbe
6. Euploea batesi
7. Euploea callithoe
8. Euploea climena

9. Euploea climena
10. Euploea core
11. Euploea coreta
12. Euploea corus
13. Euploea corus ♀ △
14. Euploea crameri
15. Euploea darchia
16. Euploea deheeri △

17. Euploea deione
18. Euploea diana
19. Euploea diocletianus ♂
20. Euploea diocletianus ♀
21. Euploea doubledayi
22. Euploea dufresne
23. Euploea duponcheli
24. Euploea eichhorni

PIERIDAE (3 : 4)

1. Idea d'urvillei
2. Idea hypermnestra
3. Idea jasonia
4. Idea leuconoe ♀
5. Ideopsis gaura

6. Idea lynceus
7. Euploea viola
8. Ideopsis vitrea
9. Euploea vollenhovi
10. Tellervo zoilus

11. Anaphaeis java △
12. Aoa affinis
13. Aporia agathon

1. Appias ada △
2. Aporia soracta
3. Aporia leucodyce
4. Appias albina
5. Appias cardena △
6. Appias libythea ♂
7. Appias celestina ♀
8. Appias indra ♀ △

9. Appias ithome
10. Appias lalage ♀ ♂
11. Appias celestina ♂
12. Appias libythea ♀
13. Appias lyncida
14. Appias melania ♀
15. Appias nephele
16. Appias nero

17. Appias pandrone △
18. Appias placidia
19. Appias paulina ♀ △
20. Appias wardii
21. Catopsilia scylla ▽
22. Catopsilia crocale
23. Catopsilia pomona

1. Catopsilia scylla △
2. Cepora abnormis △
3. Cepora aspasia
4. Cepora lea
5. Cepora eperia △
6. Cepora judith
7. Cepora perimale △
8. Cepora lacta △
9. Baltia shawii △
10. Delias aglaia
11. Cepora nadina ♀
12. Cepora temena △
13. Colias eogene ♂
14. Colias alpherakii ♂ ♀
15. Colias eogene ♀
16. Delias albertisi △
17. Delias agostina △
18. Delias aganippe
19. Cepora nerissa △
20. Colias marcopolo ♂ ♀
21. Colias sieversi
22. Delias argenthona
23. Delias baracasa △
24. Delias aruna ♂ ▽
25. Delias aruna ♀ △
26. Delias bagoe
27. Delias belisama △
28. Colotis etrida

1. Delias bornemanni △▽
   Delias caeneus ♀
   Delias crithoe
   Delias candida ♀
   Delias candida ♂
   Delias descombesi △
   Delias clathrata △
8. Delias ennia △
9. Delias eucharis ♀
10. Delias cuningputi △
11. Delias harpalyce △
12. Delias descombesi ▽
13. Delias gabia ♀ △
14. Delias kummeri △
15. Delias nigrina △
16. Delias harpalyce ♀
17. Delias henningia
18. Delias itamputi ♀
19. Delias hyparete
20. Delias mysis △
21. Delias nysa △

1. Delias periboea △
2. Delias rosenbergi △
3. Dercas verhuelli
4. Delias thysbe
5. Delias totila ♀
6. Dercas lycorias
7. Delias timorensis
8. Elodina perdita
9. Elodina egnatia
10. Eurema andersonii △

11. Eurema blanda △
12. Eurema candida ♀
13. Eurema laeta
14. Eurema hecabe ♀
15. Eurema libythea △
16. Eurema norbana
17. Eurema sari △
18. Eurema smilax
19. Eurema tilaha
20. Eurema tominia ♂

21. Eurema tominia ♀
22. Gandaca harina
23. Hebomoia glaucippe ♂
24. Gonepteryx zaneka
25. Ixias marianne △
26. Ixias reinwardti
27. Ixias pyrene ♂ ♀
28. Hebomoia leucippe
29. Leptosia xiphia △
30. Phrissura aegis ♂

SATYRIDAE (1 : 1)

1. Acropthalmia artemis ▽
2. Argyronympha pulchra △
3. Argyrophenga antipodum
4. Callerebia kalinda
5. Callerebia annada △

6. Bletogona mycalesis △
7. Callerebia nirmala ▽ △
8. Callerebia shallada ♀ ▽ △
9. Chazara heydenreichii ▽ △
10. Dodonidia helmsi

11. Cyllogenes suradeva
12. Coelites epiminthia
13. Coelites euptychioides
14. Coelites nothis △

1. Elymnias agondas ♀
2. Elymnias casiphone
3. Elymnias caudata
4. Elymnias ceryx
5. Elymnias cattonis
6. Elymnias cumaea
7. Elymnias cybele △
8. Elymnias dara
9. Elymnias esaca

1. Elymnias hicetas ♀
2. Elymnias malelas ♀
3. Elymnias hewitsoni

4. Elymnias hypermnestra ♀ ♂
5. Elymnias mimalon
6. Elymnias patna

7. Elymnias nesaea
8. Elymnias panthera ♂
9. Elymnias penanga ♂

1. Elymnias pealii ♀
2. Elymnias penanga ♀
3. Erycinidia gracilis △
4. Elymnias singhala
5. Elymnias vasudeva △
6. Geitoneura achanta
7. Geitoneura hobartia ♀
8. Erites angularis △
9. Erites argentina △
10. Erites elegans
11. Ethope diademoides
12. Ethope himachala
13. Eumenis mniszechi
14. Geitoneura kershawi
15. Geitoneura lathoniella ▽△
16. Geitoneura minyas
17. Geitoneura tasmanica

165

1. Harsiesis hygea △
2. Heteronympha merope ♂
3. Heteronympha merope ♀
4. Hypocysta adiante
5. Hypocysta antirius

6. Hypocysta osyris △
7. Heteronympha mirifica ♀ ♂
8. Hypocysta aroa
9. Hypocysta euphemia
10. Lamprolenis nitida △

11. Lethe chandica △
12. Lethe bhairava ▽
13. Hypocysta pseudirius
14. Lethe baladeva △
15. Lethe confusa ▽△

1. Lethe darena
2. Lethe drypetis △
3. Lethe europa ♀ ▽
4. Lethe elwesi ♂ ♀ ▽ △
5. Lethe goalpara △

6. Lethe jalaurida △
7. Lethe kansa
8. Lethe latiaris
9. Lethe serbonis △
10. Lethe mekara

11. Lethe minerva ♀
12. Lethe pulaha ♀
13. Lethe rohria △ ▽
14. Lethe scanda △
15. Lethe maitrya △

1. Lethe sidonis △
2. Lethe sinorix △
3. Lethe sura ▽
4. Lethe syrcis

5. Lethe verma ▽ △
6. Maniola lupinus
7. Melanitis amabilis △
8. Melanitis boisduvalia

9. Melanitis atrax
10. Melanitis constantia ▽

1. Melanitis leda
2. Melanitis phedima △
3. Mycalesis anapita △
4. Mycalesis anaxias
5. Melanitis zitenius
6. Mycalesis discobolus

7. Melanitis velutina
8. Mycalesis barbara
9. Mycalesis dexamenus △
10. Mycalesis duponcheli
11. Mycalesis durga
12. Mycalesis fuscum △

13. Mycalesis horsfieldi
14. Mycalesis ita
15. Mycalesis janardana △
16. Mycalesis lepcha ▽
17. Mycalesis maianeas △
18. Mycalesis lorna ♀

1. Mycalesis malsara
2. Mycalesis malsarida △
3. Mycalesis mahadeva △
4. Mycalesis messene
5. Mycalesis mestra
6. Mycalesis mineus ▽ △
7. Mycalesis mnasicles

8. Mycalesis mucia △
9. Mycalesis oroatis
10. Mycalesis orseis
11. Mycalesis phidon △
12. Mycalesis patnia
13. Mycalesis perseus △
14. Mycalesis sirius

15. Mycalesis tagala ♀
16. Mycalesis subdita △
17. Mycalesis terminus
18. Mycalesis visala △
19. Mycalesis sudra
20. Neope bhadra ♀

1. Neope yama ▽
2. Neope yama △
3. Platypthima ornata △
4. Neorina hilda
5. Neorina krishna
6. Neorina lowi
7. Pararge schakra △▽
8. Orsotriaena medus △
9. Pieridopsis virgo
10. Parantirrhoea marshalli
11. Pararge menava
12. Orinoma damaris

1. Ptychandra lorquini
2. Ptychandra schadenbergi ♀ △
3. Ragadia crisia
4. Xois sesara △
5. Ragadia crisilda
6. Rhaphicera moorei
7. Rhaphicera satricus △▽

8. Satyrus brahminus ▽△
9. Satyrus huebneri △▽
10. Ypthima avanta
11. Satyrus parisatis
12. Ypthima ceylonica
13. Ypthima aphnius
14. Ypthima chenui △

15. Ypthima baldus △▽
16. Satyrus pumilus
17. Satyrus parisatis ▽△
18. Tisiphone abeona
19. Tisiphone helena

LYCAENIDAE (3 : 4)

1. Castalius roxus △
2. Catapaecilma elegans
3. Catapaecilma major △
4. Catapaecilma subochracea △
5. Catopyrops ancyra △
6. Catopyrops keiria
7. Catochrysops panormus
8. Catochrysops strabo ♀ △
9. Celastrina akasa
10. Celastrina albocaeruleus
11. Celastrina camenae
12. Celastrina carna
13. Celastrina ceyx ♀
14. Celastrina cossaea △
15. Celastrina dilectus
16. Celastrina lavendularis △
17. Celastrina melaena △
18. Celastrina musina ♀ △

19. Celastrina nedda △
20. Celastrina puspa ♂
21. Celastrina puspa ♀
22. Celastrina quadriplaga
23. Celastrina tenella
24. Celastrina transpectus
25. Celastrina vardhana △
26. Charana hypoleuca
27. Charana jalindra ♂ ▽
28. Charana jalindra ♀ ▽
29. Cheritra freja
30. Cheritra orpheus
31. Chilades lajus △
32. Chliaria amabilis △
33. Chliaria kina
34. Chliaria othona △
35. Chrysozephyrus syla
36. Curetis bulis

37. Curetis insularis △
38. Curetis felderi
39. Curetis santana ♀
40. Curetis sperthis ♀ △
41. Cyaniriodes libna
42. Curetis thetis
43. Dacalana vidura ▽
44. Dacalana vidura △
45. Deramas livens
46. Deudorix dohertyi
47. Deudorix epijarbas
48. Deudorix epirus △
49. Deudorix eryx △
50. Deudorix hypargyria
51. Drina discophora
52. Drina maneia ▽
53. Drupadia estella △

175

1. Drina maneia △
2. Drupadia melisa
3. Drupadia scaeva
4. Eooxylides tharis △
5. Epimastidia pilumna ♀ △
6. Epimastidia staudingeri
7. Everes lacturnus △
8. Euaspa milionia △
9. Euchrysops cnejus ♂ ▽
10. Euchrysops cnejus ♀
11. Flos anniella
12. Flos apidanus ♀ △
13. Flos diardi △
14. Heliophorus androcles
15. Heliophorus bakeri ♂
16. Heliophorus bakeri ♀
17. Heliophorus brahma

18. Heliophorus ila ♀
19. Heliophorus moorei ♀ ▽ △
20. Horaga amethystus
21. Horaga lefebvrei △
22. Horaga onyx
23. Horaga selina △
24. Horaga viola △
25. Horsfieldia narada
26. Hypochlorosis antipha ♀ △
27. Hypochlorosis danis
28. Hypochlorosis humboldti
29. Hypochrysops anacletus △
30. Hypochrysops apelles
31. Hypochrysops apollo ♂ ▽
32. Hypochrysops apollo ♀ △
33. Hypochrysops architas
34. Hypochrysops arronica

35. Hypochrysops aurigena △
36. Hypochrysops byzos ♀ △
37. Hypochrysops chrysanthis ♂
38. Hypochrysops chrysanthis ♀
39. Hypochrysops delicia
40. Hypochrysops doleschallii ♀
41. Hypochrysops halyaetus △
42. Hypochrysops ignita ♀ ▽
43. Hypochrysops meeki
44. Hypochrysops narcissus ♀ △
45. Hypochrysops craterus ♀ △
46. Hypochrysops pagenstecheri ♀
47. Hypochrysops plotinus ♂ △
48. Hypochrysops plotinus ♀ ▽
49. Hypochrysops polycletus △

1. Hypochrysops polycletus ♀ ▽
2. Hypochrysops polycletus ♀ △
3. Hypochrysops pythias △
4. Hypochrysops regina △
5. Hypochrysops rex
6. Hypochrysops scintillans ♀ △
7. Hypochrysops rufinus ♀ ▽ △
8. Hypochrysops taeniata △
9. Hypochrysops theon
10. Hypolycaena cinesia △
11. Hypolycaena erylus △
12. Hypolycaena phorbas ♂
13. Hypolycaena phorbas ♀
14. Hypolycaena sipylus △
15. Hypothecla astyla ♀ △
16. Hypolycaena thecloides ▽
17. Hypolycaena thecloides △

18. Hypothecla astyla ♀ △
19. Iraota distanti △
20. Iraota lazarena
21. Iraota timoleon ▽
22. Iraota timoleon △
23. Jacoona amrita
24. Jacoona anasuja
25. Jacoona irmina ♀ △
26. Jacoona scopula
27. Jalmenus evagoras ▽
28. Jalmenus evagoras △
29. Jalmenus icilius
30. Jalmenus inous △
31. Jamides abdul
32. Jamides aleuas
33. Jamides aratus ♂ ▽
34. Jamides aratus ♀ △

35. Jamides bochus
36. Jamides caeruleas
37. Jamides celeno ♂
38. Jamides celeno ♀
39. Jamides cyta ♀ △
40. Jamides cunilda
41. Jamides elpis ▽
42. Jamides elpis △
43. Jamides euchylas
44. Jamides kankena
45. Jamides festivus ♀ △
46. Jamides lucide
47. Jamides lugine
48. Jamides malaccanus △
49. Jamides nemophila △

177

1. Ogyris oroetes ▽
2. Ogyris zosine
3. Panchala ammon △
4. Panchala paraganesa △
5. Parachrysops bicolor
6. Parelodina aroa △
7. Petrelaea dana
8. Pithecops corvus △
9. Pithecops fulgens
10. Pithecops peridesma
11. Poritia erycinoides
12. Poritia promula
13. Poritia karennia ♀ △
14. Poritia phalena
15. Poritia philota
16. Poritia sumatrae ♂
17. Poritia sumatrae ♀
18. Pseudodipsas cephenes

19. Pseudodipsas digglesii
20. Pseudodipsas eone ♀
21. Pseudodipsas myrmecophila
22. Purlisa giganteus
23. Rapala abnormis △
24. Rapala affinis ♀ △
25. Rapala drasmos
26. Rapala elcia
27. Rapala iarbas
28. Rapala kessuma △
29. Rapala manea
30. Rapala dioetas
31. Rapala nissa
32. Rapala scintilla △
33. Rapala pheretima
34. Rapala varuna ♀ ▽ △
35. Rathinda amor △
36. Remelana jangala ♂ ▽

37. Remelana jangala ♀ △
38. Ritra aurea
39. Semanga superba △
40. Simiskina phalena ♀
41. Simiskina phalia ♀
42. Simiskina pharyge
43. Simiskina pheretia △
44. Simiskina philura ♂
45. Simiskina philura ♀
46. Sinthusa chandrana ♀ ▽ △
47. Sinthusa indrasari △
48. Sinthusa malika
49. Sinthusa nasaka ♀
50. Sinthusa peregrinus △
51. Sinthusa virgo △
52. Sithon nedymond ♂ ▽ △
53. Sithon nedymond ♀ △
54. Spalgis epius △

180

NEMEOBIIDAE (1:1)

1. Thysonotis schaeffera △
2. Thysonotis stephani △
3. Una purpurea
4. Ticherra acte △
5. Una usta △
6. Virachola isocrates ♂
7. Virachola isocrates ♀
8. Zizina alsulus
9. Zizula gaika △
10. Zizina otis △
11. Zizina oxleyi △
12. Waigeum dinawa ♂ △
13. Waigeum dinawa ♀ ▽
14. Waigeum ribbei
15. Waigeum thauma
16. Yasoda pita
17. Zeltus amasa
18. Abisara celebica ♂ ▽
19. Abisara celebica ♀ △
20. Abisara echerius ♀ ♂ ▽△
21. Abisara fylla
22. Abisara kausambi
23. Abisara kausamboides △
24. Abisara neophron
25. Abisara savitri
26. Dicallaneura decorata ♂ ▽
27. Dicallaneura decorata ♀ △
28. Dicallaneura leucomelas △▽

1. Dicallaneura ribbei ♀
2. Dodona adonira △
3. Dodona deodata
4. Dodona dipoea △
5. Dodona durga
6. Dodona dracon
7. Dodona egeon
8. Dodona eugenes
9. Dodona fruhstorferi ♀
10. Dodona ouida ♂ △
11. Dodona ouida ♀ ▽
12. Dodona windu
13. Laxita damajanti ♂ ▽
14. Laxita damajanti ♀ △
15. Laxita orphna ♂ ▽
16. Laxita orphna ♀ △
17. Laxita teneta ♂ △
18. Zemeros flegyas △
19. Laxita teneta ♀ ▽
20. Laxita telesia ♂
21. Praetaxila segecia △
22. Laxita telesia ♀
23. Praetaxila weiskei ♂
24. Praetaxila weiskei ♀
25. Sospita satraps △

LIBYTHEIDAE (1:1)

HESPERIIDAE (2:3)

1. Sospita statira ♂ ▽
2. Sospita statira ♀ △
3. Stiboges nymphidia
4. Taxila haquinus ♂
5. Taxila haquinus ♀
6. Taxila thuisto △
7. Zemeros emesoides
8. Zemeros flegyas ▽

9. Libythea geoffroyi ♂
10. Libythea geoffroyi ♀
11. Libythea lepita
12. Libythea myrrha
13. Libythea myrrha
14. Libythea narina
15. Acerbas anthea
16. Aeromachus dubius

17. Aeromachus plumbeola
18. Aeromachus stigmata
19. Allora doleschalli
20. Arnetta atkinsoni △
21. Arnetta verones △
22. Ampittia dioscorides

1. Ancistroides armatus
2. Ancistroides gemmifer △
3. Ancistroides longicornis
4. Ancistroides nigrita
5. Anisynta dominula
6. Anisynta sphenosema ♀ △
7. Anisynta tillyardi △
8. Anisyntoides argenteomata △
9. Astictopterus jama
10. Baoris oceia
11. Badamia exclamationis
12. Baracus vittatus ♀ △
13. Bibasis etelka △
14. Baracus vittatus ♂ ▽

15. Bibasis gomata △
16. Bibasis harisa ♀
17. Bibasis sena △
18. Bibasis jaina
19. Bibasis oedipodea
20. Bibasis vasutana ♀ △
21. Borbo verani
22. Caprona erosula
23. Caprona ransonnetti
24. Caprona syrichthus △
25. Caltoris bromus △
26. Caltoris cahira
27. Caltoris cormasa △
28. Caltoris philippina

29. Caltoris tulsi △
30. Capila phanaeus
31. Celaenorrhinus ambareesa
32. Celaenorrhinus aurivittata
33. Celaenorrhinus asmara
34. Celaenorrhinus badia
35. Celaenorrhinus putra
36. Celaenorrhinus ladana
37. Celaenorrhinus leucocera
38. Celaenorrhinus lativittus
39. Celaenorrhinus spilothyrus
40. Chaetocneme beata
41. Chaetocneme corvus ♀
42. Chaetocneme corvus ♂

185

1. Chaetocneme critomedia
2. Chaetocneme denitza ♀
3. Chaetocneme editus
4. Chaetocneme porphyropis
5. Chamunda chamunda
6. Charmion ficulnea
7. Choaspes benjaminii △
8. Choaspes illuensis
9. Choaspes hemixanthus
10. Choaspes subcaudata △
11. Coladenia dan
12. Coladenia igna
13. Coladenia indrani
14. Croitana croites

15. Cupitha purreea △
16. Cyrina cyrina
17. Daimio bhagava ♀
18. Daimio corona
19. Darpa hanria
20. Darpa pteria
21. Eetion elia
22. Euschemon rafflesia
23. Erionota thrax
24. Exometoeca nycteris △
25. Gangara thyrsis
26. Gangara lebadea △
27. Ge geta
28. Gomalia albofasciata

29. Halpe homolea △
30. Halpe knyvetti △
31. Halpe moorei
32. Halpe wantona △
33. Halpe zema
34. Hasora badra △
35. Hasora discolor △
36. Hasora celaenus △
37. Hasora chromus △
38. Hasora hurama △
39. Hasora lizetta
40. Hasora malayana ♀
41. Hasora mus ♀

186

1. Hasora thridas △
2. Hasora schonherri ♀
3. Hasora vitta
4. Hesperilla chrysotricha
5. Hesperilla crypsargyra △
6. Hesperilla donnysa
7. Hesperilla idothea △
8. Hesperilla picta △
9. Hesperilla ornata △
10. Hidari irava △
11. Hyarotis adrastus △
12. Hyarotis microstictum
13. Iambriz obliquans
14. Iambrix salsala △
15. Ilma irvina
16. Iton semamora
17. Iton watsonii △
18. Isma bononia

19. Isma guttulifera ♀
20. Isma protoclea
21. Isma obscura ♀ △
22. Koruthaialos focula
23. Koruthaialos sindu
24. Lobocla bifasciatus
25. Lobocla liliana △
26. Lotongus avesta △
27. Lotongus calathus △
28. Lotongus onara
29. Lotongus taprobanus
30. Matapa aria △
31. Matapa celsina
32. Matapa druna
33. Mesodina aeluropis
34. Mesodina halyzia ♀ △
35. Mooreana princeps
36. Mooreana trichoneura

37. Motasingha atralba ♀ △
38. Motasingha dirphia
39. Neohesperilla xiphiphora
40. Netrocoryne thaddeus ♀ △
41. Netrocoryne repanda
42. Notocrypta curvifascia
43. Notocrypta clavata △
44. Notocrypta feishamelii
45. Notocrypta pria
46. Notocrypta quadrata
47. Notocrypta renardi
48. Notocrypta waigensis
49. Ochus subvittatus △
50. Ocybadistes walkeri
51. Odina hieroglyphica △
52. Odina sulina
53. Odontoptilum angulata

187

1. Odontoptilum pygela
2. Oerane microthrysus
3. Oreisplanus perornatus △
4. Oreisplanus munionga
5. Parnara amalia
6. Parnara guttatus
7. Pasma tasmanicus
8. Pirdana hyela ♀ △
9. Pelopidas assamensis
10. Pelopidas conjuncta ♀
11. Pelopidas mathias
12. Pelopidas sinensis
13. Pirdana distanti △
14. Pintara pinwilli ♀
15. Pithauria marsena
16. Pithauria stramineipennis
17. Plastingia aurantiaca △
18. Plastingia callineura
19. Plastingia corissa
20. Plastingia pugnans
21. Plastingia fuscicornis △
22. Plastingia helena
23. Plastingia latoia △
24. Plastingia niasana △
25. Plastingia naga △
26. Polytremis eltola
27. Potanthus dara △
28. Potanthus hetaerus △
29. Potanthus omaha △
30. Potanthus trachala ♀
31. Prusiana prusias
32. Prusiana kuhni
33. Psolos fuscula
34. Pudicitia pholus
35. Sabera caesina
36. Sabera fuliginosa
37. Satarupa gopala
38. Sarangesa dasahara
39. Scobura isota △
40. Seseria affinis
41. Signeta flammeata
42. Spialia galba
43. Suada albinus
44. Suada swerga △
45. Suastus everyx △
46. Suastus gremius ♀ △
47. Suastus migreus △
48. Suastus minuta △
49. Suniana sunias
50. Suniana tanus
51. Tagiades gana
52. Tagiades japetus
53. Tagiades lavata
54. Tagiades menaka
55. Tagiades toba

189

PAPILIONIDAE (1 : 2)

1. Bhutanitis lidderdalei
2. Chilasa clytia
3. Chilasa clytia
4. Dabasa hercules
5. Graphium clymenus
6. Graphium eurous
7. Graphium glycerion

8. Graphium sarpedon
9. Hypermnestra helios
10. Leuhdorfia puziloi
11. Papilio bianor
12. Papilio demoleus
13. Papilio elwesi
14. Papilio polytes

15. Papilio helenus
16. Papilio janaka
17. Papilio maacki
18. Papilio macilentus
19. Papilio paris

191

AMATHUSIIDAE (1:2)

1. Parnassius szechenyi
2. Parnassius tenedius
3. Sericinus telamon ♀
4. Sericinus telamon ♂
5. Troides aeacus ♂

6. Troides aeacus ♀
7. Aemona oberthueri
8. Enispe lunatus
9. Faunis aerope ♂ ▽
10. Faunis aerope ♀ ▽

11. Faunis eumeus ♀
12. Stichopthalma howqua
13. Stichopthalma neumogeni △

1

2

3

4

5

6

7

8

9

10

11

12

13

14

15

16

1. Abrota pratti ♂ ▽
2. Abrota pratti ♀ △
3. Aldania raddei
4. Apatura bieti ♂ ♀
5. Apatura fasciola
6. Apatura ulupi
7. Apatura laverna
8. Apatura leechii
9. Apatura subcoerulea ♀ ▽ △
10. Apatura schrenki ▽ △
11. Argyronome ruslana △
12. Araschnia burejana
13. Araschnia oreas
14. Apatura nycteis ♀
15. Argynnis anadyomene ♂ ♀
16. Apatura subalba

1. Araschnia prorsoides ▽△
2. Calinaga buddha
3. Cethosia biblis
4. Charaxes polyxena ♀
5. Charaxes polyxena ♂
6. Childrena childreni ♀ ▽
7. Childrena childreni ♂ △

8. Childrena zenobia
9. Calinaga lhatso
10. Clossiana angarensis △▽
11. Clossiana gong △▽
12. Clossiana hegemone
13. Clossiana jerdoni
14. Clossiana oscarus ▽△

15. Clossiana selenis
16. Fabriciana nerippe
17. Cyrestis thyodamas
18. Damora sagana ♀
19. Damora sagana ♂
20. Euphydryas sareptana △
21. Issoria gemmata

195

1. Limenitis zayla
2. Melitaea agar
3. Melitaea bellona △
4. Melitaea lutko △
5. Melitaea arcesia △
6. Melitaea pallas
7. Melitaea saxatilis
8. Melitaea sibina
9. Melitaea yuenty

10. Mesoacidalia claudia ▽△
11. Neptis arachne ▽△
12. Neptis dejeani
13. Neptis aspasia △
14. Neptis breti △
15. Neptis cydippe △
16. Neptis armandia △
17. Neptis narayana
18. Neptis pryeri △

19. Neptis radha
20. Neptis speyeri
21. Neptis themis ▽△
22. Neptis thisbe ▽
23. Neptis thisbe △
24. Neptis yerburyi △
25. Pantoporia disjuncta △
26. Pantoporia fortuna
27. Pantoporia punctata ♀△

196

1. Pantaporia punctata
2. Pantaporia sulpitia △
3. Polygonia c-aureum
4. Polygonia gigantea
5. Penthema adelma
6. Polygonia l-album
7. Penthema lisarda
8. Penthema formosanum
9. Polyura dolon △
10. Polyura narcaea
11. Polyura posidonius
12. Precis lemonias
13. Pseudergolis wedah
14. Sephisa dichroa
15. Sasakia charonda
16. Sasakia funebris
17. Thaleropis ionia
18. Timelaea albescens

197

DANAIDAE (1 : 2)

PIERIDAE (3 : 4)

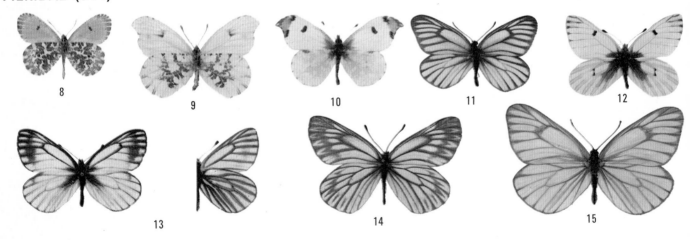

1. Timelaea maculata
2. Sephisa chandra ♀
3. Limenitis sydyi ▽△
4. Limenitis trivena
5. Mesoacidalia alexandra △

6. Helcÿra superba
7. Danaus chrysippus
8. Anthocharis bambusarum △
9. Anthocharis bieti ♀ △
10. Anthocharis scolymus

11. Aporia bieti
12. Baltia butleri
13. Aporia davidis ▽△
14. Aporia goutellei
15. Aporia hippia ♀

1. Aporia largeteaui
2. Colias christophi
3. Colias cocandica
4. Aporia lotis
5. Aporia nabellica
6. Catopsilia florella
7. Colias sagartia
8. Colias regia ♀
9. Colias aurora ♀ ♂
10. Colias sifanica ♂ ♀
11. Pieris deota △·
12. Baltia shawii ♀
13. Colias staudingeri
14. Colias stoliczkana △
15. Colias wiskotti ▽ △
16. Colotis calais
17. Colotis chrysonome
18. Colotis fausta
19. Colotis liagore
20. Colotis phisadia
21. Microzegris pyrothoe
22. Mesapia peloria
23. Colotis pleione
24. Delias belladonna
25. Gonepteryx amintha △
26. Leptidia gigantea
27. Pieris dubernardi

199

SATYRIDAE (1 : 1)

1. Acropolis thalia
2. Coenonympha saadi △
3. Aphantopus arvensis
4. Callarge sagitta
5. Coenonympha amaryllis ▽△
6. Coenonympha semenori
7. Coenonympha sunbecca △

8. Erebia alcmena
9. Coenonympha nolckeni △
10. Coenonympha mongolica
11. Erebia edda
12. Erebia herse
13. Erebia hyagriva △
14. Erebia kalmuka

15. Erebia meta
16. Erebia maurisius ▽△
17. Loxerebia phyllis
18. Erebia parmenio ▽△
19. Erebia maracandica ▽△
20. Erebia turanica ▽△
21. Erebia radians

1. Eumenis autonoe ▽△
2. Eumenis persephone ♀ ♂ ▽ △
3. Eumenis telephassa
4. Hyponephele capella
5. Hyponephele davendra ♂▽♀△
6. Hyponephele davendra ▽
7. Lethe albolineata △
8. Lethe baucis ♀ ▽
9. Lethe baucis ♂▽
10. Lethe christophi
11. Lethe diana ▽△
12. Lethe insularis △
13. Lethe dura
14. Lethe helle
15. Lethe labyrinthea △

1. Lethe lanaris △
2. Lethe isana
3. Lethe manzorum
4. Lethe marginalis △
5. Lethe mataja

6. Lethe nigrifascia
7. Lethe oculatissima ▽ △
8. Loxerebia phyllis ▽
9. Lethe proxima △
10. Lethe satyrina △

11. Lethe titania
12. Loxerebia phyllis △
13. Mandarinia regalis
14. Loxerebia sylvicola
15. Loxerebia polyphemus

1. Maniola cadusia △
2. Maniola kirghisa
3. Maniola narica
4. Mycalesis francisca
5. Maniola pulchra
6. Maniola wagneri
7. Melanargia halimede ▽△
8. Melanargia titea ▽△
9. Maniola naubidensis
10. Mycalesis gotama ▽△
11. Minois dryas
12. Neope armandii △▽
13. Neope goschkeritschii
14. Oeneis dubia
15. Neope christi △
16. Oeneis mongolica ♀
17. Oeneis sculda
18. Oeneis nanna
19. Oeneis urda ♀

1. Oeneis tarpeja ▽△
2. Palaeonympha opalina
3. Pararge climene
4. Pararge deidamia ▽△
5. Pararge episcopalis ▽△
6. Pararge eversmanni
7. Pararge felix

8. Pseudochazara anthelia
9. Pseudochazara regeli ▽
10. Pseudochazara regeli △
11. Rhaphicera dumicola △
12. Satyrus bischoffi ▽△
13. Satyrus palaearcticus
14. Pararge schrenckii

15. Satyrus sybillina
16. Satyrus thibetana
17. Triphysa phryne ♂ △
18. Ypthima asterope
19. Triphysa phryne ♀ ▽

LYCAENIDAE (3 : 4)

1. Ypthima conjuncta ▽△
2. Ypthima praenubila △
3. Ypthima iris
4. Ypthima insolita
5. Ypthima lisandra △
6. Ypthima motschulskyi △
7. Agrodiaetus erschoffi
8. Agrodiaetus poseidon
9. Apharitis acamas ▽
10. Apharitis acamas △
11. Antigius butleri ♂ ▽
12. Antigius butleri ♀ △

13. Artopoetes pryeri
14. Camena ctesia
15. Camena icetas ♀
16. Chaetoprocta odata △
17. Chrysozephyrus ataxus ♂ ▽△
18. Chrysozephyrus ataxus ♀ ▽
19. Chrysozephyrus duma ♀
20. Cordelia comes
21. Curetis acuta ♂
22. Curetis acuta ♀
23. Deudorix arata △
24. Epamera jordanus

25. Esakiozephyrus bieti △
26. Esakiozephyrus icana △
27. Euaspa forsteri
28. Everes fischeri △▽
29. Everes potanini △
30. Favonius orientalis △
31. Favonius saphirinus
32. Glaucopsyche lycormas
33. Heliophorus moorei
34. Heodes ochimus ♀
35. Heodes solskyi

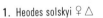

1. Heodes solskyi ♀ △
2. Japonica saepestriata ♂ △
3. Japonica saepestriata ♀ ▽
4. Lycaena caspius
5. Lycaena li ♂ △
6. Lycaena li ♀ ▽
7. Lycaena splendens
8. Lycaena standfussi △
9. Lycaena pang △
10. Lycaena tseng △
11. Lycaeides christophi △
12. Lycaeides cleobis ♂
13. Lycaeides cleobis ♀
14. Macurinea arionides △
15. Narathura japonica
16. Neolycaena tengstroemi ▽△
17. Neozephyrus taxila
18. Niphanda fusca △

19. Orthomiella pontis △
20. Praephilotes anthracias △
21. Panchala ganesa
22. Phengaris atroguttata
23. Plebejus eversmanni
24. Polyommatus alcedo
25. Polyommatus devanica
26. Polyommatus loewii ♂ ▽
27. Polyommatus loewii ♀ ▽
28. Polyommatus sieversii ♀ △
29. Rapala micans △
30. Rapala selira
31. Satsuma pluto ▽△
32. Satsuma pratti ♀
33. Shirozua melpomene ♀ △
34. Spindasis takanonis △
35. Strymon herzi ▽△
36. Strymon ledereri

37. Strymon v-album
38. Strymon sassanides △
39. Turanana anisopthalma △
40. Turanana cytis
41. Teratozephyrus hecale ♀
42. Teratozephyrus tsangkii ♀
43. Tomares callimachus △▽
44. Tomares fedtschenkoi
45. Tomares nogelii △
46. Tomares romanovi
47. Taraka hamada △
48. Ussuriana michaelis ♀
49. Vacciniina hyrcana
50. Vacciniina iris
51. Wagimo signata △▽
52. Zizeeria maha ♀ ▽
53. Zizeeria maha ♂ △

NEMEOBIIDAE (1 : 1)

1

2

3

LIBYTHEIDAE (1 : 1)

4

HESPERIIDAE (1 : 1)

5 6 7 8 9 10 11

12 13 14 15 16

17 18 19 20

21 22 23 24 25 26 27 28 29

1. Dodona henrici ▽
2. Polycaena lua △
3. Polycaena tamerlana
4. Libythea celtis
5. Abraximorpha davidii
6. Actinor radians △
7. Achalarus simplex △
8. Aeromachus inachus △
9. Ampittia dalailama △
0. Ampittia trimacula

11. Ampittia virgata
12. Astictopterus henrici ♀ △
13. Astictopterus olivascens △
14. Baoris leechii ♀ △
15. Barca bicolor
16. Bibasis aquilina
17. Bibasis septentrionis
18. Borbo zelleri △
19. Capila jayadeva
20. Capila pennicillatum

21. Capila pieridoides △
22. Capila omeia
23. Carterocephalus argyrostigma △
24. Carterocephalus avanti
25. Carterocephalus houangty
26. Carterocephalus micio
27. Carterocephalus pulchra △
28. Carterocephalus niveomaculatus
29. Celaenorrhinus pulomaya

207

1. Celaenorrhinus tibetana
2. Coladenia sheila
3. Ctenoptilon vasava
4. Daimio diversa
5. Daimio phisara
6. Daimio tethys
7. Eogenes alcides
8. Erionota grandis
9. Erynnis montanus
10. Hasora anura △
11. Halpe nephele △
12. Halpe porus △
13. Isoteinon lamprospilus △
14. Leptalina unicolor △

15. Lobocla nepos △
16. Lotongus sarala
17. Ochlodes bouddha
18. Ochlodes subhyalina ♀ △
19. Odina decoratus
20. Onryza maga △
21. Pedesta baileyi
22. Pedesta blanchardi △
23. Pedesta masunerisis
24. Pelopidas jansonis △
25. Polytremis caerulescens △
26. Polytremis pellucida
27. Potanthus flava △
28. Pyrgus breti △

29. Pyrgus thibetanus
30. Satarupa nymphalis
31. Scobura cephaloides ♀
32. Sebastonyma dolopia ♀ △
33. Seseria formosana
34. Seseria sambara
35. Sovia albipectus △
36. Sovia subflava ♀ △
37. Taractrocera flavoides △
38. Thoressa bivitta ▽
39. Thoressa bivitta △
40. Thoressa varia △
41. Thymelicus sylvatica
42. Udaspes stellata

The Text

Corrigenda —

Text

Page 236, column 2, line 17 : "Una purpurea (Druce), Brazil." should not appear.

Page 253, column 3, line 55 should not appear ; line 56 : for 17 read 16.

Page 254, column 1, line 4 : for 18 read 17 ; line 7 : for 19 read 18.

Page 257, column 1, line 44, "not arid" should read "hot arid".

Page 282, column 3, line 18, after "(see 12)" read "s/s rama (Moore) from Nilgiri Hills.".

Page 288, column 3, after line 22 insert as follows :

1. *Aporia largeteaui* (Oberth.). Ichang to Tibet. Similar : phryxe (Bsd.), N.W. India, darker ; caphusa (Moore), W. Himalayas, Tibet, very dark ; oberthuri (Leech), C. and W. China.

2. *Colias christophi* (Gr.-Gr.), Ferghana.

3. *Colias cocandica* (Ersch.). Mongolia.

4. *Aporia lotis* (Leech). W. China.

5. *Aporia nabellica* (Bsd.). Tibet, Himalayas. Similar : llamo (Oberth.), W. China, UP more streaky.

6. *Catopsilia florella* (F.). Persia to China, India, Ceylon.

7. *Colias sagartia* (Led.). Iran.

8. *Colias regia* (Gr.-Gr.). Turkestan.

9. *Colias aurora* (Esp.). Altai Mountains, S.E. Siberia to Amurland. A few subspecies. Female form chloe has grey ground colour UP.

10. *Colias sifanica* (Gr.-Gr.). Amdo.

12. *Baltia shawii* (Bates). Himalayas. Similar : butleri (Moore), Kashmir, Mongolia, S.W. China. (See Indo-Australasia also.).

13. *Colias staudingeri* (Alph.). Ferghana. Terrain : montane.

Please note that entries in the index are also affected by these corrigenda.

See over

Plates

Plate 1/13 : for Apatura iris read Limenitis reducta.

Plate 2/21 : for Ladoga camilla read Apatura iris.

Plate 2/23 : for Limenitis reducta read Ladoga camilla.

Plate 9/3 : for Agrodiaetus damon read Cyaniris helena.

Plate 18 : insert at top of plate heading SATYRIDAE (1 :1).

Plate 43 : insert at top of plate heading ACRAEIDAE (1 :2).

Plate 54 : insert at top of plate heading SATYRIDAE (1 :1).

Plate 92 : insert heading NYMPHALIDAE (3 :4).

Plate 101/8 : for $\triangle$ read ∇.

Plate 136/10 : for Troides rhadamantus read Papilio xanthicles.

Plate 136/11 : for Troides mirandus read Troides rhadamantus.

Plate 136/13 : for Papilio xanthicles read Troides mirandus.

Plate 182/2 : for Una purpurea read Thysonotis stephani.

Plate 182/3 : for Thysonotis stephani read Una purpurea.

Plate 182 : zone map should indicate Indo-Australasia.

Plate 198/12 : for Aporia goutellei read Baltia butleri.

Plate 198/14 : for Baltia butleri read Aporia goutellei.

Please note that entries in the index are also affected by these corrigenda.

See over

Europe

PLATE 1 : Papilionidae

1. *Allancastria cerisyi* (God.). Balkans, Greece, Asia Minor to Syria, Crete. Lfp : Aristolochia.

2. *Archon apollinus* (Hbst.). Greek islands, Asia Minor, Syria, Palestine, Mesopotamia. Lfp : Aristolochia. Several subspecies.

3. *Iphiclides podalirius* (L.). Central and Southern Europe through West and Central Asia to W. China, Saharan oases. Lfp : Amygdalaceae, blackthorn.

4. *Papilio alexanor* (Esp.). S. European coast to E. Persia, Syria and Palestine. Lfp : Seseli and Ferula.

5. *Papilio machaon* (L.) 'Swallowtail'. North Europe to Kamschatka, Canada, Lisbon to Yokohama, Saharan oases. Lfp : Umbelliferae. Subspecies : Many, the N. American form is aliaska. Similar : hospiton, Sardinia and Corsica ; brevicauda (Saunders), N. America.

6. *Parnassius apollo* (L.). Sierra Nevada, S. Spain to Mongolia, Scandinavia to Sicily. Terrain : montane. Lfp : Sedum and Sempervivum. Many subspecies.

7. *Parnassius mnemosyne* (L.). Pyrenees to Central Asia, Persia, Caucasus, Sweden to Greece. Terrain : montane. Lfp : Corydalis. Several subspecies.

8. *Parnassius phoebus* (F.). Alps, W., C. and S. Siberia, Mongolia. Terrain : montane. Lfp : Saxifraga and Sempervivum. Several subspecies. Similar : smintheus (Doubl.), N. America.

9. *Zerinthia polyxena* (Scop.). S. France to Asia Minor. Lfp : Aristolochia.

10. *Zerinthia rumina* (L.). Spain, Portugal, S. France, Algiers, Morocco. Lfp : Aristolochia. Variable.

Nymphalidae

11. *Aglais urticae* (L.) 'Tortoiseshell'. C. Europe through N. Asia to Amurland. Lfp : Urticaceae. Similar : caschmirensis (Koll.), Himalayas, Tibet ; milberti (Latreille). Newfoundland, Canada.

12. *Apatura ilia* (Schiff.). Portugal, C. Europe to S. Russia. Subspecies : Many, with ochreous shadings, Hungary through S. Russia. Similar : substituta (Btlr.), N. China, Korea, Japan.

13. *Limenitis reducta* (Stgr.). Europe.

14. *Araschnia levana* (L.). Summer brood = prorsa (L.). Similar : fallax (Jans.), China, Korea, Japan. (See 16 also).

15. *Argynnis paphia* (L.). W. Europe across temperate Asia to Japan, Algeria. Lfp : Violaceae, rubus. Many subspecies.

16. *Araschnia levana* (L.). C. and E. Europe through Armenia, Siberia, Amurland and Korea to Japan. Lfp : Urtica. Spring brood. (See 14 also).

17. *Boloria pales* (Schiff.). Cantabrian Mountains, Pyrenees, Alps, Carpathians, Caucasus to W. China, Himalayas, Alaska. Terrain : montane. Lfp : Violaceae. Sub-

species : Many, very variable, from fiery red to almost black.

18. *Argynnis paphia* (see 15).

19. *Argyronome laodice* (Pall.). Baltic countries across E. Europe and Asia to China, Assam to N. Burma. Several subspecies.

20. *Brenthis daphne* (Schiff.). S.W. Europe through Russia and C. Asia to China and Japan. Lfp : Viola, rubus.

21. *Brenthis hecate* (Schiff.). S.W. Europe, Russia, Asia Minor, Iran, C. Asia. Lfp : Dorycnium.

22. *Charaxes jasius* (L.). Mediterranean coasts to Greece, N. Africa, C. Africa, Senegambia to Ethiopia. Lfp : Arbutus.

23. *Boloria pales* (see 17).

24. *Brenthis ino* (Rott.). C. and N. Europe, C. Asia, N. China, Japan. Lfp : Sanguisorba, spiraea, rubus. Several subspecies.

25. *Clossiana chariclea* (Schneid.). Arctic Europe, Greenland, and America. Female very dark. Similar : freija (Thnbg.), range as chariclea and Rocky Mountains to Colorado, UN lacks zig-zag black line.

26. *Clossiana euphrosyne* (L.). W. Europe through N. and C. Asia to Korea, N. America. Several subspecies.

27. *Clossiana frigga* (Thnbg.). Scandinavia across N. Asia, Canada, Rocky Mountains S. to Colorado. Lfp : Rubus. Several subspecies.

28. *Clossiana dia* (L.). W. Europe, C. Asia to W. China. Lfp : Viola, rubus. Small. Few subspecies.

PLATE 2 : Nymphalidae

1. *Clossiana polaris* (Bsd.). In Arctic regions of Europe, Asia, Greenland and N. America. Lfp : Dryas octopetala.

2. *Clossiana selene* (see 3).

3. *Clossiana selene* (Schiff.). W. Europe, Esthonia across N. and C. Asia to Korea, N. America. Lfp : Violaceae. Many subspecies.

4. *Clossiana thore* (Hbn.). Alps, Finland, Scandinavia, through Russia and N. Asia to Japan. Lfp : Viola. Few subspecies.

5. *Clossiana titania* (Esper.). W. Europe to Altai Mountains in Siberia, Quebec to Alaska and along Rocky Mountains to New Mexico. Lfp : Viola, polygonum.

6. *Euphydryas aurinia* (Rott.). W. Europe through Russia to Korea. Lfp : Plantago. Many subspecies. Similar : taylori (Edw.), Vancouver.

7. *Euphydryas aurinia* (see 6).

8. *Euphydryas cynthia* (Hbn.). Alps. Lfp : Viola, plantago. Female resembles maturna.

9. *Euphydryas desfontainii* (Godt.). N. Africa, Spain, Pyrenees. Several subspecies.

10. *Euphydryas iduna* (Dalm.). Scandinavia through C. Siberia to Altai Mountains, Caucasus.

11. *Euphydryas maturna* (L.). C. and N. Europe across Russia to Altai Mountains. Lfp: Scrophulariaceae. Similar: intermedia (Men.), Amurland; colonia (Wright), Western N. America.

12. *Fabriciana adippe* (Schiff.). Subspecies: xanthodippe (Fixs.), Mongolia, Amurland. (See 13 and 14 also).

13. *Fabriciana adippe* (Schiff.) 'High Brown Fritillary'. W. Europe, temperate Asia to Japan, N. Africa. Lfp: Violaceae. Subspecies: Many, variable.

14. *Fabriciana adippe* (Schiff.). Subspecies: taurica (Stgr.). (See 12 and 13 also).

15. *Fabriciana elisa* (Godt.). Corsica, Sardinia. Lfp: Violets.

16. *Fabriciana niobe* (L.). W. Europe, Russia, Asia Minor to Iran. Lfp: Violaceae. Subspecies: Several, some large.

17. *Inachis io* (L.) 'Peacock'. Europe, eastwards through Asia to Japan. Lfp: Urticae.

18. *Fabriciana niobe* (see 16).

19. *Issoria lathonia* (see 20).

20. *Issoria lathonia* (L.) 'Queen of Spain'. W. Europe, N. Africa incl. Canary Islands, Central Asia, Himalayas to W. China. Lfp: Violaceae. Few subspecies.

21. *Apatura iris* (L.) 'Purple Emperor'. England to Spain, C. Europe to Asia Minor. Lfp: Salix. Few subspecies.

22. *Limenitis populi* (L.). C. Europe, S. Scandinavia, Russia. Lfp: Populus. Subspecies: ussuriensis (Stgr.), Amurland.

23. *Ladoga camilla* (L.) 'White Admiral'. C. Europe across Russia and C. Asia to China and Japan. Lfp: Lonicera.

24. *Neptis sappho* (Pallas) 'Common Glider'. E. Europe to Japan. Lfp: Lathyrus.

25. *Nymphalis antiopa* (L.) 'Camberwell Beauty'. W. Europe and N. Africa through C. Asia to Amurland, N. America, Bhutan. Lfp: Willow, Elm, Poplar. Several subspecies.

26. *Nymphalis polychloros* (L.) 'Large Tortoiseshell'. Europe. Lfp: Elm, Willow, Poplar and fruit trees. Subspecies: in Asia Minor, through Armenia to W. Himalayas and S. Siberia. Similar: erythromelas (Aust.), Algeria; californica (Bsd.), U.S.A.

27. *Nymphalis xanthomelas* (Esp.). C. and S. Europe through Asia to Amurland in China, S. to the Himalayas. Lfp: Salix. Subspecies: japonica (Stich.), Japan.

28. *Melitaea cinxia* (L.). W. Europe to Amurland, Morocco. Lfp: Viola, veronica, plantago, musa. Several subspecies. Similar: arduinna (Esp.), Danube to Asia Minor, Persia, C. Asia.

PLATE 3: Nymphalidae

1. *Melitaea diamina* (Lang.). N. Spain through C. Europe, C. Asia to Amurland.

Lfp: Veronica, Valeriana, Melampyrum. Few subspecies. Similar: protomedia (Men.), E. Siberia, China, Korea.

2. *Melitaea didyma* (see 3).

3. *Melitaea didyma* (Esp.). Portugal to Japan, N. Europe to Sahara, Himalayas. Lfp: Plantago, Scrophularia, Viola, Valerian, etc. Very many subspecies. Very variable.

4. *Melitaea phoebe* (Schiff.). Europe and N. Africa across C. Asia to N. China.

5. *Melitaea trivia* (Schiff.). S. Europe through S. Russia to Persia and W. Himalayas. Lfp: Verbascum. Several subspecies. Variable.

6. *Mellicta asteria* (Frr.). Alps, Altai Mountains.

7. *Mellicta athalia* (see 8).

8. *Mellicta athalia* (Rott.). W. Europe through temperate zone to Japan. Lfp: Plantago, Melampyrum. Many subspecies.

9. *Mellicta aurelia* (see 10).

10. *Mellicta aurelia* (Nick.). C. Europe to Ural Mountains, C. Asia, Caucasus, Amurland. Lfp: Chrysanthemum, Digitalis, Veronica, Malampyrum. Many subspecies. Very variable. Similar: britomartis.

11. *Mellicta deione* (Geyer). S.W. Europe, N. Africa.

12. *Mellicta parthenoides* (Kef.). W. Europe. Lfp: Plantago, Scabiosa. Few subspecies.

13. *Mesoacidalia aglaja* (L.) 'Dark Green Fritillary'. W. Europe across Asia to China and Japan, Morocco, Chitral. Lfp: Violaceae. Subspecies: Many, some large.

14. *Mesoacidalia aglaja* (see 13).

15. *Polygonia c-album* (L.) 'Comma'. Europe to N. Africa, C. Asia to Amurland, Himalayas. Lfp: Ribes, Urtica, Humulus, Ulmus, Honicera. Several subspecies. Similar: hamigera (Btlr.), Japan; satyris (Edw.), N. America.

16. *Polygonia egea* (Cr.). S. Europe to Armenia. Subspecies: Central Asia, Chitral, Pamir.

17. *Pandoriana pandora* (Schiff.). Canary Islands, N. Africa, S. Europe, Iran and Chitral. Lfp: Viola. Few subspecies.

18. *Vanessa atalanta* (L.) 'Red Admiral'. Europe, N. Africa, Asia Minor, Palestine, Himalayas to C. Asia, N. America to Guatemala and Haiti. Lfp: Urticae.

19. *Vanessa cardui* (L.) 'Painted Lady'. Whole world except N. and S. Arctic regions and S. America. Lfp: Urtica, Carduus, Anchusa. Several subspecies.

Pieridae

20. *Anthocharis belia* (L.). S.W. Europe, N. Africa. Lfp: Biscutella. Female white UP.

21. *Anthocharis cardamines* (L.) 'Orange Tip'. W. Europe through temperate Asia to China. Lfp: Turritis, Arabis, Sisymbrium. Many subspecies.

22. *Anthocharis cardamines* (see 21).

23. *Anthocharis damone* (Boisd.). Sicily, S. Italy, Balkans, Asia Minor to Iran. Female UP white.

24. *Anthocharis gruneri* (H.Sch.). Greece through Asia Minor to Iran. Female UP white.

25. *Aporia crataegi* (L.). W. Europe across temperate Asia to China and Japan. Lfp: Crataegus, Prunus, Pirus. Few subspecies.

26. *Colias chrysotheme* (Esp.). E. Europe to Altai Mountains. Lfp: Vicia. Similar: eurytheme (Bsd.), N. America.

27. *Colias crocea* (Geoff.) 'Clouded Yellow'. S. and C. Europe across Asia Minor to Iran, N. Africa to Cyrenaica. Lfp: Cytisus, Trefoil, Sainfoin. Several subspecies. Similar: electo (L.), E., W. and S. Africa: fieldii (Men.), India to C. China; myrmidone (Esp.), UP more reddish.

28. *Colias crocea* (see 27).

PLATE 4: Pieridae

1. *Colias erate* (see 2).

2. *Colias erate* (Esp.). E. Europe and across temperate Asia to Korea and Japan, Formosa, Abyssinia, Somalia.

3. *Colias hecla* (Lef.). Arctic Europe, Greenland, N. America. Lfp: Astragalus. Several subspecies.

4. *Colias hyale* (L.) 'Pale Clouded Yellow'. W. Europe to Altai Mountains, Abyssinia. Lfp: Vetch, Trefoil. Several subspecies. Similar: australis (Verity), FW more rounded, lemon yellow.

5. *Colias hyale* (L.), female. Has a yellow form also (see 4).

6. *Colias nastes* (Boisd.). Arctic Europe, Greenland, Labrador. Lfp: Astragalus. Few subspecies.

7. *Colias palaeno* (L.). C. and N. Europe through Siberia to Amurland and Japan, N. America. Lfp: Bog-Vaccinium. Female yellowish. Similar: melinos (Ev.), Amurland.

8. *Colias phicomone* (Esp.). Alps, Pyrenees, Hungary. Lfp: Vetches. Similar: montium (Oberth.), S.W. China, Tibet.

9. *Colotis daira* (Klug). N. Africa, Nubia to Somaliland, Spain. Many subspecies. Similar: evagore (Klug).

10. *Elphinstonia charlonia* (Douz.). Canary Islands, Morocco to Tunisia and Egypt, Sudan, Macedonia and W. Asia to Iran and Punjab. Lfp: Radish. Female white UP.

11. *Euchloe belemia* (Esp.). S.W. Europe, Asia Minor to Iran, Canary Islands, N. Africa. Several subspecies. Similar: falloui (All.), Somaliland.

12. *Euchloe pechi* (Stgr.). Algeria.

13. *Pieris mannii* (Mayer). Morocco, S. Europe to Syria.

14. *Gonepteryx cleopatra* (L.). S. Europe through Asia Minor to Syria, Madeira, N. Africa. Lfp: Rhamnus, Cathartica. Several subspecies.

15. *Gonepteryx rhamni* (L.) 'Brimstone'. Canary Islands through Europe and Asia to Japan. Lfp: Rhamnus, Vaccinium. Female white. Several subspecies.

16. *Pieris brassicae* (L.) 'Large Cabbage White'. Europe, Asia, Himalayas, N. Africa. Lfp: Brassica, Troparolum, Lepidium. Many subspecies.

17. *Euchloe tagis* (Hbn.). Portugal, Provence, Sardinia and Corsica, Algeria, Morocco. Lfp: Iberis, Biscutella.

18. *Leptidea sinapis* (L.) 'Wood White'. W. Europe through Russia to Caucasus Mountains. Lfp: Lotus, Lathyrus, Vetch. Several subspecies. Similar: duponchelli (Stgr.), S. France to Iran, faintly yellow-flushed; amurensis (Men.), N. China, Japan.

PLATE 5: Pieridae

1. *Pieris ergane* (Hbn.). S.E. France to Asia Minor and Iran. Lfp: Aethionema.

2. *Pieris krueperi* (Stgr.). Greece, Asia Minor to Iran, Pamirs. Lfp: Alyssum. Similar: deota (Nicer.), Kashmir, UNF margins not black-marked.

3. *Pontia daplidice* (L.) 'Bath White'. N. Africa, S. Europe to India and Japan. Lfp: Arabis, Reseda. Many subspecies. Similar: glauconome (Klug), Chitral, Baluchistan, UNH veins prominently yellow.

4. *Pieris napi* (L.) 'Green-veined White'. Europe across Asia to Japan, N. Africa, N. America. Lfp: Cruciferal. Very many subspecies. Similar: virginiensis (Edw.), U.S.A.

5. *Pieris rapae* (L.) 'Small Cabbage White'. Europe across Asia to Japan, N. America, Australia. Lfp: Brassica and Reseda. Many subspecies. Similar: mannii (Mayer), Morocco, S. Europe to Syria, UPF black margin reaches lower down the wing.

6. *Pontia chloridice* (Hbn.). S.E. Europe, Asia Minor, Tibet, E. Siberia, S.W. China, Montane in N. America, Oregon and California. Several subspecies.

7. *Synchloe callidice* (Hbn.). Pyrenees and Alps, Caucasus, Lebanon, Himalayas, Tibet and Mongolia. N. America montane from Alaska to California. Lfp: Erydimum, Reseda.

8. *Zegris eupheme* (Esp.). Spain, S. Russia, Asia Minor to Iran, Morocco. Female has no orange in UPF tip.

9. *Pontia daplidice* (see 3).

Satyridae

10. *Aphantopus hyperantus* (L.) 'Ringlet'. Europe to Korea. Variable in size and numbers of eye spots.

11. *Arethusana arethusa* (Esp.). W. Europe to Asia Minor, S. Russia to C. Asia, Atlas Mountains. Several subspecies.

12. *Coenonympha arcanioides* (Pierret). Morocco, Algeria, Tunisia.

13. *Berberia abdelkader* (Pier.). Oran and Morocco.

14. *Brintesia circe* (F.). Western Europe, Asia Minor, Iran, Himalayas.

15. *Coenonympha arcania* (L.). W. Europe, S. Russia, Asia Minor.

16. *Coenonympha corinna* (Hbn.). Sardinia, Corsica, Sicily, Elba.

17. *Coenonympha dorus* (Esp.). S.W. Europe, N. Africa. Variable.

18. *Coenonympha glycerion* (Borkh.). Spain, C. France, Finland, Bulgaria, Alps.

PLATE 6: Satyridae

1. *Coenonympha hero* (L.). France, Scandinavia, Central Europe and Asia to Amurland, Korea and Japan.

2. *Coenonympha iphiodes* (Stdgr.). N. and C. Spain.

3. *Coenonympha leander* (Esp.). Hungary, S. Russia, Asia Minor, Armenia, Iran.

4. *Coenonympha oedippus* (O.). W. Europe, Russia, C. Asia China, Japan.

5. *Coenonympha pamphilus* (L.). Europe, Asia Minor to Iran, Iraq, N. Africa.

6. *Coenonympha tullia* (Mueller). N.W. Europe across temperate Asia to the Pacific. Several subspecies. Similar: kodiak (Edw.), Alaska; ochracea (Edw.), Colorado, UNH two curved lighter bands.

7. *Chazara briseis* (L.). Spain, through Europe to W. Asia, Iran, Pamirs, N. Africa.

8. *Chazara prieuri* (Pierret). Spain and N. Africa. Female markings UP orange. Similar: eginus (Stgr.), Armenia, Turkestan.

9. *Erebia aethiops* (Esp.). W. Europe, Asia Minor, Urals, Caucasus. Similar: neoridas (Bsd.), S. Europe, UPF band tapers more from top to bottom.

10. *Erebia disa* (Thunb.). Arctic Europe, N. Siberia, N. America in Alaska, Yukon and circumpolar.

11. *Erebia epiphron* (Knoch.), Mountains in Europe. Lfp: grasses. Variable. Many subspecies.

12. *Erebia epistygne* (Hbn.). Spain, S.W. France.

13. *Erebia gorgone* (Bsd.). Pyrenees only. Similar: gorge (Esp.), UN lighter, smaller.

14. *Erebia ligea* (L.). Europe across Asia to Japan. Lfp: grasses. Similar: euryale (Esp.), smaller, no sexbrand UPF.

15. *Erebia melas* (Hbst.). S.E. Europe. Similar: lefebvrei (Bois), Pyrenees, variable subspecies; pluto (de Prun.), Alps, UP very black, variable subspecies.

16. *Erebia mnestra* (Hbn.). S. France, Alps.

17. *Erebia oeme* (Hbn.). Pyrenees to Upper Austria. Similar: medusa (Schiff.), Europe to Asia Minor, UP more orange background to ocelli; embla (Thnb.), Arctic Europe, Siberia, Kamschatka, UPH ocelli faint or absent; polaris (Staud.), Lapland, UNH ocelli very faint.

18. *Erebia pronoe* (Esp.). Pyrenees through S. France, Alps, Austria, Carpathians. Similar:

stirius (Godt.), S.E. Alps, UNH smooth, very dark, margin rather wavy; styx (Herr Sch.), C. and E. Alps, UNH less smooth, markings better defined.

19. *Erebia phegea* (Borkh.). Dalmatia, Iran, S. Russia to E. Siberia. Few subspecies.

20. *Erebia tyndarus* (Esp.). Mountains in S. and C. Europe. Lfp: grasses. Similar: callias (Edw.), Colorado, New Mexico; cassioides (Esp.), Pyrenees to Balkans, altajana (Stgr.), Armenia; ottomana (Herr Sch.), Greece, Balkans; iranica (Gr.Grsh.), N. Persia. Many subspecies, and very variable.

21. *Erebia tyndarus* (see 20).

22. *Erebia zapateri* (Oberth.). C. Spain.

23. *Hipparchia alcyone* (Schiff.). France across Balkans to S. Russia. Several subspecies. Similar: fagi (Scop.), larger.

PLATE 7: Satyridae

1. *Hipparchia hansii* (Aus.). Morocco, Tunis, Tripolitania.

2. *Hipparchia semele* (see 3).

3. *Hipparchia semele* (L.) 'Grayling'. W. and C. Europe, S. Russia. Lfp: grasses. Many subspecies.

4. *Hipparchia statilinus* (Hufn.). Spain through C. and S. Europe to Asia Minor, N. Africa. Lfp: grasses. Similar: fatua (Frr.), larger, UPH lunules clearer defined.

5. *Hyponephele lupinus* (Costa). S.W. Europe, N. Africa, S. Russia to Iran. Few subspecies.

6. *Hyponephele lycaon* (Kuehn.). W. Europe to C. Asia. Many subspecies.

7. *Hyponephele lycaon* (see 6).

8. *Lasiommata megera* (L.) 'Wall Brown'. W. Europe through Asia Minor to Syria. Lebanon, Iran, N. Africa.

9. *Kirinia roxelana* (Cr.). S.E. Europe, Cyprus, Syria, Iraq.

10. *Lasiommata maera* (L.). W. Europe to Asia Minor, C. Asia, Syria, Iran, Himalayas. Similar: petropolitana (F.), Pyrenees, Russia to Amur River, smaller, UPH dark transverse curly line.

11. *Lopinga achine* (Scop.). N. France through Russia, C. Asia to Amurland and Japan. Similar: catena (Leech), Central China.

12. *Maniola jurtina* (L.) 'Meadow Brown'. Canary Islands, N. Africa, Europe, Asia Minor to Iran. Several subspecies, often more brightly marked.

13. *Maniola jurtina* (see 12).

14. *Melanargia galathea* (L.) 'Marbled White'. W. Europe through S. Russia to Iran. Lfp: grasses. Few subspecies.

15. *Melanargia ines* (Hoffgg.). Spain, Portugal, N. Africa to Cyrenaica. Similar: arge (Sulz.), Italy, UP lighter, cell bar not complete.

16. *Melanargia larissa* (Gey.). Balkans, Syria, Iran. Several subspecies.

PLATE 8: Satyridae

1. *Melanargia occitanica* (Esp.). S.W. Europe, Sicily, N. Africa.

2. *Melanargia russiae* (Esp.). Portugal, Spain to S. Russia and W. Siberia. Several subspecies. Similar: parce (Stgr.), Pamirs.

3. *Pyronia cecilia* (Val.). Morocco, Spain through S. Europe to Asia Minor.

4. *Minois dryas* (Scop.). N. Spain through Europe and Asia to Japan. Lfp: grasses. Female UP paler.

5. *Oeneis glacialis* (Moll.). Alps. Lfp: grasses.

6. *Pseudochazara geyeri* (Herr. Sch.). S. Balkans to Turkestan.

7. *Oeneis jutta* (Hbn.). Scandinavia, N. Russia to Alaska, Labrador, Nova Scotia, Maine.

8. *Oeneis norna* (Thunb.). Lapland, N. Asia, arctic N. America. Similar: bore (Schneider), Lapland, male wings thinly scaled, male and female no ocelli.

9. *Pyronia bathseba* (Godt.). S.W. Europe, Morocco, Algiers. Few subspecies.

10. *Pararge aegeria* (L.) 'Speckled Wood'. W. Europe through Asia Minor, Syria to C.. Asia. Few subspecies.

11. *Pyronia janiroides* (Herr. Sch.). Algeria and Tunisia.

12. *Pyronia tithonus* (see 17).

13. *Pseudochazara hippolyte* (Esp.). Sierra Nevada, S. Russia, Asia Minor E. to China.

14. *Satyrus actaea* (see 15).

15. *Satyrus actaea* (Esp.). S.W. Europe, Asia Minor, Syria, Iran. Many subspecies.

16. *Pseudochazara mamurra* (Herr. Sch.). Greece, Asia Minor to Iran. Few subspecies.

17. *Pyronia tithonus* (L.). Spain, Europe to Caucasus.

18. *Pseudotergumia fidia* (L.). S.W. Europe, N. Africa. Similar: pisidice (Klug), Lebanon, Sinai.

PLATE 9: Lycaenidae

1. *Agriades pyrenaicus* (Bsdr.). C. Pyrenees, Cantabria. Terrain: montane. Similar: glandon (de Prunner), Sierra Nevada, Pyrenees, Alps, Balkans, broad smoky border to wings; aquilo (Bsd.), Scandinavia, arctic Asia.

2. *Agrodiaetus admetus* (Esp.). E. Europe, Asia Minor.

3. *Cyaniris helena* (Stgr.). Greece, Asia Minor, Lebanon, Iraq.

4. *Agrodiaetus damon* (Schiff.). Spain

through Europe, Russia and Armenia. Broad white streak UNH. Similar subspecies have male and female both dark brown UP. Female UP is brown.

5. *Agrodiaetus dolus* (Hnb.). S.W. Europe, Italy, Turkey to Turkestan. Female dark brown.

6. *Albulina orbitulus* (see 7).

7. *Albulina orbitulus* (Prun.). Alps, Norway to C. Asia. Female brown black UP. Several subspecies.

8. *Aricia agestis* (Bgstr.) 'Brown Argus'. Europe N. of Pyrenees to Iran, Siberia and Amurland. Many subspecies. Similar: allous (Hbn.), N. Africa, Spain, Alps, UP orange lunules faint or absent; cramera (Eschsch.), Canary Islands, Spain, Portugal, UP orange lunules large around entire margin of both wings.

9. *Aricia anteros* (Frr.). Balkans E. to Iran.

10. *Aricia nicias* (Meig.). Pyrenees, Alps, Finland, Russia. Similar: hyacinthus (Herr. Sch.), Turkey.

11. *Callophrys avis* (Chapman). S.W. Europe, N. Africa.

12. *Callophrys rubi* (L.) 'Green Hairstreak'. Europe, Asia. Lfp: Genista, Cytisus, Quercus, Sedum. Several subspecies. Similar: dumetorum (Bsd.), California; affinis (Edw.), Arizona, UNF yellowish brown.

13. *Celastrina argiolus* (L.) 'Holly Blue'. Europe, N. Africa, India, Asia to Japan, Malaysia. N. America. Lfp: Ivy and many other plants. Many subspecies, characterised by silvery white UN.

14. *Celastrina argiolus* (see 13).

15. *Cigaritis zohra* (Donzel). N. Africa. Similar: siphax (Lucas), Algeria, Tunisia, UNH outer row of silvery spots broken up; allardi (Oberth), N. Africa, UNH outer row of silvery spots in a smooth curve.

16. *Cigaritis zohra* (see 15).

17. *Cyaniris semiargus* (Rott.) 'Mazarine Blue'. Morocco, temperate Europe and Asia to Mongolia. Similar: helena (Staudinger), Greece, Asia Minor, Lebanon, Iraq, UNH has faint orange lunules.

18. *Everes argiades* (see 20).

19. *Eumedonia eumedon* (Esp.). Pyrenees to N. Cape, across Europe and Asia to Kamchatka. Lfp: Geranium. Several subspecies.

20. *Everes argiades* (Pall.) 'Short Tailed Blue'. Europe, Asia to Korea and Japan, India, Malaysia. Female brown. Many subspecies. Similar: Cupido species, no tails or orange spots.

21. *Glaucopsyche alexis* (Poda). W. Europe across Russia and C. Asia to Amurland. Few subspecies.

22. *Freyeria trochylus* (Frr.). S.E. Europe across India, Malaysia to Australia, S. Africa, E. Africa to Sudan, Arabia, Socotra. Lfp: Heliotropium. UP brown.

23. *Glaucopsyche melanops* (Bdr.). N. Africa, S.W. Europe. Similar: astraea (Frr.), Asia Minor, Kurdestan.

24. *Heodes alciphron* (Rott.). W. Europe across Asia Minor to Iran. Many subspecies.

25. *Heodes tityrus* (Poda.). W. Europe through Russia to Altai Mountains. Lfp: Rumex. Many subspecies.

26. *Heodes tityrus* (see 25).

27. *Heodes virgaurae* (L.). W. Europe to E. Siberia, North Sea to Mediterranean. Lfp: Rumex and Solidago. Many subspecies. Similar: ottomanus (Lef.) Balkans, Asia Minor, no white spots UNH.

28. *Heodes virgaurae* (see 27).

29. *Cyclirius webbianus* UN.

30. *Iolana iolas* (see 31).

31. *Iolana iolas* (O.). N. Africa, Spain, S. Europe to Asia Minor and Iran. Large.

32. *Kretania psylorita* (Frr.). Crete.

33. *Laeosopis roboris* (Esp.). Pyrenees, Spain.

34. *Lampides boeticus* (L.) 'Long Tailed Blue', 'Pea Blue'. Baltic to Mediterranean, Portugal to Japan, all Africa, Australia. Lfp: Colutea. UP dull violet blue.

35. *Lycaeides argyrognomon* (Bgstr.). France across Europe to S. Russia and Amurland, N. America. Many subspecies. Similar: idas (L.), Spain to N. Cape, UN duller yellow-blue.

36. *Lycaena dispar* (Haworth). W. Europe to Amurland.

37. *Lycaena helle* (Schiff.). C. and N. Europe across Russia and Siberia to Amurland. Lfp: Polygonum.

38. *Lycaena dispar* (see 36).

39. *Lycaena phlaeas* (see 40).

40. *Lycaena phlaeas* (L.) 'Small Copper'. Europe, N. Africa, Abyssinia, temperate Asia to Japan, Eastern N. America. Lfp: Dock and Sorrel. Many subspecies and aberrations.

41. *Lysandra albicans* (Herr. Sch.). N. Africa, Spain. Female UP is brown, very variable both in depth of colour and width and darkness of borders UP.

PLATE 10: Lycaenidae

1. *Lysandra bellargus* (see 2).

2. *Lysandra bellargus* (Rott.) 'Adonis Blue'. Europe, to Iraq and Iran.

3. *Lysandra coridon* (Poda.) 'Chalk Hill Blue'. Europe. Terrain: on chalk. Several subspecies.

4. *Maculinea arion* (L.) 'Large Blue'. W. Europe across Russia and Siberia to China. Lfp: Thymus. Attended by ants. Several subspecies. Similar: alcon (Schiff.), Spain to Central Asia, paler blue, no black spots.

5. *Maculinea teleius* (Bergs.). France, C. Europe and Asia, China, Korea, Japan. Similar: nausithous (Bergs.), N. Spain

across Europe to Urals and Caucasus, UN cinnamon brown with no marginal markings.

6. *Meleageria daphnis* (Schiff.). S. France, S. Europe to Lebanon, Syria and Iran. Female UP has wide brown borders. Few subspecies.

7. *Meleageria daphnis* (see 6).

8. *Nordmannia ilicis* (Esp.). C. and S. Europe, N. Africa. Several subspecies. Similar: acaciae (F.), smaller, paler, UN white lines less broken.

9. *Palaeochrysophanus hippothoe* (L.). W. Europe through Russia to Amurland. Several subspecies. Female of all subspecies sometimes very dark brown.

10. *Palaeochrysophanus hippothoe* (see 9).

11. *Philotes abencerragus* (Pierret). Spain, Morocco to Egypt and Jordan.

12. *Philotes baton* (Bgstr.). Spain across S. and C. Europe to Iran and Chitral. Several subspecies.

13. *Philotes baton* (see 12).

14. *Philotes bavius* (Ev.). Morocco, Algeria, Greece, Hungary, Asia Minor to S. Russia.

15. *Plebicula amanda* (see 18).

16. *Plebicula dorylas* (Schiff.). Spain, S. Europe to Asia Minor. Female black brown.

17. *Plebicula escheri* (Hbn.). Spain, S. Europe to Balkans.

18. *Plebicula amanda* (Schn.). N. Africa, Spain, Europe to W. Asia and Iran. Lfp: Vicia. Several subspecies.

19. *Plebicula escheri* (see 17).

20. *Plebejus pylaon* (see 22).

21. *Plebejus argus* (L.) 'Silver-studded Blue'. Europe, temperate Asia to Japan. Several subspecies.

22. *Plebejus pylaon* (Fisch-Waldh.). Spain E. to S. Russia and Iran. Lfp: Astragalus. Many subspecies.

23. *Polyommatus eros* (O.). Pyrenees, Alps, Apennines to C. Asia. Several subspecies. Similar: eroides (Friv.), Poland, Balkans.

24. *Polyommatus icarus* (see 25).

25. *Polyommatus icarus* (Rott.) 'Common Blue'. Canary Islands, temperate N. Africa, Europe and temperate Asia. Very many subspecies. Similar: candalus (Herr. Sch.), Asia Minor, Syria, Turkestan.

26. *Quercusia quercus* (see 27).

27. *Quercusia quercus* (L.) 'Purple Hairstreak'. England through Europe to Asia Minor and Armenia, N. Europe to the Mediterranean. Lfp: Oak. Several subspecies.

28. *Scolitantides orion* (Pall.). Spain, C. France to C. Asia, Japan.

29. *Scolitantides orion* (see 28).

30. *Strymonidia pruni* (L.) 'Black Hairstreak'.

England to Europe and Asia, Amurland and Korea. Several subspecies. Similar: mera (Leech), Japan.

31. *Strymonidia spini* (see 32).

32. *Strymonidia spini* (Schiff.). C. and S. Europe, Caucasus, Syria, Iran, Amurland, Korea, China. Lfp: Rhamnus. Similar: eximia (Fix.), Amurland, China, Mongolia, Korea; patrius (Leech), W. China; grandis (Fldr.), N. and E. China; w-album (Knoch), C. Europe to Japan, white line UNH ends in a letter W.

33. *Tarucus theophrastus* (F.). S. Europe, N. Africa, Asia Minor to W. India. Lfp: Zizyphus. UP dull blue.

PLATE 11: Lycaenidae

1. *Thecla betulae* (see 2).

2. *Thecla betulae* (L.) 'Brown Hairstreak'. N. and C. Europe through N. Asia to the Pacific. Lfp: Prunus, Amygdalus. Many subspecies. Similar: crassa (Leech), W. China; elvesi (Leech), W. and C. China, larger.

3. *Thersamonia thersamon* (Esp.). Italy and E. Europe, Asia Minor, Iraq and Iran. Several subspecies. Similar: asabinus (Herr. Sch.), Syria, Caucasus, Kurdistan; phoebus (Blach.), Morocco.

4. *Thersamonia thetis* (Klug). Balkan peninsula, Asia Minor to Iran and Iraq. Similar: lampon (Led.), Iran. With tail-less forms.

5. *Tomares ballus* (see 6).

6. *Tomares ballus* (F.). S. France, Spain, N. Africa. Lfp: Boujeania. Similar: mauritanicus (Luc.), Algeria, Morocco; romanovi (Christ.), Armenia, Iraq.

7. *Vacciniina optilete* (Knoch.). Alps, arctic Europe to Japan. Lfp: Vaccinium. Few subspecies.

8. *Zizeeria Knysna* (Tr.). S. Europe, widespread in Asia, Africa, and to Australia. Female brown UP.

9. *Zizeeria lysimon* (Hbn.).

Nemeobiidae

10. *Hamearis lucina* (L.) 'Duke of Burgundy Fritillary'. Europe.

Hesperiidae

11. *Carcharodus alceae* (Esp.). Europe, W. Asia. Similar: lavatherae (Esp.), N. Africa, S. Europe, Syria, Armenia, UP greyer brown.

12. *Carterocephalus palaemon* (Pall.) 'Chequered Skipper'. W. Europe across C. and N. Asia to Japan, N. America.

13. *Carterocephalus silvicolus* (Mei.). N. Scandinavia, Siberia, Amurland, Kamschatka. Female much darker UP and resembles abax male from W. China.

14. *Erynnis marloyi* (Bdv.). Balkans, Asia Minor, Syria, Iran to Chitral. Similar: pelias (Leech), Tibet, W. China.

15. *Erynnis tages* (L.) 'Dingy Skipper'. Europe across Russia to China. Several subspecies.

16. *Gegenes nostrodamus* (F.). S. Europe, Algeria, Asia Minor, Himalayas. Terrain: arid regions. Similar: lefebvrei (Rambr.), Cyprus.

17. *Gegenes nostrodamus* (see 16).

18. *Hesperia comma* (L.) 'Silver-spotted Skipper'. N. Africa, Spain, Europe and temperate Asia to W. North America. Lfp: grasses. Several subspecies.

19. *Hesperia comma* (see 18).

20. *Heteropterus morpheus* (Pall.). Europe through Asia to Japan. UP black.

21. *Muschampia cribrellum* (Ev.). Rumania across S. Russia to Amurland.

22. *Muschampia proto* (Esp.). N. Africa, Portugal through S. Europe to Asia Minor. Similar: staudingeri (Spr.), Iran, Iraq, C. Asia; tessellum (Hbn.), Russia to W. China; gigas (Brem.), Amurland, very large.

23. *Ochlodes venatus* (Brem.) 'Large Skipper'. W. Europe through temperate Asia to China and Japan. Many subspecies.

24. *Pyrgus alveus* (Hbn.). N. Africa, Spain to Caucasus, Siberia. Similar: cinarae (Rambr.)

25. *Pyrgus centaureae* (Rambr.). N. Scandinavia, arctic Russia, N. America to Appalachian Mountains and Rocky Mountains. Similar: andromedae (Wallgr.), Europe; cacaliae (Rambr.), montane Europe.

26. *Pyrgus fritillarius* (Poda). S. and C. Europe, S. Russia to C. Asia.

27. *Pyrgus malvae* (L.) 'Grizzled Skipper'. Europe, Asia to Amurland.

28. *Pyrgus onopordi* (Rambr.). Morocco, Algeria, Spain, S. France. Similar: cirsii (Rambr.).

29. *Pyrgus serratulae* (Rambr.). Spain, Central Europe to E. Siberia. Similar: speyeri (Stgr.), Amurland; carlinae (Rambr.), Alps.

30. *Spialia phlomidis* (Herr. Sch.). E. Europe, Asia Minor, Iran.

31. *Spialia sertorius* (Hoffmsgg.). N. Africa, S. Europe to Chitral, Tibet to Amurland. Several subspecies.

32. *Spialia sertorius* (see 32).

33. *Thymelicus acteon* (Rott.) 'Lulworth Skipper'. Canary Islands, N. Africa, S. and C. Europe to Asia Minor. Similar: hamza (Oberth.), N. Africa, Asia Minor, Cyprus, Turkestan, brighter colour.

34. *Thymelicus sylvestris* (Poda). 'Small Skipper'. Morocco, Spain, across Europe, Asia Minor to Iran. Similar: lineola (O.). 'Essex Skipper', smaller, sexbrand smaller; stigma (Stgr.), Turkestan.

North America

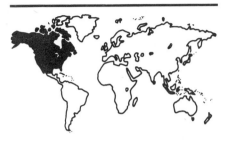

PLATE 12: Papilionidae

1. *Battus philenor* (L.). U.S.A., Cuba, Costa Rica. Variable, blue or green sheen absent.

2. *Battus polydamas* (L.). Mexico, Florida, W. Indies. Many forms. Similar: devilliers (Godt.), Cuba; archidamas (Bsd.), Chile.

3. *Eurytides marcellus* (Cr.). U.S.A. Similar: marcellinus (Dbl.), Jamaica; celadon (Lucas), Cuba; zonaria (Btlr.), Haiti.

4. *Papilio aristodemus* (Esper.). Florida, Antilles, Haiti.

5. *Papilio cresphontes* (Cr.). Mexico to Massachusetts. Similar: thoas (L.), S. America, Texas, narrower band and spots UPH; ornythion (Bsd.), Mexico, Texas; paeon (Bsd.), Colombia, Ecuador, Peru.

6. *Papilio daunus* (Bsd.). British Columbia, Alberta to Guatemala. Similar: pilumnus (Bsd.), Mexico to Guatemala.

7. *Papilio indra* (Reak.). Western U.S.A.

8. *Papilio eurymedon* (Luc.). British Columbia to Colorado.

9. *Papilio glaucus* (see 10).

10. *Papilio glaucus* (L.). Canada to Texas. Female form turnus resembles male with broader blue markings UPH. Similar: rutulus (Luc.), British Colombia to Guatemala; alexiares (Hopff.), Mexico.

11. *Papilio polyxenes* (F.). N. America, Mexico, Guatemala, Cuba. Similar: bairdi (Edw.).

12. *Papilio palamedes* (Drury). South from Virginia to Mexico.

13. *Papilio troilus* (L.). Canada to Texas. Female brownish.

14. *Papilio zelicaon* (Luc.). Arizona to Alaska. Similar: nitra (Edw.), base of UPF and UPH much darkened.

15. *Parnassius clodius* (Men.). Oregon, California. Variable.

Heliconidae

16. *Dione vanillae* (L.). Mexico, Texas, north of S. America, Bermuda. UP resembles moneta, less dark veining.

Libytheidae

17. *Libytheana carinenta* (Cr.). Canada to Florida, C. America to Buenos Aires. Several subspecies.

Danaidae

18. *Danaus eresimus* (Cr.). C. America, Texas, W. Indies.

19. *Danaus gilippus* (Cramer). N., C. and S. America, W. Indies. Similar: plexaure (Godt.), Argentina, Brazil.

20. *Danaus plexippus* (L.). Canary Islands, America, Australia. In Malaysia, India = genutia. Many subspecies. Similar: erippus (Cr.), Brazil, C. America.

PLATE 13: Nymphalidae

1. *Anaea aidea* (Guer.). Mexico to Texas.

2. *Anaea andria* (Scudder). Texas to Michigan. Similar: floridalis (Johnson & Comstock).

3. *Anartia amathea* (L.). N. and C. America, Trinidad.

4. *Anartia fatima* (F.). Tropical America to Texas.

5. *Anartia jatrophae* (Johanss.). Tropical S. America to Texas. Has seasonal forms.

6. *Asterocampa celtis* (Bsd. & Leconte). Michigan to Ontario.

7. *Asterocampa clyton* (Bsd. & Leconte). Nebraska to New York. Many subspecies. Similar: argus (Bates), Guatemala, Honduras, black tip to UPF.

8. *Asterocampa clyton* (see 7).

9. *Chlosyne acastus* (Edw.). Utah, Nevada, Montana. Similar: palla (Bsd.), British Columbia to California; whitneyi (Behr.), California to Nevada, silvery UNH.

10. *Chlosyne gabbii* (Behr.). Western U.S.A.

11. *Chlosyne harrisii* (Scudder). N. America, Canada to Illinois. Similar: nycteis (Dbl.).

12. *Chlosyne hoffmanni* (Behr.). Western U.S.A.

13. *Chlosyne janais* (Druce). Texas, Mexico, Honduras.

14. *Chlosyne lacinia* (Geyer). Mexico to Texas, C. America. Lfp: Sunflower.

15. *Chlosyne nycteis* (Dbl. & Hew.). U.S.A. Similar: gorgone (Hbn.).

16. *Chlosyne nycteis* (see 15).

17. *Clossiana alberta* (Edw.). Alberta, British Columbia.

18. *Clossiana astarte* (Dbl. & Hew.). Alberta, British Columbia.

19. *Clossiana bellona* (F.). Rocky Mountains.

20. *Clossiana improba* (Btlr.). N. Europe, N. America from Alaska to Labrador. Novaya Zemlya.

21. *Euptoieta claudia* (Cr.). N. America, Jamaica.

22. *Euptoieta hegesia* (Cr.). C. America to Texas, W. Indies, Cuba. Similar: claudia (Cr.).

23. *Euphydryas anicia* (Dbl. & Hew.). British Columbia.

24. *Euphydryas augusta* (Edw.). California. One of several subspecies of editha (Bsd.).

25. *Euphydryas chalcedon* (Dbl. & Hew.). California. Similar: baroni (Hy. Edw.), smaller.

26. *Euphydryas macglashani* (Riv.). California. This and following species are possibly only forms of chalcedon (Dbl. & Hew.), all from California. Similar: quino (Behr.); cooperi (Behr.); colon (Edw.), Washington, Oregon.

27. *Euphydryas nubigena* (Behr.). California.

28. *Euphydryas phaeton* (Drury). Eastern N. America.

29. *Euphydryas rubicunda* (Hy. Edw.). California. A subspecies of editha (Bsd.).

30. *Eunica tatila* (H. Schaff.). Florida, Jamaica, Cuba, Brazil. Few subspecies. Similar: monima (Cr.), Florida and Texas, Cuba.

31. *Junonia lavinia* (Cr.). Tropical America to S. Canada. Many forms and subspecies.

32. *Limenitis archippus* (Cr.). Canada to Mexico.

PLATE 14: Nymphalidae

1. *Limenitis astyanax* (Fab.). Florida to New England.

2. *Limenitis arthemis* (Drury). Canada to Michigan.

3. *Limenitis californica* (Btlr.). California, Arizona, Mexico. Subspecies of bredowi.

4. *Limenitis ⹀ bredowi* (Hbn.). Arizona, California, Mexico.

5. *Limenitis lorquini* (Bsd.). Western U.S.A.

6. *Limenitis weidemeyeri* (Edw.). Western parts of N. America.

7. *Mestra amymone* (Men.). Tropical C. America to Nebraska. Dry season form. Similar: dorcas (F.), Jamaica, UP yellow bordered.

8. *Metamorpha stelenes* (L.). Texas to Brazil. Several forms.

9. *Phyciodes picta* (Edw.). Mexico to Nebraska.

10. *Phyciodes phaon* (Edw.). Mexico to Georgia. UP resembles picta.

11. *Marpesia petreus* (Cr.). S. America to Kansas. Similar: eleuchea (Hbn.), Antilles, Cuba, darker.

12. *Nymphalis milberti* (Fabr.). Northern N. America, Newfoundland to Pacific.

13. *Phyciodes camillus* (Edw.). Western N. America. Similar: orseis (Edw.), Washington to Mexico.

14. *Phyciodes frisia* (Poey.). Tropical S. America to Texas. Similar: tulcis (Bates), darker, with yellow markings.

15. *Phyciodes montana* (Behr.). California, Nevada. Terrain: montane.

16. *Phyciodes texana* (Edw.). Mexico to Georgia. Similar: sitalces (G. & S.), Guatemala, UPF wider band, UPH narrower band; drymaea (G. & S.), Honduras, Panama, UNH yellower; ordys (Hew.), Mexico, larger.

17. *Phyciodes mylitta* (Edw.). Arizona, Colorado. Similar: barnesi (Skin.), Colorado, larger, less markings.

18. *Phyciodes tharos* (Drury). Mexico to Canada. Similar: batesii (Reak.), darker; pratensis (Behr.), paler UN.

19. *Phyciodes vesta* (Edw.). Mexico to Kansas.

20. *Poladryas minuta* (Edw.). Rocky Mountains, Texas, Colorado.

21. *Polygonia comma* (Harr.). Canada to Texas.

22. *Polygonia faunus* (see 15/2).

23. *Polygonia interrogationis* (F.). Mexico to Quebec.

24. *Polygonia j-album* (Bsd. & Lec.). Canada to Michigan.

25. *Polygonia orcas* (Edw.). Western N. America.

26. *Polygonia progne* (Cr.). Canada to Virginia. Very variable. Similar: gracilis (Gr. & Rob.), Canada to Michigan.

27. *Polygonia satyrus* (Edw.). Ontario to Pacific Coast of N. America.

28. *Polygonia zephyrus* (Edw.). Rocky Mountains to Pacific. Similar: chrysoptera (Ww.), California, UPH fiery yellow-red; g-argenteum (Dbl. & Hew.), Mexico.

PLATE 15: Nymphalidae

1. *Phyciodes leanira* (F. & F.) Mexico, California.

2. *Polygonia faunus* (Edw.). Canada south to Georgia, Labrador.

3. *Pyrameis tammeamea* (Esch.). Hawaii.

4. *Speyeria adiante* (Bsd.). California. Similar: artonis (Edw.).

5. *Speyeria aphrodite* (F.). Canada to Kansas.

6. *Speyeria aphrodite* (see 5).

7. *Speyeria atlantis* (Edw.). N. American Atlantic States. Similar: lais (Edw.), Alberta, British Columbia, smaller; electa (Edw.), Colorado, Montana; columbia (H. Edw.), larger.

8. *Speyeria atossa* (Edw.). California.

9. *Speyeria bremneri* (Edw.). Pacific Coast of N. America. Similar: zerene (Bsd.), California; monticola (Behr.), California, terrain: montane; rhodope (Edw.), Vancouver, British Columbia.

10. *Speyeria calgariana* (McD.). Canada.

11. *Speyeria callippe* (Bsd.). California. Similar: juba (Bsd.).

12. *Speyeria clio* (Edw.). Montana, Alberta. Terrain: montane. Similar: opis (Edw.), British Columbia, smaller; bischoffi (Edw.), Alaska.

13. *Speyeria coronis* (Behr.). California.

Similar: platina (Skin.), Utah, Idaho; snyderi (Skin.), Utah, larger.

14. *Speyeria cybele* (Fab.). N. America. Several forms, those on the Pacific Coast being paler than those from the East. Similar: aphrodite (F.).

15. *Speyeria diana* (Cr.). N. America.

16. *Speyeria diana* (see 15).

17. *Speyeria cybele* (see 14).

18. *Speyeria eurynome* (Edw.). Pacific coast of N. America. Few subspecies.

19. *Speyeria edwardsii* (Reak.). Colorado, Utah, Nevada.

20. *Speyeria halcyone* (Edw.). Colorado.

21. *Speyeria hippolyta* (Edw.). California, Oregon.

PLATE 16: Nymphalidae

1. *Speyeria hesperis* (Edw.). Colorado, Utah, Montana.

2. *Speyeria idalia* (Drury). N. America.

3. *Speyeria lais* (Edw.). Canada.

4. *Speyeria mormonia* (Bsd.). California, Nevada.

5. *Speyeria macaria* (Edw.). California, Nevada.

6. *Speyeria nevadensis* (Edw.). Utah, Nevada, Wyoming. Similar: meadii (Edw.), smaller.

7. *Speyeria notocris* (Edw.). Arizona. Similar: nokomis (Edw.), UPF sometimes very black at base.

8. *Speyeria nokomis* (Edw.). Utah, Arizona. Similar: nitocris (Edw.), Arizona; leto (Behr.), California, Alberta.

9. *Speyeria zerene* (Bsd.). California. Variable.

10. *Speyeria semiramis* (Edw.). Western N. America.

11. *Speyeria zerene* (see 9).

12. *Texola perse* (Edw.). Arizona. Similar: Dymasia dymas (Edw.), Texas; hepburni (G. & S.), Mexico.

13. *Thessalia wrightii* (see 15).

14. *Thessalia cyneas* (G. & S.). Arizona.

15. *Thessalia wrightii* (Edw.). California. Similar UP: leanira (Bsd.), California, has less yellow UN.

16. *Vanessa virginiensis* (Drury). N. America, Canary Islands, S. America to Brazil.

17. *Vanessa carye* (Hbn.). Western N. America to Brazil, Patagonia. Similar: kershawi (McCoy.), Australia, white band UPF more joined.

18. *Thessalia alma* (Strek.). Utah, Arizona. Similar: theona (Men.), Texas, C. America.

PLATE 17 : Pieridae

1. *Anteos maerula* (Fab.). Nebraska to Mexico.

2. *Ascia josephina* (Godt.). C. America to Texas.

3. *Anthocharis cethura* (Fldr.). California. Female UP yellow.

4. *Anthocharis sara* (Luc.). Western U.S.A.

5. *Anthocharis lanceolota* (Luc.). California to Alaska.

6. *Anthocharis limonea* (Btlr.). Mexico.

7. *Colias alexandra* (Edw.). Colorado.

8. *Colias boothii* (Curtis). Arctic America.

9. *Colias philodice* (Latr.). Newfoundland to Florida. Similar: chrysomelas (Hy.Edw.), California.

10. *Colias elis* (Strecker). Rocky Mountains. Similar: meadi (Edw.), Colorado, darker UP.

11. *Colias cesonia* (Stoll.). New York to S. America, Argentina. Similar: phillippa (F.), Bolivia.

12. *Colias christina* (Edw.). W. Canada. Both male and female vary in shade greatly.

13. *Colias eurydice* (Bsd.). California. Female plain yellow-green UP. Similar: helena (Reak.), Bolivia.

14. *Colias therapis* (Fldr.). California, Venezuela.

15. *Colias gigantea* (Strecker). Arctic N. America.

16. *Colias eurytheme* (Bsd.). N. America.

17. *Colias hageni* (Edw.). Canada. Male resembles marcopolo but with black dot UPF.

18. *Colias interior* (Send.). Canada, Newfoundland to Michigan.

19. *Colias pelidne* (Bsd. & Leconte). Arctic to Wyoming.

20. *Euchloe ausonides* (Luc.). Vancouver to California. Similar: creusa (Dbl. & Hew.), Rocky Mountains; hyantis (Edw.), California; both creusa and hyantis are subspecies of ausonia.

21. *Euchloe olympia* (Edw.). U.S.A.

22. *Euchloe pima* (Edw.). Arizona.

23. *Euchloe sara* (Bsd.). W. Canada.

24. *Eurema daira* (Godt.). Dry season form. (see 27).

25. *Eurema boisduvaliana* (Fldr.). Mexico, Florida.

26. *Nathalis iole* (Bsd.). Mexico, U.S.A.

27. *Eurema daira* (Godt.). Florida, Antilles, C. America. Wet season form.

28. *Eurema nicippe* (Cr.). U.S.A., Brazil, Antilles.

29. *Eurema salome* (Fldr.). Mexico to Texas.

30. *Colias scudderi* (Reak.). Rocky Mountains.

31. *Neophasia menapia* (Fldr.). Western U.S.A. to Nebraska.

32. *Neophasia terlooii* (Behr.). California. Lfp: Arbutus.

33. *Eurema lisa* (Bsd. & Lec.). Tropical America to Maine. Similar: nisa (Latreille), Brazil to Texas.

34. *Paramidea genutia* (F.). Massachusetts to Texas.

35. *Phoebis agarithe* (Bsd.). Mexico, Kansas, to Paraguay. Similar: argante (F.), Cuba, female resembles avellaneda male.

36. *Pieris cruciferarum* (Bsd.). California.

37. *Eurema mexicana* (Bsd.). C. America to Michigan.

38. *Pontieuchloia beckeri* (Edw.). U.S.A.

39. *Pontieuchloia protodice* (Bsd. & Lec.). Canada, U.S.A. to Guatemala.

40. *Pontieuchloia protodice* (see 39).

PLATE 18 : Satyridae

1. *Cercyonis meadii* (Edw.). Colorado to Montana.

2. *Cercyonis paulus* (Edw.). California, Nevada. Similar: UP charon (Edw.), Western N. America, UN darker, less lines UNF.

3. *Cercyonis pegala* (F.). N. America to Mexico. Several forms. Similar: alope (F.), Texas, smaller and male has two eye spots UPF.

4. *Cercyonis sthenele* (Bsd.). California.

5. *Coenonympha california* (Dbl. & Hew.). Western U.S.A.

6. *Coenonympha elko* (Edw.). Nevada to Vancouver.

7. *Coenonympha inornata* (Edw.). Newfoundland, Canada, Montana.

8. *Gyrocheilus patrobas* (Hew.). Mexico, Arizona. Similar: form tritonia (Edw.).

9. *Erebia episodea* (Btlr.). Alaska to Colorado. Terrain: montane.

10. *Erebia rossii* (Curtis). Arctic America and Asia. Similar: disa (Thunb.), Alaska, UPH grey scaling, UPF top ocellus bipupilled.

11. *Erebia theano* (Tauschenberg). N. America, Altai Mountains.

12. *Euptychia areolatus* (Abbot & Smith). N. America.

13. *Oeneis bore* (Hbn.). N. America, Norway, N. Russia. Similar: ammon (Elwes), Altai Mountains.

14. *Coenonympha haydeni* (Edw.). Montana, Colorado.

15. *Gnodia portlandia* (F.). N. America. Similar: creola (Skn.). UPF dark streaks between the veins.

16. *Euptychia cymele* (Cramer). N. America. Similar: periphas (Godt.), Brazil, Uruguay, only one eye-spot UPF; ocelloides (Schaus.), Brazil, smaller.

17. *Euptychia gemma* (Huebner). N. America. Similar: phocion (Fab.), N. America, UNH markings larger and with orange line around them.

18. *Hermeuptychia hermes* (F.). N. America, C. America to S. Brazil.

19. *Euptychia mitchelli* (French). N. America.

20. *Euptychia henshawi* (Edw.). Colorado and Arizona to Mexico. Similar: hedemanni (Feld.), Costa Rica, larger and darker.

21. *Euptychia rubricata* (Edw.). N. America, Guatemala. Similar: pellonia (Godm.), Mexico.

22. *Neominois ridingsii* (Edw.). Colorado. Similar: dionysius (Scudder.), larger, paler.

23. *Oeneis chryxus* (Dbd.). N. America. Similar: hora (Gr-Gr.), Tian Shan.

24. *Oeneis brucei* (Edw.). Colorado, Alberta. Similar: semidea (Say.), New Hampshire, Colorado, Labrador, UNH no dark line, less transparent.

PLATE 19 : Satyridae

1. *Oeneis ivallda* (Mead.). California.

2. *Oeneis macounii* (Edw.). N. America.

3. *Oeneis melissa* (F.). N. America, Lapland, Siberia. UP resembles bore.

4. *Oeneis nevadensis* (Fldr.). Vancouver to California. Terrain: montane. Few subspecies, paler or darker UP.

5. *Oeneis uhleri* (Reak.). Colorado, N. Dakota. Similar: alberta (Elw.), Alberta.

6. *Satyrodes eurydice* (Johans.). N. America.

7. *Paramecera xicaque* (Reak.). Mexico.

Lycaenidae

8. *Agriades podarce* (Fldr.). California, Nevada, Colorado. Similar: aquilo (Bsd.), Arctic America, small; rustica (Edw.), Colorado northwards, larger than aquilo, lighter blue.

9. *Atlides halesus* (Cr.). South of U.S.A., Mexico, Costa Rica.

10. *Callipsyche behrii* (Edw.). Rocky Mountains.

11. *Cyaniris pseudargiolus* (Cr.). Alaska to Panama. Several forms and subspecies.

12. *Everes amyntula* (Bsd.). Pacific States of U.S.A. Similar: comyntas (Godt.), Canada to Costa Rica.

13. *Everes comyntas* (Godt.). Canada to Pacific and C. America. Similar: amyntula (Bsd.).

14. *Erora laeta* (Edw.). Quebec to Arizona Mexico and C. America.

15. *Eumaeus atala* (Poey). S. America to Florida, Cuba.

16. *Feniseca tarquinius* (F.). Nova Scotia to Carolina and Florida.

17. *Brephidium exilis* (Bsd.). Venezuela to Pacific and Nebraska, Mexico, C. America to Venezuela. Similar: pseudopea (Morrison), Georgia, Florida.

18. *Erora laeta* (see 14).

19. *Glaucopsyche antiacis* (Bsd.). California, Nevada, Arizona. Similar: couperi (Grt.), Newfoundland, Labrador, darker UN.

20. *Glaucopsyche lygdamus* (Doubleday). Newfoundland to Georgia.

21. *Glaucopsyche xerces* (Bsd.). California.

22. *Hemiargus ammon* (Luc.). Florida, Cuba, S. America.

23. *Hemiargus ceraunus* (F.). C. America to Texas. Similar: thomasi (Clench).

24. *Hypaurotis crysalus* (Edw.). California to S. Colorado.

25. *Hemiargus isola* (Reak.). Mexico to Nebraska. Similar: zachaeina (Btlr.), Antilles, C. America to S. Brazil, UN lighter colour.

26. *Hemiargus isola* (see 25).

27. *Hemiargus thomasi* (Clench). Florida, Bahamas. Similar: ceraunus (F.).

28. *Incisalia augustinus* (Westw.). Newfoundland to Michigan. Similar: polios (Cork & Watson), Canada, Vancouver, New Hampshire.

29. *Incisalia irus* (Godt.). Canada to Texas. Similar: henrici (Gr. & R.).

30. *Incisalia niphon* (Hbnr.). Nova Scotia to Florida. Lfp: Pines. Similar: eryphon (Bsd.), British Columbia, Wyoming.

31. *Incisalia polios* (Cork & Watson). Quebec to Texas. Similar: irus (Godt.).

32. *Icaricia lycea* (Edw.). Rocky Mountains. Subspecies of icaroides (Bsd.), California.

33. *Icaricia pheres* (Bsd.). Pacific States of U.S.A. Several similar species.

34. *Leptotes cassius* (Cr.). S. America to Texas. Similar: marinus (Reak.), Mexico, Kansas, more blue coloured UP; theonus (Luc.), C. America, Northern S. America, darker UN.

35. *Lycaeides melissa* (Edw.). Rocky Mountains, Kansas to Manitoba.

36. *Lycaeides melissa* (see 35).

37. *Lycaeides shasta* (Edw.). Rocky Mountains.

38. *Lycaeides aster* (Edw.). Newfoundland.

39. *Lycaena epixanthe* (Bsd. & Lec.). Newfoundland to Kansas.

40. *Lycaena arota* (Bsd.). California. Similar: virginiensis (Edw.), California to Colorado, UN has white marginal lunules.

41. *Lycaena gorgon* (Bsd.). California, Nevada.

42. *Lycaena helloides* (Bsd.). Michigan to Maine and Canada. Similar: dorcas (Kirby), Canada to Maine.

43. *Lycaena heteronea* (Bsd.). Colorado to California.

44. *Lycaena mariposa* (Reak.). Rocky Mountains, California. Similar: zeroe (Bsd.), California, Colorado, UNH almost unspotted; helloides (Bsd.), Michigan to Maine and Canada, UNH reddish; dorcas (Ky.), Arctic N. America, small, UN redbrown ground colour.

45. *Lycaena mariposa* (see 44).

PLATE 20: Lycaenidae

1. *Lycaena rubidus* (Edw.). California, Oregon. Similar: cupreus (Edw.), smaller, more spotted UN.

2. *Lycaena snowi* (Edw.), Rocky Mountains. Subspecies of cupreus (Edw.).

3. *Lycaena thoe* (Bsd.). Atlantic States of N. America, Colorado.

4. *Lycaena thoe* (see 3).

5. *Lycaena xanthoides* (Bsd.). California. Similar: dione (Scudd.), Iowa; editha (Mead), Nevada, much smaller.

6. *Mitoura grunus* (Bsd.). California.

7. *Mitoura gryneus* (Hbn.). U.S.A.

8. *Mitoura nelsoni* (Bsd.). California, Colorado.

9. *Mitoura saepium* (Bsd.). Pacific States of N. America.

10. *Mitoura spinctorum* (Bsd.). Colorado to Mexico.

11. *Mitoura xami* (Reak.). Vancouver, California to Mexico. Similar: rhodope (G. & S.), Mexico.

12. *Phaedrotus sagittigera* (Fldr.). Rocky Mountains.

13. *Philotes battoides* (Behr.). California.

14. *Philotes enoptes* (Bsd.). Pacific States of U.S.A. Similar: glaucon (Edw.), UP broader black border.

15. *Philotes sonorensis* (Fldr.). California to N. Mexico.

16. *Plebejus acmon* (Westw.). W. America.

17. *Plebejus aquila* (Bsd.). Circumpolar, Hudson Bay to Labrador. Similar: saepiolus (Bsd.).

18. *Plebejus saepiolus* (Bsd.). S. Canada, Pacific States of U.S.A. Female UP sometimes blue at wing base. Similar: aquila (Bsd.).

19. *Plebejus saepiolus* (see 18).

20. *Satyrium fuliginosa* (Edw.). California Utah, Nevada.

21. *Strymon acis* (Drury). Florida, Antilles.

22. *Strymon falacer* (Godt.). Canada to Texas. Similar: alcestis (Edw.).

23. *Strymon avalona* (Wright). California.

24. *Strymon cecrops* (F.). Florida to New York. Similar: beon (Cr.).

25. *Strymon columella* (F.). Texas south to C. America. Similar: bubastus (Cr.), Brazil, UN spots darker.

26. *Strymon edwardsi* (Saunders). N. America. Similar: oslari (Dyar), Arizona, very pale UP; alcestis (Edw.), Texas, UN white markings linear.

27. *Strymon favonius* (Abbot & Smith). South of N. America. Similar: ontario (Edw.), Canada to Texas; acis (Drury), Antilles, Florida, two white dots UNH.

28. *Strymon leda* (Edw.). Texas, Arizona. Similar: ines (Edw.), Arizona, smaller, UN dark; clytie (Edw.), Texas.

29. *Strymon liparops* (Bsd. & Lec.). U.S.A. Similar UN: caryaevorus (McDunnough), Canada to north of U.S.A.

30. *Strymon m-album* (Bsd. & Lec.). S. America to Kansas. Similar: vibidia (Hew.), Costa Rica, UN markings more diffuse; punctium (H.Sch.), Guianas, UNF no white stripe.

31. *Strymon martialis* (H.Sch.). Florida, Cuba, Jamaica. Similar: coelebs (H.Sch.), Haiti, Cuba.

32. *Strymon melinus* (Hbn.). Canada to C. America and Brazil. Similar: autolycus (Edw.), Texas, Missouri, Kansas, orange spots UP more extensive.

33. *Strymon ontario* (Edw.). Texas.

34. *Strymon titus* (F.). Southern part of U.S.A.

35. *Thecla adenostomatis* (Edw.). California.

36. *Thecla dryope* (Edw.). California, Nevada, Utah. Similar: sylvinus (Bsd.), California, more yellow at end of UPH; putnami (Edw.), terrain: montane.

37. *Thecla grunus* (Bsd.). California, Nevada. Lfp: Habrodias.

38. *Thecla loki* (Skinner). California.

Nemeobiidae

39. *Apodemia mormo* (Fldr.). California to New Mexico. Few subspecies. Similar: palmerii (H.Edw.), Mexico, much smaller; stalachtioides (Btlr.), Brazil, brown stripes in margin UP.

40. *Apodemia walkeri* (Godm. & Salvin). Texas to Mexico.

41. *Emesis ares* (H.Edw.). Arizona.

42. *Emesis muticum* (McAlpine). Western

N. America to Ohio. Similar: rawsoni (McAlpine).

43. *Emesis nemesis* (Edw.). Texas. Dry season form of nilus (Fldr.).

44. *Lasaia sessilis* (Schaus). Texas, Mexico.

45. *Lephelisca virginiensis* (Guerin). Florida to Ohio, Mexico, C. America. Similar: borealis (Grote & Robinson), larger.

46. *Lephelisca wrighti* (Holl.). Texas, California.

47. *Lymnas cephise* (Men.). Mexico, C. America, Texas.

PLATE 21 : Hesperiidae

1. *Achalarus lyciades* (Geyer). New England to Texas, C. America. Similar UP: advena (Mab.), C. America, no white UN; casica (H.Sch.), Mexico, UP white edge conspicuous, transparent marking very small.

2. *Amblyscirtes aenus* (Edw.). Central and Western U.S.A. Similar: erna (Freeman).

3. *Amblyscirtes belli* (Freeman), Central and Southern U.S.A. Similar: lerida (Freeman), Lower Mississippi, UPF spots yellowish.

4. *Amblyscirtes carolina* (Skin.). Georgia to Virginia. Terrain: Swamps and marshes E. U.S.A.

5. *Amblyscirtes cassus* (Edw.). Arizona.

6. *Amblyscirtes fimbriata* (Plotz). Colorado to Mexico.

7. *Amblyscirtes eos* (Edw.). Texas.

8. *Amblyscirtes oslari* (Skinner). W. U.S.A. and Rocky Mountains.

9. *Ancyloxipha numitor* (F.). Canada to Florida and Texas. Similar: melanoneura (Fldr.), Colombia, blackened veins UP; arene (Edw.), Arizona southwards, very small, pale UPF.

10. *Amblyscirtes nysa* (Edw.). Texas, Kansas.

11. *Amblyscirtes vialis* (Edw.). Canada to Texas to Pacific.

12. *Amblyscirtes textor* (Hbn.). Virginia to Georgia and Texas.

13. *Amblyscirtes exoteria* (H.Sch.). Arizona, Mexico.

14. *Atalopedes campestris* (Bsd.). Tropical America, U.S.A. Similar UP: mesogramma (Latr.), UNH broad white band; Mellana gala (G. & S.), Mexico.

15. *Atrytone arogos* (Bsd. & Lec.). Eastern U.S.A.

16. *Atrytone aspa* (Bsd. & Lec.). Florida, Alabama. Similar: dion (Edw.), widespread in U.S.A., UNH light longitudinal streaks.

17. *Atrytone conspicua* (Edw.), Northern U.S.A. Similar: berryi (Bell), Florida, UNH no light spots.

18. *Atrytone dion* (Edw.). Canada to Nebraska.

19. *Atrytonopsis deva* (Edw.). Florida, Carolina, Mexico.

20. *Atrytonopsis hianna* (Sed.). Central and Eastern U.S.A. Similar: turneri (H. A. Freeman), Kansas, Oklahoma, grey-brown.

21. *Atrytone logan* (Edw.). Central and Eastern U.S.A.

22. *Atrytone pilatka* (Edw.). Florida north to Virginia.

23. *Autochton cellus* (Bsd. & Lec.). C. America to New York.

24. *Calpodes ethlius* (Cr.). S.E. States of U.S.A. through C. America to Argentina and W. Indies. Lfp: Canna. Similar: evansi (H. A. Freeman), Mexico.

25. *Chioides albofasciatus* (Hew.). C. America to Texas. Similar: zilpa (Btlr.), S. Texas, UNH white patch but no band.

26. *Celotes nessus* (Edw.). Arizona to Mexico.

27. *Codactractus alcalus* (Hew.). Arizona, C. America. Similar: aminias (Hew.), Brazil, Paraguay, darker UP and UN, no white patch UNH; carlos (Evans), C. America, dots slightly smaller.

28. *Cogia hippalus* (Edw.). Arizona to Guatemala.

29. *Copaeodes aurantiaca* (Hew.). Southern U.S.A. to Panama and Cuba. Similar: wrightii (Edw.), California, larger, brighter; myrtis (Edw.), Arizona, dusky edges UP.

30. *Copaeodes minima* (Edw.). Southern U.S.A. Similar: simplex (Fldr.), Mexico, paler.

31. *Ephyriades brunnea* (H. Sch.). Cuba, Florida.

32. *Epargyreus clarus* (Cr.). Canada to S. America. Similar: antaeus (Hew.), Brazil, unspecked wing fringes; zestos (Geyer), Antilles, Florida, no white band UNH.

33. *Erynnis albomarginatus* (G. & S.). Mexico to Colombia. Similar: pacuvius (Lintner), W. and S. U.S.A., smaller.

34. *Erynnis funeralis* (Scd. & Bur.). Western U.S.A. to Mexico and Colombia. Similar: clitus (Edw.), Arizona, New Mexico.

35. *Erynnis horatius* (Scd. & Bur.). U.S.A. Similar: juvenalis (F.), Canada, U.S.A.; meridianus (Bell), Western U.S.A.; zarucco (Lucas), Cuba, Texas, Florida; propertius (Scd. & Bur.), Western U.S.A.

36. *Erynnis icelus* (Scd. & Bur.). Canada, New Mexico.

37. *Erynnis martialis* (Scd.). Canada to Alabama.

38. *Erynnis persius* (Scd.). E. and W. U.S.A. to Canada. Similar: baptisiae (Forbes), Eastern U.S.A.; lucilius (Scd. & Bur.), S. U.S.A. to Mexico.

39. *Heliopetes ericetorum* (Bsd.). California, Arizona.

PLATE 22 : Hesperiidae

1. *Hesperia attalus* (Edw.). Southern U.S.A.

2. *Hesperia laurentina* (Lyman). Canada, Minnesota.

3. *Hesperia leonardus* (Harris). Canada south to Florida.

4. *Hesperia metea* (Scd.). U.S.A.

5. *Hesperia pawnee* (Dodge) (flies August/ September). Colorado. Similar: ottoe (Edw.) (flies June/July), Central U.S.A., narrower smoky margins UP.

6. *Lerodea eufala* (Edw.). Florida to Virginia and Nebraska, Mexico to Paraguay and Antilles. A great many very similar species in C. America, only differing in UN.

7. *Hylephila phylaeus* (Drury). S. America to Michigan and West Indies. Similar: fasciolata (Blch.), Chile, smaller, deeper colour.

8. *Hesperia ruricola* (Bsd.). S.W. U.S.A. Similar: nevada (Scd.), Colorado, more green colour UN.

9. *Hesperia sassacus* (Harris). U.S.A. Similar: harpalus (Edw.), Nevada.

10. *Hesperia uncas* (Edw.). Western U.S.A.

11. *Ochlodes snowi* (Edw.). Colorado to Mexico.

12. *Oarisma garita* (Reak.). N. America. Similar: edwardsii (Barnes), N. America, UN uniformly yellow.

13. *Megathymus cofaqui* (Strecker). Georgia, Florida.

14. *Megathymus smithi* (Drc.). Arizona.

15. *Megathymus streckeri* (Skinner). Colorado, New Mexico, Arizona. Male is smaller and darker.

16. *Lerema accius* (Alb. & Sm.). C. America, U.S.A. to Massachusetts. Similar: parumpunctata (H.Sch.), Venezuela, Brazil, larger, UNH rosy edged; lochius (Plotz), Venezuela, only 3 white spots UPF.

17. *Megathymus yuccae* (Bsd. & Lec.). Florida to Georgia. Similar: leussleri (Holland).

18. *Oarisma powesheik* (Parker). Western N. America to Mexico.

19. *Ochlodes sylvanoides* (Bsd.). Pacific States of U.S.A. Similar: agricola (Bsd.), California, smaller, darker.

20. *Oligoria maculata* (Edw.). Southern Atlantic States of U.S.A.

21. *Panoquina panoquin* (Scd.). Florida north to New Jersey. Terrain: salt marshes. Similar: panoquinoides (Skinn.), Cuba, Florida, Texas, Dominica, lacks long yellow streak UNH.

22. *Panoquina ocola* (Edw.). Florida to Ohio, Mexico to Peru, Trinidad. Similar: hecebolus (Scd.), Paraguay, Peru, darker UP.

23. *Pholisora aepheus* (Edw.). New Mexico, Arizona to Mexico. Similar: libya (Scd.),

Nevada to California, white spots apex UPF more distinct.

24. *Pholisora hayhurstii* (Edw.). U.S.A. Subspecies of mazans (Reak.), C. America.

25. *Pholisora mejicanus* (Reak.). Canada to Texas.

26. *Plestia dorus* (Edw.). Arizona to Mexico. Similar: elwesi (G. & S.), C. America.

27. *Poanes aaroni* (Skin.). New Jersey.

28. *Poanes hobomok* (Harris). E. Canada to Alabama. Similar: zabulon (Bsd. & Lec.), UNH more yellow.

29. *Poanes massasoit* (Scd.). Massachusetts.

30. *Poanes viator* (Edw.). Eastern U.S.A. Similar: aaroni (Skinner), smaller, resembles Atrytone logan.

31. *Polites baracoa* (Lucas). Antilles, Florida, Cuba. Similar: chispa (Wright), California, much smaller, UN olive grey; Hylephila ignorans (Plotz), Venezuela, orange patch UPH.

32. *Polites manataaqua* (Scd.). Central and Eastern U.S.A. Subspecies of origenes (F.).

33. *Polites mystic* (Scd.). Central and Eastern U.S.A.

34. *Polites peckius* (Kirby). U.S.A. and Canada.

35. *Polites sabuleti* (Bsd.). California.

36. *Polites themistocles* (Latreille). Canada to Florida.

37. *Polites verna* (Edw.). Eastern U.S.A.

38. *Polites vibex* (Geyer). Tropics to Central U.S.A., West Indies. Similar: sulfurina (Mab.), Brazil, Guiana, smaller and darker; phormio (Mab.), Brazil.

39. *Problema byssus* (Edw.). Kansas to Florida.

40. *Pyrgus communis* (Grote). Canada to Mexico. Similar: caespitalis (Bsd.), California, Oregon, Nevada, UNH brownish.

41. *Pyrgus ruralis* (Bsd.). California.

42. *Pyrgus scriptura* (Bsd.). Colorado to Mexico.

43. *Pyrgus syrichtus* (F.). C. America, Florida, Antilles. Similar: scriptura (Bsd.), California, Arizona, Montana, UPH unicolorous grey-white; philetas (Edw.), UNH yellowish.

44. *Systasea zampa* (Edw.). Mexico to California.

45. *Thorybes pylades* (Scd.). Canada to Texas, Atlantic States of U.S.A.

46. *Thorybes bathyllus* (Abbot & Smith). S. of U.S.A. Similar: mexicana (H.Sch.), Arizona to Panama, smaller, fewer spots UPF.

47. *Wallingrenia otho* (Abbot & Smith). E. Canada to Texas.

South and Central America

1. *Battus belus* (Cr.). Amazon, Guianas, Guatemala. Several forms lack white markings UPH. Similar: laodamus (Fldr.), Mexico to Colombia; lycides (Cr.), Guatemala to Bolivia.

2. *Battus crassus* (Cr.). Costa Rica to Rio de Janeiro.

3. *Battus madyas* (Dbl.). Peru, Bolivia. Similar: philetas (Hew.), Ecuador, Peru.

4. *Battus polystictus* (Btlr.). Brazil, Paraguay, Argentina. Similar: eracon (Godm. & Salv.), Mexico.

5. *Battus zetes* (Ww.). Haiti.

6. *Baronia brevicornis* (Salv.). Mexico.

7. *Euryades duponchelli* (Luc.). Argentina. Similar: corethrus (Bsd.), tailless.

8. *Euryades corethrus* (Bsd.).

9. *Eurytides agesilaus* (Guer.). Orinoco, Amazon to Bolivia. Similar: glaucolaus (Bates).

10. *Eurytides ariarathes* (Esp.). Colombia to Bolivia. Very variable.

11. *Eurytides asius* (F.). Brazil.

12. *Eurytides belesis* (Bates). Mexico to Nicaragua.

13. *Eurytides dolicaon* (Cr.). Colombia to S. Brazil. Several subspecies. Similar: callias (R. & J.).

14. *Eurytides telesilaus* (Fldr.). Colombia to Paraguay, Bolivia. Similar: earis (R. & J.), Ecuador.

15. *Eurytides epidaus* (Dbl.). Mexico to Honduras.

16. *Eurytides euryleon* (Hew.). Colombia, Ecuador. Female larger white and rose areas. Several subspecies. Similar: harmodius (Dbl.).

17. *Eurytides iphitas* (Hbn.). Brazil.

18. *Eurytides lacandones* (Bates). Guatemala, Panama, E. Andes to Bolivia.

19. *Eurytides leucaspis* (Godt.). Colombia to Bolivia. Similar: dioxippus (Hew.).

20. *Eurytides lysithous* (Hbn.). Brazil, Paraguay. Many forms, with varying amount of white UP.

21. *Eurytides marchandi* (Bsd.). Costa Rica to Ecuador. Similar: thyastes (Drury), Ecuador to Bolivia, discal band deep yellow; calliste (Bates), C. America, discal band pale yellow.

22. *Eurytides microdamas* (Burm.). Paraguay, S. Brazil.

23. *Eurytides pausanias* (Hew.). Colombia, Amazon, Bolivia.

24. *Eurytides orabilis* (Btlr.). Guatemala, Colombia, Costa Rica.

PLATE 24: Papilionidae

1. *Eurytides phaon* (Bsd.). Mexico to Venezuela. Variable, sometimes no marginal spots UP.

2. *Eurytides philolaus* (Bsd.). Mexico to Nicaragua.

3. *Eurytides protesilaus* (L.). Mexico to S. Brazil. Many subspecies. Similar: molops (R. & J.).

4. *Eurytides protodamas* (Godt.). Brazil.

5. *Eurytides salvini* (Bates). Guatemala, Honduras.

6. *Eurytides stenodesmus* (R. & J.). Paraguay, Brazil.

7. *Troides rhadamantus* (Lucas). Philippines.

8. *Papilio aglaope* (Gray). Amazon, E. Andes, Ecuador and Peru. Few subspecies.

9. *Papilio anchisiades* (Esper.). Central America. Lfp: citrus. Variable. Similar: isidorus (Dbl.), E. Andes, Bolivia to Ecuador, less rosy mauve on UPH; rhodostictus (Btlr. & Druce), Ecuador to Costa Rica, small white patch UPF.

10. *Papilio andraemon* (Hbn.). Cuba, Bahamas.

11. *Papilio androgeus* (see 12).

12. *Papilio androgeus* (Cr.). Mexico, W. Indies to S. Brazil. Similar: laodocus (F.), Brazil.

13. *Papilio bachus* (Fldr.). Colombia to Bolivia.

14. *Papilio birchalli* (Hew.). Panama, Colombia.

15. *Papilio cacicus* (Luc.). Venezuela, Colombia, Ecuador. Female has orange patch UPF and no band UPH.

16. *Papilio caiguanabus* (Poey.). Cuba.

17. *Papilio chiansiades* (Ww.). E. Andes, Ecuador, Peru. Female larger with larger patches UPF and UPH.

18. *Papilio cleotas* (Gray). C. America to Venezuela. Several subspecies. Females have broader markings UP.

19. *Papilio epenetus* (Hew.). W. Ecuador, W. of Andes.

20. *Papilio garamas* (Hbn.). C. America. Female larger, broader bands especially UPF.

21. *Papilio erostratus* (Ww.). Mexico, Guatemala, Honduras. Female resembles Papilio pharnaces female but larger red spots UPH.

22. *Papilio euterpinus* (Godm. & Salv.). Colombia to Peru.

PLATE 25: Papilionidae

1. *Papilio hectorides* (Esp.). Brazil and Paraguay. There is an all-black female form.

2. *Papilio hectorides* (see 1).

3. *Papilio homerus* (F.). Jamaica. Male resembles garamas (Hbn.).

4. *Papilio hellanichus* (Hew.). Uruguay, Argentina, Brazil. Similar: scamander (Bsd.), Brazil, much narrower bands UP.

5. *Papilio hyppason* (Cr.). Guianas, Amazon, Peru, Bolivia. Female white diffuse patch UPF central or plain black UPF.

6. *Papilio lycophron* (Hbn.). Mexico to S. Brazil. Few subspecies.

7. *Papilio oxynius* (Hbn.). Cuba.

8. *Papilio machaonides* (Esp.). Haiti.

9. *Papilio pelaus* (F.). Jamaica, Cuba, Haiti.

10. *Papilio pharnaces* (Dbl.). Mexico. Female larger with larger UPH markings. Similar: Eurytides thymbraeus (Bsd.), Mexico, Honduras.

11. *Papilio thersites* (F.). Jamaica.

12. *Papilio torquatus* (Cr.). Mexico to Brazil (tropical). Several forms of females. Similar: garleppi (Stgr.), Upper Amazon.

13. *Papilio torquatus* (see 12). Other female forms have yellow bands UPH and no white patch UPF.

14. *Papilio victorinus* (Dbl.). Central America. UNH spots are red.

15. *Papilio warscewiczi* (Hopff.). Ecuador to Bolivia. A few subspecies.

16. *Papilio xanthopleura* (Godm. & Salv.). Upper Amazon.

17. *Papilio zagreus* (Dbl.). Venezuela, Colombia to Bolivia. Similar: ascolius (Fldr.), Colombia, Ecuador.

18. *Parides aeneas* (L.). Guiana, Amazon and Orinoco to Peru and Bolivia. Female white patch UPF, no green, pink wide band UPH. Several subspecies.

19. *Parides agavus* (Drury). Brazil, Paraguay.

20. *Parides anchises* (L.). Colombia to Paraguay. Female whiter patch UPF. Several subspecies. Similar: drucei (Btlr.), Amazon; erithalion male (Bsd.), Colombia, much smaller red patches UPH.

PLATE 26: Papilionidae

1. *Parides arcas* (Cr.). Mexico, Venezuela, Guianas. Several subspecies, including amphus (Bsd.).

2. *Parides ascanius* (Cr.). Rio de Janeiro, Brazil.

3. *Parides chabrias* (Hew.). Ecuador, Peru. Female brownish.

4. *Parides childrenae* (Gray). Guianas, Orinoco, Bolivia. Similar: sesostris (Cr.) lacks red streak UPH and white dot UPF.

5. *Parides columbus* (H. Sch.). Colombia. Similar: orabilis (Butler), Costa Rica,

Ecuador, black bar does not cross UPF but is short.

6. *Parides coelus* (Bsd.). Cayenne.

7. *Parides cutorina* (Stgr.). Amazon, Ecuador, Peru. Male resembles Parides gratianus.

8. *Parides erithalion* (Bsd.). Colombia, Panama, Costa Rica. Few forms.

9. *Parides erlaces* (Gray). Peru, Bolivia, Argentina. Female round white patch UPF, no green, wide orange band UPH. Similar: lacydes (Hew.), Ecuador, white spots.

10. *Parides gundlachianus* (Feld.). Cuba.

11. *Parides iphidamas* (F.). Central America. Resembles Parides erithalion and Parides lycimenes.

12. *Parides iphidamas* (see 11).

13. *Parides lycimenes* (Bsd.). Guatemala, Ecuador. Several forms.

14. *Parides lysander* (Cr.). Amazon, Guianas. Female resembles Parides sesostris female. Similar: echemon (Hbn.), Guianas, wings more pointed, UPF patch more circular.

15. *Parides montezuma* (Westw.). Mexico to Nicaragua. Female no white scent pouch. Similar: perrhebus (Bdr.), complete series of red lunules UPH.

16. *Parides neophilus* (Hbn.). Colombia to Paraquay, S. Brazil. Female UPF no green. Several forms.

17. *Parides nephalion* (Godt.). Brazil, Paraguay.

18. *Parides orellana* (Hew.). Upper Amazon. Female resembles polyzelus male.

19. *Parides phalaecus* (Hew.). Ecuador. Similar: diodorus (Hopff.), Brazil; proneus (Hbn.), Argentina.

20. *Parides phosphorus* (Bates). Colombia, Guianas, Peru. Similar: subspecies gratianus (Hew.), white flecks in green patch UPF.

21. *Parides photinus* (Dbl.). Mexico to Costa Rica. Female lacks white scent pouches UPH.

22. *Parides polyzelus* (Fldr.). Mexico, Guatemala, Honduras. Female no white scent pouch UPH.

23. *Parides sestris* (Cr.). Similar: childrenae (Gray), Colombia, Ecuador, white spots UPF tip.

24. *Parides timias* (Gray). Ecuador. Male resembles neophilus, but red patch UPH sharply defined.

25. *Parides triopas* (Godt.). Amazon, Guianas. Similar: hahneli (Stgr.), larger, tailed, pale patches base of UPF.

26. *Parides tros* (Fabr.). Brazil.

27. *Parides vertumnus* (Cr.). Colombia, Bolivia. Male resembles phosphorus, but has white dot in green patch UPF. Several subspecies.

28. *Parides zacynthus* (F.). Rio de Janeiro.

PLATE 27: Morphidae

1. *Morpho achilles* (L.). Colombia, Paraguay, Brazil, Surinam. Several subspecies.

2. *Morpho aega* (Hbn.). Brazil. Similar: adonis (Cr.), Guianas, Cayenne.

3. *Morpho anaxibia* (Esp.). S. Brazil. UP as rhetenor, female as cypris, but without white.

4. *Morpho catenarius* (Perry). S. Brazil.

5. *Morpho aega* (see 2).

6. *Morpho cypris* (Ww.). Colombia, Panama.

7. *Morpho deidamia* (Hbn.). Surinam, Bolivia, Amazon.

8. *Morpho didius* (Hpffr.). Peru, Bolivia. Similar: amathonte (Deyr.), Colombia, Ecuador.

9. *Morpho granadensis* (Fldr.). Colombia, C. America to Ecuador. UP resembles deidamia.

10. *Morpho hercules* (Dalm.). Brazil. Similar: theseus (Deyr.), C. America, hind wing teethed.

11. *Morpho menelaus* (see 12).

12. *Morpho menelaus* (L.). Guianas to Bolivia.

13. *Morpho laertes* (Druce). Rio de Janeiro. UP resembles catenarius.

•
14. *Morpho portis* (Hbn.). Brazil, Uruguay. Similar: lympharis (Btlr.), Peru; aurora (Ww.), Bolivia.

15. *Morpho patroclus* (Fldr.). Peru, Bolivia.

PLATE 28: Morphidae

1. *Morpho peleides* (Koll.). Mexico, C. America, to Venezuela, Trinidad. Extremely variable. Similar: leontius (Fldr.), Venezuela, Bolivia; vitrea (Btlr.), Colombia, Bolivia.

2. *Morpho peleides* (see 1).

3. *Morpho perseus* (Cr.). Guianas, Colombia to Bolivia, Andes and Amazon. Similar: hecuba (L.), Surinam, L. Amazon, very large.

4. *Morpho polyphemus* (Dbl. & Hew.). Mexico, C. America.

5. *Morpho rhetenor* (Cr.). Surinam, Peru. Similar: cypris (Ww.), Colombia, C. America, UP has white bands.

6. *Morpho rhetenor* (see 5).

Brassolidae

7. *Caligo beltrao* (Ill.). Brazil.

8. *Brassolis sophorae* (L.). Colombia, Paraguay, Argentina. Similar: ardens (Stich.), Peru; astyra (Godt.), Brazil, Venezuela; granadensis (Stich.), Colombia, Ecuador, broader orange band.

9. *Caligo atreus* (Koll.). Venezuela, Colombia, Honduras.

10. *Caligo martia* (Godt.). Brazil.

11. *Caligo idomeneus* (L.). Brazil, Surinam.

12. *Caligo memnon* (Fldr.). C. America, Venezuela. Similar: eurilochus (Cr.), Surinam, Guianas. Lfp: Banana.

PLATE 29: Brassolidae

1. *Caligo memnon* (see 28/12).

2. *Eryphanis aesacus* (H. Sch.). C. America. Male UP resembles reevesi.

3. *Caligo teucer* (L.). Amazon, Peru, Colombia. Similar: illioneus (Cr.); oileus (Fldr.), Venezuela.

4. *Catoblepia xanthus* (L.). Ecuador, Peru, Guianas. Similar: xanthicles (G. & S.), Bolivia, orange edge to UPH.

5. *Dasyopthalma creusa* (Hbn.). Brazil. Similar: vertebralis (Btlr.).

6. *Dasyopthalma creusa* (see 5).

7. *Dynastor darius* (F.). Guatemala to Brazil.

8. *Eryphanis polyxena* (Meerb.). C. America, S. America to Paraguay. Many races.

9. *Eryphanis reevesi* (Dbl. & Hew.). Brazil.

10. *Narope cyllabarus* (Ww.). Cayenne, Colombia, Bolivia, Amazon.

11. *Narope cyllastros* (Dbl. & Hew.). Rio de Janeiro to Panama. Similar: panniculus (Stich.), Bolivia, darker brown sex-patch UPF; cyllarus (Ww.), S. Brazil, orange ground colour.

12. *Opoptera aorsa* (Godt.). Amazon, Ecuador, Rio de Janeiro. Similar: bracteolata (Stich.), Bolivia, darker, broader orange edge to UPH.

13. *Opoptera sulcius* (Stgr.). S. Brazil. Similar: fruhstorferi (Rober), Brazil, white band UPF; fumosa (Stich.), Rio de Janeiro, much narrower bands UP.

14. *Osiphanes batea* (Hbn.). Brazil. Many races.

15. *Opsiphanes berecynthia* (Cr.). Peru, Bolivia Brazil.

16. *Opsiphanes berecynthia* (see 15).

17. *Opsiphanes boisduvalii* (Ww.). Mexico to Honduras.

18. *Opsiphanes cassiae* (L.). Surinam, Colombia, Brazil, C. America. Lfp: Banana. Many races.

19. *Opsiphanes quiteria* (Cr.). C. America, Paraguay, Guianas. Many races. Similar: cassina (Fldr.).

20. *Opsiphanes tamarindi* (Fldr.). Mexico, Venezuela.

21. *Penetes pamphanis* (Ww.). Brazil.

22. *Selenophanes cassiope* (Cr.). Guianas, Brazil, Peru.

PLATE 30: Nymphalidae

1. *Adelpha abia* (Hew.). Brazil, Argentina, Paraguay. Similar: fessonia (Hew.), C. America.

2. *Adelpha alala* (Hew.). Venezuela, Ecuador, Bolivia. Variable, several forms. Similar: corcyra (Hew.), Colombia to Ecuador, white UPF narrower.

3. *Adelpha arete* (Men.). Brazil.

4. *Adelpha boreas* (Btlr.). Colombia to Bolivia. Similar: irma (Fruhst.), Bolivia, Peru, smaller, UNF band yellowish; salmoneus (Btlr.), C. America, Colombia, broader band UPF.

5. *Adelpha celerio* (Btlr.). C. America, Colombia, Ecuador.

6. *Adelpha cocala* (Cr.). Guianas, C. America to Brazil. Several subspecies. Similar: boeotia (Fldr.), C. America, Brazil, isolated spots at tip of UPF; aethalia (Fldr.), Colombia, Ecuador, Peru; euboea (Fldr.).

7. *Adelpha cytherea* (L.). C. America to Bolivia, Trinidad. Very variable, many forms.

8. *Adelpha demialba* (Btlr.). Costa Rica, Panama.

9. *Adelpha epione* (Godt.). Andes from Colombia to Bolivia.

10. *Adelpha erotia* (Hew.). C. America, Ecuador, Peru. Many forms. Similar: trinita (Kaye), much smaller.

11. *Adelpha felderi* (Bois.). Polochic Valley.

12. *Adelpha iphicla* (L.). Mexico, C. America, Trinidad, Brazil. Many subspecies and forms.

13. *Adelpha irmina* (Dbl.). Venezuela, Bolivia, Peru.

14. *Adelpha isis* (Drury). S. Brazil.

15. *Adelpha lara* (Hew.). Venezuela, Peru, Bolivia, Colombia. Similar: isis (Drury), S. Brazil.

16. *Adelpha leuceria* (Druce). Mexico to Panama.

17. *Adelpha melona* (Hew.). Guianas, Trinidad, Upper Amazon.

18. *Adelpha nea* (Hew.). Guianas, Peru. UP resembles melona (Hew.).

19. *Adelpha olynthia* (Fldr.). Colombia, Peru.

20. *Adelpha plesaure* (Hbn.). Guianas Bolivia, Brazil.

21. *Adelpha plylaca* (Bates). Mexico to Bolivia, Trinidad.

22. *Adelpha serpa* (Bsd.). Panama, C. America, Paraguay, Amazon, Venezuela, Bolivia. Several forms.

23. *Adelpha serpa* (see 22).

PLATE 31: Nymphalidae

1. *Adelpha syma* (Godt.). Paraguay, Argentina.

2. *Adelpha thoas* (Hew.). Amazon, Peru, Bolivia.

3. *Adelpha tracta* (Btlr.). Costa Rica, Panama.

4. *Adelpha zalmona* (Hew.). Costa Rica, Panama, Colombia.

5. *Adelpha zea* (Hew.). Mexico, C. America, Paraguay. UP resembles serpa.

6. *Agrias aedon* (Hew.). Colombia.

7. *Agrias amydon* (Hew.). Colombia to C. Brazil.

8. *Agrias claudia* (Schulz.). Surinam, Brazil.

9. *Agrias hewitsonius* (Bates). Ecuador, Peru, Amazon.

10. *Agrias narcissus* (Stgr.). Venezuela, Surinam.

11. *Agrias phalcidon* (Hew.). Lower Amazon.

12. *Agrias sardanapalus* (Bates). Upper Amazon.

13. *Anaea artacaena* (Hew.). C. America.

14. *Anaea appias* (Hubn.). Brazil.

15. *Anaea ates* (Druce). Bolivia, Peru, Ecuador. UP as Anaea glauce.

16. *Anaea aureola* (Bates). Guatemala, Panama, Colombia. Female has broad white band UPF.

17. *Anaea callidryas* (Fldr.). Guatemala, Panama. Female has tails.

18. *Anaea chaeronea* (Fldr.). Colombia, Panama. Female as female zelica, but orange band UP broader.

19. *Anaea chrysophana* (Bates). C. America, Peru, Brazil. Similar: halice (Godt.), Brazil, only the female is tailed and has yellow brown UP; ryphea (Cr.), C. America, Northern S. America; phidile (Hbn.), Costa Rica to S. Brazil, only the female is tailed and resembles glycerium; erythema (Bates); euryphile (Fldr.), Mexico to Brazil, shorter tails.

20. *Anaea echemus* (Dbl. & Hew.). Cuba.

PLATE 32 : Nymphalidae

1. *Anaea cyanea* (S. & G.). Ecuador. Female markings bright orange.

2. *Anaea electra* (Ww.). Mexico to Panama.

3. *Anaea panariste* (Hew.). Colombia.

4. *Anaea glycerium* (Dbl. & Hew.). C. America to Venezuela. Similar: moretta (Druce), N. Brazil, female has white spots UPF; verticordia (Hbn.), Cuba, Haiti, longer tails.

5. *Anaea lineata* (Salv.). Bolivia, Peru, Ecuador. Female resembles chaeronea female but has broader marginal band UPH; female is tailed.

6. *Anaea octavius* (Fabr.). Nicaragua.

7. *Anaea onophis* (Fldr.). Guatemala, Colombia, Ecuador, Peru. Similar: pithyusa (Fldr.), Mexico to Costa Rica; eubaena (Bsd.), C. America, paler UN, less clearly marked; lemnos (Druce), Peru, reddish UN; appias (Hbn.), S. Brazil, Colombia, greyish UN; arginussa (Hbn.), Peru to S. Brazil, greenish UN with white marginal dots UNH.

8. *Anaea morvus* (F.). C. America, Peru, Bolivia. Similar: oenomais (Bsd.), Mexico, Panama; xenocles (Ww.), more blue spots UPF. Several subspecies and forms.

9. *Anaea nessus* (Latr.). Colombia, Ecuador, Peru, Venezuela. Female has white patches UPF.

10. *Anaea eribotes* (F.). Lower Amazon, Guianas. Female has blue ground UP. Similar: porphyrio (Bates), Peru; leonida (Cr.), less orange UP.

11. *Anaea glauce* (Fldr.). Upper Amazon, Colombia. Several subspecies.

12. *Anaea panariste* (Hew.). Colombia. Two forms, both rare.

13. *Anaea tyrianthina* (S. & G.). Bolivia and Peru. Similar: titan (Fldr.), Colombia, tailed, female yellower.

14. *Anaea polyxo* (Druce). Colombia, Peru, Bolivia. UP as aureola. Similar: divina (Stgr.), UP markings greenish.

15. *Anaea vicinia* (Stgr.). Bolivia, Upper Amazon.

16. *Anaea sosippus* (Hpffr.). Peru, Ecuador.

17. *Anaea xenocles* (Ww.). Guatemala to Rio de Janeiro.

18. *Anaea pasibula* (Dbl. & Hew.). Colombia.

PLATE 33 : Nymphalidae

1. *Anaea zelica* (Salv.). C. America. Male as chaeronea, but UPF band narrower.

2. *Anartia lytrea* (Godt.). Cuba, Antilles.

3. *Atlantea perezi* (H.-Schaff.). Cuba. Similar: seitzi (Rob.), Jamaica.

4. *Antillea pelops* (Drury). Jamaica, Puerto Rico.

5. *Bolboneura sylphis* (Bates). Mexico. UP shot violet-blue.

6. *Anaeomorpha splendida* (Roths.). Peru.

7. *Batesia hypochlora* (Fldr.). Upper Amazon, Ecuador. Similar: chrysocantha (S. & G.), Peru, UNH yellow green.

8. *Baeotus japetus* (Stgr.). Amazon, Peru. UP resembles baeotus.

9. *Baeotus baeotus* (Dbl. & Hew.). Amazon, Colombia.

10. *Callicore aegina* (Fldr.). Ecuador, Colombia. Similar UN: guatemalana (Bates), Guatemala; mionina (Hew.); brome (Bsd.).

11. *Callicore atacama* (Hew.). Panama, Colombia, Peru. Similar: lyca (Dbl. & Hew.), Mexico, C. America.

12. *Callicore brome* (Bsd.). Colombia. Similar: denina (Hew.), Colombia; mionina (Hew.), Colombia; tolina (Hew.), Peru, Brazil; faustina (Bates), Panama; aegina (Fldr.), Ecuador, Colombia.

13. *Callicore clymena* (Cram.). Guatemala.

14. *Callicore codomannus* (F.). Colombia, Ecuador, Brazil. Several forms. Similar: cynosura (Dbl. & Hew.), Peru, Bolivia; pitheas (Latr.), Panama, Venezuela, broader red bands UP.

15. *Callicore excelsior* (Hew.). Upper Amazon, Ecuador, Peru. Orange band varies in size.

16. *Callithea leprieuri* (Feisth.). Surinam, Lower Amazon. Similar: depuiseti (Fldr.), Peru, broader light blue bands UP.

17. *Callicore faustina* (Bates). Panama. Similar UN: denina (Hew.); tolina (Hew.); pacifica (Bates), C. America.

18. *Callicore hydaspes* (Drury). Brazil, Paraguay. UP resembles zelphanta. Similar: hesperis (Guer.), broader scarlet band UPF.

19. *Callicore maimuna* (Hew.). Amazon, Trinidad.

20. *Callidula pyramus* (F.). Colombia to S. Brazil, Trinidad. Similar: thysbe (Dbl.), lacks sheen UP, UP more orange area.

21. *Callicore pitheas* (Latr.). Panama, Venezuela. UP resembles codomannus. Similar UN: aretas (Hew.), Venezuela, but much larger red areas UP.

22. *Callicore sorana* (Godt.). Brazil, Paraguay, Bolivia.

23. *Callicore texa* (Hew.). Colombia. Similar: lepta (Hew.), Upper Amazon, no orange patch UPH; pygas (Godt.), Brazil, Colombia, Bolivia; titania (Salv.), Guatemala, Honduras.

PLATE 34 : Nymphalidae

1. *Callicore patelina* (Hew.). Guatemala. Similar: aretas (Hew.).

2. *Callicore zelphanta* (Hew.). Upper Amazon. Similar: hytaspes (Drury); hesperis (Guer.), Colombia, Peru, Bolivia; pyracmon (Godt.), Brazil, Guianas, whole base of UPF dark red.

3. *Callithea adamsi* (Lathy), Peru. Similar: degandii (Hew.), Upper Amazon, UP greenish margins broader, especially UPH.

4. *Callizona acesta* (L.). C. America to Guiana. Few subspecies.

5. *Callithea batesii* (Hew.). Upper Amazon. Similar: markii (Hew.), male more vivid blue UPH.

6. *Callithea markii* (Hew.). Colombia, Upper Amazon.

7. *Chlosyne narva* (F.). Mexico to Venezuela. Female larger, yellower. Similar: Atlantea perezi (H. Sch.), Cuba, UPF markings

brown-red; Atlantea seitzi (Rob.), Jamaica, paler than perezi.

8. *Callithea sapphire* (Hbn.). Lower Amazon. Female broad yellow band UPF, resembles batesii female.

9. *Callithea sonkai* (Honr.). Upper Amazon. Similar: degandii (Hew.); optima (Btlr.), Peru and Ecuador, UP margins more diffuse and very bright sheen; salvini (Stgr.), broader margins UP, brighter blue sheen.

10. *Catagramma aphidna* (Hew.). Venezuela.

11. *Catonephele autinoe* (Godt.). Amazon, Brazil. Similar: sabrina (Hew.), Brazil; chromis (Dbl. & Hew.), Honduras to Bolivia; godmani (Stich.), C. America; salambria (Fldr.), Colombia, Peru, Bolivia. Females as female nyctimus except sabrina has orange dusting UPF tip.

12. *Catonephele numilia* (Cr.). Amazon, C. America, Brazil. Several forms.

13. *Catonephele numilia* (see 12).

14. *Catonephele nyctimus* (Ww.). Mexico to Venezuela and Ecuador. Similar: salacia (Hew.), Amazon; acontius (L.), Colombia, Guianas, Paraguay, Brazil, brown scent patch UPH; orites (Stich.), Panama, Venezuela, shorter orange patches UP. Females all as nyctimus.

15. *Catonephele nyctimus* (see 14).

16. *Chlosyne erodyle* (Bates). C. America. Similar: poecile (Fldr.), Guatemala, Mexico, Colombia, yellow markings UPF.

17. *Myscelia antholia* (Godt.). Antilles, Similar: sophronia (Godt.), Brazil.

18. *Chlosyne ehrenbergii* (Hbn.). Mexico.

19. *Chlosyne lacinia* (Hbn.). Venezuela, Colombia, Trinidad.

20. *Chlosyne eumeda* (G. & S.). Mexico.

21. *Chlosyne marina* (Hbn.). Mexico. Similar: endeis (G. & S.), less red UPH.

22. *Chlosyne melanarge* (Bates). Guatemala.

PLATE 35: Nymphalidae

1. *Coea acheronta* (F.). Mexico, West Indies to S. Brazil.

2. *Coenophlebia archidona* (Hew.). Colombia, Peru, Bolivia.

3. *Colobura dirce* (L.). Antilles, S. America, Guianas.

4. *Consul hippona* (F.). Guianas, C. America to S. Brazil.

5. *Cybdelis mnasylus* (Dbl. & Hew.). Venezuela.

6. *Cyclogramma bachis* (Dbl.). Mexico.

7. *Diaethria astala* (Guer.). Mexico to Colombia. Similar: gabaza (Hew.), Colombia, no white dot UPF.

8. *Diaethria candrena* (Godt.). Brazil, Argentina.

9. *Diaethria clymena* (Cr.). S. America. Similar: janeira (Fldr.), S. Brazil; anna (Guer.), Mexico, UNH whitish; marchalli (Guer.), Colombia, Venezuela, UNH brownish; euclides (Latr.), Colombia, Peru, broader bands UP; lidwina (Fldr.), Peru; panthalis (Honr.), Venezuela, much less red UNF; eluina (Hew.), Brazil, narrow marginal band UNH; dodone (Guer.), Colombia, broad band UPF, no markings UPH.

10. *Diaethria eupepla* (Salv. & Godm.). C. America.

11. *Cyclogramma pandama* (Dbl. & Hew.). Mexico to Panama.

12. *Diaethria clymena* (see 9).

13. *Diaethria metiscus* (Dbl. & Hew.). Venezuela.

14. *Diaethria neglecta* (Salv.). Guatemala, Colombia, Peru.

15. *Didonis biblis* (F.). Mexico to S. America to Paraguay. Several subspecies.

16. *Doxocopa agathina* (Ev.). Guiana, N. Brazil, Amazon. UP resembles vacuna, female has orange band UPF. Similar: kallina (Stgr.), Brazil, UP only, female brown.

17. *Doxocopa callianira* (Men.). Nicaragua. Similar: elis (Fldr.), Colombia and Ecuador, with yellow band on UPF.

18. *Doxocopa cherubina* (Fldr.). C. America to Bolivia. Female resembles Cirrochroa species. Similar: seraphina (Hbn.), S Brazil; clothilda (Fldr.), Colombia, broad bands UP.

19. *Doxocopa clothilda* (Fldr.). Nicaragua.

20. *Doxocopa cyane* (Latr.). Colombia. Female UP resembles Adelpha species. Similar: burmeisteri (G. & S.), Argentina.

21. *Doxocopa felderi* (G. & S.). Colombia, Venezuela, Bolivia, Peru. Female green band UP. Similar: zunilda (Godt.), S. Brazil, female red band UP. The females are very different.

22. *Doxocopa griseldis* (Fldr.). Upper Amazon, Peru.

23. *Doxocopa lavinia* (Btlr.). Bolivia and Peru. Male UP resembles cherubina but has a reddish shine.

24. *Doxocopa pavonii* (Latr.). Mexico to Bolivia. Similar: vacuna (Godt.), Brazil, Paraguay, orange spots UPF; mentas (Bsd.), C. America, female resembles Adelpha thessalia.

25. *Doxocopa laure* (Drury). Mexico to Venezuela. Similar: griseldis (Fldr.), Amazon, Peru, larger; druryi (Hbn.), Cuba; selina (Bates), Brazil, orange spot UPF disconnected from white band. Females of laure and druryi resemble male selina.

26. *Doxocopa zalmunna* (Btlr.). Brazil.

PLATE 36: Nymphalidae

1. *Doxocopa zunilda* (Godt.). Brazil.

2. *Doxocopa zunilda* (see 1).

3. *Dynamine agacles* (Dalm.). Venezuela, Trinidad, Brazil, C. America. Similar: maeon (Dbl. & Hew.), Brazil, two bars UNH; athemon (L.), Brazil, one bar UNH; coenus (F.), Brazil, Paraguay, Bolivia, larger, narrow black margins UPH, blue gloss base of UPF; theseus (Fldr.), Mexico, C. America to Venezuela, broad black margins UP; limbata (Btlr.), Bolivia, white spot in UPH black margin.

4. *Dynamine agacles* (see 3).

5. *Dynamine arene* (Hbn.). Lower Amazon. UP resembles racidula (Hew.), Amazon.

6. *Dynamine anubis* (Hew.). Amazon. Similar: pieridoides (Fldr.), Colombia, Venezuela, Panama, narrower black edge UPH.

7. *Dynamine artemisia* (F.). S. America.

8. *Dynamine chryseis* (Bates). Nicaragua, Upper Amazon. Similar: sosthenes (Hew.), Nicaragua, smaller black tip UPF.

9. *Dynamine dyonis* (Hbn.). Mexico, Honduras. Similar: zetes (Men.), Antilles.

10. *Dynamine erchia* (Hew.). Upper Amazon.

11. *Dynamine geta* (G. & S.). Peru and Bolivia. Similar: setabis (Dbl. & Hew.), Bolivia, Amazon, white dots in black tip UPF; ines (Godt.), Colombia; hecuba (Schaus.), Amazon, larger, black bar. UPH. Females have white patches UPF.

12. *Dynamine gisella* (Hew.). Panama, Colombia, Bolivia, Amazon. Females resemble mylitta females.

13. *Dynamine glauce* (Bates). C. America, Amazon, Bolivia.

14. *Dynamine mylitta* (Cr.). S. and C. America. UP resembles thalassina. Similar: egaea (F.), Paraguay.

15. *Dynamine mylitta* (see 14).

16. *Dynamine myrrhina* (Dbl.). Argentina, Brazil, Paraguay.

17. *Dynamine myrrhina* (see 16).

18. *Dynamine racidula* (Hew.). Amazon.

19. *Dynamine salpensa* (Fldr.). C. and S. America. Resembles tichia UP. Similar: sara (Bates), Amazon; racidula (Hew.), Amazon. These resemble tithia UP also.

20. *Dynamine thalassina* (Bsd.). C. America, Colombia. UN resembles mylitta, female resembles Neptis species.

21. *Dynamine tithia* (Hbn.). Brazil.

22. *Dynamine zenobia* (Bates). Amazon.

23. *Ectima liria* (F.). Venezuela, Peru. Similar: rectifascia (Btlr. & Dr.), C. America, narrower band UPF; iona (Hew.), Bolivia, no white dots apex UPF and band lunular.

24. *Epiphile adrasta* (Hew.). Mexico to Panama. Similar: chrysites (Latr.), Colombia. Venezuela, narrower markings.

25. *Epiphile dilecta* (Stgr.). Bolivia. Female UP brown with white band UPF. Similar: dinora (Fassli), Colombia, no sheen, larger, wider bands; fassli (Weym.), Peru; hubneri (Hew.), Brazil, UPH broadly orange brown; chrysites (Latr.), Colombia, no sheen, female similar.

26. *Epiphile epicaste* (Hew.). Colombia. Female has blue band UPF. Similar: boliviana (Rober), Bolivia, broader orange bands UP; dinora (Fassli), Peru, orange bands very broad, whole appearance lighter.

27. *Epiphile eriopis* (Hew.). Colombia.

28. *Epiphile plusios* (G. & S.). C. America. Similar: orea female, orange band narrower; epimenes female white band.

29. *Epiphile orea* (Hbn.). Brazil. Similar: plusios (G. & S.), Panama, UPH opalescent green; negrina (Fldr.), Colombia, UPF both orange bands unbroken; epimenes (Hew.), Colombia, only one orange band UPF; electra (Stgr.), Venezuela, light band UPH.

30. *Epiphile lampethusa* (Dbl. & Hew.). Colombia and Bolivia.

31. *Eunica alcmena* (Dbl. & Hew.). Mexico, C. America. UN resembles clytia, female UP brown with white band UPF. Similar: eurota (Cr.), Colombia, Guianas, blue iridescence UPH is more extensive.

32. *Eunica anna* (Cr.). Amazon. Similar: concordia (Hew.), smaller, but larger iridescent area UPH.

PLATE 37: Nymphalidae

1. *Eunica augusta* (Bates). C. America. Similar: olympias (Feld.), male no white bar UPF.

2. *Eunica augusta* (see 1).

3. *Eunica bechina* (Hew.). Colombia, Brazil, Amazon. Similar: careta (Hew.), Amazon.

4. *Eunica caelina* (Godt.). Parana, Rio Grande.

5. *Eunica caresa* (Hew.). Peru.

6. *Eunica careta* (Hew.). Colombia to Peru, Venezuela. Similar: caralis (Hew.), Colombia to Peru, lighter edges to UP.

7. *Eunica chlorochroa* (Salv.). Peru.

8. *Eunica clytia* (Hew.). Peru, Amazon. Violet reflection. Similar: veronica (Bates).

9. *Eunica elegans* (Salv.). Peru. UP blue iridescence central both wings.

10. *Eunica margarita* (Godt.). Brazil.

11. *Eunica mygdonia* (Godt.). Brazil, Trinidad. Similar: careta (Hew.), Colombia to Peru.

12. *Eunica norica* (Hew.). Colombia. Similar: sophonisba (Cr.), Amazon, Colombia, blue margin to bottom half of UPF; chlorochroa (Salv.), Peru, UPH band green.

13. *Eunica macris* (Godt.). Brazil, Paraguay.

14. *Eunica orphise* (Cr.). Guianas to Peru. Similar: amelia (Cr.).

15. *Eunica venusia* (Fldr.). Colombia. Similar: excelsa (G. & S.), Panama, brown UN.

16. *Eunica venusia* (see 15).

17. *Gnathotriche exclamationis* (Koll.). Colombia, Venezuela. Similar: sodalis (Stgr.), two bands of greenish spots UPH.

18. *Hamadryas amphinome* (L.). Guianas, Peru, Bolivia, C. America. Similar: arinome (Luc.).

19. *Hamadryas arethusa* (Cr.). Mexico to Bolivia. Females with white band UPF, few forms. Similar: arete (Dbl.), Brazil, male more blue spots UP, female narrower white band UP.

PLATE 38: Nymphalidae

1. *Hamadryas atlantis* (Bates). Mexico, Guatemala. Similar: lelaps (G. & S.), paler green-grey.

2. *Hamadryas chloe* (Cr.). Peru, Brazil. Several subspecies.

3. *Hypna clytemnestra* (Cr.). Surinam, Bolivia. Similar: rufescens (Btlr.), Venezuela, reddish brown UPH; iphigenia (H.-Schaff.), Cuba.

4. *Hamadryas februa* (Hbn.). Panama to Pernambuco. UP resembles feronia. Many forms and subspecies.

5. *Hamadryas feronia* (L.). C. America, Brazil. UN resembles februa. Few subspecies. Similar: epinome (Fldr.), Brazil, Paraguay, paler.

6. *Hypanartia dione* (Latr.). Northern S. America. Similar: arcaei (G. & S.), Panama, wide orange edge to UPF.

7. *Hypanartia kefersteinii* (Dbl.). Venezuela, Colombia, Amazon. Similar: splendida (Roths.), Peru, larger and paler.

8. *Hamadryas fornax* (Hbn.). Venezuela, C. Mexico. UP as februa. Similar: alicia (Bates), as chloe UP.

9. *Hypanartia godmanii* (Bates). Mexico, C. America to Colombia.

10. *Historis orion* (F.). C. and S. America.

11. *Hypanartia lethe* (F.). Mexico to Brazil. Similar: bella (F.), Brazil, UPF white spots – lethe has yellow spots.

12. *Libythina cuvieri* (Godt.). Amazon.

13. *Issoria inca* (Stgr.). Bolivia.

14. *Issoria cytheris* (Drury). Chile. Several subspecies, including falklandia (Watk.), from Falkland Islands with white speck on edge of UPF.

15. *Lucinia sida* (Hbn.). Cuba, Haiti, Jamaica.

16. *Marpesia chiron* (F.). Antilles, Mexico to S. of S. America. Similar: themistocles (F.), Brazil, no white spots UPF; norica (Hew.), Ecuador and Peru, stripes obscure.

17. *Marpesia coresia* (Godt.). C. and S. America to Peru.

18. *Marpesia harmonia* (Dbl. & Hew.). Mexico. Similar: berania (Hew.), darker lines UPF.

PLATE 39: Nymphalidae

1. *Marpesia iole* (Drury). C. America to Ecuador and Peru. Male resembles marcella with wider dark margins UP. Similar: hermione (Fldr.), Guatemala, Peru, wider orange band UP.

2. *Marpesia livius* (Kirby). Ecuador, Bolivia, Peru.

3. *Marpesia marcella* (Fldr.). C. America and north of S. America. Similar: corinna (Latr.), Colombia, Amazon, narrower band UPF, tails orange; corita (Ww.), Mexico, C. America, UN dark brown.

4. *Marpesia marcella* (see 3).

5. *Marpesia merops* (Bsd.). Costa Rica to Bolivia.

6. *Marpesia crethon* (F.). North part of S. America. Similar: orsilochus (F.).

7. *Metamorpha epaphus* (Latr.). Mexico to Brazil and Peru. Similar: trayja (Hbn.), Brazil, UPF no red-brown; superba (Bates), C. America, Mexico, broader bands.

8. *Metamorpha sulpitia* (Cr.). North of S. America to Peru.

9. *Microtia elva* (Bates). Mexico, C. America.

10. *Mestra teleboas* (Men.). Antilles.

11. *Mestra hypermnestra* (Hbn.). Brazil, Paraguay. Similar: bogotana (Fldr.), Colombia, Venezuela, yellow tip to UPF; aurantia (Weeks).

12. *Myscelia ethusa* (Bsd.). Mexico. Similar: leucocyana (Fldr.), Venezuela, shining blue, paler.

13. *Myscelia orsis* (Drury). Brazil. Female resembles Catonophele nyctimus female.

14. *Myscelia orsis* (see 13).

15. *Napeocles jucunda* (Hbn.). Amazon to Bolivia.

16. *Nica flavilla* (Hbn.). C. America, Venezuela, Paraguay, Peru. Similar: canthara (Dbl.), Venezuela, UPF orange spot on black tip; sylvestris (Bates), Peru, darker bars UN.

17. *Nessaea batesii* (Fldr.). Guianas, Venezuela. Similar: aglaura (Dbl. & Hew.), Mexico, Guatemala, narrow orange strip UPH; regina (Salv.), Venezuela, Colombia, no orange UPH.

18. *Nessaea obvinus* (L.). Colombia, Ecuador, Peru, Amazon, Bolivia. Similar: aglaura (Dbl. & Hew.), no black tip to UPF.

19. *Nessaea obvinus* (see 18).

20. *Nessaea regina* (Salvin). Venezuela.

21. *Panacea divalis* (Bates). Colombia.

22. *Panacea procilla* (Hew.). Colombia, Upper Amazon.

23. *Panacea prola* (Dbl. & Hew.). Colombia, Venezuela, Ecuador. Similar: chalcothea (Bates), Colombia, UPH blue band clearly marked.

PLATE 40: Nymphalidae

1. *Panacea regina* (Bates). Upper Amazon, Ecuador. UP resembles prola.

2. *Peria lamis* (Cr.). N. of S. America.

3. *Perisama bonplandii* (Guer.). Colombia. Similar: morona (Hew.), Peru and Bolivia, UNF redder.

4. *Perisama cabirnia* (Hew.). Bolivia, Peru. Similar: guerini (Feld.), Colombia, UNH white, UNF black, white tip; yeba (Hew.), Colombia, UN as guerini, but narrow red costa to UNH.

5. *Perisama calamis* (Hew.). Bolivia. Similar: zurita (Fruh.), UN, Ecuador.

6. *Perisama cecidas* (Hew.). Ecuador, Peru. Similar: diotima (Hew.), Bolivia, Ecuador, Colombia, much less red UNF.

7. *Perisama chaseba* (Hew.). Bolivia. UN resembles calamis.

8. *Perisama cloelia* (Hew.). Peru. Similar: tryphena (Hew.), Colombia, spots UP yellow green; vitringa (Hew.), Amazon, paler UN.

9. *Perisama cloelia* (see 8).

10. *Perisama humboldtii* (Guer.). Venezuela, Colombia, Peru. UP as cabirnia. Similar: lucrezia (Hew.), Colombia, UN ground colour brownish; goeringi (Dru.), Venezuela, no red UNF; comnena (Hew.), Peru, no black dots UNH; oppelii (Latr.), Colombia, yellow UN; xanthica (Hew.), Peru, UPH black.

11. *Perisama lebasii* (Guer.). Colombia.

12. *Perisama nyctimene* (Hew.). Ecuador.

13. *Perisama patara* (Hew.). Venezuela.

14. *Perisama priene* (Hpff.). Peru, Bolivia, Colombia. Similar: lebasii (Guer.), UP markings green; cabirnia (Hew.), Peru, Bolivia, less red UNF; cotyora (Hew.), Bolivia, no red UNF.

15. *Perisama vaninka* (Hew.). Colombia, Peru. Similar: euriclea (Dbl. & Hew.), Colombia, Venezuela, UNF less red.

16. *Phyciodes acralina* (Hew.). Peru, Colombia, Bolivia. Similar: actinote (Salv.), Peru; perilla (Hew.), Peru, UPF band yellow.

17. *Phyciodes actinote* (Salv.). Bolivia.

18. *Phyciodes aequatorialis* (Stgr.). Ecuador. Similar: simois (Hut.), Brazil, smaller, lighter brown.

19. *Phyciodes alsina* (Hew.). Nicaragua. Female additional spots UPF.

20. *Phyciodes angusta* (Hew.). Colombia. Similar: polina (Hew.), Ecuador, Colombia, Peru.

21. *Phyciodes annita* (Stgr.). Venezuela. Similar: morena (Stgr.), Peru, UN blackish.

22. *Phyciodes callonia* (Stgr.). Peru.

23. *Phyciodes castilla* (see 24).

24. *Phyciodes castilla* (Fldr.). Colombia. Similar: mundina (Druce), Peru, broader red band UPF.

25. *Phyciodes catula* (Hpff.). Peru, Bolivia. Similar: oalena (Hpff.), markings white; ithra (Kirby), Argentina, larger.

26. *Phyciodes clio* (L.). C. America, Colombia, Ecuador, Peru. Similar: nauplia (L.), Guianas, larger spots UPF; perna (Hew.), Rio de Janeiro, yellowish markings.

27. *Phyciodes clio* (see 26).

28. *Phyciodes corybassa* (Hew.). Bolivia. Similar: perilla (Hew.), Ecuador, Bolivia.

29. *Phyciodes drusilla* (Stgr.). Argentina.

30. *Phyciodes elaphiaea* (Hew.). Ecuador and Peru. Similar: crithona (Salv.); aceta (Hew.), Colombia, markings smaller.

31. *Phyciodes emerantia* (Hew.). Colombia. Similar: sestia (Hew.), Colombia, wing tip spots UPF orange.

32. *Phyciodes eranites* (Hew.). Panama, Colombia. Similar: carme (Dbl. & Hew.), Venezuela, much darker; aveyrona (Bates), Venezuela, Amazon, very long forewings; philyra (Hew.), Mexico, larger.

33. *Phyciodes etia* (Hew.). Ecuador and Peru.

34. *Phyciodes eunice* (Hbn.). Brazil. Greatly resembles Eueides isabella. Similar: pelonia (Hew.). Ecuador and Peru, no yellow band UPH; olivencia (Bates), Upper Amazon, no yellow band UPH or UPF.

35. *Phyciodes eutropia* (Hew.). Panama. Similar: nigripennis (Salv.), Costa Rica, markings not clearly defined.

36. *Phyciodes fulviplaga* (Btlr.). Costa Rica Panama. Similar: diallus (G. & S.), Guatemala, female white markings UP.

37. *Phyciodes geminia* (Hpff.). Peru.

38. *Phyciodes ianthe* (F.). Brazil, Bolivia. Similar: abas (Hew.), Colombia; hera (Cr.). Guianas, wider bands; myia (Hew.), Mexico, C. America, no white in cell UPF; ofella (Hew.), Colombia, Panama, broad white band UPF.

39. *Phyciodes ildica* (Hew.). Ecuador. Similar: moesta (Salv.), Colombia, UPH has orange inner edge.

PLATE 41: Nymphalidae

1. *Phyciodes ithomoides* (Hew.). Colombia. Male UP ground colour orange brown.

2. *Phyciodes lansdorfi* (Godt.). Brazil.

3. *Phyciodes ptolyca* (Bates). Venezuela, Guatemala. Similar: faustus (Godm. & Salv.), Panama; phlegios (Godm. & Salv.), Honduras.

4. *Prepona demophon* (L.). Guianas, Amazon, Brazil. Many subspecies.

5. *Phyciodes levina* (Hew.). Colombia.

6. *Phyciodes margaretha* (Hew.). Colombia.

7. *Phyciodes murena* (Stgr.). Peru.

8. *Phyciodes nussia* (Druce). Peru.

9. *Phyciodes orthia* (Hew.). Paraguay and Brazil. Similar: poltis (Godm. & Salv.), Mexico; berenice (Fldr.), Peru; sejona (Schaus), larger band and markings; drusilla (Fldr.), Venezuela and Colombia.

10. *Phyciodes otanes* (Hew.). Guatemala. Similar: cyno (Godm. & Salv.), Mexico.

11. *Phyciodes letitia* (Hew.). Ecuador, Colombia. Variable, female has yellow ground UP.

12. *Phyciodes quintilla* (Hew.). Ecuador.

13. *Phyciodes saladillensis* (Giacom.). Argentina. Similar: ursula (Stgr.), Bolivia.

14. *Phyciodes sestia* (Hew.). Colombia. Also has an orange female form. Similar: cocla (Druce), Costa Rica, UPF no orange.

15. *Phyciodes teletusa* (Godt.). Brazil.

16. *Phyciodes verena* (Hew.). Bolivia, Peru.

17. *Polygonia zephyrus* (Edw.).

18. *Polygrapha cyanea* (S. & G.) Ecuador, Peru.

19. *Prepona antimache* (Hbn.). C. America to Paraguay and Brazil. Many forms and subspecies. UP resembles demophon.

20. *Prepona laertes* (Hbn.). C. America to Brazil, Paraguay. Many forms and subspecies.

21. *Zaretis isidora* (Cr.). Guiana, Colombia, Paraguay. Few forms.

22. *Zaretis isidora* (see 21).

23. *Prepona buckleyana* (Hew.). Colombia, Peru, Bolivia. Similar: praeneste (Hew.), UPF with additional red spots and broader orange band.

24. *Phyciodes leucodesma* (Fldr.). Colombia, Venezuela.

25. *Phyciodes liriope* (Cr.). S. America. Many subspecies. Similar: palia (Nov.), paler.

26. *Phyciodes nigrella* (Bates). Guatemala. Similar: niveonotis (Butt.), UP markings larger and whiter.

27. *Phyciodes northbrundii* (Weeks). Bolivia.

PLATE 42: Nymphalidae

1. *Prepona chromus* (Guer.). Colombia, Venezuela.

2. *Prepona deiphile* (Godt.). C. Brazil.

3. *Pyrameis myrinna* (Dbl.). Brazil, Ecuador.

4. *Prepona meander* (Cr.). Guianas, Mexico to Brazil. Many races and subspecies. UP as demophon.

5. *Prepona neoterpe* (Hour.). C. America, Peru.

6. *Pyrrhogyra edocla* (Dbl. & Hew.). C. America. UN resembles neaerea. Similar: otolais (Bates), smaller, wider bands; nasica (Stgr.), Colombia, green band does not reach inner margin UPH.

7. *Pyrrhogyra neaerea* (L.). Mexico, C. America, Amazon. Several subspecies. UP resembles edocla, markings white. Similar: catharinae (Stgr.), Bolivia, with white border spots UP.

8. *Prepona pheridamas* (Cr.). Colombia Guianas to Brazil.

9. *Prepona pylene* (Hew.). Brazil. Similar: eugenes (Bates), Brazil, Bolivia.

10. *Siderone nemesis* (Ill.). Colombia, Venezuela, Antilles, Brazil. Similar: thebais (Fldr.), Colombia; mars (Bates), Panama, Colombia, Peru, very broad red band UPF.

11. *Prepona xenagoras* (Hew.). Bolivia. UP resembles deiphile UP.

12. *Pycina zamba* (Dbl. & Hew.). Colombia, Venezuela to Ecuador and Peru. UP resembles coea acheronta.

13. *Smyrna blomfildia* (F.). Venezuela to Peru and Paraguay. Similar: karwinskii (Hbn.), Mexico, C. America.

14. *Temenis laothoe* (Cr.). Mexico to Paraguay and Peru. Many forms.

15. *Temenis pulchra* (Hew.). Colombia, Peru.

16. *Texola elada* (Hew.). Mexico. Similar: pelops (Drury), Jamaica, Puerto Rico.

17. *Vila azeca* (Dbl. & Hew.). Bolivia and Peru. Similar: cacica (Stgr.), Ecuador, UPH blue bar clear outline, UPF more white dots; emilia (Cr.), Guianas, Amazon, UPF white patch large, narrow band UPH.

PLATE 43: Acraeidae

1. *Actinote alalia* (Fldr.). Brazil. Similar: quadra (Schaus.).

2. *Actinote alcione* (Hew.). Colombia, Bolivia, Peru. Many subspecies.

3. *Actinote anteas* (Dbl.). Guatemala to Venezuela. Form straminosa (Jord.). Form anteas resembles dicaeus. Similar: thalia (L.), Guianas, darker; cedestes (Jord.), Ecuador, paler UPF; guatemalena (Bates), Mexico to Colombia, much darker.

4. *Actinote callianthe* (Fldr.). Ecuador, Venezuela. UP resembles ozomene.

5. *Actinote demonica* (Hpffr.). Ecuador, Peru, Bolivia.

6. *Actinote dicaeus* (Latr.). Ecuador, Peru.

Several forms and subspecies. Similar: callianira (Hbn.), Colombia, Venezuela, UPF brighter orange.

7. *Actinote equatoria* (Bates). Guatemala, Bolivia, Venezuela. Many forms and subspecies.

8. *Actinote eresia* (Fldr.). Colombia to Bolivia.

9. *Altinote erinome* (Fldr.). Peru, Bolivia. Similar: abana (Hew.), larger and paler orange UPF.

10. *Actinote guatemalena* (Bates). Guatemala.

11. *Actinote hylonome* (Dbl.). Venezuela, Colombia.

12. *Actinote laverna* (Dbl.). Venezuela. Similar: leontine (Weym.), Ecuador, Peru, UPF band narrower, more yellow; momina (Jord.), Peru, UPF band wider, more diffuse.

13. *Actinote leucomelas* (Bates). Mexico, Panama. Females broken yellow band UPF.

14. *Actinote mamita* (Schaus), Argentina, Paraguay. Similar: canutia (Hpffr.), Paraguay, Brazil, slight orange colouring.

15. *Altinote neleus* (Latr.). Ecuador, Colombia. Similar euryleuca (Jord.), smaller, resembles neleus female.

16. *Actinote ozomene* (Godt.). Colombia, Ecuador.

17. *Actinote parapheles* (Jord.). Paraguay, Brazil.

18. *Actinote pellenea* (Hbn.). Venezuela, Paraguay, Argentina, Brazil. UP resembles dicaeus. Several subspecies.

19. *Actinote stratonice* (Latr.). Colombia, Ecuador, Venezuela.

20. *Actinote terpsinoe* (Fldr.). Peru, Bolivia.

21. *Altinote radiata* (Hew.). Ecuador, Peru.

Heliconidae

22. *Anetia cubana* (Salv.). Cuba, Haiti. UN resembles insignis UP.

23. *Anetia insignis* (Salv.). Costa Rica, C. America, Mexico.

24. *Anetia numidia* (Hbn.). Cuba. UP resembles Argynnis species.

25. *Dione juno* (Cr.). Mexico.

26. *Dione moneta* (Hbn.). Northern S. America. Several subspecies. Similar: vanillae (L.), numerous black dots UP, paler.

27. *Dryadula phaelusa* (L.). C. America to Argentina.

28. *Dryas julia* (F.). C. and S. America to Texas, Cuba, Jamaica, Peru, Paraguay.

29. *Eueides cleobaea* (Hbn. & G.). Cuba, Puerto Rico, C. America. A form of melphis (Cr.).

30. *Eueides isabella* (Cr.). Colombia, Peru, Ecuador, Venezuela. Several forms and

subspecies. Similar: dianassa (Hbn.), which copies exactly Heliconius narcaea.

31. *Eueides lineatus* (S. & G.). Costa Rica, C. America.

32. *Eueides lybia* (F.). C. America. Apical spot UPF varies yellow, orange, white.

33. *Eueides pavana* (Men.). Brazil, Colombia. Female UP ground colour grey white.

34. *Heliconius aliphera* (Godt.). C. America to S. Brazil.

35. *Heliconius amaryllis* (Fldr.). Costa Rica, Panama, Colombia. Several forms, form rosina (Bsd.) has yellow bar UPH.

36. *Heliconius anderida* (Hew.). C. America, Venezuela. Several forms and subspecies, including fornarina (Hew.), Guatemala, black and lemon yellow.

37. *Heliconius antiochus* (L.). Northern S. America. The white bands UPF are sometimes yellow.

38. *Heliconius aoede* (Hbn.). Amazons, Guianas, Venezuela, Bolivia. Some forms lack the orange rays UPH.

PLATE 44: Heliconidae

1. *Heliconius aristiona* (Hew.). Bolivia and Peru. Twenty different forms.

2. *Heliconius atthis* (Dbl. & Hew.). Ecuador. Mimics Tithorea pavonii.

3. *Heliconius burneyi* (Hbn.). Guianas to Peru and Bolivia. Terrain: tree-top dweller. Similar: egeria (Cr.). UPF yellow broken into smaller spots. Several forms.

4. *Heliconius charitonia* (L.). S. and C. America, to S. Carolina and W. Indies. A dwarf form is found in Peru. Similar: nattereri (Fldr.), Brazil, broader bands.

5. *Heliconius cydno* (Dbl. & Hew.). C. America. Many forms, including galanthus (Bat.), white band UPF; chioneus (Bat.), larger, white band UPF; epicydnides (Stgr.), wider white band UPH; temerinda (Hew.), Colombia, yellow band UPH.

6. *Heliconius cyrbia* (Godt.). Ecuador, Colombia.

7. *Heliconius doris* (L.). Peru, Bolivia, Trinidad, Venezuela. Very variable, many forms and subspecies, with blue green, yellow green, and reddish rays on the UPH.

8. *Heliconius eanes* (Hew.). Bolivia and Peru. Exactly resembles Heliconius vesta. Form aides (Stich.) has no red on UPF. Similar: heliconoides (Fldr.), Colombia, red stripes shorter UP.

9. *Heliconius edias* (Hew.). C. America, Ecuador, Venezuela. Tropical S. America.

10. *Heliconius erato* (L.). Form venusta.

11. *Heliconius ethra* (Latr.). Brazil.

12. *Heliconius hecale* (Fab.). Colombia. An exact copy of Tithocea hecalesia. C. American form formosus (Bat.) has UPH plain red-brown.

13. *Heliconius hermathena* (Hew.). Amazon.

14. *Heliconius heurippa* (Hew.). Colombia. Few forms, including wernickei (Stgr.), white band UPH.

15. *Heliconius hortense* (Guer.). Honduras to Ecuador. Similar: clysonimus (Latr.), Venezuela to Ecuador, narrower bands, brilliant red UPH band.

16. *Heliconius ismenius* (Latr.). Colombia to Honduras. An exact copy of Melinaea messatis. Similar: eucoma (Hbn.), Peru to Panama. Many forms, smaller and more washed out colour.

17. *Ituna lamirus* (Latr.). Eastern Andes. Similar: phenarete (Dbl. & Hew.), Bolivia, Peru, paler; ilione (Cr.), Brazil, smaller.

18. *Heliconius melpomene* (L.). Guianas, Brazil, Ecuador. Form lucia (Cr.). Many forms and subspecies, many with additional yellow spotting UPF and red-orange streaks UPH, including: bari (Oberth.), Guianas, many yellow spots UPF, orange streaks UPH; thelxiope (Hbn.), Amazon, red base UPF and red streaks UPH; penelopeia (Stgr.), Bolivia, orange band UPF and orange streaks UPH.

19. *Heliconius metharme* (Erichs.). Northern S. America.

20. *Heliconius nanna* (Stich.). Brazil. Similar: beschkei (Men.).

21. *Heliconius narcaea* (Godt.). Brazil. Few forms.

22. *Heliconius novatus* (Bat.). Bolivia, Peru.

23. *Heliconius numata* (Cr.). Guianas, Amazon. Several subspecies.

24. *Heliconius pardalinus* (Bat.). Ecuador, Peru, Bolivia, Amazon.

25. *Heliconius petiverana* (Dbl. & Hew.). Mexico to Venezuela. Form viculata (Riff.) has no yellow band UPH and resembles melpomene.

26. *Heliconius phyllis* (F.). Argentina to Paraguay and Peru, Guianas and Amazon. A form of erato (L.). Very many forms, subspecies and aberrations; mostly with broken yellow or orange bands UPF and orange rays on UPH. Forms anacreon (Sm. & Ky.) and ottonis (Riff.) have a trace of the yellow band UPH as well as red rays.

27. *Heliconius quitalena* (Hew.). Bolivia and Peru. Similar patterns: ennius (Weym.), Amazon; sergestus (Weym.), Peru, black apex UPF, no yellow spots.

28. *Heliconius vicini* (L.). Guianas, Amazon, Trinidad. Similar: procula (Dbl.), Venezuela, Colombia.

29. *Heliconius sapho* (Drury). Colombia, Ecuador, C. America. Form leuce (Dbl.). Similar: eleuchia (Hew.), whitish margin UPH.

30. *Heliconius sara* (F.). Panama, Colombia, Venezuela. Similar: leucadia (Bat.), Ecuador. Several subspecies, some with yellow edge UPH.

31. *Heliconius silvana* (Cr.). Venezuela, Guianas, Brazil. Several forms.

32. *Heliconius tales* (Cr.). Amazon, Guianas. Similar: Eueides heliconioides (Fldr.), Colombia and Ecuador, larger markings UPF.

33. *Heliconius telesiphe* (Dbl.). Peru and Bolivia. Form sotericus (Salv.), Ecuador and Peru, has a yellow band on UPH.

PLATE 45: Heliconidae

1. *Heliconius vetustus* (Btlr.). Guianas, Lower Amazon.

2. *Heliconius vibilia* (Godt.). Brazil, Colombia.

3. *Heliconius vulcanus* (Btlr.). Colombia, Panama.

4. *Heliconius wallacei* (Reak.). Guianas to Peru. Some subspecies have UPF bands yellow.

5. *Heliconius xanthocles* (Bat.). Guianas, Ecuador, Peru. Form vola (Stgr.) has additional white spot tip of UPF.

6. *Heliconius xenoclea* (Hew.). Ecuador, Peru. Form plesseni (Riff.) has markings UP white.

7. *Philaethria dido* (L.). C. America to S. Brazil.

8. *Podotricha euchroia* (Dbl. & Hew.). Venezuela, Ecuador, Peru, Bolivia. UP resembles Dione juno (Cr.).

Ithomiidae

9. *Aeria eurimedia* (Cr.). Guianas, Lower Amazon. Similar: olena (Weym.), C. Brazil, no white dots UN.

10. *Athesis dercyllidas* (Hew.). Colombia and Ecuador.

11. *Athyrtis mechanitis* (Fldr.). Peru.

12. *Callithomia hezia* (Hew.). C. America. Similar: phagesia (Hew.), Ecuador, regular separate spots, yellower UP; panamensis (G. & S.), yellow patch UPH.

13. *Callithomia schulzi* (Hsch.). Peru, Brazil.

14. *Callithomia villula* (Hew.). Colombia.

15. *Ceratinia dorilla* (Bates). C. America. Many similar species including poecila (Bates), C. America.

16. *Ceratinia jolaia* (Hew.). Colombia.

17. *Ceratinia nise* (Cram.). Peru. Form peruensis (Hsch.).

18. *Ceratinia nise* (Cr.). Guianas, Venezuela, Peru. (see 17 also).

19. *Corbulis cymo* (Hbn.). Guianas. Similar: Oleria egra (Hew.).

20. *Corbulis ocalea* (Dbl. & Hew.). Venezuela, Trinidad, Colombia. Similar:

gephira (Hew.), Colombia, C. America, whitish markings UP longer; chrysodonia (Bates), Upper Amazon.

21. *Corbulis oreas* (Weym.). Brazil. Similar: mirza (Hew.), Ecuador, less white UPF; cassotis (Bates), Guatemala, whiter apex; oriana (Hew.), Amazon, UP dark markings broad and diffuse.

22. *Corbulis orolina* (Hew.). Peru, Upper Amazon. Similar: oncidia (Bates), Upper Amazon, white dusting UP.

23. *Corbulis virginia* (Hew.). Amazon.

24. *Dircenna dero* (Hbn.). Brazil to Argentina. Similar: mantura (Hew.), Bolivia; loreta (Hsch.), Ecuador, no black bar in UPH.

25. *Dircenna klugi* (Hbn.). C. America. Similar: relata (Btlr. & Druce), Costa Rica, black base to forewing; jemina (Hbn.), Colombia, Venezuela.

26. *Dircenna vandona* (Hsch.). Ecuador. Similar: lorica (Weym.), Guianas.

27. *Dircenna varina* (Hew.). Ecuador. Similar: lenea (Cr.), Guianas.

28. *Dircenna visina* (Hsch.). Ecuador. Similar: marica (Fldr.), Venezuela.

29. *Dygoris dircenna* (Fldr.). Colombia, Bolivia. The large black spot UPH is sometimes small or absent.

30. *Elzunia humboldti* (Latr.). Ecuador, Colombia.

31. *Episcada salvinia* (Bates). Guatemala. Several similar species including clausina (Hew.), Bolivia, yellow spot UPF; mira (Hew.), Ecuador.

32. *Episcada sylpha* (Hsch.). Venezuela. Similar: polita (Weym.), Colombia, darker edge UP and larger yellow spot; hymenaea (Prittw.), C. Brazil; sao (Hbn.), Brazil, darker; cora (Bang-H.), Bolivia, lighter.

33. *Epithomia alpho* (Fldr.). C. America, Venezuela. Similar: agrippina (Hew.).

34. *Epithomia methonella* (Weym.). Brazil, Paraguay.

35. *Eutresis hypereia* (Dbl. & Hew.). C. America, Peru. Terrain: montane.

36. *Forbestra truncata* (Btlr.). Ecuador, Andes.

37. *Garsaurites xanthostola* (Bates). Amazon River.

38. *Godyris crinippa* (Hew.). Bolivia. Similar: cleomella (Hew.), Colombia, Ecuador, Peru, slightly more black markings UP.

39. *Godyris duillia* (Hew.). Colombia, Bolivia, Ecuador. Similar: Hypoleria alphesiboea (Hew.), Ecuador, smaller.

40. *Godyris gonussa* (Hew.). Colombia. Male resembles Dygoris dircenna (Fldr.). Similar: zygia male (Godm. & Salv.), Costa Rica.

41. *Godyris hewitsoni* (Husch.). Bolivia, Ecuador.

PLATE 46: Ithomiidae

1. *Godyris zavaletta* (Hew.). Colombia, Peru.

2. *Heterosais giulia* (Hew.). Colombia, Venezuela.

3. *Heterosais nephele* (Bates). Upper Amazon, Ecuador, Colombia. Similar: edessa (Hew.), Brazil, very small white spot UPF.

4. *Hyalenna perasippa* (Hew.). Ecuador, Colombia. Similar: Hypalenna dirama (Hsch.), Bolivia, smaller; lobusa (Hsch.), much smaller.

5. *Hyalenna teresita* (Hew.). Ecuador. Many similar species from the same area, only varying very slightly from each other, including Pteronymia apuleia (Hew.), yellow brown costa UPF; Corbulis coenina (Hew.).

6. *Hyaliris fenestella* (Hew.). Venezuela. A subspecies of euclea.

7. *Hyaliris vallonia* (Hew.). Brazil.

8. *Hypoleria albinotata* (Btlr.). Colombia. Similar: Velamysta cruxifera (Hew.).

9. *Hypoleria andromica* (Hew.). Venezuela, Colombia, Ecuador, Trinidad. Similar: nero (Hew.), C. America.

10. *Hypoleria libethris* (Fldr.). Colombia to Peru. Several forms. Similar: lydia (Weym.), Ecuador, resembles Pteronymia apuleia.

11. *Hypoleria morgane* (Hbn. & G.). Mexico and Honduras.

12. *Hypoleria ortygia* (Weym.). Ecuador. Resembles Godyris cleonica. Similar: enigma (Hsch.), Bolivia, Colombia.

13. *Hypoleria oto* (Hew.). Mexico.

14. *Hyposcada abida* (Hew.). Colombia. Similar: aesion (Godm. & Salv.) Panama, smaller, with large white dot UPF.

15. *Hyposcada adelphina* (Bates). C. America. Similar: consobrina (Godm. & Salv.).

16. *Hyposcada fallax* (Stgr.). Peru.

17. *Hyposcada kezia* (Hew.). Amazon. Similar: anchialia (Hew.), Peru, more spots UPF.

18. *Hyposcada sinilia* (H.Sch.). Colombia.

19. *Hypothiris angelina* (Hsch.). Ecuador, Amazon, Peru.

20. *Hypothiris antea* (Hew.). Ecuador.

21. *Hypothiris antonia* (Hew.). Ecuador.

22. *Hypothiris callispila* (Bates). C. America. Similar: decumana (Godm. & Salv.), C. America, larger, whiter spots.

23. *Hypothiris catilla* (Hew.). Bolivia. Similar: pyrippe (Hpffr.), Peru.

24. *Hypothiris honesta* (Weym.). Ecuador. Similar: meterus (Hew.), Upper Amazon, no yellow bar UPF, very black UPH; mamercus (Hew.), Ecuador, less black UPH.

25. *Hypothiris lycaste* (F.). C. America. Very variable.

26. *Hypothiris mergelena* (Hew.), Colombia.

27. *Hypothiris metella* (Hpffr.). Peru.

28. *Hypothiris ninonia* (Hbn.). Colombia, Amazon.

29. *Hypothiris ocna* (H.Sch.). Colombia, Ecuador. Similar: statilla (Hew.), Peru; coeno (Hew.), Colombia, Venezuela, no orange tip UPH.

30. *Hypothiris oulita* (Hew.). Peru.

31. *Hypothiris philetaera* (Hew.). Colombia. Similar: ignorata (Hsch.), Amazon.

32. *Hypothiris thea* (Hew.). Amazon River.

33. *Hypothiris tricolor* (Salvin). Peru and Bolivia.

34. *Ithomia agnosia* (Hew.). C. America, Venezuela, Peru. Similar: drymo (Hbn.), Colombia; ardea (Hew.), Bolivia.

35. *Ithomia celemia* (Hew.). C. America. Similar: heraldica (Bates), Costa Rica.

36. *Ithomia derasa* (Hew.). Nicaragua, Ecuador. Similar: amarilla (Hsch.), . UPH veins not blackened; aquinea (Hpffr.), Peru, no white spots in border and broader black borders.

37. *Ithomia diasia* (Hew.), Colombia. Similar: hyala (Hew.), broader wings; ossuna (Hsch.), orange tip UPH.

38. *Ithomia eilara* (Hew.). Bolivia, Peru. Similar: eleonora (Hsch.), Bolivia, additional black smudge UPF.

39. *Ithomia epona* (Hew.). Ecuador. Terrain: montane. Similar: xenos (Bates), Costa Rica; ulla (Hew.), Colombia; larger, no black spot UPF cell.

40. *Ithomia lagusa* (Hew.). Colombia. Similar: peruana (Salv.), Peru, more yellowish, broader black edges; linda (Hew.), Ecuador, no black bars UPF.

41. *Ithomia oenanthe* (Weym.). Colombia. Similar: terra (Hew.), wider black borders.

42. *Ithomia patilla* (Hew.). C. America.

43. *McClungia salonina* (Hew.). Bolivia, Paraguay, Ecuador.

44. *Mechanitis doryssus* (Bates). C. America, Venezuela. Subspecies of polymnia.

45. *Mechanitis lycidice* (Bates). C. America. Similar: franis (Reak.), Colombia; elisa (Guer.), Ecuador, Peru, Bolivia.

46. *Mechanitis lysimnia* (F.). Minas Geraes. Subspecies albescens.

47. *Mechanitis macrinus* (Hew.). C. America.

48. *Mechanitis mantineus* (Hew.). W. Andes in Ecuador.

49. *Mechanitis messenoides* (Fldr.). Ecuador, Peru, Bolivia.

50. *Mechanitis nesaea* (Hbn.). Brazil.

PLATE 47: Ithomiidae

1. *Mechanitis polymnia* (L.). Guianas, Brazil. Similar: pannifera (Btlr.).

2. *Melinaea idae* (Fldr.). Colombia and Ecuador. Similar: paraiya (Reak.), Guianas, Amazon, Brazil.

3. *Melinaea lilis* (Dbl. & Hew.). C. America, Trinidad, Venezuela.

4. *Melinaea mediatrix* (Weym.). Amazon River, Guianas. Subspecies of mneme (L.).

5. *Melinaea messatis* (Hew.). Colombia, Panama, Bolivia. Similar: parallelis (Btlr.), Panama, black bar UPH well defined and long.

6. *Melinaea messenina* (Fldr.). Colombia and Ecuador.

7. *Melinaea satevis* (Dbl. & Hew.). Bolivia. Black marking UPH very variable.

8. *Melinaea scylax* (Salv.). Costa Rica.

9. *Melinaea zaneka* (Btlr.). Ecuador.

10. *Miraleria cymothoe* (Hew.). Venezuela and Colombia. Similar: sylvella (Hew.), Ecuador, white patch UP greatly reduced, veining orange.

11. *Napeogenes corena* (Hew.). Peru, Ecuador.

12. *Napeogenes duessa* (Hew.). Peru and Ecuador.

13. *Napeogenes duessa* (see 12).

14. *Napeogenes cranto* (Fldr.). Colombia. Similar: larilla (Hew.), Ecuador, no yellow; harbona (Hew.), Ecuador, smaller; lycora (Hew.), Ecuador, smaller; glycera (Godm.), Ecuador, larger, ground colour white.

15. *Napeogenes flossina* (Btlr.). Colombia, Ecuador. Several similar species with narrow orange edges to wings, e.g. ithra (Hew.); sylphis (Guer.).

16. *Napeogenes inachia* (Hew.). Guianas, Lower Amazon. Similar: cyrianassa (Dbl. & Hew.), Amazon River, Colombia.

17. *Napeogenes larina* (Hew.). Colombia. Similar: aethra (Hew.), Ecuador, yellow spots UPF.

18. *Napeogenes peridia* (Hew.). Colombia. Similar: amara (Godm.), C. America, far fewer small spots UPF and UPH; tolosa (Hew.), C. America, far fewer larger spots UPF.

19. *Napeogenes pharo* (Fldr.). Amazon River, Ecuador. Similar: osuna (Hew.), Bolivia.

20. *Napeogenes stella* (Hew.). Colombia and Ecuador.

21. *Napeogenes sulphurina* (Bates). River Amazon, Brazil. Similar: verticilla (Hew.), Bolivia; thira (Guer.), Bolivia and Peru, grey, not yellow.

22. *Oleria aegle* (F.). Guianas.

23. *Oleria astraea* (Cr.). Guianas, C. America. Similar: egra (Hew.), Amazon; brighter, broader orange band UPH; aquata (Weym.), Brazil; narrower black margins, no orange.

24. *Oleria deronda* (Hew.). Peru, Bolivia.

25. *Oleria estella* (Hew.). Ecuador, Venezuela, Colombia.

26. *Oleria ida* (Hsch.). Ecuador. Several similar species, including lerda (Hsch.), Peru, orange edging complete UP.

27. *Oleria makrena* (Hew.). Venezuela, Colombia. Similar: tabera (Hew.), Ecuador, wider black margins; quadrata (Hsch.), Ecuador, smaller; zea (Hew.), Mexico.

28. *Oleria orestilla* (Hew.). E. Andes in Colombia and Ecuador. Terrain: high altitude.

29. *Oleria priscilla* (Hew.). Upper Amazon.

30. *Oleria susiana* (Fldr.). Colombia, Ecuador. UP black and white. Similar: attalia (Hew.), Bolivia and Peru; solida (Weym.), Ecuador.

31. *Oleria tigella* (Weym.). Ecuador. Several similar species including agarista (Fldr.), smaller white spots UPF.

32. *Oleria zelica* (Hew.). W. Andes, Ecuador.

33. *Olyras montagui* (Btlr.). Eastern Andes.

34. *Olyras praestans* (Godm. & Salv.). C. America.

35. *Pseudoscada aureola* (Bates). Amazon.

36. *Pseudoscada florula* (Hew.). Cayenne. Similar: Corbulis cymo (Hbn.).

37. *Pseudoscada seba* (Hew.). Ecuador, Bolivia, Venezuela, Peru. Similar: adasa (Hew.), S. Brazil.

38. *Pteronymia apuleia* (Hew.). Ecuador.

39. *Pteronymia latilla* (Hew.). Venezuela, Colombia. Similar: notilla (Btlr. & Druce), C. America, UPF all darkened; barilla (Hsch.), Ecuador, UP darker.

40. *Pteronymia laura* (Stgr.). Colombia. Similar: aletta (Hew.), yellow band and spots; Corbulis vanilia (H.Sch.), Colombia; Pseudoscada lavinia (Hew.), Colombia.

41. *Pteronymia lilla* (Hew.). Ecuador. Similar: primula (Bates), Amazon; auricula (Hsch.), Colombia, broader black margins.

42. *Pteronymia picta* (Salvin). Colombia and Venezuela.

43. *Pteronymia tigranes* (Godm. & Salv.). C. America. Many similar species differing but slightly.

44. *Pteronymia veia* (Hew.). Venezuela and Colombia.

45. *Pteronymia zerlina* (Hew.). Peru and Ecuador. UP resembles Ithomia oenathe.

46. *Rhodussa viola* (Hsch.). Upper Amazon.

47. *Sais zitella* (Hew.). Amazon. Similar: paraensis (Hsch.), Amazon, Guianas, Venezuela, broader orange band.

48. *Scada gazoria* (Godt.). Brazil.

PLATE 48: Ithomiidae

1. *Scada kusa* (Hew.). Ecuador. Similar: ethica (Hew.), Ecuador, paler black marking UP; perpuncta (Kaye), Peru, black patches UP; zibia (Hew.), C. America, yellower; theaphia (Bates), Ecuador, Guianas.

2. *Scada zemira* (Hew.), Ecuador.

3. *Thyridia confusa* (Btlr.). Guianas, Amazon, Peru. Similar: themiste (Hbn.).

4. *Tithorea hermias* (Godm. & Salv.). Amazon. Several very similar species including: harmonia (Cr.), Guianas and Trinidad, black bar UPH uniform width; furia (Stgr.), Ecuador to Venezuela.

5. *Tithorea pinthias* (Godm. & Salv.). Panama, C. America.

6. *Tithorea tarricina* (Hew.). Colombia. Similar: irene (Drury), Jamaica.

7. *Velamysta torquatilla* (Hew.). Bolivia. Similar: Veladyris pardalis (Salv.), Andes, high altitudes, fewer spots; cruxifera (Hew.), Ecuador, smaller, UPF orange sheen; cyricilla (Hew.), Bolivia, orange front edge UPF.

8. *Xanthocleis aedesia* (Dbl. & Hew.). Colombia, Venezuela. Similar: melantho (Bates), C. America, much darker; psidii (L.), Guianas, Amazon River, Ecuador, much paler.

9. *Xanthocleis menophilus* (Hew.). Colombia to Peru.

Danaidae

10. *Lycorea ceres* (Cr.). Cuba, Haiti, Trinidad, Guianas.

11. *Lycorea cleobaea* (Godt.). C. America to Bolivia. Similar: eva (F.), smaller, orange discal band; halia (Hbn.), yellow disc UPH.

12. *Danaus cleophile* (Godt.). Haiti, Cuba, Jamaica.

Pieridae

13. *Anteos clorinde* (Gdt.). Brazil to Texas.

14. *Appias drusilla* (Cr.). Brazil to Florida. Male resembles albina.

15. *Anteos menippe* (Hbn.). Tropical America.

16. *Ascia buniae* (Hbn.). Brazil, Peru. Similar: amaryllis (F.), Jamaica, smaller.

17. *Ascia monuste* (L.). Argentina to Texas. Variable. Similar: sevata (Fldr.), Venezuela, C. America.

18. *Catasticta bithys* (Hbn.). Mexico to S. Brazil.

19. *Catasticta colla* (Dbl.). Bolivia, Peru.

Similar: chelidonis (Hopff.), more yellow UP; hopfferri (Stgr.), smaller.

20. *Catasticta pharnakia* (Fruhst.). Peru. Female has red patch.

21. *Ascia sincera* (Weym.). Ecuador.

22. *Catasticta flisa* (H.-Sch.). Colombia.

23. *Catasticta chrysolopha* (Koll.). Ecuador. Similar: apaturina (Btlr.).

24. *Catasticta uricaecheae* (Fldr.). Colombia. Similar: vulnerata (Btlr.), Ecuador, less red UPH.

PLATE 49: Pieridae

1. *Catasticta nimbice* (Bsd.). Mexico, Guatemala. Similar: pinava (Dbl.), Bolivia, Peru; bryson (G. & S.), Panama, much less black UP, veins stand out.

2. *Catasticta notha* (Luc.). Venezuela. Similar: corcyra (Fldr.), Venezuela, Bolivia, UPF wing tip plain black, UN less markings; pieris (Hopff.), Peru.

3. *Catasticta froujadei* (Dognin). Bolivia. Similar: clara (Rob.), Ecuador.

4. *Catasticta semiramis* (Luc.). Colombia. Similar: niobe (Rob.), Bolivia, UP suffused black.

5. *Catasticta sisamnus* (F.). Peru. Female yellow instead of white.

6. *Catasticta straminea* (Btlr.). Peru. Similar: theresa (Btlr. & Dre.), Panama, veins more black and clear UP.

7. *Catasticta teutile* (Dbl.). Mexico.

8. *Catasticta tomyris* (Fldr.). Colombia and Venezuela. Similar: toca (Dbl.), Bolivia, Colombia, smaller; tamina (Rob.), Peru.

9. *Catasticta troezenides* (Rob.). Colombia. Similar: hebra (Luc.).

10. *Charonias eurytele* (Hew.). Ecuador, Colombia.

11. *Charonias theano* (Bsd.). Brazil.

12. *Colias antarctica* (Stgr.). Tierra del Fuego.

13. *Colias cynops* (Btlr.). Haiti. Male resembles cesonia.

14. *Colias dimera* (Dbl. & Hew.). Colombia, Peru, Ecuador. Terrain: high altitudes.

15. *Colias dinora* (Ky.). Ecuador. Terrain: high altitudes.

16. *Colias dimera* (see 14).

17. *Colias flaveola* (Bl.). Chile and Bolivia. Terrain: montane.

18. *Colias lesbia* (F.). S. Brazil.

19. *Colias vautieri* (Guer.). Chile.

20. *Dismorphia amphione* (Cr.). C. America, Guianas. Several subspecies. Similar: astynome (Dalm.), Brazil, much less orange UPF, yellow markings clearer defined.

21. *Dismorphia erythroe* (Felder). Colombia.

22. *Dismorphia cornelia* (Fldr.). Mexico. Very variable ground colour orange to pale yellow.

23. *Dismorphia cretacea* (S. & K.). S. Brazil. A form of litinia (Cram.). Similar: mercenaria (Fldr.), Venezuela; marion (G. & S.), Nicaragua.

24. *Dismorphia cubana* (H.-Sch.). Cuba.

25. *Dismorphia cordillera* (Bates). Amazon River.

26. *Dismorphia foedora* (Luc.). Venezuela, Peru. Similar: virgo (Bates), Guatemala, Costa Rica, male UPF band broken into spots, or thinner.

27. *Dismorphia ithomia* (Hew.). Ecuador. Similar: pinthaeus (L.), UP without white dots in black margins.

28. *Dismorphia leonora* (Hew.). Ecuador. Similar: lewyi (Luc.), Venezuela, Colombia, Ecuador, no yellow spot; critomedia (Hbn.), white median band.

29. *Dismorphia lua* (Hew.). Colombia, Ecuador, Peru.

30. *Dismorphia medora* (Dbl.). Colombia, Venezuela. Similar: pallidula (Btlr.), Costa Rica, markings white; arcadia (Fldr.), less yellow, 3 spots UPF beyond bar; othoe (Hew.), Ecuador, smaller.

31. *Dismorphia lysis* (Hew.). Ecuador.

PLATE 50: Pieridae

1. *Dismorphia melia* (Godt.). Brazil.

2. *Dismorphia mirandola* (Hew.). Ecuador, Colombia. Similar: carthesis (Hew.), Ecuador; zaela (Hew.), orange spots on FW.

3. *Dismorphia nemesis* (Latr.). C. America, Venezuela, Peru. Similar: cinerascens (Salv.), Costa Rica, grey-blue.

4. *Dismorphia orise* (Bsd.). Guianas, Bolivia.

5. *Dismorphia rhetes* (Hew.). Colombia, Bolivia, Ecuador.

6. *Dismorphia spio* (Godt.). Antilles.

7. *Dismorphia theonoe* (Hew.). Ecuador. Similar: siloe (Hew.), Colombia, red-brown on UPH.

8. *Dismorphia theucharila* (Dbl.). Venezuela. Similar: avonia (Hew.), Ecuador, UP ground colour yellow.

9. *Dismorphia theugenis* (Dbl.). Bolivia, Peru. Similar: melite (L.), Brazil, more orange coloured, UPF spots coalesced into a bar.

10. *Eroessa chilensis* (Guer.). Chile. Terrain: high altitudes.

11. *Eucheira socialis* (Ww.). Mexico.

12. *Eurema albula* (Cr.). Venezuela, Brazil, Trinidad. Similar: deflorata (Koll.), Colombia.

13. *Eurema arbela* (Hbn.). Mexico to S. Brazil. Several subspecies.

14. *Eurema atinas* (Hew.). Bolivia, Peru. Terrain: high altitudes.

15. *Eurema deva* (Dbl.). S. Brazil, Chile. Similar: leuce (Bsd.), S. Brazil, Uruguay, Trinidad.

16. *Hesperocharis agasicles* (Hew.). Bolivia and Peru.

17. *Dismorphia fortunata* (Lucas). Mexico. Similar: antherize (Hew.), Mexico, longer white bar UPF; avonia (Hew.), Ecuador, yellowish; pinthaus (L.), Guianas, Amazon River; theonoe (Hew.), Ecuador. three white patches UPF.

18. *Dismorphia sororna* (Btlr.). Costa Rica. Similar: cordillera (Fldr.), Colombia.

19. *Dismorphia sororna* (see 18).

20. *Eurema gratiosa* (Dbl. & Hew.). Honduras, Venezuela, Trinidad.

21. *Eurema messalina* (F.). Jamaica.

22. *Eurema elathea* (Cr.). Surinam, Brazil, Trinidad. Several subspecies. Similar: mycale (Fldr.), Brazil.

23. *Eurema limbia* (Fldr.). Venezuela.

24. *Eurema hyona* (Men). San Domingo.

25. *Eurema proterpia* (F.). S. America to Texas, Antilles. Variable. Female ground colour yellow buff. Similar: gundlachia (Poey.), tailed.

26. *Eurema neda* (Godt.). Guianas, Venezuela, Nicaragua. Similar: nise (Cr.), Surinam, Dominica; venusta (Bsd.), Jamaica, Colombia, Trinidad; musa (F.), S. America.

27. *Eurema phiale* (Cr.). Colombia, Bolivia.

28. *Eurema reticulata* (Btlr.). Peru.

29. *Eurema sybaris* (Hopff.). Peru.

PLATE 51: Pieridae

1. *Eurema thymetus* (Bsd.). S. Brazil. Syn. of leuce (Bsd.).

2. *Eurema westwoodi* (see 3).

3. *Eurema westwoodi* (Bsd.). Mexico. Several subspecies including: dina (Poey.), from Bahamas, smaller with UP unmarked.

4. *Hesperocharis anguitia* (Godt.). S. Brazil. Similar: erota (Lucas), larger.

5. *Hesperocharis aureomaculata* (Dogn.). Ecuador.

6. *Hesperocharis graphites* (Bates). Mexico.

7. *Haballia demophile* (L.). C. America. Several subspecies.

8. *Haballia locusta* (Fldr.). C. America. Female heavily marked black.

9. *Haballia mandela* (Fldr.). C. America,

Peru. UP male black tips to white wings; female yellow heavily marked black.

10. *Haballia pandosia* (Hew.). Venezuela, Peru, Trinidad. Similar: marana (Dbl.), Ecuador.

11. *Haballia pisonis* (Hew.). Colombia, Peru. Female UP ground colour yellow.

12. *Haballia tithoreides* (Btlr.). Venezuela, Ecuador.

13. *Leptophobia eleone* (D-H.). Colombia, Venezuela. Similar: smithii (Kirby), Bolivia and Peru.

14. *Kricogonia lyside* (Godt.). Puerto Rico, Texas, Venezuela, Haiti.

15. *Leptophobia caesia* (Luc.). Ecuador, C. America, Costa Rica. UP grey-blue. Similar: cinerea (Hew.), Ecuador.

16. *Leptophobia caesia* (see 11).

17. *Leptophobia eleusis* (Luc.). Colombia, Venezuela.

18. *Leptophobia euthemia* (Fldr.). Colombia, Venezuela. Several subspecies.

19. *Leptophobia subargentea* (Btlr.). Peru. UP resembles caesia. Similar: philoma (Hew.), Ecuador, Peru.

20. *Leodonta dysoni* (Dbl.). Venezuela, Colombia. Variable width to whitish markings UP. Similar: tellane (Hew.), Colombia, yellow.

21. *Leptophobia nephthis* (Hopff.). Peru, Bolivia.

22. *Leptophobia olympia* (Fldr.). Venezuela, Columbia, Peru. Similar: tovaria (Fldr.), Venezuela, Colombia.

23. *Leptophobia pinara* (Fldr.). Colombia. Similar: cinnia (Fruhst.), Ecuador, much larger black dot UPF.

24. *Leucidia brephos* (Hbn.). Venezuela to S. Brazil, Trinidad.

25. *Leucidia exigua* (Prittw.). Venezuela, Brazil, Trinidad. Similar: elvina (Godt.), Brazil.

26. *Nathalis planta* (Dbl. & Hew.). Venezuela, Colombia.

27. *Melete florinda* (Btlr.). C. America. UP resembles polyhymnia, female form orange ground colour.

28. *Melete lycimnia* (Cr.). Surinam, Venezuela to S. Brazil, C. America. Black borders UP vary. Many subspecies.

29. *Melete peruviana* (Lucas). Peru, Bolivia, Colombia. Male is white UP.

30. *Melete polyhymnia* (Fldr.). Colombia.

PLATE 52: Pieridae

1. *Melete salacia* (Godt.). Mexico, Cuba.

2. *Pereute autodyca* (Bsd.). S. Brazil. Similar: swainsoni (Gray); cheops (Stgr.), yellow band.

3. *Hesperocharis hirlanda* (Stoll.). Surinam, C. America. Similar: serda (Fruhst.), Colombia, UN more yellow.

4. *Hesperocharis idiotica* (Btlr.). Mexico, Costa Rica.

5. *Hesperocharis marchali* (Guer.). Colombia, Venezuela, Peru, Bolivia.

6. *Hesperocharis nera* (Hew.). Ecuador, Bolivia, Surinam. Few subspecies.

7. *Hesperocharis nera* (see 14).

8. *Hesperocharis nereina* (Hopff.). Peru and Bolivia. UN resembles nera.

9. *Pereute charops* (Bsd.). Mexico to N. Venezuela. UP bluish grey; female has red band UPF.

10. *Pereute leucodrosine* (Koll.). Colombia, Bolivia. Similar: callinera (Stgr.), Peru, black antennae; callinice (Fldr.), Venezuela, Colombia, Peru.

11. *Pereute swainsoni* (Gray). Brazil. UP resembles leucodrosine, without grey. Similar: autodyca (Bsd.).

12. *Phoebis orbis* (see 11).

13. *Pereute telthusa* (Hew.). Peru.

14. *Perrhybris lypera* (Koll.). Colombia, Ecuador.

15. *Perrhybris pyrrha* (F.). C. America to S. Brazil. Many subspecies. Similar: flava (Oberth.), Brazil; lorena (Hew.), S. America, male white patch tip UPF, female narrow yellow band UPF.

16. *Perrhybris pyrrha* (see 6).

17. *Phoebis cipris* (F.). S. America, Brazil, Peru.

18. *Phoebis eubule* (L.). C. and S. America.

19. *Phoebis avellaneda* (H-Sch.). Cuba. Similar: philea (L.), Cuba, UP markings much paler.

20. *Phoebis orbis* (Poey.). Haiti, Cuba. Similar: godartiana (Swains.), C. America, Puerto Rico, Haiti, UP markings yellow rather than orange. Female orbis resembles editha female.

21. *Phoebis editha* (Btlr.). Haiti.

22. *Phulia illimani* (Weym.). Bolivia. Terrain: high altitudes.

23. *Phulia nympha* (Stgr.). Bolivia. Terrain: high altitudes. Similar: nymphaea (Stgr.), smaller.

PLATE 53: Pieridae

1. *Phoebis philea* (L.). C. America to S. Brazil. Female very variable, wings sometimes appear semi-transparent.

2. *Phoebis philea* (see 1).

3. *Phoebis rurina* (Fldr.). Venezuela, Peru, C. America.

4. *Phoebis sennae* (L.). S. America, Jamaica.

5. *Phoebis statira* (Cr.). S. America, Guatemala, Texas.

6. *Pieris pylotis* (Godt.). Brazil. Similar: Leptophobia olympia (Fldr.), Venezuela, Colombia, Peru, UPF more pointed, dot tip UPF large white; Leptophobia tovaria (Fldr.), Venezuela, Colombia, slightly wider black border UPH, wings more pointed.

7. *Pieris viardi* (Bsd.). C. America.

8. *Pieris viardi* (see 7).

9. *Pierocolias huanaco* (Stgr.). Cordilleras of ·Bolivia. Terrain: very high altitude. UN as nysias.

10. *Theochila itatiayae* (Foett.). Brazil to Argentina.

11. *Pseudopieris nehemia* (Bsd.). Mexico to S. Brazil. Similar: aequatorialis (Fldr.), Bolivia, broader black tip UPF; viridula (Fldr.), Venezuela, brown sex-streak at base of UNF.

12. *Tatochila blanchardii* (Btlr.). Chile.

13. *Tatochila mercedis* (Eschsch.). Chile.

14. *Tatochila theodice* (Bsd.). Tierra del Fuego.

15. *Tatochila vauvolxemii* (Capr.). Argentina. Similar: orthodice (Weym.), Argentina, thin black bar UPF.

16. *Pierocolias nysias* (Weym.). Bolivia.

17. *Pierocolias nysias* (see 16).

18. *Dismorphia deione* (Hew.). Nicaragua.

19. *Dismorphia hippotas* (Hew.). Ecuador. Similar: deione (Hew.), Nicaragua, black veining less marked UPH.

20. *Archonias bellona* (Cr.). Guianas, Bolivia, Peru.

21. *Catasticta marcapita* (Thieme). Bolivia.

22. *Archonias tereas* (Godt.). C. America, Brazil. Similar: rosacea (Btlr.), Venezuela, white spots UPH suffused rose.

23. *Dismorphia methymna* (Godt.). Brazil.

24. *Dismorphia teresa* (Hew.). Bolivia.

25. *Catasticta teutanis* (Hew.). Peru, Ecuador. Similar: ctemene (Hew.), white; prioneris (Hopff.).

26. *Catasticta manco* (Dbl.). Bolivia, Venezuela.

27. *Catasticta manco* (see 26).

28. *Catasticta modesta* (Lucas). Peru. Similar: suasa (Rob.), Bolivia; anaitis (Hew.), Ecuador.

PLATE 54: Satyridae

1. *Altopedaliodes tena* (Thieme). Ecuador. Similar: Punapedaliodes albopunctata (Weym.), Bolivia, Peru, smaller white spots.

2. *Argyreuptychia penelope* (F.). Brazil

Surinam, Trinidad. Several very similar species.

3. *Amphidecta pignerator* (Btlr.). Colombia. Similar: calliomma (Fldr.), Colombia, Brazil, two rows of brownish white spots.

4. *Antirrhaea archaea* (Hbn.). Brazil.

5. *Antirrhaea avernus* (Hoppfer). Guianas, Amazon. Similar: philaretes (Fldr.), smaller purple dots UPH.

6. *Antirrhaea geryon* (Fldr.). Colombia. Terrain: montane, forests. Similar: geryonides (Weym.), Colombia, Ecuador, larger eye-spots; phasiane (Btlr.), Venezuela, Peru, orange surround to eye-spots; adoptiva (Weym.), Colombia.

7. *Antirrhaea miltiades* (F.). C. America.

8. *Antirrhaea phasiane* (Btlr.). Peru.

9. *Antopedaliodes antonia* (Stgr.). Bolivia, Peru.

10. *Archeuptychia cluena* (Drury). Brazil.

11. *Argyreuptychia ocypete* (F.). Amazon, Surinam, Trinidad. Similar: Euptychia myncea (Cr.), Curinam, Trinidad, smaller, with violet sheen UP.

PLATE 55: Satyridae

1. *Auca coctei* (Guer.). Chile.

2. *Argyrophorus argenteus* (Blanch.). Chile, Argentina. Terrain: montane. Similar: Punargentus lamna (Thieme), Bolivia, much smaller, UPH brown.

3. *Caeruleuptychia coelestis* (Btlr.). Amazon. Similar: caerulea (Btlr.), lighter blue; cyanites (Btlr.), larger.

4. *Bia actorion* (L.). Surinam, Amazon.

5. *Caerois chorinaeus* (F.). Guianas, Amazon.

6. *Caeruleuptychia lobelia* (Btlr.). Bolivia, Ecuador.

7. *Caeruleuptychia coelica* (Hew.). Ecuador.

8. *Caerois gerdrudtus* (F.). Costa Rica, Panama. Subspecies vespertilio (Thieme), Ecuador.

9. *Calisto pulchella* (Lathy). Haiti. Similar: hysius (Godt.), smaller.

10. *Calisto zangis* (F.). Jamaica, Guianas. Similar: nubila (Lathy), Puerto Rica, no scent scales UPF.

11. *Cepheuptychia angelica* (Btlr.). Brazil. UP brown, male UP as cephus.

12. *Cepheuptychia cephus* (F.). Surinam, Colombia to S. Brazil. Female brown UP.

13. *Cepheuptychia glaucina* (Bates). Mexico, Guatemala, Bolivia. Female brown UP.

14. *Cheimas opalinus* (Stgr.). Venezuela.

15. *Chilanella stelligera* (Btlr.). Chile, Agentina. Terrain: high altitudes.

16. *Chloreuptychia agatha* (Btlr.). Amazon, Colombia. UP resembles tolumnia. Similar: chloris (Cramer).

17. *Chloreuptychia agaya* (Btlr.). Amazon. Female UP brown.

18. *Chloreuptychia arnaea* (F.). C. America, Trinidad.

19. *Chloreuptychia tolumnia* (Cr.). Surinam, Lower Amazon, Brazil.

20. *Cithaerias aurorina* (Weym.). Amazon.

PLATE 56: Satyridae

1. *Cithaerias esmeralda* (Doubleday). Amazon.

2. *Cithaerias menander* (Drury). C. America, Colombia. Female resembles pellucida. Similar: pireta (Cr.), Ecuador, larger.

3. *Cithaerias philis* (Cr.). Surinam, Amazon. Similar: pyropina (Godm. & Salv.), Bolivia, Peru, larger, broad margin to UPH, red rather than mauve.

4. *Corades argentata* (Btlr.). Bolivia.

5. *Corades cybele* (Btlr.). Colombia, Peru. Similar: sareba (Hew.), Bolivia, more orange.

6. *Corades cistene* (Hew.). Venezuela, Colombia, Ecuador. Similar: medeba (Hew.), Bolivia.

7. *Corades enyo* (Hew.). Venezuela, Colombia, Ecuador, Peru, Bolivia.

8. *Corderopedaliodes pandates* (Hew.). Bolivia. Similar: napaea (Bates), Guatemala, UPH dull red margin; phila (Hew.), Bolivia, orange band UPF.

9. *Corades pannonia* (Hew.). Colombia, Venezuela. Similar: albomaculata (Stgr.), UPF has two small white dots at tip.

10. *Corades iduna* (Hew.). Bolivia, Peru. Similar: peruviana (Btlr.), Colombia, Ecuador, single spot middle UPF; chelonis (Hew.), spots UPF orange.

11. *Corades ulema* (Hew.). Colombia. Similar: chirone (Hew.).

PLATE 57: Satyridae

1. *Daedalma dinias* (Hew.). Bolivia. Similar: dora (Stgr.), Colombia, no orange patch.

2. *Dioriste cothonides* (Gr. Sm.). Costa Rica, Panama. UP as tauropolis.

3. *Dioriste leucospilos* (Stgr.). Peru, Ecuador, Bolivia.

4. *Dioriste tauropolis* (Dbl. & Hew.). Mexico to Nicaragua. UN as cothonides.

5. *Eretris calisto* (Fldr.). Colombia. Similar: decorata (Fldr.), Colombia, UNH shining band broader.

6. *Drucina championi* (G. & S.). Guatemala.

7. *Drucina leonata* (Btlr.). Costa Rica Panama.

8. *Drucina venerata* (Btlr.). Peru, Bolivia.

9. *Dulcedo polita* (Hew.). C. America.

10. *Elina lefebvrei* (Guer.). Chile, Argentina, Uruguay. Similar: vanessoides (Blanch.), smaller, orange ground; nemynioides (Blanch.), white patch UNH.

11. *Eretris apuleja* (Fldr.). Ecuador, Venezuela, Peru. Similar: porphyria (Fldr.), Venezuela, no orange patch UNH; hulda (Btlr.-Druce), small orange patch UNH.

12. *Erichthodes erichtho* (Btlr.). Cayenne, Surinam, Trinidad, Brazil. UP dark brown. Similar: fumata (Btlr.), Brazil UN darker, blue spots UNH do not shine; amalda (Weymer), Amazon.

13. *Erichthodes julia* (Stgr.). Bolivia, Peru, Colombia. Terrain: high altitudes.

14. *Eteona tisiphone* (Bsd.). Rio de Janeiro.

15. *Eteona tisiphone* (see 14).

PLATE 58: Satyridae

1. *Euptychia ambigua* (Btlr.). Brazil, Ecuador. Similar: griseldis (Weymer), Amazon, thin marginal lines UPH.

2. *Euptychia gera* (Hew.). Lower Amazon. Similar: nortia (Hew.), Upper Amazon, darker.

3. *Euptychia mermeria* (Cr.). C. America to Brazil. Variable, UP olive brown, unmarked.

4. *Euptychia philodice* (G. & S.). C. America.

5. *Euptychia innocentia* (Fldr.). Venezuela, UP pale brown unmarked.

6. *Euptychia polyphemus* (Btlr.). C. America. Several similar species including: necys (Godt.), Brazil, darker; quantius (Godt.), Brazil, white dots larger; Pharneuptychia boliviana (Hayward), Bolivia, olive brown UP.

7. *Etcheverinus chilensis* (Guer.). Chile, Patagonia to Magellan Straits.

8. *Euptychia grimon* (Godt.). Brazil. Similar: Parypthimoides phronius (Godt.); modesta (Btlr.), Brazil, UN less clearly marked.

9. *Euptychia harmonia* (Btlr.). Ecuador, Colombia. Similar: Ypthimoides phineus (Btlr.), Peru, Venezuela, UN much darker.

10. *Euptychia maepius* (Godt.). Guianas, Brazil. Similar: Ypthimoides erigone (Btlr.), Brazil, Peru, broader discal band.

11. *Euptychia mollina* (Hbn.). C. America Venezuela. Few similar species.

12. *Euptychia ocelloides* (Schaus.). Paraguay, Brazil.

13. *Euptychia paeon* (Godt.). Rio de Janeiro.

14. *Euptychia phares* (Godt.). Venezuela, Brazil. Many subspecies.

15. *Euptychia picea* (Btlr.). Amazon, Peru, Surinam.

16. *Euptychia salvini* (Btlr.). Panama and Peru. Similar: hygina (Btlr.), Brazil.

17. *Euptychia terrestris* (Btlr.). Amazon, Surinam, Trinidad. Similar: Argyreuptychia palladia (Btlr.); Argyreuptychia labe (Btlr.), C. America, red-yellow border.

18. *Euptychoides saturnus* (Btlr.). Venezuela, Colombia, Bolivia, Brazil. Similar: vesta (Btlr.); fida (Weym.), Colombia; nossis (Hew.), Ecuador.

19. *Faunula patagonica* (Mat.). Patagonia.

20. *Godartiana byses* (Godt.). Brazil. Similar: muscosa (Btlr.), Paraguay, Brazil, larger, UN darker.

21. *Haetera piera* (L.). Guianas, Amazon, Brazil. Similar: macleannania (Bates), C. America, rosy tinge to UPH markings; hypaesia (Hew.), Colombia, Ecuador, Peru, Bolivia, black and white margin to UPH.

22. *Junea doraete* (Hew.). Colombia, Peru. UP resembles dorinde.

PLATE 59: Satyridae

1. *Junea dorinde* (Fldr.). Ecuador, Peru. Similar: gideon (Thieme), paler brown UP.

2. *Lymanopoda labda* (Hew.). Colombia, Ecuador. UP brown unmarked.

3. *Lymanopoda nivea* (Stgr.). Ecuador, Colombia. Similar: galactea (Stgr.), Bolivia, black spots UPH, UPF rounded; huilana (Weym.), Colombia, small black discal dots UNH.

4. *Junea whitelyi* (Druce). Peru, Bolivia, Ecuador. UP resembles doraete. Similar: dorinde (Fldr.), Colombia, Ecuador; emilia (Btlr.), markings indistinct, UP resembles dorinde.

5. *Lasiophila circe* (Fldr.), Colombia. Similar: palades (Hew.), Ecuador; zapatoza (Ww.), Venezuela, much smaller; orbifera (Btlr.), Bolivia, Peru, bright brown red, large spots.

6. *Lymanopoda obsoleta* (Ww.). Colombia, Venezuela, Peru, Bolivia. UP brown unmarked. Similar: albofasciatus (Rober), Ecuador, white bar UNH.

7. *Lasiophila cirta* (Fldr.). Peru. Terrain: high altitude.

8. *Lasiophila phalaesia* (Hew.). Ecuador, Bolivia, Peru. Similar: persepolis (Hew.), Ecuador, UP bands dull orange-brown.

9. *Lasiophila prosymna* (Hew.). Colombia, Ecuador.

10. *Lymanopoda albomaculata* (Hew.). Colombia, Bolivia, Peru. Few forms. Similar: apulia (Hopffer), Bolivia, white bar UNH, no white spots; affineola (Stgr.), Bolivia, small white marginal spots UP.

11. *Lymanopoda acraeida* (Btlr.). Ecuador, Peru, Bolivia. Similar: venosa (Btlr.), UP brown unmarked.

12. *Lymanopoda cinna* (G. & S.). Guatemala.

13. *Magneuptychia batesii* (Btlr.). Amazon, Peru, Surinam.

14. *Lymanopoda panacea* (Hew.). Ecuador, Peru, Colombia. Few forms.

15. *Lymanopoda samius* (Dbl.). Colombia. Terrain: montane. Similar: caeruleata (G. & S.), UNF brown and black, UP darker blue.

16. *Magneuptychia cluena* (Drury). Brazil.

PLATE 60: Satyridae

1. *Magneuptychia lea* (Cr.). Surinam and Brazil.

2. *Magneuptychia libye* (F.). C. America, Jamaica.

3. *Magneuptychia nortia* (Hew.). Peru, Amazon, Cayenne.

4. *Magneuptychia ocnus* (Btlr.). Amazon, Peru. Similar: juani (Stgr.), Ecuador, UPH ocelli larger.

5. *Magneuptychia ocnus* (see 4).

6. *Magneuptychia tricolor* (Hew.). Amazon, Peru, Ecuador, Surinam.

7. *Manerebia cyclopina* (Stgr.). Bolivia, Peru.

8. *Manataria hercyna* (Hbn.). Mexico to S. Brazil. Similar: maculata (Hpff.), C. America to S. Brazil, brighter, smaller.

9. *Maniola limonias* (Phil.). Chile. Similar: Neomaenas monachus (Blanch.), Chile, less reddish.

10. *Megeuptychia antonoe* (Cr.). C. America, Amazon. Similar: Euptychia sabina (Fldr.), smaller.

11. *Neomaenas edmondsii* (Btlr.). Brazil.

12. *Neomaenas haknii* (Mabille). Chile, Patagonia.

13. *Mygona irmina* (Dbl.). Venezuela Colombia.

14. *Mygona paeania* (Hew.). Ecuador.

15. *Neomaenas poliozona* (Fldr.). Chile. Similar: reedi (Btlr.), Chile.

16. *Neomaenas servilia* (Wallgr.). Valparaiso, Chile.

17. *Mygona prochyta* (Hew.). Bolivia, Peru. UP dark brown.

18. *Mygona thammi* (Stgr.). Peru.

19. *Neomaenas servilia* (see 16).

PLATE 61: Satyridae

1. *Oressinoma typhla* (Dbl. & Hew.). Colombia, Venezuela, Ecuador, Peru. Similar: sorata (Salvin), Bolivia, Peru, white zig-zag lines UPH margins clearer.

2. *Oxeoschistus pronax* (Hew.). Peru and Bolivia. Similar: duplex (Godm.), larger, darker spots.

3. *Oxeoschistus protagenia* (Hew.). Colombia, Ecuador, Peru, Bolivia. Similar: euryphile (Btlr.), Costa Rica, Panama.

4. *Oxeoschistus puerta* (Ww.). Colombia Venezuela, Costa Rica. Similar: isolda (Thieme), Ecuador, dark red band; submaculatus (Btlr. & Druce), Colombia, broader brighter orange band UPH.

5. *Oxeoschistus simplex* (Btlr.). Colombia, Ecuador. UP resembles pronax.

6. *Pampasatyrus quies* (Berg.). Argentina, Patagonia, Uruguay.

7. *Panarche callipolis* (Hew.). Bolivia. Similar: ulema (Hew.), Bolivia, two yellow stripes UNH; chirone (Hew.), Ecuador, one yellow stripe UNH.

8. *Parataygetis lineata* (Godm.). Colombia. Similar: tiessa (Hew.), Ecuador, UPH has faint lunule, UN no white lines.

9. *Pareuptychia hesione* (Sulz.). C. America and Brazil. Similar: metaleuca (Bsd.), Colombia, Bolivia, narrower white bands.

10. *Paryphthimoides poltys* (Pritter). Venezuela, Brazil. Similar: eous (Btlr.), Brazil, Paraguay, only one largish lunule UPH.

11. *Pedaliodes albonotata* (Godm.). Venezuela.

12. *Pedaliodes empusa* (Fldr.). Colombia, Peru. Similar: simpla (Thieme), Ecuador, Peru, small; poetica (Stgr.), Bolivia.

13. *Pedaliodes piletha* (Hew.). Venezuela, Paraguay, Colombia. Similar: phazania (Sm.), Ecuador, Colombia, UNH creamy band broader; prytanis (Hew.), Ecuador, UNH band very small.

14. *Pedaliodes praxithea* (Hew.). Bolivia, Ecuador. Similar: triaria (G. & S.), Costa Rica, smaller; phila (Hew.), Peru, Bolivia, even smaller, band on UNH short.

15. *Pedaliodes jeptha* (Thieme). Colombia. Similar: muscosa (Thieme), Bolivia, Colombia, less whitish powdering UNH.

16. *Pedaliodes juba* (Stgr.), Ecuador, Similar: parrhaebia (Hew.), Ecuador. broader orange bands UP.

PLATE 62: Satyridae

1. *Pedaliodes pactyes* (Hew.). Bolivia. Few forms. Similar: chrysataenia (Hpffr.), Peru, no orange line UPH; antonia (Stgr.), Bolivia, white markings UPH well developed.

2. *Pedaliodes pammenes* (Hew.). Bolivia.

3. *Pedaliodes paneis* (Hew.). Peru, Colombia, Bolivia. Similar: philonis (Hew.), Ecuador, Peru.

4. *Pedaliodes pelinna* (Hew.). Ecuador. Similar: ochrotaenia (F.), Colombia, bands UP less clear-cut.

5. *Pedaliodes pelinaea* (Hew.). Ecuador. Similar: philotera (Hew.), Colombia, more reddish UN.

6. *Pedaliodes perperna* (Hew.). C. America.

7. *Pedaliodes peucestas* (Hew.). Colombia, Peru, Ecuador. Several similar species, including: porrima; lyssa (Burmeister), Argentina, UPF band very narrow.

8. *Pedaliodes phaeaca* (Stgr.). Venezuela. Similar: thiemei (Stgr.), Colombia, broader bands UPF and UPH; peruda (Hew.), Amazon, very broad orange bands both wings UP.

9. *Pedaliodes phaedra* (Hew.). Colombia. Similar: pylas (Hew.), Colombia, no white patch UPH; porrima (Stgr.), Bolivia, no white patch UPH, white band UPF.

10. *Pedaliodes pheres* (Thieme). Ecuador. Bolivia, Peru. Similar: tyro (Thieme), smaller orange marking UNH.

11. *Pedaliodes phrasiclea* (Hew.). Colombia, Ecuador, Peru, Bolivia. UP as polusca. Similar: naevia (Thieme), Ecuador, very dark UN.

12. *Pedaliodes physcoa* (Hew.). Bolivia, Peru.

13. *Pedaliodes pisonia* (Hew.). Venezuela, Ecuador, Peru, Bolivia.

14. *Pedaliodes plotina* (Hew.). Venezuela. Similar: hopfferi (Stgr.), Peru, longer orange band.

15. *Pedaliodes polusca* (Hew.). Peru, Bolivia, Colombia. Similar: ferratiles (Btlr.), paler wing margins UP.

PLATE 63: Satyridae

1. *Pedaliodes porcia* (Hew.). Ecuador, Colombia, Peru. UP as pammenes.

2. *Pedaliodes poesia* (Hew.). Colombia, Ecuador. Similar: japhleta (Btlr.), Venezuela, large white patch UNH; hewitsoni (Stgr.), Bolivia, red brown UNF, UNH extensively dusted white; perisades (Hew.), Bolivia, red brown UNF, no white spot UNF.

3. *Pedaliodes tena* (Hew.). Colombia Ecuador.

4. *Penrosada lena* (Hew.). Colombia. Several similar species, including: lisa (Weym.), Peru, orange band UPH; luttela (Weeks), Colombia, UNH white band broken up and small ocelli UPH; staudingeri (Forst.), Peru, no white bar UNH.

5. *Pierella helvina* (Hew.). Colombia. Similar: incanescens (Godm. & Salv.), C. America, red patch UPH more extensive; pacifica (Niepelt), Ecuador, UP dark, large red and white patch UPH.

6. *Pherepedaliodes pheretiades* (Sm. & Ky.). Bolivia. Similar: Pedaliodes prosa (Stgr.), no white patch UNF; Praeponophila emma (Stgr.), 4 white spots UPF; panthides (Hew.), red brown UNF, UP unmarked.

7. *Pharneuptychia phares* (Godt.). Argentina, Brazil, Venezuela.

8. *Pierella hortona* (Hew.). Amazon, Ecuador.

9. *Pierella hyceta* (Hew.). Amazon, Bolivia, Peru. Similar: cercye (Hew.), Ecuador, Bolivia, larger lunules UPH; latona (Fldr.),

Bolivia, large bright orange patch UPH, large lunules.

10. *Pierella lena* (L.). Surinam, Guianas, Brazil. Similar: hyalinus (Gmel.), Surinam, Trinidad, Amazon, hind wing semi-tailed.

11. *Pierella nereis* (Drury). S. Brazil.

12. *Pierella astyoche* (Erichs.). Guianas, Amazon. Similar: luna (F.), C. America, 2 lunules UPH, which is dull grey brown.

13. *Pindis pellonia* (Godm.). Mexico, Guatemala.

PLATE 64: Satyridae

1. *Pierella rhea* (F.). Amazon, Rio de Janeiro. Similar: lamia (Sulz.), Surinam, Colombia, Cayenne.

2. *Posttaygetis penelea* (Cr.). C. America to Brazil. Similar: Pseudodebis valentina (Cr.), C. America, Amazon, no yellow band UNH; Taygetis kerea (Btlr.), eye spots UNH very faint; Taygetis inornata (Fldr.), Colombia, small white dots UNH.

3. *Praefaunula armilla* (Btlr.). Brazil. UP brown unmarked.

4. *Praepedaliodes phanias* (Hew.). Paraguay, Brazil, Peru, Ecuador. UP all dull brown. Similar: Muscopedaliodes amussis (Thieme), Colombia, white dots UNH; Panyapedaliodes panyasis (Hew.), Venezuela, Colombia, brighter, lighter markings UN; Panyapedaliodes drymaea (Hew.), Bolivia, Peru, darker UN than panyasis.

5. *Pronophila cordillera* (Ww.). Bolivia.

6. *Punargentus lamna* (Thieme). Bolivia.

7. *Proboscis orsedice* (Hew.). Ecuador, Peru. Similar: propulea (Hew.), Colombia, UPF strongly falcate.

8. *Pronophila orcus* (Latreille). Colombia, Bolivia, Peru.

9. *Quilaphoetosus monachus* (Blch.). Chile.

10. *Pronophila rosenbergi* (Lathy). Peru. UPF white band.

11. *Pronophila timanthes* (Salvin). Costa Rica, Panama, Ecuador.

12. *Spinantenna tristis* (Guer.). Chile.

13. *Pseudomaniola gerlinda* (Thieme). Bolivia. Similar: ilsa (Thieme), Colombia UN ocelli diffuse; mena (Gr.-Sm.), Bolivia, orange spot UNF.

14. *Pseudomaniola phaselis* (Hew.). Colombia and Venezuela. Similar: gigas (G. & S.), Guatemala, larger, has similar UN but orange margin to UPH; loxo (Dogmn.), Colombia, no silver spots UN.

15. *Splendeuptychia ashna* (Hew.). Bolivia, Peru, Colombia, Ecuador. Terrain: montane. Similar: Euptychia ordinata (Weym.).

16. *Satyrotaygetis satyrina* (Bates). C. America. Very variable.

PLATE 65: Satyridae

1. *Pronophila theleba* (Dbl. & Hew.). Venezuela, Colombia, Ecuador, Peru, Bolivia. UN resembles orchus.

2. *Splendeuptychia cosmophila* (Hbn.). Brazil. Similar: telesphora (Btlr.), Peru.

3. *Steroma bega* (Ww.). Venezuela, Colombia, Bolivia. Similar: modesta (Weym.), Argentina, much paler brown UP; superba (Btlr.), much larger; zibia (Btlr.), white patch UNH; also Steremnia species.

4. *Splendeuptychia furina* (Hew.). Amazons. Similar: itonis (Hew.), larger white area UPH.

5. *Taygetis albinotata* (Btlr.). Bolivia.

6. *Taygetis andromeda* (Cr.). C. America, Trinidad to S. Brazil.

7. *Taygetis celia* (Cr.). C. America. Similar: uncinata (Weym.), Mexico.

8. *Taygetis chrysogone* (Dbl. and Hew.). Colombia, Venezuela, Peru.

9. *Vareuptychia usitata* (Btlr.). C. America. Similar: Ypthimoides castrensis (Schaus), Brazil.

10. *Ypthimoides celmis* (Godt.). Brazil, Argentina, Paraguay. Similar: angularis (Btlr.), Brazil, darker UN; and several other species.

11. *Vareuptychia themis* (Btlr.), C. America. Similar: divergens (Btlr.), Amazon. UP unmarked.

12. *Taygetis sylvia* (Bates). Panama, Bolivia, Upper Amazon. Variable. Similar: salvini (Stgr.), Colombia, Panama, no white on UN.

13. *Taygetis rectifascia* (Weym.). Brazil. UP brown unmarked.

14. *Ypthimoides renata* (Cr.). C. America, Colombia, Paraguay. Several forms.

PLATE 66: Satyridae

1. *Taygetis virgilia* (Cr.). C. America, Trinidad to S. Brazil. Similar: angulosa (Weym.), Brazil, wings and markings angled.

2. *Taygetis xenana* (Btlr.). Peru, Surinam, Brazil. Similar: echo (Cr.), Surinam, Trinidad, Amazon, large black brown area UPF.

3. *Ypthimoides poltys* (Prittw.). Bolivia, Amazon.

4. *Ypthimoides modesta* (Btlr.). Venezuela, Bolivia, Peru. Several similar species, including: Euptychia perfuscata (Btlr.), Brazil, darker; Euptychia alcinoe (Fldr.), Colombia, lighter.

5. *Taygetis ypthima* (Hbn.). Brazil. Variable. Several subspecies.

6. *Tetraphlebia glaucope* (Fldr.). Brazil.

7. *Thiemeia phoronea* (Dbl.). Bolivia, Venezuela.

8. *Nelia nemyrioides* (Bl.). Chile. UP brown, large sex-brand UPF, female has orange patch UPF.

Lycaenidae

9. *Arawacus linus* (F.). Colombia, Venezuela, Bolivia, Trinidad. Similar: togarna (Hew.), Mexico to Bolivia, narrower markings UP/UN.

10. *Arawacus phaea* (G. & S.). C. America. Similar: leucogyna (Fldr.), Colombia, narrower black margin UPH. Females of both species resemble female linus.

11. *Arawacus sito* (Bsd.). Mexico to Nicaragua. Similar: melibaeus (F.), no red lobe UNH; phaenna (G. & S.), Guatemala.

12. *Atlides bacis* (G. & S.). Panama. Similar: melidor (Druce), Peru; atys (Cr.), Panama to Colombia, UN markings more distinct.

13. *Atlides getus* (F.). C. America, Amazon, Guianas, Trinidad. Similar: caranus (Stoll.), C. America; silumena (Hew.), Colombia, UN markings diffuse; didymaon (Cr.), Brazil, small, UN much less red; neora (G. & S.), Mexico to Colombia, very small, very intense blue.

14. *Atlides carpasia* (Hew.). Mexico, Guatemala. Similar: inachus (Cr.), Panama, Peru, Amazon, Guianas, UN markings more restricted.

15. *Atlides polybe* (L.). Mexico to S. Brazil and Argentina, Trinidad. UN resembles scamander UN.

16. *Atlides scamander* (Hbn.). Panama.

17. *Bithys phoenissa* (Hew.). Nicaragua, Panama, Colombia to Amazon.

18. *Callicista albata* (Fldr.). Panama, Colombia, Venezuela, Trinidad. Similar: sedecia (Hew.), Mexico, Guatemala.

19. *Callicista angelia* (Hew.). Cuba, Jamaica. Similar: limenia (Hew.), Cuba, W. Indies, paler UN, no orange brown UPF; angerona (G. & S.), W. Indies, larger red patch UNH.

PLATE 67: Lycaenidae

1. *Callicista bubastus* (Cr.). Northern S. America, Dominica, Grenada: no tails. Southern N. America to Panama (form eurytulus, Hbn.): tailed. Similar to bubastus: sapota (Hew.), Peru; Similar to eurytulus: argona (Hew.), Brazil, Argentina, Paraguay.

2. *Callicista ligia* (Hew.). Colombia. Similar: limenia (Hew.), Cuba, Jamaica, Haiti.

3. *Callicista yojoa* (Reak.). Mexico to Amazon. Similar: alea (G. & S.), Mexico, UN more ochreous; mulucha (Hew.), Guatemala, Amazon, UNH whitened margin; veterator (Druce), Paraguay.

4. *Calycopis atrius* (H.Sch.). Guatemala to Amazon, Trinidad. Similar: calor (Druce), Brazil.

5. *Calycopis badaca* (Hew.). Panama, Colombia, Brazil, Trinidad. Several similar species.

6. *Calycopis beon* (see 7).

7. *Calycopis beon* (Cr.). Southern U.S.A., C.

America to Brazil. Many similar species, including : amplia (Hew.), Nicaragua, Guianas, Colombia ; nortia (G. & S.), Guatemala ; guzanta (Schs.), Mexico ; lorina (Hew.), Venezuela ; cyanus (Drt.), Bolivia ; talama (Schs.), S. Brazil.

8. *Calycopis cinniana* (Hew.). Amazon, Trinidad.

9. *Calycopis cleon* (F.). Trinidad, Amazon, Brazil. Several similar species.

10. *Calycopis demonassa* (Hew.). Mexico to Amazon, Trinidad. Similar : buphonia (Hew.), Colombia, broader bands UN.

11. *Callipsyche dindymus* (Cr.). Bolivia, Peru, Trinidad. UN grey white. Similar : villia (Hew.), Honduras to Amazon, UN yellow-brown ; proba (G. & S.), Panama, UN whitish, markings faint.

12. *Calycopis hesperitis* (Btlr.). Mexico to Brazil and Trinidad. UN dark brown. Several similar species, including : camissa (Hew.), Guatemala to Peru, UN more olive, red spot larger ; gedrosia (Hew.), Amazon, UN dark line very black ; capeta (Hew.), Nicaragua, Colombia, black-brown UP ; aruma (Hew.), Guianas to Brazil, paler UN.

13. *Calycopis hesperitis* (see 12).

14. *Calycopis orcidia* (Hew.). Mexico to Brazil. Similar : myrsina (Hew.), Nicaragua to Colombia ; smaller, better defined basal brown area UN ; tabena (G. & S.), Mexico, Guatemala ; UP brown, UN bands yellower ; canacha (Hew.), Venezuela, Colombia, UN brown bands narrower.

15. *Calycopis phrutus* (Hbn.). Guianas, Trinidad, Peru. Similar : inoa (G. & S.), Mexico, UN markings less distinct ; zilda (Hew.), C. America to Brazil.

16. *Calycopis vesulus* (Cr.). Guianas to Amazon, Trinidad. Several similar species.

17. *Eumaeus debora* (Hew.). Mexico, Guatemala. Similar : minyas (Hbn.), Mexico to Brazil, much smaller, fewer spots UNH but red dot.

18. *Hemiargus hanno* (Stoll.). Mexico, Antilles, C. America.

19. *Lamprospilus genius* (Hbn.). Surinam to Brazil.

20. *Oenomaus ortygnus* (Cr.). Mexico to Brazil, Trinidad.

21. *Oenomaus rustan* (Stoll.). Honduras to Brazil. UN resembles ortygnus UN. Similar : polama (Schaus), no sex mark UPF, smaller spots UN.

22. *Panthiades pelion* (Cr.). Brazil, Ecuador, Trinidad. Similar : paphlagon (Fldr.), Colombia, Peru, Venezuela ; ochus (G. & S.), Mexico, C. America, markings UN more diffuse ; boreas (Fldr.), Colombia, Amazon, UN markings yellow, more red.

23. *Parachilades speciosa* (Stgr.). Peru and Bolivia.

24. *Polyniphes dumenilii* (Godt.). Venezuela, Trinidad, Colombia. Similar UN : tadita (Hew.), but UP ground colour blue not white.

25. *Pseudolucia chilensis* (Blch.). Chile.

26. *Pseudolucia faga* (Dogn.). Ecuador, Peru. UP brown.

27. *Strymon azia* (Hew.). Mexico to Brazil and Paraguay.

28. *Strymon bazochii* (Godt.). Brazil to Texas, Trinidad.

29. *Strymon pastor* (Btlr. & Druce). Texas to C. America ; Similar : pseudolongula (Clench), Venezuela.

30. *Strymon simaethis* (Drury). Antilles. Similar : telea (Hew.), Mexico to Paraguay ; crethona (Hew.), Cuba, Jamaica, larger.

31. *Strymon telea* (H.Sch.). Brazil to Texas.

32. *Siderus tephraeus* (Hbn.). Mexico to Amazon. Similar : leucophaeus (Hbn.), Brazil, Venezuela, Trinidad .

33. *Theclopsis eryx* (Cr.). Guianas, Brazil, Ecuador, Peru, Bolivia. Similar : curtira (Schs.), Venezuela, UP markings slightly brown ; demea (Hew.), Nicaragua, Colombia, UP black margin very narrow.

34. *Theclopsis eryx* (see 33).

35. *Thecla aegides* (Fldr.). C. America to Venezuela. Similar : cyda (G. & S.), Costa Rica ; adamsi (Druce), Peru, narrow black margins UP ; UN resembles comae UN in both species.

36. *Thecla agricolor* (Btlr.). Mexico to Panama. UP as herodotus.

37. *Thecla americensis* (Blch.). Chile. Similar : tucumana (Druce), Argentina ; eurytulus (Hbn.), Argentina.

38. *Thecla aphaca* (Hew.). Paraguay, Brazil.

39. *Thecla atesa* (Hew.). Panama to Amazon. Similar : maculata (Lathy), Amazon, UN eye-spot has two pupils.

40. *Thecla auda* (Hew.). Colombia, Panama. UN resembles sala UN.

41. *Thecla bagrada* (Hew.). Venezuela.

42. *Thecla barajo* (Reak.). Mexico to Panama. Similar : viridicans (Fldr.), Colombia, lustrous green UP ; theia (Hew.), Ecuador, smaller, darker UN ; erybathis (Hew.), Mexico, broader white stripes UN.

43. *Thecla bassania* (Hew.). Costa Rica, Mexico. Similar : keila (Colombia), UN paler, almost white ; marmoris (Druce), Venezuela, UNF has additional curly line.

44. *Thecla bitias* (Cr.). Mexico to Amazon.

45. *Thecla brescia* (Hew.). Mexico to Nicaragua. Several similar species, including : ergina (Hew.), Jamaica.

46. *Thecla busa* (G. & S.). Mexico to Costa Rica. UN resembles undulata.

47. *Thecla cadmus* (Fldr.). Panama, Northern S. America. UN as comae. This is female platyptera. Similar : timaeus (Fldr.), Colombia, Bolivia, bluer UP, only one line UNF.

48. *Thecla caesaries* (Druce), Guianas, Colombia. Similar : ledaea (Hew.), Amazon.

49. *Thecla calesia* (Hew.). Venezuela, Ecuador, Colombia.

50. *Thecla calus* (Godt.). Colombia.

51. *Thecla comae* (Druce). Colombia. Similar : ion (Druce), Colombia, blue discal spot UNF ; auda (Hew.), Colombia, UN duller brown, lines less distinct.

52. *Thecla celida* (Lucas). Cuba.

53. *Thecla commodus* (Fldr.). Colombia. Similar : elongata (Hew.), Ecuador, Bolivia.

54. *Thecla conchylium* (Druce). Paraguay. Similar species, some tailed.

PLATE 68 : Lycaenidae

1. *Thecla crines* (Druce). Cayenne.

2. *Thecla critola* (Hew.). Guianas. Few similar species.

3. *Thecla cupentus* (Cr.). Nicaragua to Brazil. Similar : cambes (G. & S.), Mexico, Guatemala, UN slightly violet shot.

4. *Thecla draudti* (Lathy). C. America. UN resembles teresina UN.

5. *Thecla emendatus* (Druce). Bolivia. Similar : calchinia (Hew.), Amazon ; carnica (Hew.), Amazon, darker blue UP ; and several other species.

6. *Thecla doryasa* (Hew.). Colombia, Panama, Amazon. Similar : nota (Druce), Colombia, lighter straw-coloured UN ; seos (Schs.), Costa Rica.

7. *Thecla elongata* (Hew.). Colombia, Peru

8. *Thecla ducalis* (Westwood). Brazil.

9. *Thecla emessa* (Hew.). Amazon. Similar : genena (Hew.), Amazon, paler green UP ; eliatha (Hew.), bright blue UP but UN similar.

10. *Thecla endymion* (Cr.). Colombia. Similar : cyphara (Hew.), Mexico to Venezuela, UPH all light brown ; denarius (Btlr.), Mexico to Panama, less orange UP ; sethon (G. & S.), Mexico to Costa Rica, no orange patch UP ; joya (Dogn.), Peru, orange patches middle of wings UP.

11. *Thecla erema* (Hew.). Guatemala, Guianas, Amazon. Similar : olbia (Hew.), Amazon, paler UN, broader black borders UP ; avoca (Hew.), white markings pronounced UN, bright blue, smaller sex spot UPF.

12. *Thecla ericusa* (Hew.). Venezuela. Similar : legytha (Hew.), Cayenne.

13. *Thecla eunus* (G. & S.). Guatemala, C. America.

14. *Thecla falerina* (Hew.). Guianas, Amazon. UN similar : elika (Hew.), Brazil, larger ; carteia (Hew.), Ecuador, greyer.

15. *Thecla fusius* (G. & S.). C. America.

16. *Thecla gibberosa* (Hew.). Colombia,

Bolivia. Similar: numen (Druce), Guianas, UPF broadly blue, no 'hump' on forewing; phydela (Hew.), UPF and UPH blue except for UPH margin. Females of all three species lack the blue and the hump.

17. *Thecla gabatha* (Hew.). Guatemala, Honduras, Colombia. Similar: sylea (Hew.), Amazon.

18. *Thecla galliena* (Hew.). Nicaragua to Brazil. Similar: lophis (Druce), Ecuador.

19. *Thecla crambusa* (Hew.). Brazil, Bolivia. Similar: goleta (Hew.), Colombia; binangula (Schaus), Argentina, Brazil, UN very pale markings, male UPH slightly blue.

20. *Thecla badeta* (Hew.). Guianas, Brazil, Colombia. Similar: gabina (G. & S.), Mexico to Amazon, UNH smaller red dot; oleris (Druce), Paraguay, UN very vivid green, UP darker blue. A few other very similar species.

21. *Thecla halciones* (Btlr. & Druce). Mexico to Amazon. Several similar species.

22. *Thecla hemon* (Cr.). C. America to Guianas and Amazon.

23. *Thecla herodotus* (F.). Mexico to Amazon, Argentina. Similar: amyntor (Cr.), Mexico to Brazil, larger, fewer spots UNH; fusius (G. & S.), Mexico to Panama, UP brown; pastor (Btlr.), Mexico to Panama, brown spots on margin UNH; acaste (Pritww.), Brazil, white transverse line UNH; remus (Hew.), Brazil, red-brown transverse band UNH.

24. *Thecla herodotus* (see 23).

25. *Thecla hesperitis* (Btlr. & Druce). Costa Rica, Panama.

26. *Thecla jada* (Hew.). Mexico and Guatemala. Similar: malina (Hew.), Brazil, UN much more brown.

27. *Thecla janias* (Cr.). Mexico, C. America, Northern S. America.

28. *Thecla jebus* (Godt.). Mexico to S. Brazil, Peru.

29. *Thecla laudonia* (Hew.). Amazon, Colombia. UN is greenish. Similar: phegeus (Hew.), sky blue.

30. *Thecla lausus* (Cr.). Nicaragua to Amazon.

31. *Thecla lenitas* (Druce). Brazil to Paraguay. Similar: strenua (Hew.), Brazil.

32. *Thecla lisus* (Stoll.). Guatemala to Bolivia. Similar: orsina (Hew.), C. America, UN markings less distinct, UNF bands slightly broader.

33. *Thecla literatus* (Druce). Paraguay. Similar: nugar (Schs.), Mexico to Bolivia.

34. *Thecla longula* (Hew.). Colombia, Ecuador, Bolivia. UN resembles fusius UN.

35. *Thecla loxurina* (see 36).

36. *Thecla loxurina* (Fldr.). Colombia, Bolivia, Peru, Venezuela. Similar: amatista (Dogn.), Peru, Colombia.

37. *Thecla lycabas* (Hew.). Panama, Colombia, Amazon.

38. *Thecla malvina* (Hew.). Brazil. Many similar species from Brazil very difficult to separate.

39. *Thecla marsyas* (L.). Panama to S. Brazil. Female UP vivid blue. Similar: damo (Druce), lighter blue, more silvery.

40. *Thecla mavors* (Hbn.). Mexico to Amazon. Similar: ella (Stgr.), Colombia, Ecuador, no scent spot UPF, female brown; triquetra (Hew.), Panama, Guianas, Brazil, only one tail.

41. *Thecla megacles* (Cr.). Brazil, Colombia, Venezuela. Similar: scopas (G. & S.), Mexico, Nicaragua.

42. *Thecla minyia* (Hew.). Guianas, Amazon. Similar: porthura (Druce), Panama to Colombia, UN more ochreous; rocena (Hew.), Colombia to Amazon, more green marking UNH; atena (Hew.), Guatemala to Amazon, no red UN; melleus (Druce), Colombia, broad black apex UPF, no red UN; ravus (Druce), Amazon, UN margins coppery.

43. *Thecla monica* (Hew.). Venezuela, Colombia. Male UP resembles theocritus. Similar: crines (Druce), Colombia, paler UNF.

44. *Thecla meton* (Cr.). Mexico to Brazil.

45. *Thecla mirma* (Hew.). Colombia, Peru, Ecuador. Similar: arria (Hew.), Colombia, Peru, deeper blue; mishma (Hew.), Colombia, brilliant blue UP; oxida (Hew.), Ecuador, Peru, UP violet blue.

46. *Thecla mycon* (G. & S.). Colombia, Amazon. Few similar species.

47. *Thecla mantica* (Druce). Brazil. Similar: teueria (Hew.), Demerara, larger red marks UNH; casmilla (Hew.), Paraguay, UN much less distinct markings.

48. *Thecla myrtillus* (Cr.). Venezuela.

49. *Thecla myrtusa* (Hew.). Colombia, Bolivia, Amazon. Several very similar species.

50. *Thecla ocrisia* (Hew.). C. America, Mexico to Paraguay.

51. *Thecla ophelia* (Hew.). Bolivia, Amazon. Similar: athymbra (Hew.), Amazon, doubled scent patch UP; amplus (Druce), French Guiana, two black dots UNH.

52. *Thecla orcynia* (Hew.). Mexico to Northern S. America. Similar: ahola (Hew.), Mexico, Colombia, Venezuela, four white lines UNH.

53. *Thecla oreala* (Hew.). Brazil. Similar: lucena (Hew.), Venezuela, smaller; canitus (Druce), Paraguay, very small.

PLATE 69: Lycaenidae

1. *Thecla orgia* (Hew.). Mexico to Amazon. Similar: vilidia (Hew.), darker UN. A few other very similar species.

2. *Thecla orgia* (see 1).

3. *Thecla orobia* (Hew.). Panama to Amazon.

4. *Thecla pedusa* (Hew.). Guianas.

5. *Thecla phaleros* (L.). Mexico to S. Brazil. Female UP brown grey. Similar: battus (Cr.), Mexico to Colombia, red lobes to UPH; erybathis (Hew.), Mexico, Honduras.

6. *Thecla velina* (Hew.). Amazon. Similar: phobe (G. & S.), Mexico, Guatemala.

7. *Thecla pholeus* (Cr.). Guianas, Colombia, Brazil. Similar: selina (Hew.), Brazil, Ecuador; bactriana (Hew.), Amazon, UPF light-ringed scent spot; hyacinthus (Cr.), W. Indies, UP paler blue.

8. *Thecla platyptera* (Fldr.). Colombia, Venezuela, Peru.

9. *Thecla palegon* (Cr.). Mexico to S. Brazil.

10. *Thecla polibetes* (Cr.). Mexico to Brazil. Similar: thyrea (Hew.), Panama to Amazon, very broad black margins UPF.

11. *Thecla parthenia* (Hew.). Mexico to Nicaragua.

12. *Thecla sala* (Hew.). Colombia. UP resembles auda, but darker blue. Similar: maraches (Druce), darker green UN.

13. *Thecla satyroides* (Hew.). Amazon, Brazil.

14. *Thecla seudiga* (Hew.). Brazil, Bolivia. Similar: jambe (G. & S.); carnica (Hew.), Mexico to Amazon.

15. *Thecla serapio* (G. & S.). Mexico, Panama. Similar: bebrycia (Hew.), Mexico, Guatemala, less blue UP.

16. *Thecla strephon* (F.). Amazon. Many very similar subspecies.

17. *Thecla spurius* (Fldr.). Guianas, Colombia, Bolivia. Similar: ellida (Hew.), Venezuela to S. Brazil, no scent spot.

18. *Thecla talayra* (Hew.). Mexico to Brazil. UP brilliant blue, narrow black borders, small scent spot UPF, as thabena. Similar: beera (Hew.), Ecuador, Brazil, darker UN.

19. *Thecla tagyra* (Hew.). Amazon.

20. *Thecla tamos* (G. & S.). Costa Rica, Panama. Similar: matho (G. & S.), Guianas to Bolivia, white band UNH narrower; clarina (Hew.), Mexico to Panama, white band UNH very thin.

21. *Thecla tarama* (Hew.). Brazil. Similar: tegaea (Hew.), Brazil, row of black dots UNF.

22. *Thecla telemus* (Cr.). C. America to Guianas. Similar: episcopalis (Fasse), Andes, UP is greenish, but UN similar with wide brown bands; tagyra (Hew.), Amazon, larger, greener blue.

23. *Thecla telemus* (see 22).

24. *Thecla terentia* (Hew.). Amazon.

25. *Thecla teresina* (Hew.). Colombia. UP resembles draudti UP.

26. *Thecla teucria* (Hew.). Amazon. Similar: tegula (Hew.).

27. *Thecla thabena* (Hew.). Guianas, Amazon. Similar: temesa (Hew.), UP very dark blue.

28. *Thecla thales* (F.). Nicaragua to S. Brazil. UN similar: arpoxias (G. & S.), Panama to Bolivia, no white dots UNF.

29. *Thecla thales* (see 28).

30. *Thecla thargelia* (Burm.). Argentina.

31. *Thecla theocritus* (F.). Mexico to Colombia. Similar: augustula (Ky.), Mexico to Panama, brownish margin to UFW.

32. *Thecla thespia* (Hew.). Peru. Similar UN: bosora (Hew.). Ecuador.

33. *Thecla tiasa* (Hew.). Cayenne, French Guiana.

34. *Thecla tiasa* (see 33).

35. *Thecla timaeus* (Fldr.). Colombia.

36. *Thecla tolmides* (Fldr.). Mexico, Guatemala to Panama. Similar: perpenna (G. & S.), Panama, UN only; danaus (Fldr.), Colombia, Bolivia, Peru, UN blue lines clearer, wings darker.

37. *Thecla trebula* (Hew.). Mexico to Colombia to Amazon. Similar: orcilla (Hew.), Ecuador, Colombia, Bolivia; pisis (G. & S.), Costa Rica, Trinidad, UP dull blue; (G. & S.), Colombia, UPH less bright, UNH tail spots blue, not red.

38. *Thecla una* (Hew.). Venezuela, Guianas. Similar: vena (Druce), Peru; gamma (Druce), Argentina; coronta (Hew.), Mexico to Guianas, larger.

39. *Thecla undulata* (Hew.). Colombia, Brazil. Male UP resembles busa, but is more greenish blue.

40. *Thecla velentina* (Berg.). Argentina. Similar: badaca (Hew.), Brazil, UN much darker; rufofusca (Hew.), Mexico, W. Indies, UN markings less distinct; sangala (Hew.), Mexico, much smaller.

41. *Thecla verania* (Hew.). Ecuador, Bolivia, Amazon. Similar: fabulla (Hew.), Guianas, Venezuela, UNH red dots smaller; ceglusa (Hew.), Amazon, only one large red dot UNH.

42. *Theorema eumenia* (Hew.). C. America, Colombia.

43. *Theorema eumenia* (see 42).

44. *Theritas cypria* (Geyer). Mexico, C. America to Colombia. UP greenish, resembles imperialis.

45. *Theritas coronata* (Hew.). Guatemala to Ecuador. Female red lobes UPH. Similar: gabriela (Cr.), Colombia, Amazon, long narrow stripe UNF; batesii (Hew.), Brazil, UNH bands straighter and more uniform; sumptuosa (Druce), grey scent patch on UPF; ornatrix (Druce), Guianas, two scent patches on UPF; candidus (Druce), Colombia; UNH markings very distinct and broad; regalis (Cr.), Mexico to Amazon, darker margins to UPH.

46. *Theritas imperialis* (Cr.). Nicaragua to Northern S. America.

47. *Tmolus basalides* (Geyer). Mexico to Brazil, Trinidad. Similar: arola (Hew.), Brazil, UPH light blue; cardus (Hew.), Brazil, UN browner; tigonia (Schs.), Peru.

48. *Tmolus basalides* (see 47).

49. *Tmolus cydrara* (Hew.). Mexico to Amazon.

50. *Tmolus celmus* (Cr.). Mexico to S. Brazil.

51. *Zizula tulliola* (G. & S.). Mexico to S. Brazil. Subspecies cyna (Edwards) in Texas.

52. *Tmolus echion* (L.). Mexico to S. Brazil. Similar: crolinus (Btlr.), Mexico to Panama; philinna (Hew.), Mexico to S. Brazil, Trinidad, two scent spots vertically above each other UPF.

PLATE 70: Nemeobiidae

1. *Alesa amesis* (Cr.). Guianas. UN as UP, male dark blue. Similar: prema (Godt.), Colombia, Amazon.

2. *Amarynthis meneria* (Cr.). Guianas, Ecuador, Peru.

3. *Amphiselenis chama* (Stgr.). Columbia, Venezuela.

4. *Ancyluris aulestes* (Cr.). S. America. Variable, male resembles colubra but red stripes narrower. Similar: meliboeus (F.), Colombia to Peru, Bolivia, also variable.

5. *Ancyluris formosa* (Hew.). Ecuador, Peru. Similar: miranda (Hew.), Ecuador, larger blue patch UPH.

6. *Ancyluris colubra* (Sndrs.). Venezuela to Peru. Similar: mira (Hew.), Bolivia, Peru, broader bands.

7. *Ancyluris formosissima* (Hew.). Peru. Similar: aristodorus (Mor.), Amazon, narrower bands.

8. *Ancyluris huascar* (Sndrs.). Colombia.

9. *Ancyluris inca* (Sndr.). Mexico, C. America, Colombia.

10. *Ancyluris jurgensenii* (Sndrs.). C. America, Mexico. Male resembles huascar.

11. *Ancyluris meliboeus* (F.). Amazon, Peru.

12. *Ancyluris meliboeus* (see 11).

13. *Anteros acheus* (Stoll.). S. America. UP as formosus.

14. *Anteros allectus* (Ww.). C. America, Colombia, Ecuador.

15. *Anteros allectus* (see 14).

16. *Anteros bracteata* (Hew.). Amazon, Brazil.

17. *Anteros carausius* (Ww.). C. America,

Mexico. Similar: bracteata (Hew.), no white spots UP; renaldus (Stoll.), one white spot UP.

18. *Anteros formosus* (Cr.). S. America.

19. *Apodemia carteri* (Holl.). Bahamas.

20. *Apodemia nais* (Edw.). Mexico.

21. *Argyrogramma holosticta* (G. & S.). C. America, Peru, Trinidad. Similar: stilbe (Godt.), Brazil, darker.

22. *Argyrogramma saphirina* (Stgr.). Bolivia and Peru. Exactly the same as male UN, male UP is blue.

23. *Argyrogramma sulphurea* (Fldr.). Mexico.

24. *Argyrogramma trochilia* (Ww.). Colombia, Lower Amazon. UN resembles female UP.

25. *Argyrogramma trochilia* (see 24).

26. *Astraeodes areuta* (Ww.). Brazil, Bolivia, Peru.

27. *Argyrogramma venilia* (Bates). Lower Amazon. Similar: crocea (G. & S.), C. America, darker; occidentalis (G. & S.), Colombia, smaller, larger black apex UPF.

28. *Audre epulus* (Cr.). Brazil, Argentina.

29. *Audre albinus* (Fldr.). Panama to Venezuela.

30. *Audre dovina* (Schs.). Argentina, Bolivia. Similar: aurinia (Hew.), Brazil, Uruguay, white spots in band on UPF.

31. *Audre aurinia* (Stichel). Brazil and Paraguay.

32. *Audre chilensis* (Fldr.). Andes in Chile, Argentina. Similar: cisandina (Seitz), Chile; consquinia (Giacomelli), Brazil.

33. *Audre erostratus* (Ww.). Venezuela, Colombia, Panama.

34. *Audre erostratus* (see 33).

35. *Baeotis melanis* (Hbn.). Brazil. Similar: eufrepas (Bates), Guianas, second thin outer stripe UP.

36. *Baeotis nesaea* (G. & S.). Peru, Bolivia, Panama, Costa Rica. Similar: bacaenis (Hew.), Ecuador, Bolivia, Peru, broader black borders UP; creusis (Hew.), Bolivia, Peru, markings UP white.

37. *Baeotis zonata* (Fldr.). Mexico, C. America, Trinidad. Similar: capreolus (Stich.), Colombia, black bands UP broken by yellow markings.

38. *Barbicornis acroleuca* (Berg.). Paraguay.

PLATE 71: Nemeobiidae

1. *Barbicornis melanops* (Btlr.). Brazil and Paraguay. Several forms and subspecies. Similar: mona (Ww.), Brazil, orange margin UPH.

2. *Brachyglenis esthema* (Fldr.). Panama to

Colombia and Brazil. Similar: dodone (G. & S.). Costa Rica, Panama, darker, more pointed FW; dinora (Bates), much paler.

3. *Calliona argenissa* (Stoll.). New Grenada, Cundinamarea.

4. *Calliona irene* (Ww.). Lower Amazon. Similar: siaka (Hew.), Orinoco, Amazon, red margin UPH and blue sheen UP; latona (Hew.), Amazon, UPH scarlet inner margin and no white patch.

5. *Callistium cleadas* (Hew.). Guianas, Amazon.

6. *Calociasma lilina* (Btlr.). Mexico to Panama. Similar: ictericum (G. & S.), Peru, ground colour yellow buff.

7. *Calydna cabira* (Hew.). Amazon. Two large white dots UPF.

8. *Calydna cabira* (see 7).

9. *Calydna calyce* (Hew.). Amazon. Similar: lusca (Hbn.), Mexico to Peru, darker; sturnula (Hbn.), Guianas, Brazil, larger white dot UPF; euthria (Ww.), very small and dark.

10. *Calydna catana* (Hew.). Venezuela, Amazon. Female as cabira but no white band UPF. Similar: hira (Godt.), Peru, Amazon.

11. *Calydna cea* (Hew.). Amazon.

12. *Calydna charila* (Hew.). N. Brazil, Peru. Female brown and yellow speckled.

13. *Calydna punctata* (Fldr.). Ecuador, Peru, Bolivia. Similar: chaseba (Hew.), Amazon.

14. *Calydna thersanda* (Stoll.). Guiana, Brazil. Similar to female: charila male (Hew.); similar: lusca (Geyer), Brazil, no blue edge UPH.

15. *Caria chrysame* (Hew.). Bolivia, Peru. Similar: sponsa (Stgr.), large black patch at apex UPF and brighter green.

16. *Caria domitianus* (F.). Guadeloupe, Mexico, Venezuela, Texas. Similar: rhacotis (G. & S.), Honduras to Colombia.

17. *Caria lampeto* (G. & S.). C. America to Bolivia. Similar: mantinea (Fldr.), Ecuador, Bolivia; trochilus (Er.), Guianas, Amazon to Peru, no red UNF; castalia (Men.), Brazil, Peru; UN brownish; colubris (Hbn.), Brazil, Peru, brown bar UPF.

18. *Caria stillaticia* (Dyar). Mexico.

19. *Cariomothis erotylus* (Stich.). Peru, Bolivia. Similar: poeciloptera (G. & S.), UP markings orange and smaller.

20. *Cariomothis erythromelas* (Sepp.). Surinam, Guianas.

21. *Cartea vitula* (Hew.). Amazon, Peru.

22. *Chalodeta epijessa* (Pritt.). Brazil, Guianas.

23. *Catocyclotis aemulius* (F.). Costa Rica, Ecuador, Brazil. Similar: Echenais elpinice (Godm.), Bolivia, Colombia, smaller, no orange on UPF.

24. *Chalodeta chaonitis* (Hew.). Guianas, Bolivia.

25. *Chamaelimnas briola* (Bates). S. America. Similar: doryphora (Stich.), Argentina, UPH yellow bar narrower and elongate; cercides (Hew.), Venezuela, UPH with black edge only.

26. *Chamaelimnas joviana* (Schs.). Peru, Bolivia.

27. *Chamaelimnas splendens* (Sm.). Bolivia. Similar: tircis (Fldr.), no blue reflection UPH; pausa (Godm.), Brazil, Bolivia, Peru, very narrow band UPF.

28. *Chamaelimnas villagones* (Hew.). C. America to Peru. Similar: ammon (Cr.), Guianas, Colombia, UPF more yellow, black bar only; pausa (Godm.), Brazil, UPH unmarked.

29. *Charis anius* (Cr.). C. America, Brazil, Bolivia. Similar: cleonus (Stoll.), Guianas to Bolivia, white fringes UPH; hermodora (Fldr.), Colombia, Venezuela, Panama, brown UN.

30. *Charis anius* (see 29).

31. *Charis cadytis* (Hew.). S. Brazil, Paraguay.

32. *Charis chrysus* (Cr.). Mexico, C. America, Amazon. UP blackish, white spots on FW. Similar: acanthoides (H. Schaff.), Guianas, Amazon, HW has many tails.

33. *Charis gyas* (Cr.). C. America to Brazil. Red forelegs. Similar: gamelia (G. & S.); myrtea (G. & S.), black forelegs.

34. *Charis gynea* (Godt.). Amazon, Colombia, Brazil. Similar: Chalodeta chaonitis (Hew.), Guianas, Bolivia.

35. *Charis thedora* (Fldr.). Brazil, Bolivia, Peru.

36. *Chimastrum argentea* (Bates). C. America. Similar: carnutes (Hew.), Colombia, has dark lines UPF in the form of a cross.

37. *Chorinea faunus* (F.). Guianas, Trinidad, Venezuela. Similar: amazon (Sndrs.), broader black band UP; batesii (Sndrs.), Amazon, very long tails, no black band UPH; sylphina (Bates), Ecuador, Peru, Bolivia, long red base to UPH.

38. *Calydna caieta* (Hew.). Amazon, Peru.

39. *Colaciticus johnstoni* (Dannatt). S. America. Similar: jordani (Seitz), black bar UPF; banghaasi (Seitz), black bar UPF and UPH.

40. *Calydna calamisa* (Hew.). Amazon.

41. *Comphotis irrorata* (Godm.). Guianas.

42. *Corrachia leucoplaga* (Schaus.). Costa Rica.

43. *Cremna actoris* (Cr.). Guianas to Bolivia. A few forms, some with blue spots. Similar: alector (Hbn. & G.), Guianas to S. Brazil, wider bands.

44. *Crocozona coecias* (Hew.). Bolivia, Peru, Amazon. Similar: pheretima (Fldr.), Colombia, no red stripe UPH; fasciata (Hopff.), Peru, Bolivia, red patch, not stripe, UPF.

PLATE 72: Nemeobiidae

1. *Cyrenia martia* (Ww.). Panama to Bolivia.

2. *Dinoptotis orphana* (Stich.). Amazon.

3. *Echenais bolena* (Btlr.). Brazil, Paraguay.

4. *Diopthalma telegone* (Bsd.). C. America, Venezuela to Peru.

5. *Diopthalma telegone* (see 4).

6. *Dysmathia portia* (Bates). Guianas, Trinidad.

7. *Echenais leucophaea* (Hbn.). Brazil. Similar: tinea (Bates), Brazil, smaller.

8. *Echenais micator* (Seitz). Peru.

9. *Echenais penthea* (Cr.). Amazons.

10. *Echenais aminias* (Hew.). Venezuela, Amazon.

11. *Echenais leucocyana* (Hbn. & G.). Guiana, Amazon. Similar: alector (Btlr.), Amazon, Bolivia, Trinidad, larger, browner.

12. *Echenais zerna* (Hew.). Brazil, Bolivia. Similar: glauca (G. & S.), Costa Rica, much paler blue, fewer stripes; curulis (Hew.), Bolivia, Ecuador, bright blue.

13. *Ematurgina bifasciata* (Meng.). Brazil, Argentina, Paraguay. Similar: axena (Hew.), S. Brazil, broader bands UP.

14. *Emesia progne* (Godm.). Peru.

15. *Echenais pulcherrima* (Btlr.). Amazon, Peru. Female has white bands UPF and UPH. Similar: penthea (Cr.), Guianas, Amazon, less white on UPH.

16. *Echenais senta* (Hew.). Amazon.

17. *Emesis brimo* (G. & S.). Colombia, Peru, Bolivia, Trinidad.

18. *Emesis cypria* (Fldr.). Mexico, C. America. Similar: heterochroa (Hopff.), Bolivia, Peru, paler broader band UPF.

19. *Emesis lucinda* (see 20).

20. *Emesis lucinda* (Cr.). C. America to Brazil. Many forms, but UN markings vary little, male markings similar to female but no white patch, male UP has blue reflection. Similar: eurydice (Godm.), Ecuador, UN has dark border.

21. *Emesis mandana* (Cr.). Mexico, C. America to S. Brazil. Similar: fatima (Cr.), Colombia to Brazil, bright brown-red; ocypore (Hbn. & G.), Peru, Amazon, nut-brown.

22. *Emesis tenedia* (Fldr.). Mexico to S. Brazil. Several subspecies. Similar UP: guppyi (Kaye), Colombia, Trinidad, Venezuela, UNF orange-yellow band.

23. *Emesis velutina* (G. & S.). C. America to Colombia.

24. *Emesis zela* (Btlr.). Mexico, C. America, Venezuela, Colombia.

25. *Esthemopsis clonia* (Fldr.). C. America to Amazon. Similar: Uraneis ucubis (Hew.).

26. *Esthemopsis jessi* (Btlr.). Brazil, Bolivia.

27. *Esthemopsis sericina* (Bates). Amazon. Similar: lithosina (Bates), Amazon, more hyaline streaks; celina (Bates), much smaller.

28. *Esthemopsis thyatira* (Hew.). Bolivia, Colombia, Brazil. Female UP markings yellow-orange. Similar: inaria (Ww.), Brazil, no black streak UPF, female UP markings orange.

29. *Eunogyra satyrus* (Ww.). S. America.

30. *Eurybia latifasciata* (Hew.). Colombia, Peru.'

31. *Eurybia leucolopha* (Thieme). Ecuador, Peru, Bolivia.

32. *Eurybia carolina* (Godt.). Brazil. Similar: pergaea (Hbn. & G.).

33. *Eurybia halimede* (Hbn.). C. America to Bolivia and Brazil.

34. *Eurybia juturna* (Fldr.). Bolivia, Peru, Guianas. Similar: donna (Fldr.), Colombia, wings brown, orange edge UPH.

PLATE 73: Nemeobiidae

1. *Eurybia lycisca* (Ww.). C. America, Colombia, Peru.

2. *Eurybia nicaeus* (F.). Guianas to S. Brazil. Several subspecies, some with violet lustre. Similar: dardus (F.), Guianas, Amazon, larger eye-spot UPF; lamia (Cr.), C. and S. America, marginal rings separate.

3. *Eurybia patrona* (Weym.). C. America to Ecuador.

4. *Euselasia aurantia* (Btlr. & Dr.). Panama. Similar: mys (H.Sch.), C. America, red UP duller.

5. *Euselasia chrysippe* (Bates). C. America.

6. *Euselasia amphidecta* (G. & S.). C. America, Colombia.

7. *Euselasia angulata* (Bates). Guianas, Colombia to Rio de Janeiro.

8. *Euselasia argentea* (Hew.). C. America, Colombia. Male UP as hieronymi. Similar: hahneli (Stgr.), yellower and UP bright red.

9. *Euselasia authe* (Godm.). Bolivia, Peru.

10. *Euselasia cafusa* (Bates). Guianas, Ecuador, Trinidad.

11. *Euselasia corduena* (Hew.). C. America to C. Brazil.

12. *Euselasia erythraea* (Hew.). Colombia, Amazon. Similar: zena (Hew.), smaller red spot UPH.

13. *Euselasia euboea* (Hew.). Guianas to Bolivia.

14. *Euselasia eucrates* (Hew.). Ecuador. Similar: eubule (Fldr.), Mexico to Costa

Rica, 3 small spots on UPF; leucorrhoa (G. & S.).

15. *Euselasia eugeon* (Hew.). Amazon to Bolivia, Argentina.

16. *Euselasia euoras* (Hew.). Ecuador.

17. *Euselasia euphaes* (Hew.). Amazon.

18. *Euselasia euriteus* (Cr.). Amazon. Several forms. UN resembles gelon UN. Similar: eutychus (Hew.), Colombia, Amazon, narrower bands, brown UN.

19. *Euselasia euryone* (Hew.). Guianas, Ecuador, Peru, Bolivia.

20. *Euselasia eusepus* (Hew.). Mexico to S. Brazil. UP blackish brown with blue gloss. Several subspecies. Similar: urites (Hew.); bettina (Hew.), C. America to Ecuador, UN more bronze coloured.

21. *Euselasia gelanor* (Cr.). Guianas, Amazon, Bolivia. UP black, blue reflection. Similar: crotopus (Cr.), C. America to Bolivia, faintly red in middle of UPF.

22. *Euselasia gelon* (Stoll.). Guianas.

23. *Euselasia gyda* (Hew.). C. America, Amazon to Bolivia. Female white UP.` Similar: praeclara (Hew.), Ecuador, UP shot with green; opalescens (Hew.), Amazon, darker green irridescence.

24. *Euselasia hieronymi* (G. & S.). Mexico, C. America. Similar: pusilla (Fldr.), UN silvery white.

25. *Euselasia labdacus* (Cr.). Guianas, Colombia, Trinidad to Bolivia. UP resembles eucrates female.

26. *Euselasia lisias* (Cr.). Colombia, Guianas, Amazon.

27. *Euselasia melaphaea* (Hbn.). Northern S. America.

28. *Euselasia arbas* (Cr.). Guianas, Colombia. Several forms.

29. *Euselasia orfita* (Cr.). Guianas, Ecuador, Bolivia, Amazon. A few subspecies and forms.

30. *Euselasia pellonia* (Stich.). Brazil. Male bright blue.

31. *Euselasia subargentea* (Lathy.). Colombia. UP blackish brown.

32. *Euselasia thucydides* (F.). Brazil. Similar: teleclus (Stoll.), UN resembles subargentea UN.

33. *Euselasia uzita* (Hew.). Guianas, Amazon. Female has white spot UPF.

34. *Euselasia uzita* (see 33).

PLATE 74: Nemeobiidae

1. *Hades hecamede* (Hew.). Ecuador.

2. *Hades noctula* (Ww.). Mexico, C. America, Venezuela. UP black.

3. *Helicopis acis* (F.). Northern S. America.

4. *Helicopis cupido* (L.). Trinidad, Eastern S. America to C. Brazil. Many forms. Very similar: endymion (Cr.), UP black margins finer.

5. *Hyphilaria nicias* (Stoll.). Guianas to Bolivia. Similar: anthias (Hew.), Colombia to Guianas, white spots instead of patches UP.

6. *Hyphilaria anophthalma* (Fldr.). Colombia, Ecuador. Female UP black and white stripes.

7. *Hyphilaria parthenis* (Ww.). Guianas, Bolivia. Male resembles anophthalma.

8. *Imelda glaucosmia* (Hew.). Colombia, Ecuador.

9. *Hermathena candidata* (Hew.). Amazon to Bolivia.

10. *Ithomeis astrea* (Fldr.). Venezuela, Brazil. Similar: mimica (Bates), Colombia, Ecuador, broad orange margins; corena (Fldr.), Colombia, narrow orange margin UPH.

11. *Ithomeis eulema* (Hew.). Costa Rica, Panama.

12. *Ithomiola callixena* (Hew.). Ecuador.

13. *Ithomiola cascella* (Hew.). Colombia. Similar: floralis (Fldr.), Bolivia, no orange UPF.

14. *Lasaia meris* (Cr.). Mexico to Amazon. Very variable and many subspecies. Similar: agesilas (Latr.), C. America, Brazil, no white spot UPH; sessilis (Schs.), Mexico, bluer; moeros (Stgr.), Peru, fewer markings UP.

15. *Lasaia meris* (see 14).

16. *Lasaia oileus* (Godm.). S. America.

17. *Juditha lamis* (see 18).

18. *Juditha lamis* (Stoll.). Mexico to Brazil. Variable. Similar: Nymula calyce female (Fldr.); Nymula mycone female (Hew.); Nymphidium azanoides (Btlr.), C. America to Peru, white band UPF pointed, very little red band UPH.

19. *Lemonias agave* (G. & S.). Costa Rica to Colombia, Trinidad.

20. *Lemonias glaphyra* (Ww.). Paraguay, Brazil. Few forms.

21. *Lemonias thara* (Hew.). Guianas, Amazon. Similar: pulchra (Lathy), Ecuador and Peru, lighter blue; Polystichtis pione (Bates), Brazil, small and dark.

22. *Lemonias zygia* (Hbn.). Guiana, Venezuela, Brazil.

23. *Lepricornis melanchroia* (Fldr.). Mexico. Similar: strigosus (Stgr.), Panama, Colombia, Venezuela, UPF band of broad white dashes, UP streaked white; incerta (Stgr.), Colombia to Peru, hyaline streaks UP.

24. *Leucochimona philemon* (Cr.). Guianas, Amazon. Similar: lagora (H. Schaff.), C. America, eye spot towards edge of UPF; matisca (Hew.), Amazon, Peru, Bolivia, eye spot in middle of UPF.

25. *Lucillella camissa* (Hew.). Ecuador.

26. *Lymnas aegates* (Hew.). Bolivia, Peru, Argentina. Similar: hellapana (Rob.), darker, with broader white band UPF; melander (Cr.), Guianas, Brazil, darker with yellow band UPF; ubia (Fldr.), Venezuela, Guianas, with red spots and wider margin UPH.

27. *Lymnas ambryllis* (Hew.). Northern S. America. Similar: erythra (Men.), Brazil, markings orange.

28. *Lymnas pulcherrima* (H. Schaff.). Surinam.

29. *Lymnas cinaron* (Fldr.). Colombia to S. Brazil.

30. *Lymnas iarbas* (F.). Venezuela, Ecuador, Trinidad. Variable. Similar: marathon (Fldr.), Venezuela, no red spots UP.

31. *Lymnas pixe* (Bsd.). C. America, Mexico to S. Brazil. Several forms. Similar: alena (Hew.), yellow tip UPF and yellow margin UPH; passiena (Hew.), Colombia, Bolivia, no red spots.

32. *Lymnas xarifa* (Hew.). Northern S. America. Similar: unxia (Hew.), larger orange patch UPF.

PLATE 75: Nemeobiidae

1. *Lyropteryx appollonia* (Ww.). Ecuador to Bolivia and Brazil. Similar: terpsichore (Ww.), many red spots from UN show through UP.

2. *Lyropteryx lyra* (Saund.). Panama, Colombia.

3. *Melanis agyrtus* (Cr.). C. America to S. Brazil. Similar: Panara phereclus (L.), north of South America, wider orange band UPF; Panara thisbe (F.), north of South America, orange band UPH and UPF.

4. *Menander coruscans* (Btlr.). Bolivia, Amazon.

5. *Mesene crocella* (Bates). C. America.

6. *Mesene epaphus* (Stoll.). Northern S. America. Several forms. Similar: epalia (Godt.), narrow black edges UP, bright vermilion.

7. *Menander hebrus* (Cr.). Guianas, Colombia, Amazon. Few forms.

8. *Menander hebrus* (see 7).

9. *Menander menander* (Cr.). Northern S. America, Trinidad. Similar: nitida (Btlr.), S. and W. Brazil, UP as coruscans.

10. *Mesene hya* (Ww.). Amazon. Few forms.

11. *Mesene margaretta* (White). Colombia, Venezuela, Bolivia.

12. *Mesene nepticula* (Mschlr.). Amazon, Guianas, Ecuador.

13. *Mesene phareus* (Cr.). S. America. Very variable. Similar: pyrippe (Hew.), wide black borders UP; bomilcar (Stoll.), Guianas, even wider black borders UP; hyale (Fldr.), Colombia, small, very wide black borders UP.

14. *Mesene silaris* (G. & S.). Nicaragua, Venezuela, Peru.

15. *Mesenopsis bryaxis* (Hew.). C. America to Bolivia. Similar: albivitta (Lathy), S. Brazil, UPF orange ground colour, UPH black.

16. *Mesopthalma idotea* (Ww.). Guianas, Amazon.

17. *Mesosemia calypso* (Bates). Amazon. Similar: maeotis (Hew.), Guiana, darker markings UP; nina (Hbst.), Guianas to Peru, darker markings still, only base of UPF blue.

18. *Mesosemia ephyne* (Cr.). Guianas, Amazon, Peru. Similar: coclestis (G. & S.), C. America.

19. *Mesosemia eumene* (Cr.). Guianas, Ecuador, Peru, Bolivia. Several forms, varying in blue sheen. Similar: macella (Hew.), smaller, no blue gloss.

20. *Mesosemia gaudiolum* (Bates). Mexico to Costa Rica.

21. *Mesosemia loruhama* (Hew.). Peru.

22. *Mesosemia ibycus* (Hew.). Guianas, Peru, Colombia. Similar: cippus (Hew.), Amazon region, larger.

23. *Mesosemia machaera* (Hew.). Western S. America. UP resembles philocles. Similar: zonalis (G. & S.), C. America, Colombia, broader bands UP; magete (Hew.), Amazon, lighter brown.

24. *Mesosemia macrina* (Fldr.). Colombia. Similar: zikla (Hew.), Ecuador, white stripe UPF broader.

25. *Mesosemia melpia* (Hew.). Amazon. UN same as UP. Similar: myrmecias (Stich.), Guianas, Bolivia.

26. *Mesosemia messeis* (Hew.). Amazon, Ecuador, Bolivia, Peru. Female brown with white bands UP.

27. *Mesosemia metuana* (Hew.). Colombia, Ecuador. Similar: ama (Hew.), Ecuador, white band UNF.

28. *Mesosemia mevania* (Hew.). Colombia, Peru.

29. *Mesosemia minos* (Hew.). Amazon, Brazil. Similar: melaene (Hew.).

30. *Mesosemia odice* (Godt.). Argentina, Brazil. Similar: rhodia (Godt.).

31. *Mesosemia ahava* (Hew.). Peru. Similar: olivencia (Bates), Peru, thin short black stripes UPH.

32. *Mesosemia orbona* (Godm.). Guianas, Colombia. Similar: antaerice (Hew.), Guianas, Trinidad, narrower stripes; menoetes (Hew.), as antaerice but darker; epidius (Hew.), northern S. America.

33. *Mesosemia philocles* (L.). C. America. Very variable. Similar: jeziela (Btlr.), Colombia to Ecuador.

34. *Mesosemia sifia* (Bsd.). Guianas, Ecuador, Colombia, Amazon. Similar: zonalis (G. & S.), Nicaragua, white bands UP much broader.

35. *Mesosemia ulrica* (Cr.). Northern S. America. Female brown UP with white band FW and HW. Similar: asa (Hew.), black margins UP, female only white band UPF.

36. *Mesosemia zanoa* (Hew.). Colombia. Similar: metope (Hew.), Guianas, Amazon, with white on UPH.

37. *Mesosemia zorea* (Hew.). Peru, Bolivia, Ecuador.

PLATE 76: Nemeobiidae

1. *Metacharis lucius* (F.). Guianas. Similar: nigrella (Bates), Venezuela to Peru, male UN grey blue, female dull yellow UN.

2. *Metacharis ptolomaeus* (F.). Amazon to S. Brazil. UP resembles lucius. Similar: cuparina (Bates), Colombia to Peru, UN as UP, NOT blue.

3. *Methonella cecilia* (Cr.). Panama, C. America to Ecuador. Several forms.

4. *Mimocastina rothschildi* (Seitz). Guianas.

5. *Necyria bellona* (Ww.). Bolivia, Peru, Brazil. Similar: duellona (Ww.), Ecuador, less red markings; saundersi (Hew.), Colombia, broad orange band UPF.

6. *Nahida coenoides* (Hew.). Ecuador. Similar: trochois (Hew.), Ecuador, orange inner margin UPH.

7. *Napaea beltiana* (Godm.). Guianas, Colombia, Brazil.

8. *Napaea eucharila* (Bates). Guianas to Bolivia. Similar: phryxe (Fldr.), grey; sylva (Mschlr.), Guianas, paler, bluish.

9. *Monethe albertus* (Fldr.). Colombia to Bolivia. Similar: alphonsus (F.), Brazil; rudolphus (G. & S.), Nicaragua, smaller yellow dotting UPF.

10. *Napaea nepos* (F.). Guianas to Peru and Paraguay.

11. *Napaea theages* (G. & S.), C. America, Colombia. Similar: lucilia (H. Druce), Guianas, without white patch UPF.

12. *Napaea umbra* (Bsd.). Mexico, C. America.

13. *Necyria manco* (Sndrs.). Colombia.

14. *Necyria zaneta* (Hew.). C. America.

15. *Nelone cadmeis* (Hew.). Panama to S. Brazil. UP resembles hypochalybe. Similar: incoides (Schs.), Argentina, Bolivia, Peru, very much smaller, brownish.

16. *Nelone hypochalybe* (Fldr.). C. America to Peru.

17. *Nelone hypochalybe* (see 16).

18. *Nymphidium mantus* (Cr.). Guianas, Trinidad, Venezuela, Brazil.

19. *Notheme eumeus* (F.). Guianas, Amazon to Paraguay, Brazil. Few subspecies.

20. *Nymphidium azanoides* (Btlr.). C. America to Peru.

21. *Nymphidium cachrus* (F.). Colombia Amazon, Guianas, Trinidad. Many forms.

22. *Nymphidium lisimon* (Stoll.). Guianas, Peru. Female half the size of azanoides female. Similar: olinda (Bates), C. America, Colombia, no red UP; baeotia (Hew.), Guianas, Amazon, smaller than olinda.

23. *Nymphidium caricae* (L.). Guianas, Colombia. Similar: omois (Hew.), Amazon, much smaller; acherois (Bsd.), Guiana to S. Brazil, much broader unbroken orange margins UP.

24. *Nymphidium ninias* (Hew.). Amazon. Similar: leucosia (Hbn.), Amazon, UP markings pale yellow.

25. *Nymphidium onaeum* (Hew.). C. America to Colombia, Venezuela, Trinidad. Similar: chione (Bates), Amazon to S. Brazil, no red or yellow UP.

26. *Nymula agle* (Hew.). Guianas.

27. *Nymula calyce* (Fldr.). S. America. Similar: gela (Hew.), Guianas, Lower Amazon, UP bands pale yellow; pelops (F.), Venezuela, Colombia, UP pale yellow band fills the wings.

28. *Nymula chaonia* (Hew.). Brazil.

29. *Nymula mycone* (Hew.). Mexico, Guatemala, Honduras. Female has broad white bands UP.

30. *Nymula nymphidioides* (Btlr.). Central America. Similar: ethelinda (Hew.), C. and S. Brazil, UPF unmarked; nycteus (G. & S.), C. America, snow white.

31. *Nymula orestes* (Cr.). Guianas, Amazon, Ecuador.

PLATE 77: Nemeobiidae

1. *Nymula phliasus* (Cr.). Guianas. Similar: phillone (Godt.), no orange UPF tip; victrix (Rebel), Rio de Janeiro, narrower white bands UP.

2. *Nymula phylleus* (Cr.). Guianas, Amazon.

3. *Nymula tytia* (Cr.). Guianas, Ecuador, Peru. Similar: abaris (Cr.), Guianas, Amazon, no band UPH margin.

4. *Nymula tytia* (see 3).

5. *Orimba alemaeon* (Hew.). Ecuador, Colombia.

6. *Orimba cruentata* (Btlr.).

7. *Orimba epitus* (see 8).

8. *Orimba epitus* (Cr.). Guianas.

9. *Orimba jansoni* (Btlr.). C. America, Ecuador. Female has orange band UPF.

10. *Orimba tapaja* (Sndrs.). Santarem, Amazon. Very variable.

11. *Orimba terias* (Godm.). Paraguay. UP resembles cruentata female.

12. *Orimba tapaja* (see 10).

13. *Orimba tutana* (Godt.). Brazil. Similar:

monotone (Stich.), Brazil, UN brown streaks only.

14. *Ourochnemis archytes* (Stoll.). Paraguay.

15. *Pachythone gigas* (G. & S.). Panama.

16. *Pachythone palades* (Hew.). S. Brazil. Similar: pasides (Hew.), lighter UP, no yellow band UNF.

17. *Pachythone lateritia* (Bates). Northern S. America, Trinidad.

18. *Panara phereclus* (L.). Brazil, Peru, Guianas.

19. *Pandemos pasiphae* (Cr.). Guianas, Colombia, Peru, Amazon. Female dull white.

20. *Parcella amarynthina* (Fldr.). Argentina to Colombia. Female has round yellow patches UP.

21. *Parnes nycteis* (Ww.). Panama to Amazon. Similar: philotes (Ww.), Guianas, larger.

22. *Peropthalma tullius* (F.). C. and S. America.

23. *Periplacis glaucoma* (Hbn. & G.). Brazil. Similar: splendida (Btlr.), larger but duller, UN whitish; Menander purpurata (G. & S.), C. America, darker brown UN.

24. *Phaenochitonia bocchoris* (Hew.). Brazil.

25. *Phaenochitonia cingulus* (Stoll.). Surinam to Bolivia.

26. *Phaenochitonia sophistes* (Bates). Peru.

27. *Polystichtis apotheta* (Bates). Guianas, Colombia, Brazil. Similar: martia (Godm.), Colombia, larger markings.

28. *Phaenochitonia phoenicura* (G. & S.). C. America to Colombia. Similar: arbuscula (Mosch.), Guianas.

29. *Pheles heliconides* (H. Schaff). Guianas, Amazon.

30. *Polystichtis argenissa* (Stoll.). Colombia, Panama. Female grey brown with orange band UPF.

31. *Polystichtis emylius* (Cr.). Guianas, Trinidad, Amazon, Peru. Female dark brown with orange band UPF. Similar: cilissa (Hew.), C. America, UP markings orange.

32. *Polystichtis florus* (Stgr.). Ecuador to Venezuela. Female resembles lasthenes female but broad yellow band UP.

33. *Polystichtis laobotas* (Hew.). Colombia and Panama.

34. *Polystichtis latona* (Hew.). Amazon.

35. *Polystichtis lasthenes* (Hew.). Mexico and Honduras.

PLATE 78: Nemeobiidae

1. *Polystichtis lucianus* (F.). Panama, Venezuela, Guianas, Trinidad. Similar: cilissa

(Hew.), C. America, UP yellower, female pale yellow.

2. *Polystichtis porthaon* (Dolman). Amazon.

3. *Polystichtis rhodope* (Hew.). Amazon, Trinidad.

4. *Polystichtis thara* (Hew.). Peru. Similar: pione (Bates) Guianas, very small brown area UP.

5. *Polystichtis zeanger* (Stoll.). Guianas, Trinidad, Amazon. Very variable. Similar: caecina (Fldr.), Peru, larger blue patch UPF.

6. *Polystichtis siaka* (Hew.). Brazil.

7. *Pseudopeplia grande* (G. & S.). Colombia.

8. *Rhetus arcius* (L.). Mexico to S. Brazil.

9. *Pretus preta* (Cr.). C. America, Bolivia.

10. *Symmachia hippea* (H. Schaff.). Guianas.

11. *Symmachia leopardina* (Fldr.). Amazon.

12. *Rhetus dysonii* (Sndrs.). Panama, Peru, Bolivia. Similar: periander (Cr.), Guianas to S. Brazil, white stripe UPF.

13. *Riodina lycisca* (Hew.). S. Brazil.

14. *Riodina lysippus* (L.). Guianas, Venezuela, Amazon.

15. *Riodina lysistratus* (Burm.). Argentina, S. Brazil.

16. *Rodinia calpharnia* (Sndrs.). Upper Amazon. Similar: delphinia (Stgr.), Lower Amazon, blue base to UPF.

17. *Roeberella calvus* (Stgr.). Peru. Similar: gerres (Thm.), Colombia; Dinoplotis orphana (Stich.), UNH yellow grey.

18. *Stichelia dukinfieldia* (Schs.). S. Brazil. Variable.

19. *Semomesia croesus* (F.). Northern S. America. UP female is brown with broad white bands. Several forms and subspecies. Similar: macaris (Hew.), Amazon, Peru, smaller, dark markings narrower.

20. *Setabis gelasine* (Bates). Colombia, Amazon. Female yellow bands and patch UPF, yellow patch UPH. Similar: Orimba lagus (Cr.), Guianas, Ecuador, Amazon, female yellow band UPF, male smaller white area UPF.

21. *Stichelia sagaris* (Cr.). Guianas, Amazon to S. Brazil. Female has only orange band UPF. Similar: Phaenochitonia iasis (Godm.), UP bands more reddish.

22. *Symmachia asclepia* (Hew.). C. America, Ecuador.

23. *Setabis pythia* (Hew.). Colombia, Bolivia, Amazon. Similar: Orimba butleri (Bates).

24. *Siseme alectryo* (Ww.). Colombia, Brazil. Several forms.

25. *Siseme aristoteles* (Latr.). Colombia, Ecuador. Few forms.

26. *Siseme luculenta* (Ersch.). Peru.

27. *Siseme pallas* (Latr.). Colombia, Venezuela. Similar: neurodes (Fldr.), Peru, Bolivia, Colombia, much whiter; pedias (Godm.), bluish reflection; pseudopallas (Weym.), bands UP are yellow.

28. *Siseme peculiaris* (Druce). Peru.

29. *Stalachtis calliope* (L.). Guianas. Similar: magdalenae (Ww.), Colombia, two rows of white dots UPF.

30. *Stalachtis euterpe* (L.). Guianas, Lower Amazon. UPH sometimes lacks orange band.

31. *Symmachia jugurtha* (Stgr.). Colombia.

32. *Stalachtis phlegia* (Cr.). Guianas to C. Brazil. Several forms. Similar: susanna (F.), S. Brazil, orange band at apex of UPF.

33. *Styx infernalis* (Stgr.). Peru.

34. *Symmachia cleonyma* (Hew.). Nicaragua, Colombia.

35. *Stalachtis phaedusa* (Hbn.). Amazon, Guianas. Similar: zephyritis (Dolm.), Guianas, white powdered surface UNH; lineata (Guer.), Lower Amazon, orange tip UPF, no orange margin UPH.

PLATE 79: Nemeobiidae

1. *Symmachia menetas* (Drury). S. Brazil. Similar: rubina (Bates), Mexico to Colombia.

2. *Symmachia praxila* (Ww.). S. Brazil. Male is probator. Similar: norina (Hew.), Amazon.

3. *Symmachia probator* (Stoll.). Guianas, Amazon, Trinidad.

4. *Symmachia threissa* (Hew.). Nicaragua. Similar: hetaerina (Hew.), Amazon, markings yellow; arcuate (Hew.), Amazon, some red on UPF.

5. *Symmachia triangularis* (Thm.). Colombia.

6. *Symmachia tricolor* (Hew.). Amazon, Colombia.

7. *Teratophthalma axilla* (Druce). Bolivia, Peru. Similar: massidia (Hew.), Ecuador.

8. *Teratophthalma marsena* (Hew.). Ecuador, Peru. Similar: phelina (Fldr.), Colombia.

9. *Syrmatia dorilas* (Cr.). S. America.

10. *Themone pais* (Hbn.). Brazil, Venezuela, Guianas, Peru. A few subspecies.

11. *Theope eudocia* (Ww.). Colombia, Guianas, Venezuela, Trinidad.

12. *Theope barea* (G. & S.). Panama to Amazon, Trinidad. Similar: excelsa (Bates), Amazon, Guianas, twice as large.

13. *Tharops trotschi* (G. & S.). Colombia.

14. *Theope basilea* (Bates). C. America. Similar: terambus (Godt.), S. Brazil, smaller; eleutho (G. & S.), Panama, broader black margins UPH.

15. *Theope foliorum* (Bates). Venezuela, Trinidad, Amazon.

16. *Theope lycaenina* (Bates). Brazil, Trinidad.

17. *Theope matuta* (G. & S.). C. America to Amazon.

18. *Theope pieridoides* (Fldr.). Brazil, Trinidad.

19. *Theope pedias* (H. Schaff.). C. America to S. Brazil, Mexico. Similar: sericea (Bates), Amazon, larger.

20. *Theope publius* (Fldr.). Panama to Amazon. UP resembles virgilius.

21. *Theope virgilius* (F.). C. America. Very variable. Similar: talna (G. & S.), Honduras, marginal row of dots UNH; cratylus (G. & S.), Panama, no blue spots in black apex UPF.

22. *Theope simplicia* (Bates). Brazil.

23. *Theope syngenes* (Bates). Brazil, Trinidad. UP as virgilius.

24. *Theope theritas* (Hew.). Amazon.

25. *Theope thestias* (Hew.). C. and S. America.

26. *Theope thootes* (Hew.). C. America to Amazon, Trinidad. Similar: thentis (G. & S.), C. America, UN with dark shading.

27. *Thisbe irenea* (Stoll.). Guianas, Colombia, Venezuela, Trinidad.

28. *Thisbe molela* (Hew.). Venezuela, Guianas. Female resembles irenea.

29. *Thisbe irenea* (see 27).

30. *Thisbe lycorias* (Hew.). Mexico, C. America. A few forms.

31. *Voltinia theata* (Stich.). Ecuador, Colombia.

32. *Uraneis hyalina* (Bates). Amazon to Bolivia.

33. *Zabuella tenella* (Burm.). Argentina.

34. *Thysanota galena* (Bates). Guianas, Amazon.

35. *Xenandra helius* (Cr.). Guianas, Trinidad, Venezuela, Brazil. Female has golden yellow band UPF.

36. *Xinias cynosema* (Hew.). Bolivia.

37. *Uraneis zamuro* (Thieme). Colombia, Ecuador.

38. *Xenandra prasinata* (Thieme). Colombia. Similar: Lymnas pulcherrima (H. Schaff.), Surinam, additional white dashes UPF.

39. *Zelotaea phasma* (Bates). Amazon, Brazil. Colour varies to brownish grey.

PLATE 80: Hesperiidae

1. *Ablepsis azines* (Hew.). Amazon.

2. *Ablepsis vulpinus* (Hbn.). Brazil.

3. *Achalarus albociliatus* (Mab.). Mexico to Colombia. UP black-brown. Similar: casica (H.Sch.).

4. *Achlyodes busirus* (Stoll.). Mexico to Paraguay. Male UP/UN black.

5. *Achlyodes pallida* (Fldr.). Colombia.

6. *Achlyodes thraso* (Hbn.). Mexico to Paraguay, Antilles. Similar: ulpianus (Poey), Brazil and Cuba, UNH dusted blue grey; papinianus (Poey), Trinidad and Cuba.

7. *Aethilla later* (Mab.). Peru.

8. *Aethilla echina* (Hew.). Mexico to Colombia and Ecuador. A few similar species. UP is blackish brown.

9. *Aegiale hesperiaris* (Wkr.). Mexico. Lfp: Agare.

10. *Aecas aecas* (Stoll.). Panama to Brazil and Trinidad.

11. *Aethilla lavochrea* (Btlr.). C. and S. America. UP resembles memmius.

12. *Aethilla memmius* (Btlr.). Venezuela. Similar: gigas (Mab.), Ecuador, pale brown wing tips UPF.

13. *Aguna asander* (Hew.). Mexico to Brazil. Similar: Epargyreus exadeus (Cr.), S. America, reduced markings UP and UN; Proteides maysii (Luc.), Cuba.

14. *Aguna cholus* (Plotz). Brazil. Similar: ganna (Mschlr.), Venezuela, smaller, greener sheen UPH; coelus (Stoll.), Brazil, much wider white band UNH.

15. *Aides aestria* (Hew.). Brazil. Similar: dysoni (G. & S.), Honduras.

16. *Aides aegita* (Hew.). Brazil.

17. *Aides epitus* (Stoll.). Panama to Brazil. Similar: elara (G. & S.), Mexico; Paraides ocrinus (Plotz), green hairs base of UPH.

18. *Alera vulpina* (Fldr.). Colombia.

19. *Amenis baroni* (G. & S.). Peru.

20. *Amenis pionia* (Hew.). Colombia.

21. *Anastrus obscurus* (Hbn.). S. America. Similar: petius (Mschlr.), Guianas.

22. *Anastrus sempiternus* (Btlr. & Druce). Mexico to Amazon. Similar: simplicior (Plotz), Brazil, Paraguay, Trinidad, UNH brown.

23. *Anisochoria albida* (Mab.). Bolivia.

24. *Anisochoria polysticta* (Mab.). Mexico to Guianas and Peru. Similar: minorella (Mab.), Bolivia, smaller and paler.

25. *Anthoptus epictetus* (F.). Mexico to S. America. Similar: tryhana (Kaye), Trinidad; several similar species in Brazil.

26. *Antigonus decens* (Btlr.). Peru.

27. *Antigonus emorsa* (Fldr.). Mexico.

28. *Antigonus liborius* (Plotz). Argentina, Uruguay. Female much paler.

29. *Antigonus nearchus* (Latr.). Mexico to S. Brazil. Similar: erosus (Hbn.), female UP much paler.

30. *Autochton bocus* (Plotz). Guianas, Colombia, Trinidad, Brazil.

31. *Apaustus gracilis* (Fldr.). Mexico to Venezuela. UP brown unmarked.

32. *Apaustus menes* (Stoll.). Panama to Brazil.

33. *Appia appia* (Evans). Argentina. Similar UP: Linka lina (Plotz), Bolivia.

34. *Ardaris eximia* (Hew.). Venezuela. Similar: Metardaris cosinga (Hew.), Bolivia, Peru.

35. *Argon argus* (Mschlr.). Panama to Colombia, Trinidad, Argentina. Similar: Decinea percosius (G. & S.), Mexico, Panama, Trinidad.

36. *Argopteron aureipennis* (Bluch.). Chile.

37. *Aroma aroma* (Hew.). Costa Rica to Amazon. Similar: henricus (Stgr.), Panama.

38. *Argopteron puelmae* (Calvert). Chile. UN as aureipennis.

39. *Arteurotia tractipennis* (Btlr. & Druce). Venezuela.

40. *Asbolis capucinus* (Lucas). Antilles, Florida, Cuba, Colombia.

41. *Artines aquilina* (Plotz). Brazil. Similar: aepitus (Hbn.), Brazil.

42. *Artines atizies* (G. & S.). Panama to Venezuela, Brazil, Trinidad.

43. *Aspitha agenoria* (Hew.). Surinam to Bolivia.

44. *Aspitha leander* (Boullet). Colombia.

45. *Astraptes alardus* (Stoll.). Mexico to Colombia and Brazil. Similar: megalaurus (Mab.), Mexico, hind wing produced to a tail.

46. *Astraptes anaphus* (Cr.). Mexico to S. America. Similar: chiriquensis (Stgr.), Panama to Colombia, darker UP, deep blue wing bases, no yellow; elorus (Hew.), Brazil, Colombia, Bolivia, UP resembles chiriquensis; ampyx (G. & S.), Mexico to Amazon, inner margin UNF lighter, much less yellow UNH; Thymele gallius (Mab.), Colombia, tiny white dots at apex UPF.

47. *Astraptes apastus* (Cr.). Guianas, Brazil, Peru.

48. *Astraptes aulestes* (Stoll.). Colombia, Brazil to Paraguay. Similar: egregius (Btlr.), Mexico to Colombia, Trinidad, UPF dots almost invisible; briccius (Plotz), Brazil, Trinidad, UPF dots almost form a band, ending in a point.

49. *Astraptes creteus* (Cr.). Mexico to Amazon and Brazil. Several subspecies. UP resembles alardus.

PLATE 81 : Hesperiidae

1. *Atarnes sallei* (Fldr.). Mexico to Costa Rica.

2. *Atrytonopsis zaovinia* (Dyar). Mexico, Costa Rica. Similar: ovinia (Hew.), Nicaragua; pittacus (Edw.), Arizona, markings smaller; python (Edw.), New Mexico, UP markings yellowish.

3. *Astraptes fulgerator* (Walch). Mexico to Brazil, Colombia, Trinidad. Similar: naxos (Hew.), S. Brazil; brevicauda (Plotz), Panama, UPF band narrow; fulminans (H.Sch.), Mexico to Brazil, UNH basal half almost black; dinora (Plotz), Peru, Bolivia, Venezuela, UN dull black, UNH with few spots; enotrus (Cr.), Guianas, Colombia, Brazil, Peru, Trinidad, yellowish spot middle of UNH; Orneates aegiochus (G. & S.), Costa Rica to Panama, Colombia, small yellow spot UNH, margin UNH yellowish.

4. *Astraptes hopferi* (Plotz). C. America, Peru.

5. *Astraptes naxos* (Hew.). Brazil, Colombia.

6. *Astraptes pheres* (Mab.). Brazil, Colombia, Peru, Paraguay.

7. *Astraptes talus* (Cr.). C. and S. America.

8. *Augiades crinisus* (Cr.). S. America, Amazon region. Similar: epimetha (Plotz), much smaller markings UP.

9. *Bella cupreiceps* (Mab.). Mexico to Bolivia and Trinidad. Similar: Staphylus aurocapilla (Stgr.), Mexico to Argentina, and several Bolla species.

10. *Bungalotis midas* (Cr.). Guianas, Trinidad, Bolivia, Peru, Colombia. Brown female wide white hyaline band UPF. Similar: Dyscophellus ramusis (Cr.), female has hyaline dots; Salatis salatis (Cr.), Colombia, Brazil, male less spots than ramusis; diophorus (Mosch.), Surinam, male UP yellow brown, female spots smaller and more numerous.

11. *Burca braco* (H.Sch.). Panama to Brazil, Cuba.

12. *Burca undulatus* (H.Sch.). Mexico to Brazil.

13. *Butleria elwesi* (Evans). Chile.

14. *Butleria facetus* (Plotz). Argentina and Chile. Several similar species. UP resembles elwesi.

15. *Butleria fruticolens* (Btlr.). Chile. Several similar species. UP resembles elwesi.

16. *Buzyges idothea* (Godm.). Costa Rica.

17. *Cabares paterculus* (H.Sch.). Panama to S. America.

18. *Cabares potrillo* (Luc.). Mexico, C. America, Cuba, Texas. Similar: Polyctor enops (G. & S.), Mexico, Honduras.

19. *Cabirus procas* (Cr.). Guianas to Peru.

20. *Cabirus procas* (Cr.) (see 19 also). Some females have more stripes UP and some have none UPH.

21. *Calliades phrynicus* (Hew.). Brazil.

22. *Callimormus alsimo* (Mosch.). C. America, Trinidad.

23. *Callimormus corades* (Fldr.). Mexico to Brazil and Trinidad.

24. *Camptopleura theramenes* (Mab.). Brazil. Similar: termon (Hpff.), Bolivia, UPH paler brown.

25. *Carrhenes canescens* (Fldr.). Mexico to Colombia. Similar: fuscescens (Mab.), Mexico to Honduras, UN markings more pronounced; calidius (G. & S.), UN whiter; meridensis (G. & S.), Costa Rica, Venezuela, UNH bluish.

26. *Carrhenes unifasciata* (Fldr.). C. America.

27. *Carystoides basochis* (Latr.). C. America, Amazon, Trinidad. Similar: cathaea (Hew.), no spot UNH.

28. *Carystoides maroma* (Mschlr.), Guianas. Similar: noseda (Hew.), Trinidad.

29. *Carystus jolus* (Stoll.). Brazil.

30. *Carystus phorcus* (Cr.). Guianas, Trinidad.

31. *Charidia lucaria* (Hew.). Guianas, Colombia, Bolivia. Female has large whitish patches UPH.

32. *Cacropterus aunus* (F.). Mexico to Paraguay. Similar: oryx (Fldr.), N. Brazil, almost twice as large; bipunctatus (Gmel.), Mexico to Brazil, two white dots at apex UPF; lunulus (Plotz), Brazil, three white apical dots UPF; zonilis (Mab.), C. America to Colombia, UNH bands broad and banded with lighter colour; cinctus (H.Sch.), Mexico to Brazil, four dots at apex UPF; vertilucis (Btlr.), Guatemala to Colombia, yellow-grey fringes and margin on hind-wing.

33. *Cecropterus neis* (Hbn.). Mexico to Brazil. Similar: itylus (Hbn.), Guianas, Trinidad, Brazil, white band even narrower, especially on UNF.

34. *Celaenorrhinus eligius* (Cr.). Mexico to S. America and Trinidad. Similar: fritz-gartneri (Bail.), Mexico and C. America, UPH lighter colour with dull spots.

35. *Charidia empolaeus* (Ww.). Brazil.

36. *Celaenorrhinus shema* (Hew.). Guianas. Similar: monartrus (Plotz), Mexico to Panama, smaller, fewer, spots.

37. *Chiomara asychis* (Cr.). California, Mexico to Argentina and the Antilles.

38. *Chioides catillus* (Cr.). C. America. Similar: myrto (Mab.), Haiti, UNH more silvery.

39. *Chioides jethira* (Btlr.), Peru.

40. *Chiomara mithrax* (Mschlr.), Mexico to Brazil, Trinidad, Cuba. Similar: punctum (Mab.), S. America, paler blue grey. UPH pale grey brown.

41. *Chloeria psittacina* (Fldr.). Colombia to S. Peru.

42. *Choranthus radians* (Lucas). Florida, Antilles. Female very dark. Similar: haitensis (Skinner), Antilles, UN brighter orange.

43. *Choranthus vitellius* (F.). Amazon, W. Indies. Similar: magdalia (H.Sch.), Cuba, much smaller.

44. *Chrysoplectrum perniciosus* (H.Sch.). Colombia, Brazil.

45. *Chrysoplectrum pervivax* (Hbn.). Surinam. Similar: otriades (Hew.), Brazil, no white spots UNF.

46. *Clito bibulus* (Riley). Brazil.

47. *Clito clito* (F.). Guianas, Brazil.

48. *Cobalus calvina* (Hew.). Ecuador.

49. *Cobalus virbius* (Cr.). Brazil, Trinidad. Similar: fidicula (Hew.), Honduras, Costa Rica, Panama, smaller white patch UPH; Orthos gabinus, (G. & S.), Mexico, UPH no spot.

50. *Codactractus imalena* (Btlr.). Costa Rica to Colombia. Similar: bryaxis (Hew.), Mexico to Guatemala, UPH and base of UPF yellow brown; cyda (G. & S.), Mexico to Honduras, UP light brown; arizonensis (Skinner), Arizona.

51. *Cogia abdul* (Hayw.). Brazil. Similar: hassan (Btlr.), Brazil, smaller.

52. *Cogia calchas* (H.Sch.). Paraguay to Texas. Similar: outis (Skinner).

53. *Cogia eluina* (G. & S.). Mexico and C. America. Similar: calchas (H.Sch.). Texas to Paraguay.

54. *Conga zela* (Plotz). Argentina.

PLATE 82: Hesperiidae

1. *Conognathus platon* (Fldr.). Amazon.

2. *Corticea epiberus* (Mab.). Mexico to Brazil and Trinidad. Similar: corticea (Plotz), Mexico, larger, UN hardly marked; lyzias (Plotz), C. America, yellow markings brighter, more extensive.

3. *Cumbre cumbre* (Schaus). Argentina.

4. *Croniades machaon* (Dbl. & Hew.). Brazil. Similar: pieria (Hew.), Bolivia, UP ground colour yellow.

5. *Cycloglypha thrasybulus* (F.). Mexico to S. Brazil, Trinidad. Similar: tisias (G. & S.), Costa Rica to Amazon, markings clearer and more linear.

6. *Cyclosemia anastomosis* (Mab.). Mexico to Brazil. Similar: herennius (Cr.)., Surinam, darker shining blue UNH.

7. *Cymaenes tripunctus* (H.Sch.). Colorado, Mexico to Brazil.

8. *Cynea cynea* (Hew.). Mexico to Colombia, Venezuela, Trinidad. Similar: megalops (G. & S.), without white patch UNF.

9. *Cynea irma* (Mosch.). Mexico to Colombia, Brazil, Trinidad.

10. *Dalla agathocles* (Fldr.). Colombia. Many similar species.

11. *Dalla caenides* (Hew.). Venezuela. Several similar species.

12. *Dalla caicus* (Hew.). Venezuela.

13. *Dalla cyprius* (Mab.). Bolivia.

14. *Dalla cypselus* (Fldr.). Colombia. Similar: cupavia (Mab.), Bolivia, markings UP yellow; and several other species.

15. *Dalla dimidiatus* (Fldr.). Venezuela, Colombia, Bolivia.

16. *Dalla dognini* (Mab.). Ecuador. Several similar species.

17. *Dalla eryonas* (Hew.). Panama to Brazil. Several similar species.

18. *Dalla epiphaneus* (Fldr.). Venezuela. Similar: polycrates (Fldr.), Colombia, Peru, smaller dots UPH.

19. *Dalla hesperioides* (Fldr.). Colombia.

20. *Dalla ibhara* (Btlr.). Ecuador, Bolivia, Peru, Brazil. Several similar species with or without white dots on brown UP, including: plancus (Hpff.), Peru, larger pale markings UNF; quadristriga (Mab.), Bolivia, UN warm brown; crithote (Hew.), Ecuador, many white spots UPF.

21. *Dalla jelskyi* (Ersch.). Peru, Bolivia.

22. *Dalla semiargentea* (Fldr.). Colombia.

23. *Damas clavus* (Erichs.). Panama to Amazon.

24. *Dardarina daridaeus* (Godm.). Brazil. Several similar species.

25. *Dardarina dardaris* (Hew.). Mexico.

26. *Decinea percosius* (G. & S.). Mexico, Panama, Trinidad. Many very similar species, mostly from C. America and Northern S. America.

27. *Diaeus lacaena* (Hew.). Mexico to Costa Rica and Panama.

28. *Dion carmenta* (Hew.). Brazil. UP blackish brown with veins prominent.

29. *Dion rubrinota* (Druce). Peru, Bolivia, Colombia. Similar: gemmatus (Btlr.), Costa Rica, Panama, UP blackish brown, UPF light coloured wing tip.

30. *Drephalys alcmon* (Cr.). Amazons.

31. *Drephalys oriander* (Hew.). Amazons.

32. *Drephalys phoenicoides* (Mab. & Btlr.). Brazil.

33. *Dyscophellus euribates* (Stoll.). Surinam.

34. *Ectomis cythna* (Hew.). Guianas.

35. *Dyscophellus porcius* (Fldr.). C. America to Peru and Colombia. Similar: sebaldus (Cr.), Guianas, warm brown colour; fulvius (Mab.), Colombia, fiery yellow colour.

36. *Dyscophellus ramusis* (Cr.). Brazil, C. America. Female has small hyaline dots.

37. *Dubiella fiscella* (Hew.). Nicaragua to Amazon. Similar: dubius (Stoll.), Guianas, broader band UNH.

38. *Ebrietas osyris* (Stgr.). Mexico to Amazon. UP as Burca undulatus, purple black with darker marks. Similar: infanda (Btlr.), Mexico to Amazon; badia (Plotz), Venezuela, UNH grey brown.

39. *Ebusus ebusus* (Stoll.). Panama to Amazon, Trinidad, Bolivia.

40. *Elbella polyzona* (Latr.). Guianas, Brazil.

41. *Elbella scylla* (Men.). Peru and Bolivia. Similar: mariae (Bell), Brazil.

42. *Enosis immaculata* (Hew.). Venezuela. A few similar species.

43. *Enosis misera* (Schs.). Brazil, Trinidad. Similar species virtually indistinguishable.

44. *Entheus lemna* (Btlr.). Brazil. Female resembles priassus female. Similar: gentius (Cr.). Colombia, orange yellow, three stripes UPF; eumelus (Cr.), C. America, smaller than gentius, three stripes UPF.

45. *Entheus priassus* (L.). S. America. Similar: dius (Mab.), Costa Rica to Colombia, larger, wider band UPF; matho (G. & S.), Guatemala, Nicaragua, Costa Rica, large red area at base UPF.

46. *Entheus priassus* (see 45).

47. *Epargyreus barisses* (Hew.). Peru, Brazil, Argentina. Variable. Similar: enispe (Hew.), Colombia, Brazil, UPF markings smaller; tmolis (Burmeister), Paraguay.

48. *Epargyreus exadeus* (Cr.). S. America.

49. *Ephyriades arcas* (Drury). Antigua, Cuba.

50. *Ephyriades zephodes* (Hbn.). Cuba, Bahamas.

51. *Eprius veleda* (G. & S.). Mexico to Panama, Trinidad. Similar small species of Mnaseas, Mnasicles, Methionopsis and Eutocus come from the Mexico to Amazon area.

52. *Eracon bufonia* (Mschlr.). Colombia.

53. *Eracon clinias* (Mab.). Fr. Guiana.

54. *Erynnis gesta* (H.Sch.). Tropical America to Texas.

55. *Erynnis heteroptera* (Plotz). Brazil. Similar: austerus (Schs.), Peru.

56. *Euphyes derasa* (H.Sch.). Brazil.

57. *Euphyes peneia* (G. & S.). Panama.

58. *Eutychide complana* (H.Sch.). Mexico to Venezuela. Similar: ochus (G. & S.), Mexico to Amazon, Trinidad.

59. *Eutychide olympia* (Plotz). Brazil.

PLATE 83: Hesperiidae

1. *Eutychide physcella* (Hew.). Brazil. UP resembles olympia. Many similar species.

2. *Falga jeconia* (Btlr.). Venezuela. Similar: sciras (G. & S.), Honduras, much larger orange area UPF.

3. *Gindanes brebisson* (Latr.). Colombia and Brazil.

4. *Gindanes brontinus* (G. & S.). Nicaragua.

5. *Gorgopas viridiceps* (Btlr.). Nicaragua to

Peru, Brazil. Similar: chlorocephala (Druce), Costa Rica, darker, green less conspicuous.

6. *Gorgythion begga* (Prittw.). Panama to Paraguay, Trinidad. Similar: pyralina (Mschlr.), Mexico to S. Brazil, no white patch UNH.

7. *Grais stigmaticus* (Mab.). Mexico to S. Brazil, Jamaica.

8. *Haemactis sanguinalis* (Dbl. & Hew.). Ecuador, Bolivia. Similar: pyrrhosphenus (Lindsay), Colombia, UP browner red, UNH white patch at bottom edge.

9. *Halotus angellus* (Plotz). C. America.

10. *Helias phalaenoides* (F.). Mexico to Paraguay, Trinidad.

11. *Heliopetes arsalte* (L.). Mexico to Paraguay and Jamaica. Similar: petrus (Hbn.), Nicaragua to Amazon, broader black tip to UPF; alana (Reak.), Mexico to Brazil, brownish spots UNH.

12. *Heliopetes domicella* (Erichs.). Arizona, Mexico to Argentina.

13. *Heliopetes laviana* (Hew.). Mexico to Argentina. Similar: ericetorum (Bsd.), Arizona.

14. *Heliopetes macaira* (Reak.). Arizona to Panama. Similar: nivella (Mab.), Mexico to Brazil, UN markings very faint; laviana (Hew.), Mexico to Argentina, larger, two large brown spots apex UNF.

15. *Heliopetes omrina* (Btlr.). Peru.

16. *Hyalothyrus neleus* (L.). S. America. Female deep brown UP and UN. Similar: nitocris (Cr.), no white UP, UPH brown, UNH white at base; infernalis (Mschlr.), UNH ochre yellow; mimicus (M. & B.), Peru, smaller.

17. *Hylephila boulleti* (Mab.). Peru.

18. *Hylephila ignorans* (Plotz). Venezuela. Terrain: montane.

19. *Justinia justinianus* (Latr.). Mexico to Brazil, Trinidad. Similar UP: Orthos lycortas (G. & S.); Phanes almoda (Hew.); Phanes rezia (Plotz), Brazil, no yellow patch UNH.

20. *Lamponia lamponia* (Hew.). S. Brazil.

21. *Lento lento* (Plotz). Colombia.

22. *Lerema lineosa* (H.Sch.). Brazil.

23. *Levina levina* (Plotz). Brazil.

24. *Lerodea edata* (Plotz). Texas, south through Mexico. Similar: tyrtaea (Plotz), Texas, south through Mexico, smaller.

25. *Librita librita* (Plotz). Mexico, Panama. Similar: heras (G. & S.), Mexico, much darker.

26. *Lucida lucia* (Capr.). Brazil.

27. *Ludens ludens* (Mab.). Panama to Venezuela.

28. *Lycas argenteus* (Hew.). Mexico to Brazil. Similar: godarti (Latr.), Panama to Brazil, larger, UN silver stripes better defined.

29. *Lychnuchus celsus* (F.). S. America.

30. *Marela tamyroides* (Fldr.). Colombia, Brazil.

31. *Mellana mella* (G. & S.). Mexico to Brazil and Trinidad. Similar: eulogius (Plotz); helva (Mschlr.), three orange dots at apex UPF.

32. *Lychnuchoides ozias* (Hew.). S. Brazil. Similar: saptine (G. & S.), Costa Rica, Panama, much browner UN, no purple, and more yellow edging UPH.

33. *Mellana perfida* (Mschlr.). Costa Rica to Colombia.

34. *Mellana villa* (Evans). Brazil.

35. *Metron chysogastra* (Btlr.). Mexico to Amazon, Trinidad.

36. *Metron oropa* (Hew.). Paraguay.

37. *Microceris variicolor* (Men.). Brazil.

38. *Milanion hemes* (Cr.). Guianas, Brazil. Similar: marciana (G. & S.), Panama, UPH band much broader.

39. *Milanion filumnus* (Mab. & Boullet). Bolivia. Similar: leucaspis (Mab.), Brazil, even larger white patch UPH.

40. *Mimoniades ocyalus* (Hbn.). Brazil. Similar: mimetes (Mab.), Guiana.

41. *Mimoniades eupheme* (G. & S.). Peru, Ecuador. Similar: subspecies versicolor (Latr.), Brazil, red band UPF narrower; periphema (Hew.), Peru, Bolivia, four bands UPF.

42. *Mimoniades nurscia* (Swns.). Ecuador, Peru. Similar: malis (G. & S.), Colombia, UP only.

43. *Mimoniades punctiger* (Mab. & Boullet). Colombia, Bolivia. Similar: minthe (G. & S.), Bolivia, no apical spot UPF; pityusa (Hew.), Colombia, Peru, broader, more diffuse orange bands UP.

44. *Misius misius* (Mab.). Amazons.

45. *Mnasilus penicillatus* (G. & S.), Mexico to Brazil.

46. *Mnasitheus chrysophrys* (Mab.). C. America. UP brown. Several very similar species.

47. *Mnestheus ittona* (Btlr.). Panama to Bolivia.

48. *Moeris remus* (F.). Mexico to Brazil, Trinidad.

49. *Moeris striga* (Geyer). Mexico to Argentina.

50. *Moeris moeris* (Mosch.). Amazons.

51. *Molo heraea* (Hew.). Panama to Amazon. Subspecies of mango (Guinee). Similar: nebrophone (Schs.), Costa Rica, Panama, orange colour is browner.

52. *Molo humeralis* (Mab.). Brazil, Colombia. Subspecies of mango (Guinee). Similar: Zalomes biforis (Weym.), Ecuador.

53. *Monca telata* (H.Sch.). Mexico to Venezuela and Trinidad. Similar: Cymaenes fraus (G. & S.), UNH three dark bands.

54. *Morys cerdo* (Bsd.). Mexico to S. America, Trinidad. Some similar species.

55. *Morys etelka* (Schs.). Trinidad. Similar: Mnasitheus simplicissimus (H.Sch.), Trinidad; Penicula cocoa (Kaye), Trinidad, UPH more golden green, larger.

56. *Morvina morvus* (Plotz). Brazil. UNH tends to become whitened. These closely resemble Myrinia species.

57. *Morys lyde* (G. & S.). Mexico to Costa Rica.

58. *Mycteris crispus* (H.Sch.). Guatemala to Colombia. Similar: cambyses (Hew.), Bolivia.

59. *Mylon melander* (Cr.). Mexico to Paraguay. Similar: ozema (Btlr.), Mexico to S. Brazil, smaller, less dark.

60. *Mylon pulcherius* (Fldr.). Mexico to Brazil and Trinidad. Similar: lassia (Hew.), UPH paler.

61. *Myscelus amystis* (Hew.). Bolivia.

62. *Myscelus assaricus* (Cr.). Guianas.

63. *Myscelus draudti* (Riley). Bolivia. UP as phoronis, but darker, more orange.

64. *Myscelus illustris* (Mab.). Peru, Bolivia.

65. *Myscelus belti* (G. & S.). C. America.

66. *Myscelus phoronis* (Hew.). Colombia, Bolivia, Peru.

67. *Myscelus rogersi* (Kaye). Trinidad.

PLATE 84: Hesperiidae

1. *Myscelus santhilarius* (Latr.). Guianas to Brazil, Amazon.

2. *Mysoria galgala* (Hew.). Colombia, Brazil.

3. *Mysoria thasus* (Stoll.). Surinam, C. America.

4. *Nascus phocus* (Cr.). Mexico to Brazil, Trinidad. Similar: Discophellus euribates (Stoll.); phintias (Schs.), Costa Rica, UPH more ochre.

5. *Nastra ethologus* (Hayward). Argentina.

6. *Nascus broteas* (Cr.). Guianas, Brazil.

7. *Nascus caepio* (H.Sch.). Honduras to Colombia and Trinidad. Similar: cephise (Hew.), Brazil, yellow spots FW form a band.

8. *Naevolus naevolus* (G. & S.). Mexico to Brazil.

9. *Mysoria venezuelae* (Scudd.). Mexico to Colombia. Similar: Amenis ambigua (Mab. & Boullet), Brazil. Subspecies of barcastus (Sepp.), Surinam.

10. *Neoxeniades luda* (Hew.). Honduras to Guianas. Similar: molion (G. & S.), Mexico, only 2 spots UPF.

11. *Nerula fibrena* (Hew.). Venezuela.

12. *Niconiades xanthaphes* (Hbn.). Mexico to Brazil. Similar: caeso (Mab.), Trinidad, Brazil, Mexico; mikko (Hayward), Argentina; merenda (Mab.), Panama, to Venezuela and Brazil, smaller, apical dots UPF very faint; sabaea (Plotz), Brazil, Colombia, smaller dots UPH.

13. *Niconiades bromius* (Stoll.). Guianas. UP dark brown. Several similar species.

14. *Niconiades ephora* (H.Sch.). Mexico, Colombia, Guianas, Trinidad. Many similar species, all very similar, including: Thespius macareus (H.Sch.), rounder wings; bromias (G. & S.), UNH bands clearer.

15. *Noctuana haematospila* (Fldr.). Mexico to Colombia. Similar: stator (G. & S.). Mexico to Colombia and Trinidad, UN scarlet spots much smaller.

16. *Nyctelius ares* (Fldr.). Mexico to Brazil, Trinidad, W. Indies. Subspecies of nyctelius (Latr.).

17. *Nosphistia perplexus* (Mab.). Brazil.

18. *Nyctelius nyctelius* (Latr.). Mexico, Brazil, W. Indies, Cuba, Trinidad, Texas. Very variable. UP resembles Panoquina eradnes UP.

19. *Ocella albata* (Mab.). Colombia, Bolivia, Peru.

20. *Oechydrus chersis* (H.Sch.). Bolivia.

21. *Oeonus pyste* (G. & S.). Mexico. UP as Onaphas columbaria. Onophas

22. *Ocyba calathana* (Hew.). C. & S. America.

23. *Onophas columbaria* (H.Sch.). Panama to Brazil and Trinidad.

24. *Onenses hyalophora* (Fldr.). Mexico to Panama. Onaphas

25. *Orneates aegiochus* (G. & S.). Costa Rica to Panama, Colombia. Similar UP: Astraptes fulgerator.

26. *Orphe vatinius* (G. & S.). Guianas, Peru, Amazon. Similar: gerasa (Hew.), Colombia, Amazon.

27. *Orses cynisca* (Swains.). Mexico to Colombia, Brazil, Trinidad. Female has white band UPF. Similar: itea (Swains.), male and female, Brazil, UN light grey veining.

28. *Orthos orthos* (Godm.). Panama.

29. *Ouleus fridericus* (Hbn.). Panama to Brazil. Similar: calavius (G. & S.), Guatemala, Panama, Nicaragua, brown black UP and UN.

30. *Ouleus narycus* (Mab.). Ecuador.

31. *Ouleus simplex* (G. & S.). Mexico.

32. *Ouleus terreus* (Schs.). Venezuela, Trinidad. Subspecies of fridericus, UN uniform brown.

33. *Oxynetra erythrosoma* (Mab.). Amazon.

34. *Oxynetra felderi* (Hpff.). Brazil to Peru. Similar: confusa (Mab.), Peru, larger apical spot UPF; hopfferi (Stgr.), Panama, no apical spot UPF.

35. *Oxynthes corusca* (H.Sch.). Mexico, Panama to Brazil.

36. *Paches loxus* (Dbl. & Hew.). Mexico to Panama. Female brown UP; Similar: polla (Mab.), Mexico to Costa Rica, UPF no blue.

37. *Pachyneuria obscura* (Mab.). Colombia, Peru, Bolivia.

38. *Pachyneuria eremita* (Plotz). S. America. UP resembles Burca undulatus, dusted lavender grey.

39. *Panoquina eradnes* (Cr.). Guatemala to Colombia and Brazil. Similar: luctuosa (H.Sch.), Brazil, UNH white broad patch.

40. *Papias microsema* (G. & S.). Mexico to Brazil, Trinidad. Several similar species.

41. *Paracarystus hypargyra* (H.Sch.). Guianas, Brazil.

42. *Paracarystus menetries* (Latr.). Colombia, Brazil. Similar: koza (Btlr.), Brazil, smaller spots UP; rona (Hew.), Brazil, UNH bands stand out brightly.

43. *Potamanaxas thestia* (Hew.). Ecuador.

44. *Paramimus stigma* (Fldr.). Panama to Colombia. Similar: scurra (Hbn.), Brazil.

45. *Paraides anchora* (Hew.). Brazil, Trinidad. Similar: brino (Cr.), Surinam, smaller silver patch UNH; dysoni (Godm.). Honduras, silver patches UNH broken up; destria (Hew.), Argentina, very large silver patch UNH.

46. *Parphorus decora* (H.Sch.). Mexico to Brazil, Trinidad. UN resembles storax UN. Several very similar species.

47. *Parphorus storax* (Mab.). C. America to Amazon, Trinidad. UP as decora, but markings faint.

48. *Potamanaxas flavofasciata* (Hew.). Ecuador, Bolivia. Similar: xantholeuce (Mab.), Panama, yellow band also on UPH.

49. *Potamanaxas laoma* (Hew.). Bolivia. A few subspecies. Similar: latrea (Hew.), much darker markings.

50. *Potamanaxas melicertes* (G. & S.). Panama, Costa Rica. Similar: pammenes (G. & S.), Nicaragua, wider band UPF; unifasciata (Fldr.), Colombia, UPF has five dots at apex.

51. *Pellicia costimacula* (H.Sch.). Mexico to Brazil. Similar: dimidiata (H.Sch.); and several other species.

PLATE 85: Hesperiidae

1. *Pellicia zamia* (Plotz). S. America.

2. *Penicula cocoa* (Kaye). Trinidad. Several similar species.

3. *Perichares agrippa* (G. & S.). Nicaragua, Trinidad.

4. *Perichares butus* (Moshler). Guianas.

5. *Perichares lindigiana* (Fldr.). Colombia and Venezuela.

6. *Perichares lotus* (Btlr.). Mexico to Venezuela and Trinidad.

7. *Perichares philetes* (Gmelin). Mexico.

8. *Phanes abaris* (Mab.). Ecuador. Similar: rezia (Plotz), Brazil, UNH darker markings.

9. *Phanes almoda* (Hew.). Brazil, Guiana. Similar: alteus (Geyer), Brazil, small yellow patch UNH; trogon (Evans), Bolivia, smaller markings UP.

10. *Phanus vitreus* (Stoll.). Mexico to S. America. Similar: marshalli (Kirby).

11. *Pheraeus argynnis* (Plotz). Brazil. Similar: odila (Plotz), Brazil, no white spots UNH; and several other species.

12. *Piruna gyrans* (Plotz). Mexico. Few similar species.

13. *Phareas coeleste* (Dbl. & Hew.). Colombia, Brazil.

14. *Phocides batabano* (Lucas). Tropical America, Cuba. Female UP is brown. Lfp: Mangrove.

15. *Phocides oreides* (Hew.). Peru, Bolivia. Similar: charonotis (Hew.), Bolivia; pigmalion (Cr.), Colombia, blue and green markings instead of orange UP.

16. *Phocides pialia* (Hew.). Mexico to Brazil. Subspecies maximus.

17. *Phocides polybius* (F.). Brazil to Argentina. Similar: lilea (Reak.), Mexico to Brazil, paler UN.

18. *Phocides thermus* (Mab.). C. America.

19. *Poanopsis puxillius* (Mab.). Mexico.

20. *Phocides urania* (Ww.). Mexico. Similar: vida (Btlr.), Panama, Costa Rica, UPF top half completely black.

21. *Polygonus lividus* (Latr.). Brazil to Florida. Subspecies of leo (Gmelin). Similar: manueli (Bell & Comstock).

22. *Polyctor fera* (Weeks). Bolivia.

23. *Polyctor polyctor* (Prittw!). Mexico to S. Brazil.

24. *Polythrix auginus* (Hew.). Guianas Colombia, Brazil. Similar: octomaculata (Sepp.), Mexico to Amazon; alciphron (G. & S.), Mexico, larger, white band UNH; asine (Hew.), Mexico to Nicaragua, additional white spots at bottom edge of UPF.

25. *Polythrix decurtata* (H.Sch.). Colombia, Brazil.

26. *Polythrix gyges* (Evans). Venezuela, Peru. Several similar species.

27. *Polythrix metallescens* (Mab.). Brazil.

28. *Polythrix roma* (Evans). Peru, Amazons. Similar: asine (Hew.), C. America.

29. *Pompeius athenion* (Hbn.). Mexico to Brazil. UP blackish brown.

30. *Pompeius chittara* (Schs.). Trinidad, C. America.

31. *Pompeius dares* (Plotz). Brazil to Mexico. A few similar species.

32. *Porphyrogenes omphale* (Btlr.). Amazon to Bolivia. Subspecies of passalus (H.Sch.).

33. *Porphyrogenes vulpecula* (Plotz). Brazil. Similar: zohra (Mosch.), Venezuela; despecta (Btlr.), Brazil, much smaller.

34. *Proteides maysii* (Luc.). Cuba.

35. *Proteides mercurius* (F.). Arizona to S. America. Several forms.

36. *Pseudosarbia phaenicola* (Berg.). Brazil, Argentina.

37. *Psoralis exclamationis* (Mab.). Bolivia.

38. *Pyrrhocalles antiqua* (H.Sch.). Haiti, Cuba, Jamaica.

39. *Pyrrhopyge arax* (Evans). Bolivia.

40. *Pyrrhopyge amyclas* (Cr.). Guianas.

41. *Pyrrhopyge bixae* (L.). Similar: phidias (L.). S. America, narrower white margin UNH.

42. *Pyrrhopyge chalybea* (Scudder). Mexico, C. America, Venezuela.

PLATE 86: Hesperiidae

1. *Pyrrhopyge creona* (Druce). Peru. Similar UP: telassina (Stgr.), Peru, UN plain brown.

2. *Pyrrhopyge creon* (Druce). C. America.

3. *Pyrrhopyge decipiens* (Mab.). Ecuador. Several similar species.

4. *Pyrrhopyge erythrosticta* (G. & S.). Central America, Colombia. Similar: maculosa (Hew.), Brazil, no red spot UPF.

5. *Pyrrhopyge hygieia* (Fldr.). Ecuador. Similar: aesculapius (Stgr.), C. America, narrower yellow edge UPH, more vivid blue.

6. *Pyrrhopyge jonas* (Fldr.). Mexico.

7. *Pyrrhopyge kelita* (Hew.). Bolivia, Peru, Ecuador.

8. *Pyrrhopyge markena* (Hew.). Ecuador. Similar: schausi (Bell), Ecuador, narrow orange UNH; sadia (Evans), Peru.

9. *Pyrrhopyge latifasciata* (Btlr.). Colombia and Peru. Similar: selina (Evans), Brazil, larger white area UNH.

10. *Pyrrhopyge araxes* (Hew.). Mexico to Colombia.

11. *Pyrrhopyge pelota* (Plotz). Brazil, Paraguay, Argentina.

12. *Pyrrhopyge rubricollis* (Sepp.). Surinam. Several similar species. Similar: crida (Hew.), Colombia, long white band UPF.

13. *Pyrrhopyge sergius* (Hpffr.). Colombia, Peru, Brazil.

14. *Pyrrhopyge spatiosa* (Hew.). Ecuador, Colombia. Similar: cosyra (Druce), Bolivia

and Peru, yellow markings; Aspitha aspitha (Hew.), white band only UPF; staudingeri (Plotz), Peru, Bolivia, only 2 small spots and white band UPF.

15. *Pyrrhopygopsis agaricon* (Druce). Colombia.

16. *Pyrgus trisignatus* (Mab.). Argentina and Chile.

17. *Pyrgus veturius* (Plotz). Brazil.

18. *Pyrrhopygopsis socrates* (Men.). Brazil, Trinidad. UP steely blue. Subspecies crakes (Mab. & Bon.) has a white area UNH.

19. *Pyrdalus corbulo* (Cr.). Guianas.

20. *Pythonides amaryllis* (Stgr.). Guatemala, Panama, Colombia, Brazil. Similar: lerina (Hew.), Guianas, UPF band broken up, small; lancea (Hew.), Brazil, no white spots at apex of UPF.

21. *Pythonides assecla* (Mab.). Brazil. Subspecies of grandis (Mab.).

22. *Pythonides lusorius* (Mab.). Brazil. Subspecies of herennius (Gey.).

23. *Pythonides proxenus* (G. & S.). Mexico, C. America. Subspecies of herennius (Gey.).

24. *Quadrus cerealis* (Stoll.). Mexico to S. America. Similar: Urbanus lucida (Plotz), Colombia, UNH blue much paler.

25. *Quadrus contubernalis* (Mab.). Mexico to Colombia and Brazil. Similar: deyrollei (Mab.), French Guiana, smaller, but broader blue bands UPH.

26. *Quadrus lugubris* (Fldr.). Mexico to Colombia, Trinidad, Brazil. Similar: truncata (Hew.), Bolivia, larger.

27. *Quinta cannae* (H.Sch.). Mexico to Argentina.

28. *Rhinthon chiriquensis* (Mab.). Mexico, Guatemala, Panama.

29. *Ridens biolleyi* (Mab.). Costa Rica.

30. *Ridens mephitis* (Hew.). Bolivia, C. America. Similar: tristis (Drandt), Bolivia, UP unmarked brown; bridgmani (Weeks), Ecuador, UP brownish, narrow band UPF; harpagus (Fldr.), Colombia, has long tails to UPH, like biolleyi.

31. *Ridens ridens* (Hew.). Panama to Brazil. Similar: Urbanus miltas (G. & S.), Mexico, white band UNH reduced to a spot; crison (Godm. & Salv.), C. America, UPF band broad and compact.

32. *Sabina sabina* (Plotz). Brazil.

33. *Sacrator polites* (G. & S.). Colombia. Similar: Megaleas syrna (G. & S.), Costa Rica, smaller orange markings UPH.

34. *Salatis fulrius* (Plotz). Colombia, Peru.

35. *Saliana salius* (Cr.). Mexico to Argentina and Trinidad. Similar: chiomara (Hew.), Panama to Amazon, UN reddish brown with lighter marginal areas; Tisias lesueuri (Latr.), Brazil, UN lighter violet brown.

36. *Salatis salatis* (Cr.). Colombia, Brazil.

37. *Saliana placens* (Btlr.). Panama to Colombia. Similar: Damas polles (G. & S.), Nicaragua to Brazil, UN markings faint; several similar species with markings generally paler, UP always paler.

38. *Saliana triangularis* (Kaye). Trinidad.

39. *Saturnus tiberius* (Mschlr.). Mexico to Colombia, Guianas, Trinidad. Few similar species. Similar: Pompeius chittara (Schs.), Trinidad, no yellow UPF margin.

40. *Sarbia damippe* (Mab. & Boullet). Brazil. Similar: catomelaena (Mab.), Brazil, UP bands very narrow; pertyi (Plotz), Brazil, body yellowish; martii (Plotz), Brazil, diffuse, broader yellow markings UPH; xanthippe (Lat.), Brazil, yellow bands UP more broken.

PLATE 87: Hesperiidae

1. *Sarmientoia phaselis* (Hew.). Venezuela to Argentina. Similar: eriopis (Hew.), Amazons, male darker, UP markings smaller; female UPF band wide and complete.

2. *Serdis venezuelae* (Ww.). Venezuela.

3. *Serdis viridicans* (Fldr.). Colombia. Similar: tractifascia (Fldr.), Colombia, Venezuela.

4. *Serdis statius* (Plotz). Venezuela.

5. *Sophista aristoteles* (Dbl. & Hew.). Amazon.

6. *Sophista latifasciata* (Spitz). Brazil.

7. *Sostrata cronion* (Fldr.). Brazil.

8. *Sostrata grippa* (Evans). Ecuador.

9. *Sostrata lucullea* (Hew.). Brazil, Trinidad. Subspecies of festiva (Erichs.).

10. *Sostrata scintillans* (Mab.). Mexico to Brazil, Trinidad. Similar: leuchorrhoa (G. & S.), Panama to Colombia, UNH bluish white area; pusilla (G. & S.), Nicaragua, Panama, UP blacker, smaller.

11. *Spathilepia clonius* (Cr.). Mexico and S. America, Texas.

12. *Spioniades artemides* (Cr.). Panama to S. Brazil, Trinidad. Similar: abbreviatus (Mab.), Nicaragua, Bolivia, often larger, or with more white UNH; libethra (Hew.), Amazon, UNH blue-washed.

13. *Staphylus mazans* (Reak.). Mexico, Venezuela, Trinidad. Many scarcely separable species.

14. *Synapte lunata* (Plotz). Costa Rica to Brazil and Trinidad. Subspecies of silius (Latr.), Mexico to Brazil.

15. *Synapte syraces* (G. & S.). Mexico to Guatemala.

16. *Synole elana* (Plotz). Brazil.

17. *Synole hylaspes* (Stoll.). Brazil.

18. *Synapte malitiosa* (H.Sch.). C. America, West Indies, Texas. Some subspecies without yellow.

19. *Talides sergestus* (Cr.). Mexico to

Brazil, Trinidad. Similar: alternata (Bell), Panama, UP wings fringed bright orange.

20. *Tarsoctenus papias* (Hew.). Amazons. Female resembles corytus female, but markings ochre not red.

21. *Tarsoctenus corytus* (Cr.). Surinam to Colombia. Similar: guadialis (Hew.), Panama, male resembles papias male.

22. *Tarsoctenus plutia* (Hew.). Amazon.

23. *Tarsoctenus praecia* (Hew.). Brazil.

24. *Telemiades amphion* (Hbn.). Mexico to Brazil. Similar: logonus (Hew.), Brazil, UP markings smaller.

25. *Telemiades avitus* (Cr.). Guianas, Amazon. Similar: Ablepsis azines (Hew.), Amazon.

26. *Telemiades ceramina* (Plotz). Surinam. Similar: squanda (Evans), S. Brazil, only apical dots UPF; nicomedes (Mosch.), Colombia, UNH flushed with white.

27. *Telles arcalaus* (Stoll.). Panama, Amazon, Trinidad. UP as Xeniades pteras.

28. *Thargella fuliginosa* (G. & S.). Nicaragua, Guianas, Trinidad. UP blackish brown.

29. *Theagenes aegides* (H.Sch.). Mexico to Colombia. Subspecies of albiplaga (Fldr.). Similar: dichrous (Mab.), Argentina, no white patch UPH, yellow UPF much less.

30. *Thespieus dalman* (Latr.). Mexico to Colombia, Peru. Similar: ethemides (Burm.), Argentina.

31. *Thespieus himella* (Hew.). Brazil. Many similar species from Peru and Brazil.

32. *Thespieus macareus* (H.Sch.). Mexico to Venezuela. UN resembles othna. This is the 'standard' UP for genus Thespieus. There are many similar species.

33. *Thespieus opigena* (Hew.). Ecuador, Peru.

34. *Thespieus othna* (Btlr.). Mexico, Brazil. UP as macareus. Similar: tapayuna (Zikan), Colombia, smaller.

35. *Thoon modius* (Mab.). C. America.

36. *Thoon taxes* (Godm.). Panama. A few similar species.

37. *Thracides nanea* (Hew.). Trinidad.

38. *Thracides phidon* (Cr.). Panama to Brazil, Trinidad.

39. *Thracides phidon* (see 38).

40. *Timochares trifasciata* (Hew.). Mexico to Argentina.

41. *Timochreon satyrus* (Fldr.). Panama to S. Brazil.

42. *Tirynthia conflua* (H.Sch.). Nicaragua to Brazil.

43. *Tisias quadrata* (H.Sch.). Brazil.

44. *Tisias lesueur* (Latr.). Brazil. UN ground colour dark olive green.

45. *Tromba xanthura* (G. & S.). Honduras, Panama, Colombia.

46. *Typhedanus ampyx* (G. & S.). Venezuela, Mexico. Similar: Ocyba calathana (Hew.), C. and S. America, broader yellow tip to hindwing.

47. *Typhedanus undulatus* (Hew.). Mexico to Brazil.

48. *Typhedanus galbula* (Plotz). Brazil.

49. *Urbanus chalco* (Hbn.). S. America. Similar: dominicus (Plotz), smaller, narrower tail; brachius (Hbn.), Mexico to Brazil, short, broad tail, broader white patch; albicuspis (H.Sch.), Colombia, Brazil, broader white marking UN, tail more pointed.

50. *Typhedanus orion* (Cr.). C. America.

PLATE 88: Hesperiidae

1. *Turesis lucas* (F.). Panama to S. America, Antilles.

2. *Urbanus corydon* (Btlr.). Mexico to Brazil, Jamaica, Haiti.

3. *Urbanus dorantes* (Stoll.). California to Venezuela. Similar: galbula (Plotz), Brazil, UNF inner margin whitened; santiago (Luc.), Venezuela, Cuba, Grenada, smaller spots, UN much darker; cenis (H.Sch.), Colombia, shorter tails.

4. *Urbanus doryssus* (Swainson). S. & C. America.

5. *Urbanus proteus* (L.). U.S.A., C. America, S. America. Similar: metophis (Latr.), S. America, shorter broader tail; harpagus (Fldr.), Colombia, very large, markings white UPF.

6. *Urbanus simplicius* (Stoll.). Texas to C. and S. America.

7. *Udranomia kikkawai* (Weeks). Venezuela.

8. *Udranomia spitzi* (Hayw.). Matto Grosso.

9. *Wallengrenia drury* (Latr.). E. U.S.A. to Brazil. Subspecies of otho (Abbot and Smith) which is very variable, many subspecies. Similar: gemma (Plotz), Antilles, Dominica, UP mostly orange yellow; misera (Lucas), Bahamas, Honduras, UP very dark

10. *Wallengrenia ophites* (Mab.). Antilles. Subspecies of otho.

11. *Vacerra egla* (Hew.). Mexico, Nicaragua, Panama. Similar: litana (Hew.), Mexico to Amazon, base of wings ochreous; caniola (H.Sch.), Costa Rica, UPH spots less distinct.

12. *Vacerra hermesia* (Hew.). Peru.

13. *Vehilius clavicula* (Plotz). Brazil.

14. *Vehilius labdacus* (G. & S.). Mexico to Venezuela and Trinidad.

15. *Vehilius venosus* (Plotz). Mexico to Brazil and Trinidad. Similar: illudens (Mab.), Mexico to Colombia, no band of spots UPH. A few similar species.

16. *Vehilius vetula* (Mab.). Brazil.

17. *Vettius artona* (Hew.). Nicaragua to Brazil and Trinidad.

18. *Jemadia gnetus* (F.). Colombia, Guianas, Brazil. Many similar species, also similar: Myscelus pardalina (Fldr.), Colombia.

19. *Jemadia hospita* (Btlr.). Colombia to Brazil. Several forms. Similar: Granila paseas (Hew.), Brazil, hind wings toothed; hewitsoni (Mab.), Colombia, broader white band UPF.

20. *Jera tricuspidata* (Mab.). Ecuador.

21. *Vettius fantasos* (Cr.). Mexico to Brazil, Trinidad. Lfp: Grasses.

22. *Vettius coryna* (Hew.). Mexico to Bolivia.

23. *Vettius lafrenaye* (Latr.). Panama to Brazil. Similar: crispa (Evans), Amazon, larger white patch UPH.

24. *Vettius marcus* (F.). Panama to Brazil, Guianas, Trinidad. Similar: aurelius (Plotz), C. America, Venezuela, Brazil, UPH white area larger; diversus (H.Sch.), Nicaragua to Brazil, UNH veining less marked.

25. *Vettius marcus* (see 24).

26. *Vettius phyllus* (Cr.). Panama to Brazil and Trinidad.

27. *Vlasta extrusus* (Fldr.). Colombia. Similar: affinis (Mab. and Boullet), Guianas, smaller.

28. *Vinius arginote* (Draudt). Brazil, Amazon. Similar: nicomedes (Mab.), Brazil, much darker.

29. *Vinius tryhana* (Kaye). Trinidad.

30. *Virga cometho* (G. & S.). Mexico.

31. *Xeniades orchamus* (Cr.). Surinam.

32. *Zariaspes mythecus* (G. & S.). Mexico. Similar: Copaeodes simplex (Fldr.), Mexico, very small; mys (Hbn.), Mexico to Paraguay, much broader black borders UP.

33. *Xeniades pteras* (G. & S.). Panama, Colombia, Venezuela, Trinidad. Subspecies of chalestra (Hew.), Colombia, Brazil.

34. *Xenophanes tryxus* (Cr.). Argentina to Texas.

35. *Zera scybis* (G. & S.). Mexico to Bolivia. Similar: phila (G. & S.), Panama, no blue UNH; pelopea (G. & S.), Mexico to Amazon, UN brown, UP narrow dark band; erisichton (Plotz), Ecuador, Bolivia, one or two rows of black spots UNH, narrow dark band UP.

36. *Zopyrion satyrina* (Fldr.). Colombia. UP brown. Similar: sandace (G. & S.), UN markings less distinct, but brighter.

37. *Zenis minos* (Latr.). Mexico to Brazil and Trinidad. Similar: jebus (Plotz), Brazil.

38. *Zera hyacinthinus* (Mab.). C. America to Peru. Similar: menedemus (G. & S.), Panama, Trinidad, no light area UNF; Cabares paterculus (H.Sch.), Panama to S. America, greater light areas UNF.

Africa

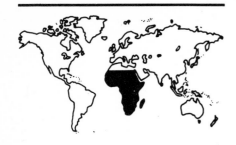

PLATE 89: Papilionidae

1. *Graphium agamedes* (Westw.). Ghana, N. Congo. Terrain: forest. Similar: adamastor (Bsd.), W. Africa.

2. *Graphium almansor* (Honr.). W. Africa, Congo, Uganda, Abyssinia, W. Kenya.

3. *Graphium antheus* (Cr.). W., C. and E. Africa south to Natal. Similar: porthaon (Hew.), E. Africa to Natal; junodi (Trim.), E. Africa, markings creamy.

4. *Graphium auriger* (Btlr.). W. Africa, Gabon. Similar: ucalegon (Hew.), Congo, Uganda; fulleri (Smith), Cameroons; ucalegonides (Stdgr.), W. Africa, Congo; simoni (Aur.), Cameroons, Congo.

5. *Graphium hachei* (Dew.). Cameroons, Angola, Congo. Similar: mobii (Suff.). UPH broader black band.

6. *Graphium colonna* (Ward.). E. Africa south to Natal.

7. *Graphium endochus* (Bsd.). Madagascar.

8. *Graphium cyrnus* (Bsd.). Madagascar.

9. *Graphium evombar* (Bsd.). Madagascar.

10. *Graphium auriger* (Btlr.). Congo. Similar: odin (Strand.), Congo, smaller, white markings clear cut.

11. *Graphium illyris* (Hew.). W. Africa, Congo. Terrain: forest.

12. *Graphium kirbyi* (Hew.). Kenya, Tanzania.

13. *Graphium latreillianus* (Godt.). W. Africa, Congo.

14. *Graphium leonidas* (F.). W., C., E. and S. Africa.

15. *Graphium levassori* (Oberth.). Comoro Islands.

16. *Graphium philonoe* (Ward.). E. Africa. Lfp: Anona.

17. *Graphium policenes* (Cr.). W. Africa, C. and E. Africa south to Natal. Similar: Papilio polistratus (Smith), E. Africa to Natal; nigrescens (Eimer), Cameroons, Congo.

18. *Graphium pylades* (F.). W., C., E. and S. Africa. Similar: morania (Angas.), Rhodesia to S. Africa.

19. *Graphium ridleyanus* (White). W. Africa, Congo to Uganda.

20. *Graphium tynderaeus* (F.). W. Africa, Congo. There is a variety with orange markings.

21. *Papilio antimachus* (*Drury*). *W. Africa, Congo.*

22. *Papilio constantinus* (Ward.). Natal to Abyssinia. Low flying. Similar: euphranor (Trim.), S. Africa, high flying.

23. *Papilio antenor* (Drury). Madagascar.

24. *Papilio charopus* (Westw.). W. Africa to Congo. Similar: hornimani (Dist.), narrower bands; oribazus (Bsd.), narrow bands, smaller, brighter.

25. *Papilio cynorta* (F.). W. Africa, C. Africa to W. Kenya, Ethiopia. Several forms, mimics Bernatistes. Similar: plagiatus (Auriv.) Nigeria, N. Congo.

26. *Papilio bromius* (Dbl.). Similar: nireus (L.); sosia (R. & J.); brontes (Godm.)

PLATE 90: Papilionidae

1. *Papilio dardanus* (Brown). Female form trophonissa (Auriv.). (See 2 also.)

2. *Papilio dardanus* (Brown). E., W., C. and S. Africa. Lfp: citrus, etc. Many subspecies. Many female forms. Female antinorii (Oberth.) resembles male.

3. *Papilio dardanus* (Brown). Female form hippocoon (F.). (See 2 also.)

4. *Papilio delalande* (Godt.). Madagascar. Similar: mangoura (Hew.), Madagascar.

5. *Papilio demodocus* (Esp.). W., C., E. and S. Africa, Mauritius. Lfp: Calodendron, Teclea, citrus. Similar: erithonioides (Smith), Madagascar.

6. *Papilio echerioides* (Trim.). E., W., C. and S. Africa. Similar: jacksoni (E. Sh.), Kenya, Uganda, E. Congo, highland forest, whiter; fulleborni (Karsch), Tanzania, Malawi, smaller white spots; sjostedti (Auriv.), Tanzania, very narrow white bands; zoroastres (Druce), C. and E. Africa, spots UPF more separate.

7. *Papilio echerioides* (see 6).

8. *Papilio epiphorbas* (Bsd.). Madagascar.

9. *Papilio gallienus* (Dist.). S. Nigeria to Congo.

10. *Papilio hesperus* (Westw.). W. Africa, Congo, Uganda, Zambia. Terrain: forest. Similar: pelodorus (Btlr.), Tanzania, Malawi, complete row of yellow spots UPH.

11. *Papilio hornimani* (Dist.). Kenya, Tanzania. Terrain: highland forest. Similar: charopus (Westw.), W. Africa to Congo; oribazus (Bsd.), Madagascar.

12. *Papilio jacksoni* (E. Sh.). Similar: Female forms resemble this type: echerioides (Trim.), large orange patch UPH, larger violet markings UPF; fulleborni (Karsch), no submarginal dots UPH; sjostedti (Auriv.), one submarginal dot UPH; zoroastres (Druce), smaller orange patch UPH; homeyeri (Plotz), subspecies of zoroastres.

13. *Papilio lormieri* (Dist.). Nigeria, Congo, Uganda to W. Kenya.

14. *Papilio phorcas* (Cr.). Kenya, Uganda, Congo. Several subspecies. Female brown with yellow-green band.

15. *Papilio mackinnoni* (E. Sh.) E. Africa. Terrain: highland forest.

16. *Papilio mnestheus* (Drury). W. Africa.

17. *Papilio nireus* (L.). W., C., E. and S. Africa. Several subspecies. Similar: sosia (R. & J.), Sierra Leone to Uganda, broader band, spots on UPF margin ; bromius (Dbl.), W. Africa, Congo to Kenya, even broader band.

18. *Papilio nobilis* (Rog.). Kenya, Uganda, Tanzania, S. Sudan. Terrain : highland forest. Female with brown dots UP margins.

19. *Papilio ophidicephalus* (Oberth.). Kenya, E. Africa to S. Africa. Lfp : citrus.

20. *Papilio mechowianus* (Dew.). W. Africa to Congo. Similar : andronicus (Ward), Cameroons, very wide white bands UP.

PLATE 91 : Papilionidae

1. *Papilio rex* (Oberth.). Ethiopia, E. Africa, Cameroons, E. Congo. Lfp : Calodendron. Similar : mimeticus (Rothsch.).

2. *Papilio zalmoxis* (Hew.). W. Africa and Congo. Form rippon has brown UP.

3. *Papilio zenobia* (F.). W. Africa, Congo, south to Angola. Forest species.

PLATE 92 : Nymphalidae

1. *Antanartia abyssinica* (Fldr.). Kenya, Abyssinia.

2. *Antanartia delius* (Drury). Sierra Leone to Congo.

3. *Antanartia hippomene* (Hbn.). E. Africa, Cameroons.

4. *Antanartia schaeneia* (Trim.). E. Africa.

5. *Apaturopsis cleocharis* (Hew.). Angola, Congo, Uganda, Rhodesia. Similar : kilusa (Smith), Madagascar, much paler brown UP ; ionia (Everson.), much less black UP.

6. *Ariadne enotrea* (Cr.). Sierra Leone to Angola.

7. *Ariadne pagenstecheri* (Suff.). Cameroons to E. Africa. Similar : actisanes (Hew.), Cameroons, Congo, larger.

8. *Asterope amulia* (Cr.). Sierra Leone to Angola.

9. *Asterope benguelae* (Chapm.). Congo.

10. *Asterope boisduvali* (Wall.). Sierra Leone to E. Africa and south to Natal, north to Abyssinia.

11. *Asterope madagascariensis* (Bsd.). Madagascar.

12. *Asterope morantii* (Trim.). Natal. Female UP as natalensis female UP.

13. *Asterope natalensis* (Bsd.). Transvaal to Natal.

14. *Asterope natalensis* (see 13).

15. *Asterope occidentalium* (Mab.). Sierra Leone to Abyssinia, Angola.

16. *Asterope pechueli* (Dew.). Congo to Zambia. Similar : Crenidomimas concordia (Hopff.), E. Africa.

17. *Asterope trimeni* (Auriv.). Congo, Angola, E. Africa to Cape. Female UP as natalensis female UP.

18. *Aterica galene* (Brown). W., C. and E. Africa to Abyssinia. Form theophane (Hopff.), E. Africa, resembles rabena.

19. *Aterica rabena* (Bsd.). Madagascar.

20. *Bebearia absolon* (F.). Cameroons, Congo. Similar : zonana (Btlr.), Ghana to Congo ; mandinga (Fldr.), Senegal to Congo ; oxione (Hew.), Nigeria to Angola.

21. *Bebearia arcadius* (F.). Sierra Leone to Ghana.

22. *Bebearia barombina* (Stgr.). Cameroons.

23. *Bebearia comus* (Ward.). Cameroons to Congo. Female larger, white tip UPF. Similar : cinaethon (Hew.), Gaboon.

PLATE 93 : Nymphalidae

1. *Bebearia carshena* (Hew.). Ghana to Congo and Uganda.

2. *Bebearia cutteri* (Hew.). Liberia to Cameroons. Several forms.

3. *Bebearia cutteri* (see 2).

4. *Bebearia iturina* (Karsch.). Congo. Similar : chriemhilda (Stgr.), Uganda ; congolensis (Caproun.), Congo to Uganda, brighter red-brown.

5. *Bebearia demetra* (Godt.). Sierra Leone to Cameroons.

6. *Bebearia elphinice* (Hew.). Gaboon.

7. *Bebearia laetitia* (Plotz). Sierra Leone to Gaboon.

8. *Bebearia tentyris* (Hew.). Sierra Leone to Congo.

9. *Bebearia laetitia* (see 7).

10. *Bebearia mardania* (F.). Ghana to Congo and Uganda. Similar : plistonax (Hew.), Lagos to Angola.

11. *Bebearia mardania* (see 10).

12. *Bebearia nivaria* (Ward.). Cameroons, Congo. Similar : flaminia (Stgr.), white tip to UPF.

13. *Bebearia octogramma* (Gr.Sm.). Cameroons.

14. *Bebearia sophus* (F.). Sierra Leone to Angola. A few forms.

15. *Bebearia partita* (Auriv.). Cameroons, Congo.

16. *Bebearia phantasia* (Hew.). Nigeria to Congo.

17. *Bebearia phranza* (Hew.). Congo, Nigeria.

18. *Bebearia phantasia* (see 16).

19. *Bebearia senegalensis* (H.Sch.). W. Africa to Mozambique and Kenya.

20. *Bebearia staudingeri* (Auriv.). Cameroons, Gaboon.

PLATE 94 : Nymphalidae

1. *Bebearia theognis* (Hew.). Ghana. Similar : cocalia (F.), Cameroons to Congo.

2. *Byblia acheloia* (Wallengr.). Throughout Africa. Several forms.

3. *Catacroptera cloanthe* (Cr.). S. and E. Africa, Abyssinia.

4. *Catuna crithea* (Drury). Sierra Leone to Uganda.

5. *Charaxes acraeoides* (Druce). Cameroons.

6. *Charaxes ameliae* (Doumet). W. Africa to Nyasaland.

7. *Charaxes achaemenes* (Fldr.). S., C. and E. Africa to Abyssinia. UN as etisippe (Godt.), female as saturnus male. (See 6/3.)

8. *Charaxes anticlea* (Drury). Sierra Leone to Uganda. Male UP similar to protoclea, but much smaller, UPH spots silver centred.

9. *Catuna sikorana* (Rogenh.). E. Africa.

10. *Charaxes bebra* (Roths.). Nigeria to Tanzania.

11. *Charaxes baumanni* (Rghfr.). Kenya, Nyassa.

12. *Charaxes analava* (Ward.). Madagascar. UP yellow, dark margins yellow dotted.

13. *Charaxes ameliae* (see 6).

14. *Charaxes boueti* (Feisth.). Gambia to Mombasa. Few subspecies. Female yellower, lighter UP. Similar : cynthia (Btlr.).

15. *Charaxes bohemanni* (see 16).

16. *Charaxes bohemanni* (Fldr.). S. W. Africa to Congo.

17. *Charaxes brutus* (Cr.). Sierra Leone, Nigeria. Similar : angustus (Rothsch.) ; ansorgei (Rothsch.), Kenya.

PLATE 95 : Nymphalidae

1. *Charaxes candiope* (Godt.). Sierra Leone to Abyssinia and Natal. Similar : antambonlon (Luc.), Madagascar ; cowani (Btlr.), Madagascar.

2. *Charaxes castor* (Cr.). W., C. and E. Africa.

3. *Charaxes castor* (see 2).

4. *Charaxes cithaeron* (Fldr.). Natal to Kenya. Similar : violetta (Smith), Delagoa Bay to Mombasa.

5. *Charaxes cithaeron* (see 4).

6. *Charaxes etesippe* (see 9).

7. *Charaxes doubledayi* (Auriv.). Sierra Leone to Congo. Similar : mycerina (Godt.).

8. *Charaxes druceanus* (Btlr.). Congo, E. Africa, Zambia to Transvaal.

9. *Charaxes etesippe* (Godt.). Sierra Leone to E. Africa. Few subspecies.

10. *Charaxes cynthia* (Btlr.). W. Africa. Male UP resembles lucretius (Cr.).

11. *Charaxes ethalion* (Bsd.). Kenya, Uganda. Male as etheocles.

12. *Charaxes etheocles* (Cr.). W., C. and E. Africa to Transvaal. Many forms and subspecies. Very variable.

PLATE 96: Nymphalidae

1. *Charaxes etheocles* (see 95/12).

2. *Charaxes eudoxus* (Drury). Congo.

3. *Charaxes protoclea* (Feisth.). Senegambia, C. Africa, E. Africa. Few subspecies.

4. *Charaxes eupale* (Drury). Sierra Leone to Nyasaland.

5. *Charaxes guderiana* (Dew.). Angola to Kenya. Female resembles saturnus male. (See 97/3 also.)

6. *Charaxes protoclea* (see 3).

7. *Charaxes hadrianus* (Ward.). Nigeria, Congo.

8. *Charaxes hildebrandti* (Dew.). Ghana, W. Africa.

9. *Charaxes jahlusa* (Trim.). S. Africa to Transvaal and Nyasaland. Similar: kenyensis (J. & T.), darker, UPF tips more broadly darkened.

10. *Charaxes kahldeni* (Hom. & Dew.). Cameroons to Angola. Has a form with brown markings UP.

11. *Charaxes laodice* (Drury). Ghana to Angola.

12. *Charaxes lichas* (Dbl.). Sierra Leone, Congo. Similar: bebra (Rothsch.), Cameroons to Tanganyika, black tip UPF much smaller.

13. *Charaxes lucretius* (Cr.). W. Africa. Terrain: forest.

14. *Charaxes lucretius* (see 13).

15. *Charaxes nichetes* (Smith). Cameroons to Angola, Nyasaland.

16. *Charaxes numenes* (Hew.). Sierra Leone to Uganda. Similar: tiridates (Cr.).

17. *Charaxes nobilis* (Druce). Nigeria, Congo. Similar: superbus (Arn. Schultze).

PLATE 97: Nymphalidae

1. *Charaxes numenes* (see 96/16).

2. *Charaxes paphianus* (Ward.). Sierra Leone to Angola. Similar: jahlusa (Trim.).

3. *Charaxes pelias* (Cr.). Cape Province, S. Africa. Similar: saturnus (Btlr.), W., C. and E. Africa, and other subspecies.

4. *Charaxes pollux* (Cr.). W., C. and E. Africa. Similar: phoebus (Btlr.), Abyssinia.

5. *Charaxes smaragdalis* (Btlr.). W. Africa. UN as bohemanni (Fldr.).

6. *Charaxes tiridates* (Cr.). Sierra Leone to Uganda. Similar: bipunctatus (Rothsch.), W. Africa; numenes female similar to tiridates female.

7. *Charaxes tiridates* (see 6).

8. *Charaxes violetta* (Gr.Sm.). Africa.

9. *Charaxes violetta* (see 8).

10. *Charaxes xiphares* (Cr.). S. Africa to Natal. Similar: nandina (Rothsch.), Kenya.

11. *Charaxes xiphares* (see 10).

12. *Charaxes zelica* (Btlr.). Nigeria, Cameroons, Angola.

13. *Charaxes zingha* (Stoll.). Sierra Leone to Congo.

14. *Charaxes zoolina* (Westw.). S. and E. Africa to Abyssinia. Form neanthes (Hew.) is ochre brown.

15. *Charaxes zoolina* (see 14).

16. *Charaxes zingha* (see 13).

PLATE 98: Nymphalidae

1. *Cirrochroa niasica* (Honrath). Nias, Kalim Bungo.

2. *Cymothoe alcimeda* (Godt.). S. Africa to Transvaal and Natal, Rhodesia.

3. *Cymothoe anitorgis* (Hew.). Nigeria, Cameroons. Male UP as coccinata. Similar: angulifascia (Auriv.).

4. *Cymothoe anitorgis* (see 3).

5. *Cymothoe beckeri* (H.Sch.). Nigeria to Congo.

6. *Cymothoe beckeri* (see 5).

7. *Cymothoe caenis* (Drury). Sierra Leone, Congo to Uganda. Several female forms. Similar: coranus (Smith), E. Africa to Natal.

8. *Cymothoe caenis* (see 7).

9. *Cymothoe capella* (see 11).

10. *Cymothoe cloetensi* (Seeldr.). Congo. Female resembles lucasi female; male lucasi has dark markings UPH.

11. *Cymothoe capella* (Ward.). Cameroons, Congo.

12. *Cymothoe coccinata* (Hew.). Nigeria, Congo to Uganda.

13. *Cymothoe coccinata* (see 12).

14. *Cymothoe elabontas* (Hew.). Ghana to Congo.

15. *Cymothoe confusa* (Auriv.). Nigeria, Congo to Uganda. Male resembles egesta male.

16. *Cymothoe egesta* (Cr.). W. Africa.

17. *Cymothoe fumosa* (Stgr.). Congo. Similar: haynae (Dew.), Congo. Female resembles hesiodotus female but narrower white band UPF.

PLATE 99: Nymphalidae

1. *Cymothoe fumana* (Westw.). W. Africa. Male resembles hypatha male but wings undulate.

2. *Cymothoe hesiodotus* (Stgr.). Africa.

3. *Cymothoe jodutta* (Westw.). Congo.

4. *Cymothoe hyarbita* (see 6).

5. *Cymothoe hypatha* (Hew.). Ghana to Cameroons. Female resembles fumana female.

6. *Cymothoe hyarbita* (Hew.). Nigeria, Cameroons. Similar: reinholdi (Plotz), male darker margins UP, female narrower white band UPF.

7. *Cymothoe jodutta* (see 3).

8. *Cymothoe lucasi* (Doumet). Nigeria to Gaboon.

9. *Cymothoe lurida* (Btlr.). Ghana to Angola. Female resembles hesiodotus female.

10. *Cymothoe lucasi* (see 8).

11. *Cymothoe theobene* (Dbl. & Hew.) Nigeria, Angola and Uganda.

12. *Cymothoe oemilius* (Doumet). Nigeria to Gaboon.

13. *Cymothoe pluto* (Ward.). Cameroons, Congo. Similar: kinugnana (Smith). E. Africa.

14. *Cymothoe preussi* (Stgr.). Cameroons, Nigeria.

15. *Cymothoe preussi* (see 14).

16. *Cymothoe melanjae* (B.B.). E. Africa, Nyasaland. Female resembles weymeri.

PLATE 100: Nymphalidae

1. *Cymothoe theobene* (see 99/11).

2. *Cymothoe weymeri* (Suff.). Nigeria, Cameroons. Similar: herminia (Smith), narrower, lighter brown marking UP.

3. *Cynandra opis* (Dr.). Sierra Leone to Uganda.

4. *Cyrestis camillus* (F.). Sierra Leone to Abyssinia. Similar: elegans (Bsd.), Madagascar.

5. *Euphaedra aureola* (Kirby). Nigeria, Cameroons.

6. *Euphaedra ceres* (F.). Sierra Leone, Nigeria, Cameroons. Several subspecies, some with white bands.

7. *Euphaedra cyparissa* (Cr.). Sierra Leone to Congo. Similar: themis (Hbn.), UP golden brown.

8. *Euphaedra edwardsi* (Hoeven.). Ghana to Congo.

9. *Euphaedra eleus* (Drury). Sierra Leone through Congo to Uganda, Angola. Several subspecies, often with spots in UPF cell. Similar: zampa female (Westw.).

10. *Euphaedra francina* (Godt.). Sierra Leone.

11. *Euphaedra eupalus* (F.). Sierra Leone, W. Africa. Similar UP : harpalyce (Cr.).

12. *Euphaedra eusemoides* (Sm. & Kirby). Congo. Similar : zaddachi (Dew.), Cameroons, Congo to E. Africa.

13. *Euphaedra gausape* (Btlr.). Ghana, Sierra Leone to Congo.

14. *Euphaedra harpalyce* (Cr.). Sierra Leone to Cameroons. Similar : eupalus (F.).

15. *Euphaedra imperialis* (Lindemans). Nigeria, Cameroons. Similar : luperca (Hew.).

PLATE 101 : Nymphalidae

1. *Euphaedra inanum* (Btlr.). Sierra Leone to Angola.

2. *Euphaedra judith* (Weymer). W. Africa.

3. *Euphaedra medon* (L.). Sierra Leone to Angola and Congo. Variable shades of colouring.

4. *Euphaedra medon* (see 3).

5. *Euphaedra neophron* (Hpff.). E. Africa south to Natal. Similar : ellenbecki (Pag.). Abyssinia.

6. *Euphaedra perseis* (Drury). Sierra Leone, Liberia. Similar : elephantina (Stgr.), slightly redder UP.

7. *Euphaedra preussi* (Stgr.). Cameroons to Uganda.

8. *Euphaedra sarita* (Sharpe). Congo, Abyssinia.

9. *Euphaedra spatiosa* (Mab.). Cameroons, Nigeria through Congo to Uganda. Similar : losinga (Hew.), white band UNH ; wardi (Druce), Nigeria, Cameroons.

10. *Euphaedra themis* (Hbn.). Sierra Leone to Congo, Angola. Very variable.

11. *Euphaedra xypete* (Hew.). Sierra Leone to Angola. Several subspecies.

12. *Euphaedra xypete* (see 11).

13. *Euphaedra zampa* (Westw,). Sierra Leone. Similar : eleus male (Drury), red patch UPH more extensive and diffuse.

14. *Euryphene abasa* (Hew.). Nigeria, Cameroons, Congo.

15. *Euryphene amaranta* (Karsch.). Cameroons, Uganda. Female UP resembles gambiae female UP.

PLATE 102 : Nymphalidae

1. *Euryphene ampedusa* (see 2).

2. *Euryphene ampedusa* (Hew.). Ghana to Nigeria.

3. *Euryphene aridatha* (Hew.). Nigeria, Cameroons. Male resembles abasa male.

4. *Euryphene atossa* (Hew.). Nigeria, Congo.

5. *Euryphene atrovirens* (Mab.). Cameroons, Gaboon. Male resembles abasa male but purple suffusion thicker. Similar : atropurpurea (Auriv.).

6. *Euryphene camarensis* (Ward.). Cameroons, Congo. Female resembles goniogramma female but UPF more heavily marked.

7. *Euryphene doriclea* (Drury). Sierra Leone to Congo.

8. *Euryphene duseni* (Auriv.). Cameroons.

9. *Euryphene gambiae* (Feisth.). Senegal to Congo.

10. *Euryphene goniogramma* (Karsch.). Cameroons, Congo.

11. *Euryphene goniogramma* (see 10).

12. *Euryphene karschi* (Auriv.). Cameroons. Female resembles iris female.

13. *Euryphene grosesmithi* (Stgr.). Cameroons. Female resembles aridatha female. Similar : pavo (Howarth), purple suffusion male UPF sharply defined.

14. *Euryphene iris* (Auriv.). Congo.

15. *Euryphene lysandra* (Stoll.). Congo, Cameroons. Similar : melanops (Auriv.), Congo, larger black dot UNH.

16. *Euryphene mawamba* (Baker). Congo.

17. *Euryphene milnei* (Hew.). Liberia to Cameroons. Female resembles iris female.

18. *Euryphene saphirina* (Karsch.). Congo.

19. *Euryphene simplex* (Stgr.). Sierra Leone. Similar : feronia (Stgr.), Sierra Leone, UPF bar white ; veronica (Cr.), Sierra Leone, Ghana ; barombina (Auriv.), Cameroons ; tadema (Hew.), Nigeria, Cameroons Gaboon.

20. *Euryphura achlys* (Hopff.). E. Africa. Similar : chalcis (Fldr.), W. Africa ; isuka (Stoneham), Uganda, brown, not greenish.

21. *Euryphura albula* (Suffert). Sierra Leone.

22. *Euryphura isuka* (Stoneham). Uganda. Male has no white UP.

23. *Euryphura nobilis* (Stgr.). Sierra Leone.

PLATE 103 : Nymphalidae

1. *Euryphura plantilla* (Hew.). Nigeria to Congo and Uganda. Female resembles albula female but no grey-blue gloss UP.

2. *Euryphura porphyrion* (Ward.). Ghana to Cameroons.

3. *Eurytela alinda* (Mab.). Cameroons. Similar : narinda (Ward.), UP markings orange, UN browner, females of both paler markings.

4. *Eurytela dryope* (Cr.). Sierra Leone to Congo.

5. *Euxanthe wakefieldi* (Ward.). E. Africa. Female resembles female eurinome, but white band UPF less broken up. Similar :

madagascariensis (Luc.), Madagascar ; eurinome (Cr.), Nigeria, Cameroons, blue band UPF more broken and macular.

6. *Euxanthe eurinome* (Cr.). Nigeria, Cameroons.

7. *Euxanthe trajanus* (Ward.). W. Africa. Similar : tiberius (Smith), Tanzania.

8. *Eurytela hiarbas* (Drury). Sierra Leone to E. Africa and south to Cape, north to Abyssinia. Several local subspecies, female lighter.

9. *Euxanthe eurinome* (Cr.). Nigeria, Cameroons.

10. *Hadrodontes varanes* (Cr.). S. Africa to Natal. Similar : fulvescens (Auriv.).

11. *Hamanumida daedalus* (F.). Africa south of Sahara.

12. *Hypolimnas antevorta* (Dist.). Tanzania. Female very large, UPH white, orange margin and zig-zag dark edging resembles dexithea.

13. *Harmilla elegans* (Auriv.). Cameroons.

14. *Hypolimnas dexithea* (Hew.). Madagascar.

15. *Hypolimnas deceptor* (Trim.). Kenya south to Natal.

PLATE 104 : Nymphalidae

1. *Hypolimnas dinarcha* (Hew.). Sierra Leone to Uganda.

2. *Hypolimnas dubia* (Pal.). W., C., E. and S. Africa. Many subspecies.

3. *Crenidomimas concordia* (Hopff.). Angola to E. Africa.

4. *Hypolimnas mechowi* (Dew.). Congo. UP resembles dinarcha.

5. *Hypolimnas salmacis* (Drury). Sierra Leone to Uganda. Female markings UP are whitish. Several local subspecies.

6. *Issoria excelsior* (Btlr.). Cameroons, Tanzania. Terrain : montane.

7. *Issoria hanningtoni* (Elwes). E. Africa. Terrain : montane. Similar : baumanni (Reb. & Rog.), Uganda, much brighter UP.

8. *Hypolimnas usambara* (Ward.). E. Africa.

9. *Lachnoptera ayresii* (Trim.). Cape to Rhodesia.

10. *Kallima rumia* (see 14).

11. *Kallima ansorgei* (Rothsch.). Cameroons to Uganda.

12. *Kallima cymodice* (Cram.). Congo. Male lacks orange band UPF.

13. *Kallima jacksoni* (E. Sharpe). Congo.

14. *Kallima rumia* (Dbl. & Westw.). Nigeria, Congo.

15. *Issoria smaragdifera* (Btlr.). Nyasaland, Rhodesia. Terrain : montane.

16. *Lachnoptera iole* (F.). Sierra Leone

17. *Neptidopsis ophione* (Cr.). Sierra Leone

to E. Africa and Abyssinia. Similar: velleda (Mab.).

18. *Neptidopsis platyptera* (Rothsch. & Jord.). E. Africa.

PLATE 105: Nymphalidae

1. *Neptis agatha* (Stoll.). Sierra Leone to E. Africa, Abyssinia, south to Natal. Variable.

2. *Neptis exalenca* (Karsch.). Cameroons, Congo. UP white band and spots. Similar: ochracea (Neave), Uganda, UP yellow band and spots.

3. *Neptis frobenia* (F.). Mauritius. Similar: mayottensis (Oberth.), Mayotte Islands; comorarum (Oberth.), Grand Comoro Island.

4. *Neptis incongrua* (Btlr.). Uganda, Nyasaland.

5. *Neptis melicerta* (Drury). Sierra Leone to Abyssinia, Angola. Similar: lermanni (Auriv.), Congo, larger.

6. *Neptis jamesoni* (Godm.). Cameroons, Congo. Similar: nebrodes (Hew.), Angola, markings UPF shorter.

7. *Neptis metalla* (Dbl. & Hew.). Sierra Leone, Congo, Madagascar.

8. *Neptis nemetes* (Hew.). Sierra Leone to Uganda, Angola.

9. *Neptis nicomedes* (Hew.). Ghana to Uganda. Similar: strigata (Auriv.).

10. *Neptis nicoteles* (Hew.). Ghana to Angola.

11. *Neptis paula* (Stgr.). Sierra Leone. Similar: trigonophora (Btlr.), E. Africa.

12. *Neptis saclava* (Bsd.). Nigeria to Abyssinia, south to Cape, Madagascar. Similar: pasteuri (Snellen), E. Africa, browner UP and UPF band narrower.

13. *Neptis seeldrayersi* (Auriv.). Nigeria, Congo. Similar: nysiades (Hew.).

14. *Palla decius* (Cr.). Sierra Leone to Angola. Similar: ussheri (Btlr.), Sierra Leone, Congo to Uganda; publius (Stgr.), UN darker, more marginal lunules, UPH white band very short.

15. *Phalanta columbina* (Cr.). Sierra Leone to Kenya, south to Natal. UP resembles phalantha, but fewer spots and brighter colour.

16. *Precis clelia* (Cr.). Throughout Africa. Many local subspecies.

17. *Precis hadrope* (Dbl. & Hew.). Ghana. Male golden yellow UP.

18. *Precis andremiaja* (Bsd.). Madagascar. Dry season form.

19. *Precis infracta* (Rog.). E. Africa.

20. *Precis andremiaja* (Bsd.). Madagascar. Wet season form.

21. *Precis antilope* (Feisth.). Congo to E. Africa, Natal to Abyssinia, Senegal. Distinct wet and dry season forms; UPH wet season form no tail, no hook to wing tip UPF.

22. *Precis archesia* (Cr.). S. Africa to Angola, E. Africa. Dry season form; very variable seasonally; UP resembles ceryne.

23. *Precis artaxia* (Hew.). Angola to E. Africa.

24. *Precis ceryne* (Bsd.). Angola to Natal and north to Abyssinia. Wet season form; dry season form is darker.

25. *Precis chorimene* (Guer.). Senegal to Congo and Abyssinia.

26. *Precis coelestina* (Dew.). Cameroons to Uganda and Somaliland. UP resembles villida.

27. *Precis eurodoce* (Westw.). Madagascar.

28. *Precis limnoria* (Klug.). E. Africa to Somaliland, Abyssinia and Arabia. Few local subspecies.

29. *Precis octavia* (Cr.). Sierra Leone to Congo, Abyssinia and Somaliland. Dry season form. Similar: natalica (Fldr.), Natal.

30. *Precis octavia* (see 29). Wet season form.

PLATE 106: Nymphalidae

1. *Precis pelarga* (F.). Senegal to Angola, Abyssinia. Wet season form.

2. *Precis pelarga* (see 1). Dry season form.

3. *Precis rhadama* (Bsd.). Mozambique, Madagascar, Mauritius.

4. *Precis sinuata* (Plotz). Sierra Leone to Uganda. Similar: milonia (Fldr.), Cameroons to Congo, larger; tugela (Trim.), Tanganyika.

5. *Precis sophia* (F.). Senegal to Congo and Uganda, south to Natal.

6. *Precis westermanni* (see 21).

7. *Pseudacraea boisduvali* (Dbl.). Sierra Leone to Congo, E. Africa to Natal. Female colourless; variable.

8. *Pseudacraea clarki* (Btlr.). Cameroons, Congo.

9. *Precis terea* (Drury). Sierra Leone to Uganda, Somaliland, Angola.

10. *Pseudacraea dolomena* (Hew.). Sierra Leone to Congo to Uganda, Angola. Several subspecies.

11. *Pseudacraea eurytus* (L.). Sierra Leone through Congo to Uganda, south to Natal. Male UP reddish brown, resembles striata.

12. *Pseudacraea glaucina* (Guer.). Madagascar.

13. *Precis tareta* (Rghfr.). Kenya. UN resembles limnoria UN.

14. *Pseudacraea imitator* (Trim.). S. Africa.

15. *Pseudacraea kuenowi* (Dew.). Congo,

Uganda. Similar: gottbergi (Dewitz), no white UPH.

16. *Pseudacraea lucretia* (see 17).

17. *Pseudacraea lucretia* (Cr.). Sierra Leone to E. Africa, Angola, Somaliland to Madagascar. Many local subspecies.

18. *Pseudacraea poggei* (Dew.). Angola, Congo, Rhodesia. Mimics Danaus chrysippus.

19. *Pseudacraea simulator* (Btlr.). Sierra Leone, Ghana.

20. *Pseudacraea semire* (Cr.). Sierra Leone to Angola.

21. *Precis westermanni* (Westw.). Ghana to Angola.

22. *Precis tugela* (Trim.). Nyasaland, south to Natal. Very variable.

23. *Pseudacraea striata* (Btlr.). Sierra Leone to Angola. Similar: ruhama (Hew.), Ghana to Angola, UPF orange median band; gottbergi (Dew.), Cameroons, Congo, no black spots.

PLATE 107: Nymphalidae

1. *Pseudacraea warburgi* (Auriv.). Cameroons, Congo.

2. *Pseudargynnis hegemone* (Godt.). Cameroons to Uganda, south to Rhodesia.

3. *Pseudoneptis coenobita* (F.). Sierra Leone to Uganda.

4. *Salamis anacardi* (L.). Sierra Leone to E. Africa, Natal to Abyssinia. Several subspecies.

5. *Salamis anteva* (Ward). Madagascar.

6. *Salamis cacta* (F.). Sierra Leone through Congo to Abyssinia. Similar: amaniensis (Vosseler), Rhodesia, Tanzania.

7. *Vanessula milca* (Hew.). Nigeria, Cameroons, Congo to Uganda.

8. *Precis natalica* (Feld.). E. Africa.

9. *Salamis parhassus* (Drury). Sierra Leone to Cape, Abyssinia.

10. *Salamis temora* (Fldr.). Nigeria to E. Africa and Abyssinia.

11. *Salamis cytora* (Dbl. & Hew.). Sierra Leone.

12. *Mesoxantha ethosea* (Drury). Sierra Leone to Angola.

13. *Palla decius* (Cramer). W. Africa.

14. *Charaxes monteiri* (Stgr.). Island of St. Thome. Male resembles smaragdalis.

15. *Charaxes thomasius* (Stgr.). Island of St. Thome. UP deep orange brown, dark termens.

PLATE 108: Acraeidae

1. *Acraea acerata* (Hew.). Ghana to E.

Africa and Abyssinia. Several races.

2. *Acraea acrita* (Hew.). 'Fiery Acraea'. Angola to Kenya. Very variable, many forms and subspecies.

3. *Acraea admatha* (Hew.). Sierra Leone to Kenya, south to Natal. Female form boopis (Wichgr.) has pale buff UP., Similar: lia (Mat.), Madagascar, small.

4. *Acraea aglaonice* (Westw.). Natal, Transvaal. There is also a whiter female form. Similar: rhodesiana (Wichgr.), Rhodesia.

5. *Acraea alciope* (Hew.). Ghana to Congo and Uganda. Several subspecies.

6. *Acraea alciope* (see 5).

7. *Acraea alicia* (E. Sharpe). Cameroons to E. Africa.

8. *Acraea althoffi* (Dew.). Cameroons to Congo and Uganda, Ghana and Nigeria. Several forms.

9. *Acraea althoffi* (see 8).

10. *Acraea amicitiae* (Heron). Uganda.

11. *Acraea anacreon* (Trim.). S. Africa, Angola to Rhodesia and E. Africa to Kenya. Female much paler.

12. *Acraea anemosa* (Hew.). E. Africa. Similar: welwitschi (Rogenh.), Damaraland, white patch UPH.

13. *Acraea asboloplintha* (Karsh.). Uganda, Ruwenzori. Terrain: high altitudes. Female has white UP instead of orange.

14. *Acraea aubyni* (Eltr.). Kenya. Female has yellow UPH.

15. *Acraea axina* (Westw.). Angola to Natal.

16. *Acraea bonasia* (F.). Sierra Leone to E. Africa.

17. *Acraea braesia* (Godm.). Tanzania, Kenya, Abyssinia.

18. *Acraea butleri* (Auriv.). Uganda.

19. *Acraea buttneri* (Rog.). Rhodesia, Congo.

20. *Acraea cabira* (Hpff.). Congo to Uganda, south to Cape.

21. *Acraea caecilia* (F.). Senegal to E. Africa and Abyssinia. Few races.

22. *Acraea caldarena* (Hew.). E. Africa, Natal to Kenya.

23. *Acraea camaena* (Drury). Sierra Leone, Nigeria.

24. *Acraea cepheus* (L.). Ghana, Sierra Leone, Angola to Sudan. Several races and subspecies.

25. *Acraea cerasa* (Hew.). Natal to Kenya. Very many forms, some without spots UP.

26. *Acraea chaeribula* (Oberth.). Congo to Kenya and Rhodesia.

27. *Acraea chilo* (Godm.). Kenya, Somalia and Abyssinia.

28. *Acraea conradti* (Oberth.). Nyasaland, Tanzania.

29. *Acraea dammii* (Vollenh.). Madagascar. Similar: cuva (Smith), Kenya, Tanzania, more orange colour, spots smaller; igati (Bsd.), Madagascar, spots very large.

30. *Acraea doubledayi* (Guer.). E. Africa to Sudan.

31. *Acraea egina* (Cr.). Senegal through Congo to E. Africa. UP resembles zetes. Several subspecies.

32. *Acraea egina* (see 31).

33. *Acraea equatorialis* (Neave). Kenya.

34. *Acraea encedon* (L.). Through Africa south of Sahara including Madagascar. Lfp: commelina. Very variable and with many forms, which mimic Danaus chrysippus in its many forms.

35. *Acraea esebria* (Hew.). Africa. Form protea (Trim.). Similar: form monteironis (Butl.). (See 36).

36. *Acraea esebria* (Hew.). Angola through Congo to E. Africa, south to Cape. Several subspecies.

37. *Acraea eugenia* (Karsch.). Angola.

38. *Acraea excelsior* (E. Sharpe). Nyasaland, Tanzania and Kenya.

39. *Acraea horta* (L.). 'Garden Acraea'. Cape to Transvaal. Lfp: Passiflora. Similar: admatha (Hew.), UPF darker grey.

40. *Acraea hova* (Bsd.). Madagascar. Female UP almost colourless.

41. *Acraea igola* (Trim.). Natal, Zululand to Tanzania. Similar: strattipocles (Oberth.), Madagascar.

42. *Acraea insignis* (Dist.). Uganda, Kenya and Tanzania. Similar: eltringhami (J. & T.), Uganda; terrain: montane; black border UPH serrated.

43. *Acraea jodutta* (F.). Senegal, Nigeria, Cameroons, Uganda, Tanzania. Female markings white.

44. *Acraea johnstoni* (Godm.). Uganda, Nyasaland, Tanzania. Form pretiosa. Several forms.

45. *Acraea kraka* (Auriv.). Cameroons, Congo.

46. *Acraea leucopyga* (Auriv.). Rhodesia, Nyasaland.

47. *Acraea lycoa* (Godt.). Sierra Leone to Nigeria, Uganda and Kenya. Female is black and white.

48. *Acraea mahela* (Bsd.). Madagascar.

49. *Acraea masamba* (Ward.). Madagascar. Similar: sambavae (Ward.), more orange at base of UPF.

50. *Acraea natalica* (Bsd.). S. and E. Africa. Similar: pseudegina (Westw.), Senegal to Nigeria.

51. *Acraea mirifica* (Lathy.). Angola to Rhodesia.

52. *Acraea neobule* (Dbl. & Hew.). Senegal to Nigeria, S. Africa, E. Africa to Sudan and Abyssinia.

53. *Acraea newtoni* (E. Sharpe). Sao Thome Island.

54. *Acraea niobe* (E. Sharpe). Sao Thome Island.

55. *Acraea nohara* (Bsd.). S. Africa, E. Africa to Kenya. Several subspecies, pale buff UP. Similar: quillemei (Oberth.), Angola, UPF blackish tip to wing; atolmis (Westw.), Angola to Rhodesia, narrow marginal bands.

PLATE 109: Acraeidae

1. *Acraea mairessei* (Auriv.). Congo, Uganda.

2. *Acraea obeira* (Hew.). Madagascar, Transvaal.

3. *Acraea oberthuri* (Btlr.). Nigeria to Congo. Similar: karschi (Auriv.); viviana (Stgr.).

4. *Acraea oncaea* (Hpff.). S. Africa, Congo, E. Africa to Abyssinia.

5. *Acraea oncaea* (see 4).

6. *Acraea oreas* (E. Sharpe). Angola to Uganda and E. Africa.

7. *Acraea orina* (Hew.). Sierra Leone to Congo and Uganda.

8. *Acraea orestia* (Hew.). Nigeria to Angola and Uganda.

9. *Acraea oscari* (Rothsch.). Abyssinia.

10. *Acraea parrhasia* (F.). Sierra Leone, Nigeria, Cameroons. UP as peneleos.

11. *Acraea peneleos* (Ward.). Sierra Leone to Congo, Uganda and Abyssinia.

12. *Acraea penelope* (Stgr.). Nigeria through Congo to E. Africa.

13. *Acraea pentapolis* (Ward.). Sierra Leone to Congo and Uganda.

14. *Acraea perenna* (Dbl. & Hew.). Sierra Leone, Angola to E. Africa and Abyssinia.

15. *Acraea periphanes* (Oberth.). Angola to Rhodesia. Several subspecies.

16. *Acraea petraea* (Bsd.). Tanzania.

17. *Acraea pharsalus* (Ward.). Senegal to Angola and east to Kenya and Tanzania. Few local subspecies. Similar: salambo (Sm.), grey.

18. *Acraea pseudolycia* (Btlr.). Angola, Rhodesia, Tanzania. Form astrigera.

19. *Acraea pseudolycia* (Btlr.), (see 18). Female form auasa (Gabriel).

20. *Acraea quirina* (Fab.). Sierra Leone to Kenya.

21. *Acraea quirinalis* (Smith). E. Congo, Uganda, Kenya and Tanzania.

22. *Acraea rabbaiae* (Ward.). Kenya south to Rhodesia, Tanzania.

23. *Acraea rahira* (Bsd.). 'Marsh Acraea'. Angola and Rhodesia south to Cape. Lfp: Erigeron, Polygonum.

24. *Acraea ranavalona* (Bsd.). Madagascar. Female UP colourless except for black and orange edge to UPH. Similar: lia (Mab.), Madagascar, UPH black border unbroken; machequena (Smith), Nyasaland, Rhodesia, larger red area UPF; obeira (Hew.), Transvaal, UP ground colour buff.

25. *Acraea safie* (Fldr.). Abyssinia. Female UPH almost no marks, very restricted markings UPF.

26. *Acraea satis* (Ward.). Rhodesia, Tanzania, Kenya.

27. *Acraea semivitrea* (Auriv.). Congo to Uganda.

28. *Acraea sotikensis* (E. Sharpe). Congo, Angola, Rhodesia, E. Africa.

29. *Acraea servona* (Godt.). Cameroons to Angola, Uganda and E. Africa north to Abyssinia. Similar: circeis (Drury), Sierra Leone to Angola.

30. *Acraea servona* (see 29).

31. *Acraea stenobea* (Wallengr.). S. Africa, Angola to Tanzania.

32. *Acraea terpsichore* (L.). Sierra Leone to E. Africa and S. Africa. Very variable, several races and subspecies.

33. *Acraea terpsichore* (see 32).

34. *Acraea uvui* (Sm.). Nigeria to Uganda and Tanzania, Angola.

35. *Acraea vesperalis* (Smith). Sierra Leone, Congo, Uganda.

36. *Acraea violarum* (Bsd.). S. Africa, Angola. Male reddish. Similar: asema (Hew.), Angola, Nyasaland, UPH marginal band not solid black.

37. *Acraea rogersi* (Hew.). Nigeria.

38. *Acraea wigginsi* (Neave). Uganda.

39. *Acraea zetes* (L.). W. Africa, C. Africa, E. Africa, south to Natal. Lfp: Passiflora. Several subspecies. Similar: pseudolycia (Btlr.).

40. *Acraea zetes* (see 39).

41. *Acraea zitja* (Bsd.). Madagascar.

42. *Acraea zonata* (Hew.). Kenya, Tanzania.

43. *Bematistes adrasta* (Weym.). Kenya, Tanganyika. Female markings white.

44. *Bematistes aganice* (Hew.). E. and S. Africa. Similar: montana (Btlr.), E. Africa, UP darker orange.

45. *Bematistes consanguinea* (Auriv.). Ghana through Nigeria and Congo to Uganda. Has a white form, albicolor (Karsch.).

46. *Bematistes elongata* (Btlr.). Cameroons, Congo. Female very large.

47. *Bematistes epaea* (Cr.). Nigeria through

Congo to E. Africa, north to Abyssinia. Many local subspecies.

48. *Bematistes epaea* (see 47).

49. *Bematistes epiprotea* (Btlr.). Nigeria to Congo.

50. *Bematistes excisa* (Btlr.). Cameroons to Congo.

51. *Bematistes poggei* (Dew.). Congo to Uganda, Abyssinia, Sudan.

PLATE 110: Acraeidae

1. *Bematistes formosa* (Btlr.). Cameroons, Congo.

2. *Bematistes indentata* (Btlr.). Cameroons to Angola. Similar: excisa (Btlr.), Cameroons, Congo.

3. *Bematistes macarioides* (Auriv.).

4. *Bematistes macaria* (Godt.). Sierra Leone. Similar: macarioides (Auriv.), Ghana; alcinoe (Fldr.), Sierra Leone to Ghana and Congo.

5. *Bematistes macarista* (E. Sharpe). Nigeria, Cameroons, Congo. Few subspecies.

6. *Bematistes macarista* (see 5).

7. *Bematistes quadricolor* (Rogerch.). E. Africa. Several subspecies. Female tends to be paler, whitish UPH.

8. *Bematistes vestalis* (Fldr.). Cameroons, Congo, Sierra Leone to Nigeria.

9. *Bematistes scalivittata* (Btlr.). Zambia.

10. *Bematistes tellus* (Auriv.). Cameroons to Uganda.

11. *Pardopsis punctatissima* (Bsd.) 'Polka Dot'. Cape to Abyssinia, Madagascar.

Danaidae

12. *Amauris albimaculata* (Btlr.). W. Africa, Congo, Uganda.

13. *Amauris ansorgei* (E. Sharpe). Kenya, E. Congo, south to Malawi. Terrain: high forest.

14. *Amauris echeria* (Stoll.). W., C. and E. Africa, south to S. Africa. Several subspecies.

15. *Danaus formosa* (Godm.). W., C. and E. Africa.

16. *Amauris hecate* (Btlr.). W., C. and E. Africa. Terrain: forest.

17. *Amauris inferna* (Btlr.). W. Africa, Congo, Uganda.

18. *Danaus mercedonia* (Karsh.). Kenya, Uganda. Similar: morgeni (Honr.).

19. *Euploea mitra* (Moore). Seychelles.

20. *Amauris niavius* (L.). W., C. and E. Africa, south to Natal.

21. *Amauris ochlea* (Bsd.). E. Africa, south to Natal. Similar: nossima (Ward.), Madagascar.

22. *Amauris phaedon* (F.). Madagascar, Mauritius. Similar: comorana (Oberth.), Comoro Islands.

23. *Amauris tartarea* (Mab.). W., C. and E. Africa. Similar: damocles (Beauv.), E. Africa; bulbifera (Smith).

24. *Amauris vashti* (Btlr.). Nigeria, Congo.

25. *Euploea euphon* (F.). Mauritius.

26. *Euploea ~oudotii* (Bsd.). Bourbon Island.

PLATE 111: Pieridae

1. *Anaphaeis anomala* (Btlr.). Socotra. Similar: antsianaka (Ward.), Madagascar.

2. *Anaphaeis aurota* (Fabr.). Africa, Arabia, Ceylon, India, Syria and Iran.

3. *Anaphaeis aurota* (see 2) = Belenois (see 9).

4. *Anaphaeis eriphia* (Godt.). E. Africa from Somalia to S. Africa. Terrain: open bush. Lfp: Capparis.

5. *Appias epaphia* (Cr.). W., E. and C. Africa, S. Africa, Madagascar. Male as phaola.

6. *Appias lasti* (Smith). Kenya, Tanzania. Mimics Mylothris trimenia.

7. *Appias phaola* (Dbl.). W. and C. Africa. Terrain: forest. Male resembles sylvia, but without orange UP.

8. *Appias sylvia* (F.). W., C. and E. Africa south to Rhodesia. Mimics Mylothris rhodope. Similar: sabina (Feld.).

9. *Belenois aurota* (F.). Throughout Africa.

10. *Belenois calypso* (Drury). W., C. and E. Africa to Tanzania.

11. *Belenois creona* (Cr.). W., C., E. and S. Africa. Several similar.

12. *Belenois creona* (see 11).

13. *Belenois gidica* (see 14).

14. *Belenois gidica* (Godt.). W., C., E. and S. Africa. Lfp: Capparis. Several subspecies. (Dry season form.)

15. *Belenois hedyle* (Cr.). Sierra Leone to Ashanti.

16. *Belenois helcida* (Bsd.). Madagascar.

17. *Belenois raffrayi* (Oberth.). Abyssinia, Kenya, Uganda, Tanzania. Terrain: montane forest.

18. *Belenois solilucis* (Btlr.). W. Africa, Congo to Uganda.

19. *Belenois subeida* (Fldr.). W., C. and E. Africa.

20. *Belenois theora* (Dbl.). W. and C. Africa and Uganda. UP female form lacta (Weym.) is yellow.

21. *Belenois theuszi* (Dew.). Cameroons, Congo.

22. *Belenois thysa* (see 23).

23. *Belenois thysa* (Hpff.). E., C. and S. Africa. Few subspecies.

24. *Belenois zochalia* (Bsd.). Abyssinia, E. Africa, S. Africa. Male similar to aurota.

25. *Catopsilia pyranthe* (L.). Africa, Arabia, India, Ceylon, Malaya. Lfp: Cassia. Similar: florella (F.), smaller, brown tinge.

26. *Colotis agoye* (Walleng.). S. and S.W. Africa, Somaliland. Terrain: arid bush. Variable.

27. *Catopsilia pyranthe* (see 25).

PLATE 112: Pieridae

1. *Catopsilia thauruma* (Reak.). Madagascar. Male UP as crocale with black spot UPF.

2. *Colotis antevippe* (Bsd.). Throughout Africa south of Sahara.

3. *Colotis aurigineus* (Btlr.). S. Sudan, E. Africa to Malawi. UP as chrysonome. Similar: doubledayi (Hpff.), W. Africa, Congo.

4. *Colotis celimene* (Lucas). E. Africa to S. Africa, S.W. Africa. Terrain: dry bush.

5. *Colotis celimene* (see 4).

6. *Colotis danae* (see 7).

7. *Colotis danae* (F.). Throughout Africa. UP resembles eupompe but with black margins UPH. Similar: guenei (Mab.), Madagascar.

8. *Colotis dissociatus* (Btlr.). Kenya, Nyasaland. Male resembles eucharis (Fabr.).

9. *Colotis ducissa* (Dogn.). Kenya. (Dry season form.)

10. *Colotis elgonensis* (E.M.S.). Highlands of Kenya, Uganda, Tanzania, Cameroons and Nigeria. Similar: glauningi (A. Schultze), W. Africa, larger.

11. *Colotis evenina* (Walleng.). E. to S. Africa.

12. *Colotis evenina* (see 11).

13. *Colotis evippe* (L.). W. Africa. There is also a white female form resembling imphale female.

14. *Colotis eris* (Klug.). W. Africa, E., C. and S. Africa, S. Arabia. Terrain: hot arid country. Few forms.

15. *Colotis eris* (see 14).

16. *Colotis erone* (Angas.). Coastal areas, Zambia, S. Africa to S.W. Africa.

17. *Colotis erone* (see 16).

18. *Colotis eucharis* (F.). Throughout Africa. Terrain: bush and semi-desert.

19. *Colotis eulimene* (Klug.). Nubia.

20. *Colotis eupompe* (Klug.). Sinai, Arabia, E. Africa, Senegal.

21. *Colotis halimede* (Klug.). W. Africa to Sudan, south to Tanzania. Terrain: semi-

desert bush. Female has additional black spots UPF. Similar: venosus (Stgr.), without any orange UP.

22. *Colotis hetaera* (Gerst.). Kenya, Tanzania. Form sulphurea: normal female has ground colour white (see 24 also).

23. *Colotis eunoma* (Hpff.). Kenya to Mozambique. Terrain: coastal, dunes. Female has black spots UPF and black edges.

24. *Colotis hetaera* (Gerst.). Kenya, Tanzania. Similar: lorti (E. Sharpe), Somaliland; puniceus (Btlr.), Tanzania.

25. *Colotis hildebrandti* (Stgr.). Kenya, Tanzania, Malawi. Few subspecies.

26. *Colotis ione* (Godt.). E. and S. Africa, S.W. Africa. Male resembles erone.

27. *Colotis mananhari* (Ward.). Madagascar.

28. *Colotis niveus* (Btlr.). Socotra.

29. *Colotis omphale* (Godt.). C., E. and S. Africa.

30. *Colotis protomedia* (Klug.). W. Africa, Sudan, Somalia, south to Tanzania. Terrain: scrub or arid bush.

PLATE 113: Pieridae

1. *Colotis regina* (Trim.). C. and E. Africa, Natal to S. Africa.

2. *Colotis ducissa* (Dogn.). Wet season form (see 112/9).

3. *Colotis subfasciatus* (Swains.). Tanzania, E. to S. Africa, Angola. Female white UP with orange or black and orange tips UPF.

4. *Colotis vesta* (Reiche.). E. Africa.

5. *Colotis pallene* (Hopff.). Rhodesia, S. and S.W. Africa. Terrain: dry bush. Male resembles evippe.

6. *Colotis zoe* (Grand.). Madagascar.

7. *Colotis zoe* (Grand.). Madagascar. This female is typical of many Colotis females.

8. *Dixeia astarte* (Btlr.). Tanzania.

9. *Dixeia doxocharina* (Bsd.). Cape to Rhodesia.

10. *Dixeia cebron* (Ward.). Cameroons. Female resembles capricornus.

11. *Dixeia capricornus* (Ward.). Cameroons. Male similar to cebron but no yellow UP.

12. *Dixeia liliana* (Smith). E. Africa.

13. *Dixeia pigea* (Bsd.). S. Sudan, C. Africa, south to S. Africa. Lfp: Capparis. Similar: doxo (Godt.); gerda (Sm. & Kirby); charina (Bsd.).

14. *Dixeia spilleri* (Spiller). Coastal districts, Kenya to Natal.

15. *Eronia leda* (Bsd.). E. and S. Africa, Angola.

16. *Eronia pharis* (Bsd.). W. African forest.

17. *Eronia cleodora* (Hbn.). C., E. and S. Africa.

18. *Eronia cleodora* (Hbn.). C., E. and S. Africa. Form dilatata (Btlr.), (see 3 also)

19. *Eurema brigitta* (Cr.). Throughout Africa. Few subspecies. Similar: stygma (Bsd.), Brazil, Cuba.

20. *Eurema brigitta* (see 19).

21. *Eurema desjardinsi* (Bsd.). Throughout Africa. Similar: regularis (Btlr.), marginal bands even but wider; mandarinula (Holl.), black border reduced to spots on HW.

22. *Eurema eximia* (Thur.). Kenya to S. Africa.

23. *Eurema hapale* (Mab.). W., C. and E. Africa south to Rhodesia, Madagascar.

24. *Eurema hecabe* (L.). Throughout Africa. Terrain: open country. (Dry season form.)

25. *Eurema hecabe* (L.). Throughout Africa. Terrain: open country, (Wet season form) (see 10 also).

26. *Leptosia alcesta* (Cr.). W. Africa to E. Africa, south to Natal and Madagascar. Few subspecies.

27. *Leptosia medusa* (Cr.). W. Africa to Congo and Uganda. Similar: immaculata (Auriv.), no spot.

28. *Mylothris bernice* (Hew.). Cameroons, Congo, Kenya, south to Rhodesia. Terrain: swamps and marshes. Similar: rubricosta (Mab.).

29. *Mylothris agathina* (see 16).

30. *Mylothris agathina* (Cr.). Congo, S. and E. Africa to Abyssinia. Lfp: Loranthus. Many similar.

PLATE 114: Pieridae

1. *Mylothris chloris* (F.). W. and C. Africa.

2. *Mylothris mortoni* (Blachier). W. Abyssinia.

3. *Mylothris ngaziya* (Oberth.). Comoro Islands.

4. *Mylothris nubila* (Moschl.). Cameroons, Gabon. Male whitish.

5. *Mylothris poppea* (Cr.). W., C. and E. Africa. Many similar.

6. *Mylothris poppea* (see 5).

7. *Mylothris rhodope* (Fabr.). W. and C. Africa. Form spica (Mosche). Male UP white, black tip to UPF.

8. *Mylothris sagala* (Smith). W., C. and E. Africa, south to Rhodesia. Many similar.

9. *Mylothris sagala* (see 8). Form knutsoni (Auriv.).

10. *Mylothris yulei* (Btlr.). E. Africa, Abyssinia to Rhodesia.

11. *Mylothris sulphurea* (Auriv.). Cameroons. Similar: ochracea (Auriv.).

12. *Mylothris trimenia* (Btlr.). S. Africa.

13. *Mylothris smithi* (Mab.). Madagascar. Similar : humbolti (Oberth.), Comoro Islands.

14. *Nepherònia argia* (F.). S.E. and S.W. Africa. Female form aurora. Male is white with black tip UPF (see 15 and 17 also).

15. *Nepheronia argia* (F.). S.E. and S.W. Africa. Form giara (Suff.).

16. *Nepheronia buqueti* (Bsd.). E. and S. Africa, Madagascar.

17. *Nepheronia argia* (F.). S.E. and S.W. Africa. Form idotea.

18. *Nepheronia thalassina* (Bsd.). W., C. and E. Africa to Transvaal. Female form verulanus has yellow UPF resembling Mylothris species.

19. *Pontia helice* (L.). Throughout Africa. Lfp : Reseda. UP as glauconome.

20. *Pseudopontia paradoxa* (Feld.). W. Africa, Congo, W. Uganda. Terrain : forest shade.

21. *Eurema brenda* (Dbl. & Hew.). W., C. and E. Africa to Uganda.

22. *Pieris brassicoides* (Guer.). Abyssinia.

PLATE 115: Satyridae

1. *Aphysoneura pigmentaria* (Karsch.). Nyasaland, Tanzania.

2. *Bicyclus auricruda* (Btlr.). Ghana to Uganda.

3. *Bicyclus campina* (Auriv.). Mt. Kilimanjaro.

4. *Bicyclus iccius* (Hew.). Nigeria, Congo, Uganda. Similar : Mycalesis sebetus (Hew.), W. Africa ; hewitsoni (Doumer), UPF violet band continued on UPH.

5. *Cassionympha cassius* (Godt.). S. Africa to Natal. Similar : Pseudonympha detecta (Trim.), UPH no ocelli ; magus (Fab.), S. Africa, warmer brown UP.

6. *Coenonympha vaucheri* (Blachier). Morocco.

7. *Coenura aurantiaca* (A.). S. Africa to Natal. Lfp : Grass. Similar : hebe (Trim.), Cape Province ; rupiflaga (Trim.), Transvaal.

8. *Coenyropsis bera* (Hew.). Uganda, Nyasaland, Rhodesia.

9. *Henotesia eliasis* (Hew.). Congo. Similar : ochracea (Lathy), Angola, no lunules UPH.

10. *Dingana bowkeri* (Trim.). S. Africa to Natal.

11. *Dingana dingana* (Trim.). Transvaal.

12. *Elymniopsis bammakoo* (Westw.). W. Africa. Terrain : forest.

13. *Henotesia ankora* (Ward.). Madagascar.

14. *Elymniopsis phegea* (F.). W. Africa.

15. *Elymniopsis ugandae* (Grunb.). Uganda.

Form rattrayi (E. Sharp) resembles bammakoo but larger white patch UPF.

16. *Eumenis atlantis* (Aust.). Morocco, Atlas Mountains.

17. *Gnophodes parmeno* (Dbl. & Hew.). Throughout Africa south of Sahara.

18. *Henotesia antahala* (Ward.). Madagascar.

19. *Henotesia ankaratra* (Ward.). Madagascar.

20. *Henotesia avelona* (Ward.). Madagascar. Similar : ankoma (Mab.), Madagascar, darker.

21. *Henotesia masikora* (Mab.). Madagascar. Similar : perdita (Btlr.), Madagascar.

PLATE 116: Satyridae

1. *Henotesia narcissus* (F.). Mauritius.

2. *Henotesia paradoxa* (Mab.). Madagascar.

3. *Henotesia strigula* (Mab.). Madagascar.

4. *Henotesia peitho* (Plotz). Ghana to Gaboon, Uganda.

5. *Henotesia perspicua* (Trim.). Congo, E. Africa to Natal.

6. *Henotesia phaea* (Karsh.). Congo.

7. *Henotesia simonsi* (Btlr.). Rhodesia.

8. *Mycalesis dubia* (Auriv.). Kenya, Uganda.

9. *Heteropsis drepana* (Dbl., Hew. & West.). Madagascar. Male is smaller and dark brown UP.

10. *Lasiommata maderakal* (Guer.). Abyssinia, N. Somaliland.

11. *Mycalesis anynana* (Btlr.). E. Africa to Transvaal.

12. *Leptoneura clytus* (L.). S. Africa to Natal.

13. *Melanitis libya* (Dist.). Senegal to Uganda.

14. *Leptoneura swanepoeli* (Van Son.). Transvaal.

15. *Leptoneura oxylus* (Trim.). S.E. Africa. Similar : swanepoeli (Van Son.), smaller blue spots in ocelli.

16. *Meneris tulbaghia* (L.). S. Africa to Natal and Rhodesia.

17. *Mycalesis aurivillii* (Btlr.). Uganda. Terrain : montane.

18. *Mintha mintha* (Geyer). Cape Province, S. Africa.

19. *Mycalesis ansorgei* (Sharpe). Uganda.

20. *Mycalesis asochis* (Hew.). Nigeria to Angola.

PLATE 117: Satyridae

1. *Mycalesis ena* (Hew.). Rhodesia, Nyasaland, Tanzania.

2. *Mycalesis evadne* (Cr.). Sierra Leone, Gaboon.

3. *Mycalesis funebris* (Guer.). Sierra Leone, Gaboon.

4. *Mycalesis golo* (Auriv.). Congo, Uganda.

5. *Mycalesis dorothea* (Cr.). Sierra Leone to Angola. Similar : Bicyclus miriam (F.).

6. *Mycalesis italus* (Hew.). W. Africa. Similar : Bicyclus xeneas (Hew.), W. Africa ; sebetus (Hew.), Uganda, UPF pale violet band.

7. *Mycalesis hewitsoni* (Doumet). Cameroons and Congo.

8. *Mycalesis italus* (Hew.). W. Africa.

9. *Mycalesis kenia* (Rogenh.). E. Africa.

10. *Mycalesis mandanes* (Hew.). Togo to Congo. Similar : auricruda (Btlr.).

11. *Mycalesis matuta* (Karsch.). Mt. Ruwenzori.

12. *Mycalesis martius* (F.). Ghana to Kenya. Male UP silky black, female UP pale brown.

13. *Mycalesis nobilis* (Auriv.). Congo to Uganda. Similar : sciathis (Hew.).

14. *Mycalesis phalanthus* (Stgr.). E. Africa. UP similar : italus (Hew.).

15. *Mycalesis obscura* (Auriv.). Nigeria, Congo. UP black-brown.

16. *Mycalesis safitza* (Hew.). Throughout Africa south of Sahara.

17. *Mycalesis safitza* (see 16).

18. *Mycalesis sandace* (Hew.). Senegal to Congo. Similar : Bicyclus mesogena (Karsch.), Uganda, larger.

PLATE 118: Satyridae

1. *Mycalesis saussurei* (Dew.). Congo, E. Africa to Uganda.

2. *Mycalesis sciathis* (Hew.). Liberia, Cameroons. Similar : analis (Auriv.), Congo ; Bicyclus taenias (Hew.), Sierra Leone, Nigeria ; ignobilis (Btlr.), Gold Coast, Congo ; nobilis (Auriv.), Congo to Uganda.

3. *Mycalesis vulgaris* (Btlr.). W. Africa to Uganda.

4. *Neita neita* (Wall.). S. Africa to Natal.

5. *Neocoenyra cooksoni* (H. H. Druce). Congo.

6. *Ypthima albida* (Btlr.). Nigeria and Cameroons, Kenya and Uganda. Terrain : montane.

7. *Neocoenyra durbani* (Trim.). Cape Province, South Africa. Similar : natalii (Bsd.), Transvaal, Rhodesia, UPF markings more diffuse, reddish UPH.

8. *Neocoenyra extensii* (Btlr.). S. Africa to Transvaal and Rhodesia.

9. *Neocoenyra gregorii* (Btlr.). Sudan, Uganda.

10. *Physcaeneura pione* (Godm.). E. Africa. Similar: leda (Gerst.).

11. *Physcaeneura leda* (Gerst.). E. Africa. Male UP resembles pione.

12. *Pseudonympha magus* (see 17).

13. *Physcaeneura panda* (Bsd.). S. Africa to Natal and Rhodesia.

14. *Paralethe dendrophilus* (Trim.). S. Africa. Few subspecies.

15. *Pseudonympha hippia* (Cr.). Cape Province, S. Africa.

16. *Pseudonympha machacha* (Riley). Basutoland.

17. *Pseudonympha magus* (F.). S. Africa to Natal and Rhodesia.

18. *Ypthima itonia* (Hew.). W. Africa, C. Africa to Abyssinia and Kenya. UP resembles philomela.

19. *Ypthima sufferti* (Auriv.). Madagascar.

20. *Ypthima triopthalma* (Mab.). Madagascar. Similar: tamatare (Bsd.), Madagascar, larger.

21. *Pseudonympha narycia* (Wallgr.). S. Africa to Transvaal and Rhodesia.

22. *Pseudonympha trimeni* (Btlr.). Cape Province, S. Africa. Similar: gaika (Riley); poetula (Trim.).

23. *Ypthima batesi* (Fldr.). Madagascar.

24. *Ypthima doleta* (Kirby). W. Africa.

25. *Neocoenyra duplex* (Btlr.). Tanzania to Somalia.

26. *Tarsocera cassus* (L.). Cape Province, Madagascar. UP as cassina.

27. *Ypthima zanjuga* (Mab.). Madagascar.

28. *Stygionympha vigilans* (Trim.). S. Africa to Natal and Rhodesia.

29. *Tarsocera cassina* (Btlr.). Cape Province. Terrain: sand dunes.

PLATE 119 : Satyridae

1. *Gnophodes chelys* (F.). W. Africa to Uganda. Female very pale brown.

2. *Gnophodes diversa* (Btlr.). Nigeria to Uganda and south to Natal.

Lycaenidae

3. *Actis perigrapha* (Karsch.). Cameroons to Congo.

4. *Actizera lucida* (Trim.). S. and E. Africa to Kenya.

5. *Actizera stellata* (Trim.). Cape, Nyasaland.

6. *Alaena amazoula* (Bsd.). Angola to Nyasaland, south to Cape.

7. *Alaena caissa* (Rbl. & Rog.). Tanzania.

8. *Alaena johanna* (E. Sharpe). Kenya, Somalia. Similar: oberthuri (Auriv.), Tanganyika.

9. *Alaena margaritacea* (Elthr.). Transvaal.

10. *Alaena nyassae* (Hew.). Nyasaland.

11. *Alaena picata* (E. Sharpe). Kenya.

12. *Alaena subrubra* (Beth.-Baker). Tanganyika.

13. *Alaena subrubra* (see 12).

14. *Aloeides aranda* (Wallengr.). Cape to Transvaal.

15. *Aloeides backlyi* (Trim.). Cape. Female has orange wing tip UPF.

16. *Aloeides conradsi* (Auriv.). Tanzania.

17. *Aloeides damarensis* (Trim.). Central S. Africa.

18. *Aloeides malagrida* (Wallengr.). Cape to Transvaal. Similar female: Phasis wallengreni (Trim.).

19. *Aloeides molomo* (Trim.). S. Africa. Variable.

20. *Aloeides pierus* (Cr.). Cape.

21. *Aloeides simplex* (Trim.). Cape.

22. *Aloeides taikosama* (Wallengr.). Cape to Kenya.

23. *Aloeides thyra* (L.). Cape to Transvaal. Many local forms. Similar: almeida (Fldr.).

24. *Anthene amarah* (Guer.). Throughout Africa, Aden.

25. *Anthene arescopa* (Beth.-Baker). Cameroons.

26. *Anthene arescopa.* (see 25).

27. *Anthene bipuncta* (Talb.). Congo.

28. *Anthene definita* (Btlr.). E. Africa, south to Cape. Similar: chirinda (Beth.-Baker), E. Africa to Cape.

29. *Anthene fasciata* (Auriv.). Sierra Leone to Congo.

30. *Anthene hades* (Beth.-Baker). Sierra Leone, Nigeria. Similar: phoenicis (Karsch.); marshalli (Beth.-Baker).

31. *Anthene hades* (see 30).

32. *Anthene hobleyi* (Neave). Kenya and Uganda.

33. *Anthene hodsoni* (Talbot). Uganda.

34. *Anthene juba* (F.). Sierra Leone to Nigeria. UP orange patches.

35. *Anthene kamilila* (Beth.-Baker). Sierra Leone.

36. *Anthene lachares* (Hew.). Sierra Leone to Gaboon. Subspecies toroensis (Stempff).

37. *Anthene lachares* (see 36).

38. *Anthene lamias* (Hew.). Sierra Leone.

39. *Anthene larydas* (Cr.). Rhodesia, Natal, Sierra Leone to Uganda.

40. *Anthene larydas* (see 39).

41. *Anthene larydas* (see 39).

42. *Anthene lasti* (Sm. & Ky.). E. Africa.

43. *Anthene lemnos* (see 44).

44. *Anthene lemnos* (Hew.). Natal to Kenya. Similar: liodes (Hew.), Nyasaland.

45. *Anthene leptines* (Hew.). Cameroons, Congo. Several similar species including: makala (Beth.-Baker), Belgian Congo, brighter; ngoko (Stampff.), Congo, wider black areas UP; rufomarginata (Beth.-Baker), Belgian Congo, almost all dark UP.

46. *Anthene levis* (Hew.). Sierra Leone to Rhodesia.

47. *Anthene ligures* (see 48).

48. *Anthene ligures* (Hew.). W. Africa, east to Tanzania.

49. *Anthene lirida* (Trim.). Cape to Abyssinia. A subspieces of butleri (Oberth.).

50. *Anthene locuples* (Sm.). Nigeria, Cameroons.

51. *Anthene lucretilis* (Hew.). Sierra Leone to Angola.

PLATE 120 : Lycaenidae

1. *Anthene lunulata* (see 2).

2. *Anthene lunulata* (Trim.). Sierra Leone to Kenya.

3. *Anthene lusones* (Hew.). Sierra Leone to Angola.

4. *Anthene lysicles* (see 5).

5. *Anthene lysicles* (Hew.). Sierra Leone to Gaboon.

6. *Anthene lyzanius* (Hew.). Sierra Leone to Angola.

7. *Anthene millari* (Trim.). Natal, Transvaal, Rhodesia. Similar: otacilia (Trim.), Cape to Uganda.

8. *Anthene musagetes* (Holl.). Sierra Leone, to Uganda, Angola. Several similar.

9. *Anthene neglecta* (Trim.). Sierra Leone to E. Africa, Natal to Abyssinia.

10. *Anthene pyroptera* (Auriv.). Cameroons, Congo.

11. *Anthene rufoplagata* (Beth.-Baker). Sierra Leone to Congo.

12. *Anthene scintillula* (Holl.). Sierra Leone to Congo. Similar: mahota (Gr.Sm.), Equatorial Africa, wider black borders UP.

13. *Anthene staudingeri* (Sm. & Ky.). Sierra Leone to Congo. Similar: minima (Trim.), Rhodesia, Natal, smaller.

14. *Anthene sylvanus* (Dr.). Sierra Leone to Angola.

15. *Anthene thyrsis* (Kirby). Gaboon, Congo. Similar: lithas (Druce), Ghana, Sierra Leone. Female form unicolor (Auriv.), Cameroons.

16. *Anthene thyrsis* (see 15).

17. *Anthene voltae* (E. Sharpe). Sierra Leone to Uganda. Female resembles arescopa female.

18. *Anthene zenkeri* (Karsch.). Cameroons, Congo. Similar: fulvus (Skempff), Cameroons, no yellow patch UPH.

19. *Aphnaeus asterius* (Plotz). Sierra Leone.

20. *Aphnaeus asterius* (see 19).

21. *Aphnaeus erikssoni* (Trim.). Angola, Rhodesia. Similar: rex, Tanzania.

22. *Aphnaeus hutchinsoni* (Trim.). S. and E. Africa.

23. *Aphnaeus marshalli* (Neave). Tanzania. UP brown.

24. *Aphnaeus orgas* (Drury). Sierra Leone to Congo.

25. *Aphnaeus orgas* (see 24).

26. *Aphnaeus questiauxi* (Auriv.). Congo.

27. *Aphnaeus rex* (Auriv.). Tanzania. Subspecies of erikssoni.

28. *Aphniolaus pallene* (Wallengr.). E. Africa to Natal.

29. *Argiolaus lalos* (Ham. Druce). Tanzania, Kenya.

30. *Argiolaus lalos* (see 29).

31. *Argiolaus silas* (Ww.). S. and E. Africa to Tanzania.

32. *Argiolaus silas* (see 31).

33. *Argyrocheila undifera* (Stgr.). Sierra Leone to Ogowe River.

34. *Paraslauga kallimoides* (S. Schultze). Cameroons.

35. *Aslauga lamborni* (Baker). Nigeria, Cameroons.

36. *Aslauga leonae* (Auriv). Sierra Leone. Female resembles vininga female.

37. *Aslauga pandora* (Schultze). S. Cameroons.

38. *Aslauga purpurascens* (Holl.). E. Africa.

39. *Aslauga vininga* (Hew.). Sierra Leone to Ogowe. Male resembles lamborni UP.

40. *Axiocerses amanga* (see 41).

41. *Axiocerses amanga* (Westw.). S. Africa, E. Africa to Kenya. Similar: mendeche (Smith), S. Africa.

42. *Axiocerses harpax* (F.). Sierra Leone, C. Africa, E. Africa to Cape. Few subspecies. UP resembles amanga, has black dots UPF.

43. *Axiocerses harpax* (see 42).

44. *Axiocerses punicea* (Smith). Kenya, Tanzania.

45. *Azanus jesous* (Guer.). E. and S. Africa.

46. *Azanus natalensis* (Trim.). Cape, Natal to Abyssinia, Congo.

47. *Azanus moriqua* (Wallengr.). Angola to Natal. Similar: mirza (Plotz), Sierra Leone to Kenya, Natal.

48. *Azanus mirza* (Plotz), Sierra Leone to Tanzania and Kenya, Natal.

49. *Baliochila aslauga* (Trim.). Angola to Kenya, south to Natal. Few similar species.

50. *Batelusia zebra* (H. Druce). Cameroons.

51. *Brephidium barberae* (Trim.). S. Africa.

52. *Brephidium metophis* (Wallengr.). S. Africa to Delagoa Bay.

53. *Cacyreus lingeus* (Cr.). Throughout Africa.

54. *Cacyreus palemon* (Cr.). S. and E. Africa. Lfp: Geranium. Similar: marshalli (Btlr.), Cape to Natal.

PLATE 121: Lycaenidae

1. *Capys alphaeus* (Cr.). S. Africa.

2. *Capys disjunctus* (Trim.). Natal, Transvaal, Cameroons. Similar: penningtoni (Riley), Natal, larger, brighter UP.

3. *Capys disjunctus* (see 2).

4. *Castalius calice* (Hpff.). Congo to Kenya, south to Natal.

5. *Castalius cretosus* (Btlr.). Abyssinia, Somalia. Several local forms.

6. *Castalius isis* (Drury). Sierra Leone to Uganda, Angola.

7. *Castalius hintza* (Trim.). S. and E. Africa.

8. *Castalius margaritaceus* (E. Sharpe). Kenya.

9. *Castalius melaena* (Trim.). S. Africa north to Kenya.

10. *Catachrysops eleusis* (Demais). Senegal, Abyssinia. Similar: contractus (Btlr.).

11. *Chloroselas pseudozeritis* (Trim.). Cape to Transvaal, Rhodesia.

12. *Citrinophila erastus* (Hew.). Ghana to Angola.

13. *Citrinophila tenera* (Ky.). Cameroons, Nigeria. Similar: similis (Ky.), Ghana.

14. *Cooksonia trimeni* (H. Druce). Rhodesia.

15. *Crudaria leroma* (Wallengr.). S. Africa to Natal and Rhodesia.

16. *Cnodontes pallida* (Trim.). Transvaal, Rhodesia.

17. *Cupidopsis cissus* (Godt.). Rhodesia, Sierra Leone to Kenya, E. Africa, S. Africa.

18. *Cupidopsis cissus* (see 17).

19. *Cupidopsis iobates* (Hopff.). S. Africa, E. Africa to Abyssinia.

20. *Deudorix virgata* (H. Druce). Sierra Leone.

21. *Dapidodigma hymen* (F.). Sierra Leone to Congo.

22. *Deloneura barca* (Smith). Angola.

23. *Deloneura millari* (Trim.). Natal, Rhodesia.

24. *Desmolycaena mazoensis* (Trim.). Rhodesia, Natal, Transvaal.

25. *Deudorix antalus* (Hpffr.). Throughout Africa, including Madagascar and Comoro Islands.

26. *Deudocix caerulea* (H. Druce). Nigeria, E. Africa.

27. *Deudorix caliginosa* (Lathy). Nigeria, Rhodesia.

28. *Deudorix dariares* (Hew.). E. Africa. Male UP as diocles, but no orange UPF.

29. *Deudorix dinochares* (Smith). E. Africa, Madagascar. Similar: livia (Klug.), E. Africa, Nigeria, Arabia; dinomenes (Smith), Sierra Leone, E. Africa.

30. *Deudorix dinochares* (see 29).

31. *Deudorix dinochares* (see 29).

32. *Deudorix diocles* (Hew.). E. Africa. Lfp: Acacia.

33. *Deudorix kafuensis* (Neave). Rhodesia.

34. *Deudorix odana* (H. Druce). Nigeria to Cameroons.

35. *Deudorix lorisona* (Hew.). Sierra Leone to Nigeria.

36. *Deudorix zela* (see 37).

37. *Deudorix zela* (Hew.). Sierra Leone, Nyasaland, Rhodesia. Male UP blue.

38. *Diopetes angelita* (Suff.). Cameroons, Congo.

39. *Diopetes angelita* (see 38).

40. *Diopetes aurivalliusi* (Stemp.). Cameroons.

41. *Diopetes catalla* (Karsch.). Togo to Cameroons.

42. *Diopetes violetta* (Auriv.). Cameroons, Gaboon. Similar: kedassa (H. Druce), Cameroons; deritas (Hew.), Togo to Cameroons.

43. *Durbania amakoza* (Trim.). Cape to Transvaal. Several subspecies.

44. *Durbania limbata* (Trim.). Natal.

45. *Durbaniella clarki* (Van Son.). Cape.

46. *Durbaniella saga* (Trim.). Cape.

47. *Eicochrysops hippocrates* (F.). Sierra Leone to Natal and Abyssinia, Madagascar.

48. *Eicochrysops mahallakoaena* (Wallengr.). S. and E. Africa. UN as messapus.

49. *Eicochrysops messapus* (God.). Cape, Rhodesia, Abyssinia.

50. *Epamera aemulus* (Trim.). Natal to Tanzania.

51. *Epamera aethria* (Karsch.). Togoland. Similar: jasis (Hew.), Gold Coast, UP dull; ognes (Auriv.), West Africa, blue.

52. *Epamera alienus* (Trim.). Transvaal to Tanzania.

53. *Epamera aphneoides* (Trim.). S. Africa to Nyasaland.

54. *Epamera bellina* (Plotz). Sierra Leone to Cameroons. Similar: sappirus (H. Druce); gemmarius (H. Druce).

55. *Epamera fontainei* (Stempff). Uganda.

PLATE 122: Lycaenidae

1. *Epamera laon* (Hew.). Ghana to Gaboon. UP as adamsi.

2. *Epamera mimosae* (Trim.). S. Africa, E. Africa to Somalia.

3. *Epamera mermis* (H. Druce). Tanzania, Kenya.

4. *Epamera nursei* (Btlr.). Arabia, Aden, Somalia.

5. *Epamera pollux* (Auriv.). Tanzania, Uganda.

6. *Epamera sappirus* (H. Druce). Sierra Leone. Male UP as bellina.

7. *Epamera sidus* (Trim.). Natal.

8. *Epamera silanus* (Smith). Kenya, Tanzania.

9. *Epamera stenogrammica* (Riley). Uganda.

10. *Epitola albomaculata* (Baker). Sierra Leone. Similar: cercene (Hew.), Cameroons, Angola; badia (Ky.), Cameroons.

11. *Epitola badura* (Ky.). Cameroons to Gaboon. UN dull brown.

12. *Epitola batesi* (H. Druce). Cameroons. Male resembles cercene male and nitida male.

13. *Epitola carcina* (Hew.). Sierra Leone.

14. *Epitola catuna* (Ky.). Cameroons. Similar: elissa (Smith), Nigeria.

15. *Epitola ceraunia* (Hew.). Sierra Leone to Gaboon.

16. *Epitola conjuncta* (Sm. & Ky.). Uganda. Similar: mengoensis (Baker), many similar species.

17. *Epitola crowleyi* (E. Sharpe). Sierra Leone to Nigeria.

18. *Epitola crowleyi* (see 17).

19. *Epitola gerina* (Hew.). Congo.

20. *Epitola hewitsoni* (Mab.). Congo.

21. *Epitola honorius* (F.). Cameroons, Congo, Sierra Leone to Ghana. Few subspecies.

22. *Epitola leonina* (Stgr.). Sierra Leone.

23. *Epitola liana* (Roche). Uganda.

24. *Epitola nigra* (Baker). Sierra Leone.

25. *Epitola nitida* (H. Druce). Cameroons.

26. *Epitola miranda* (Stgr.). Sierra Leone.

27. *Epitola posthumus* (F.). Sierra Leone to Congo.

28. *Epitola posthumus* (see 27).

29. *Epitola staudingeri* (Ky.). Sierra Leone, Gaboon.

30. *Epitola sublustris* (Baker). Sierra Leone to Nigeria.

31. *Epitola uniformis* (Ky.). Cameroons. Male resembles leonina male.

32. *Epitola viridana* (Joicey & Talbot). Sierra Leone to Nigeria.

33. *Epitolina catori* (Baker). Sierra Leone to Nigeria.

34. *Epitolina dispar* (Ky.). Ghana to Nigeria.

35. *Eresina bilinea* (Talbot). Uganda.

36. *Eresina toroensis* (Talbot). Uganda. Similar: fontainei (Stemff.), Nigeria, darker UP.

37. *Euchrysops abyssinia* (Auriv.). Abyssinia.

38. *Euchrysops albistriata* (Capr.). Sierra Leone through Congo to Uganda.

39. *Euchrysops barkeri* (Trim.). Sierra Leone to Tanzania, south to Natal. Female resembles dolorosa female.

40. *Euchrysops dolorosa* (Trim.). Natal, Transvaal, Tanganyika. Similar: subpallidus (Beth.-Baker), Kenya, Rhodesia. UP resembles barkeri.

41. *Euchrysops hypopolia* (Trim.). Natal, Transvaal. Similar: acholi (Beth.-Baker), Lake Victoria, Nyanza, male UP brown.

42. *Euchrysops kabrosae* (Beth.-Baker). Kenya.

43. *Euchrysops malathana* (Bsd.). Throughout Africa and its islands, Arabia.

44. *Euchrysops osiris* (Hpffr.). Throughout Africa.

45. *Euchrysops scintilla* (Mab.). Madagascar.

46. *Euchrysops scintilla* (see 45).

47. *Euliphyra leucyanea* (Hew.). Nigeria to Cameroons.

PLATE 123: Lycaenidae

1. *Euliphyra mirifica* (Holl.). Nigeria to Ogowe.

2. *Everes micylus* (Cr.). Sierra Leone to Nigeria. UP blue.

3. *Everes togara* (Plotz). Cameroons to Congo, Nigeria.

4. *Harpendyreus aequatorialis* (Sharpe). Tanzania, Uganda.

5. *Harpendyreus noquasa* (Trim.). Cape north to Tanzania.

6. *Harpendyreus tsomo* (Trim.). Cape.

7. *Hemiolaus ceres* (Hew.). Kenya. Similar: dolores (Suff.), UP.

8. *Hemiolaus dolores* (Suff.). E. Africa. Similar: coeculus (Hpffr.), Angola to Kenya and Tanzania.

9. *Hewitsonia similis* (Auriv.). Gold Coast to Congo. Similar: kirbyi (Dew.).

10. *Hewitsonia similis* (see 9).

11. *Hypokopelates aruma* (Hew.). Cameroons to Gaboon.

12. *Hypokopelates aruma* (see 11).

13. *Hypokopelates eleala* (Hew.). Sierra Leone to Congo. Similar: otraeda (Hew.), UP blue.

14. *Hypokopelates eleala* (see 13).

15. *Hypokopelates mera* (Hew.). Cameroons to Angola.

16. *Hypolycaena hatita* (Hew.). Sierra Leone to Congo, Angola. Similar: nigra (H. Druce), 2 white dots.

17. *Hypolycaena hatita* (see 16).

18. *Hypolycaena lebona* (Hew.). Sierra Leone to Congo. Similar: dubia (Auriv.), Cameroons.

19. *Hypolycaena liara* (H. Druce). Ghana to Congo and Uganda.

20. *Hypolycaena philippus* (F.). Throughout Africa.

21. *Hypomyrina nomenia* (Hew.). Sierra Leone to Congo.

22. *Iolaphilus calisto* (Dbl. & Hew.). Senegambia to Gaboon.

23. *Iolaphilus laonides* (Auriv.). Sierra Leone.

24. *Iolaphilus ismenias* (Klug.). Nigeria to Sudan.

25. *Iolaphilus julus* (Hew.). Sierra Leone to Nigeria.

26. *Iolaphilus julus* (see 25).

27. *Iolaphilus menas* (H. Druce). Senegambia to Gaboon. Similar: vansomereni (Stempt. & Ben.), Uganda.

28. *Iolaphilus piaggae* (Oberth.). Abyssinia.

29. *Iolaus bolissus* (Hew.). Cameroons, Congo.

30. *Iolaus eurisus* (Cr.). Sierra Leone to Cameroons.

31. *Iridana nigeriana* (Stempt.). Ivory Coast.

32. *Iridana rougeoti* (Stempt.). Gaboon.

33. *Lachnocnema bibulus* (F.). Nigeria to E. Africa, south to Cape. The larvae are carnivorous. Male UP resembles brimo male UP.

34. *Lachnocnema bibulus* (see 33).

35. *Lachnocnema brimo* (Karsch.). Nigeria, Togoland.

36. *Lachnocnema durbani* (Trim.). E. Africa, south to Cape.

37. *Lachnocnema luna* (H. Druce). Cameroons.

38. *Lachnocnema magna* (Auriv.). Cameroons and Congo.

39. *Lachnocnema niveus* (H. Druce). Cameroons.

40. *Larinopoda lagyra* (Hew.). Nigeria to Congo. Several subspecies.

41. *Larinopoda latimarginata* (Smith). Nigeria.

42. *Larinopoda lircaea* (Hew.). Nigeria.

43. *Leptomyrina boschi* (Strand.). Abyssinia.

44. *Leptomyrina hirundo* (Wallengr.). E. Africa, south to Cape.

45. *Leptomyrina lara* (L.). S. Africa, E. Africa to Abyssinia.

46. *Leptomyrina phidias* (F.). Madagascar.

PLATE 124: Lycaenidae

1. *Lepidochrysops aethiopia* (Beth.-Baker). Natal, Transvaal.

2. *Lepidochrysops ariadne* (Btlr.). Natal.

3. *Lepidochrysops caffrariae* (Trim.). Cape to Natal. Similar: trimeni (Beth.-Baker).

4. *Lepidochrysops caffrariae* (see 3).

5. *Lepidochrysops coxii* (Pinhey). S. Rhodesia.

6. *Lepidochrysops delicata* (Beth.-Baker). Rhodesia, Nyasaland.

7. *Lepidochrysops glauca* (Trim.). Transvaal, Rhodesia.

8. *Lepidochrysops giganta* (Trim.). Rhodesia. Similar: stormsi (Robbe), Tanganyika, less blue.

9. *Lepidochrysops grahami* (Trim.). Cape.

10. *Lepidochrysops ignota* (Trim.). Natal, Transvaal. Similar: pephredo (Trim.), Natal.

11. *Lepidochrysops lacrimosa* (Beth.-Baker). Natal, Transvaal. Similar: niobe (Trim.) Cape.

12. *Lepidochrysops letsea* (Trim.). Cape to Rhodesia, Somalia. Similar: cinerea (Solwezi), Kenya, UPH lunules without orange.

13. *Lepidochrysops methymna* (Trim.). Cape to Natal. Similar: puncticilia (Trim.), smaller, no dot on UPH.

14. *Lepidochrysops methymna* (see 13).

15. *Lepidochrysops nevillei* (Beth.-Baker). Rhodesia.

16. *Lepidochrysops ortygia* (Trim.). Cape to Transvaal.

17. *Lepidochrysops patricia* (Trim.). S. and E. Africa to Abyssinia.

18. *Lepidochrysops parsimon* (F.). Sierra Leone to Tanzania, Rhodesia.

19. *Lepidochrysops peculiaris* (Rogenh.). Rhodesia, Tanzania and Kenya. Similar: neavei (Beth.-Baker).

20. *Lepidochrysops peculiaris* (see 19).

21. *Lepidochrysops plebeia* (Btlr.). Natal to Rhodesia. UP similar to letsea.

22. *Lepidochrysops polydialecta* (Beth.-Baker). Nigeria.

23. *Lepidochrysops procera* (Trim.). Natal, Transvaal.

24. *Lepidochrysops tantalus* (Trim.). Natal, Transvaal.

25. *Lepidochrysops victoriae* (Karsch.). Kenya, Uganda.

26. *Lipaphnaeus aderna* (Plotz). Sierra Leone, through Congo to Uganda. Female UP yellow, black edge and spots.

27. *Lipaphnaeus ella* (Hew.). S. Africa to Tanzania.

28. *Liptena campimus* (Holl.). Cameroons.

29. *Liptena catalina* (Smith & Ky.). Sierra Leone to Cameroons.

30. *Liptena despecta* (Holl.). Cameroons. UP black.

31. *Liptena eukrines* (H. Druce). Rhodesia.

32. *Liptena fatima* (Ky.). Cameroons. Similar: allaudi (Mab.), Ghana to Cameroons; albicans (Cator.), Sierra Leone; decipiens (Ky.), Cameroons, Congo.

33. *Liptena ferrymani* (Smith & Ky.). Nigeria.

34. *Liptena helena* (H. Druce). Ghana to Cameroons. Female UP similar to female ideoides and otlauga; modesta resembles helena UN but is plain black UP.

35. *Liptena hollandi* (Auriv.). Congo.

36. *Liptena homeyeri* (Dew.). Congo to Rhodesia.

37. *Liptena ideoides* (Dew.). Uganda.

38. *Liptena ilma* (Hew.). Sierra Leone to Congo and Uganda, Angola. Few subspecies. UP dark brown unmarked.

39. *Liptena libyssa* (Hew.). Nigeria to Angola, Uganda.

40. *Liptena lybia* (Stgr.). Gaboon. Similar: melandeta (Holl.).

41. *Liptena nubifera* (H. Druce). Cameroons.

42. *Liptena opaca* (Ky.). Cameroons to Gaboon.

43. *Liptena o-rubrum* (Holl.). Cameroons.

44. *Liptena o-rubrum* (see 43).

45. *Liptena perobscura* (H. Druce). Cameroons.

46. *Liptena praestans* (Smith). Sierra Leone. Similar: flavicans (Smith & Ky.), Cameroons.

47. *Liptena otlauga* (Smith). Nigeria to Cameroons.

48. *Liptena turbata* (Ky.). Cameroons. Similar: similis (Ky.).

49. *Liptena similis* (Ky.). Cameroons. Similar: turbata (Ky.), UNF markings speckled.

PLATE 125: Lycaenidae

1. *Liptena subvariegata* (Smith & Ky.). Cameroons, Congo.

2. *Liptena subvariegata* (see 1).

3. *Liptena subvariegata* (see 1). Female subspecies aliquantum (H. Druce).

4. *Liptena undina* (Smith & Ky.). Congo.

5. *Liptena undularis* (Hew.). Nigeria to Congo.

6. *Liptena xanthostola* (Holl.). Nigeria to Uganda. Similar: evanescens (Ky.), Nigeria, Cameroons.

7. *Lipaphnaeus leonina* (E. Sharpe). Sierra Leone to Cameroons. UP resembles aderna.

8. *Lycaena abboti* (Holl.). Nyasaland, Kenya. Subspecies of phlaeas.

9. *Lycaena orus* (Cr.). S. Africa.

10. *Megalopalpus metaleucus* (Karsch.). Ghana to Cameroons. Similar: angulosus (Grunb.), Guinea, UPH broader dusky edge.

11. *Megalopalpus zymna* (Dbl. & Hew.). Ghana to Gaboon.

12. *Micropentila adelgitha* (Hew.). Cameroons.

13. *Micropentila alberta* (Stgr.). Ogowe River, Cameroons.

14. *Mimacraea apicalis* (Smith & Ky.). Togoland.

15. *Micropentila gabunica* (St. & Benson). Sierra Leone. Similar: jacksoni (Talbot), Uganda; adelgunda (Stgr.), Cameroons.

16. *Micropentila brunnea* (Ky.). W. Africa, Liberia.

17. *Micropentila mpigi* (St. & Benson). Uganda.

18. *Mimacraea eltringhami* (H. Druce). Unyoro.

19. *Mimacraea fulvaria* (Auriv.). Congo. Similar: pulverulenta (A. Schultze), Congo, and several other species.

20. *Mimacraea heurata* (Holl.). Sierra Leone.

21. *Mimacraea krausei* (Dew.). Congo.

22. *Mimacraea landbecki* (H. Druce). Cameroons. Several very similar species.

23. *Mimacraea marshalli* (Trim.). Rhodesia, Nyasaland.

24. *Mimacraea neokoton* (H. Druce). Rhodesia.

25. *Mimacraea skoptoles* (H. Druce). Rhodesia. Similar: gelinia (Oberth), Nigeria, white patch UPF.

26. *Mimeresia cellularis* (Ky.). Cameroons.

27. *Mimeresia debora* (Ky.). Cameroons.

28. *Mimeresia dinora* (Ky.). Cameroons.

29. *Mimeresia neavei* (Joicey & Talbot). Uganda.

30. *Mimeresia libentina* (Hew.). Cameroons.

31. *Mimeresia semirufa* (Smith). Sierra Leone.

32. *Myrina dermaptera* (Wallengr.). E. Africa to Natal, Rhodesia. Similar: sharpei (Baker), Uganda, larger, duller; subornata (Lathy), Nigeria, smaller, deeper and larger blue patches.

33. *Myrina silenus* (F.). Sierra Leone to Congo, Uganda and Abyssinia. Lfp: Ficus. Similar: ficedula (Trim.), S. and E. Africa, brown patch UPF reaches edge of wing.

34. *Neaveia lamborni* (H. Druce). Nigeria.

35. *Neoepitola barombiensis* (Ky.). Cameroons.

36. *Oboronia gussfeldti* (Dew.). Sierra Leone to Angola. Similar: bueronicus (Karsch.), E. Africa, UPH marginal dots well defined.

37. *Oboronia punctatus* (Dew.). Nigeria. Similar: pseudo-punctatus (Strd.), Nigeria, Cameroons, UP markings lighter.

38. *Ornipholidotos kirbyi* (Auriv.). Cameroons. Similar: sylpha (Ky.), no dots.

39. *Oxylides faunus* (Drury). Sierra Leone to Congo and Uganda, Angola.

40. *Oxylides faunus* (see 39).

41. *Syrmoptera melanomitra* (Karsch.). Cameroons. Male UP resembles Oxylides faunus.

42. *Oxylides amasa* (Hew.). Nigeria.

43. *Oraidium barberae* (Trim.). Cape to Natal. UP as Brephidium metophis.

44. *Phlyana stactalla* (Karsch.). Sierra Leone to Nigeria.

45. *Phylaria cyara* (Hew.). Cameroons, Angola to Kenya.

46. *Phlyana heritsia* (Hew.). Kenya.

47. *Ornipholidotos peucetia* (Hew.). E. Africa.

48. *Ornipholidotos muhata* (Dew.). Cameroons, Congo. Similar: perfragilis (Holl.), narrower black margin.

49. *Ornipholidotos paradoxa* (H. Druce). Cameroons.

50. *Pentila abraxas* (Dbl. & Hew.). Ghana to Cameroons. Similar: telesippe (Grunb.), Cameroons, smaller dots.

51. *Pentila aspasia* (Grunb.). Spanish Guinea. Similar: abraxas (Dbl. & Hew.), Ghana to Cameroons, broader black tip UPF.

52. *Pentila auga* (Karsch.). Cameroons, Congo.

53. *Pentila bitje* (H. Druce). Cameroons.

54. *Pentila hewitsoni* (Smith & Ky.). Nigeria, Cameroons. Similar: pardalena (H. Druce), Cameroons.

55. *Pentila laura* (Ky.). Lagos.

PLATE 126: Lycaenidae

1. *Pentila mombasae* (Smith & Ky.). Tanzania. Similar: lasti (Smith & Ky.), Kenya.

2. *Pentila occidentalium* (Auriv.). Cameroons.

3. *Pentila pauli* (Stgr.). Nigeria. Variable.

4. *Pentila petreia* (Hew.). Ghana to Uganda. Similar: UP preussi (Stgr.), Sierra Leone to Congo.

5. *Pentila phidia* (Hew.). Ghana, Togoland.

6. *Pentila preussi* (Stgr.). Sierra Leone to Congo.

7. *Pentila rotha* (Hew.). Cameroons. Similar: amenaida (Hew.), Congo, Nyasaland.

8. *Pentila torrida* (Ky.). Gaboon. Similar: tachyroides (Dew.), Cameroons, no dots.

9. *Pentila tropicalis* (Bsd.). S. Africa to Natal and Rhodesia.

10. *Phasis argyraspis* (Trim.). Cape.

11. *Phasis lycegenes* (Trim.). S. Africa to Natal.

12. *Phasis malagrida* (Wallengr.). Cape Town.

13. *Phasis sardonyx* (Trim.). Cape.

14. *Phasis sardonyx* (see 13).

15. *Phasis felthami* (Trim.). Cape. Similar: chrysaor (Trim.), smaller black spots UP.

16. *Phasis thero* (L.). Cape. Similar: clavum (Murray).

17. *Phasis wallengreni* (Trim.). Cape. Similar: malagrida (Wallengr.), Cape to Transvaal; mcmasteri (Dickson) UN silver markings less angular.

18. *Phytala elais* (Dbl. & Hew.). Ghana, Nigeria, Congo. Female UP brown.

19. *Phytala hyettina* (Auriv.). Angola.

20. *Phytala hyettoides* (Auriv.). Nigeria.

21. *Phytala intermixta* (Auriv.). Cameroons.

22. *Phytala vansomereni* (Jackson). Uganda. Female UP brown.

23. *Pilodeudorix diyllus* (Hew.). Sierra Leone to Nigeria. Similar: camerona (Plotz), Uganda; ankolensis (Stemp.), Cameroons, larger.

24. *Poecilmitis chrysaor* (Trim.). Cape. Many similar species, including: aethon (Trim.); lycegenes (Trim.); lyncurium (Trim.).

25. *Poecilmitis palmus* (Cr.). Cape Province.

26. *Poecilmitis thysbe* (L.). Cape Province. Similar: pyroeis (Trim.), UP with glaze less.

27. *Poecilmitis zeuxo* (L.). Cape. Similar: chrysaor (Trim.).

28. *Powellana cottoni* (Baker). Cameroons, Congo.

29. *Powellana cottoni* (see 28).

30. *Pseudaletis agrippina* (H. Druce). Cameroons.

31. *Pseudaletis batesi* (H. Druce). Cameroons, Sierra Leone.

32. *Pseudaletis clymenus* (H. Druce). Cameroons, Sierra Leone.

33. *Pseudaletis leonis* (Stgr.). Sierra Leone.

34. *Pseudaletis mazanguli* (Neave). Congo.

35. *Pseudonacaduba aethiops* (Mab.). Gaboon to Congo.

36. *Pseudonacaduba sichela* (Wallengr.). Cape to Rhodesia and Mozambique.

37. *Scolitantides notoba* (Trim.). Cape to Transvaal and Rhodesia. Lfp: Salvia, Mesembryanthemum.

38. *Spalgis lemolea* (H. Druce). W. Africa to Congo and Rhodesia. Similar: tintinga (Bsd.), Madagascar.

39. *Spindasis crustaria* (Holl.). Uganda.

40. *Spindasis ella* (Hew.). Natal.

41. *Spindasis homeyeri* (Dew.). Congo to Tanzania, Rhodesia. UP as mozambica.

42. *Spindasis mozambica* (Bertol.). Sierra Leone to Togo, S. Africa to Nyasaland. Similar: apelles (Oberth.).

43. *Spindasis namaqua* (Trim.). Cape.

44. *Spindasis natalensis* (Dbl. & Hew.). S. Africa to Zambia.

45. *Spindasis phanes* (Trim.). S. Africa to Transvaal.

46. *Spindasis somalina* (Btlr.). Somalia.

47. *Spindasis subaureus* (Gr.Sm.). Nigeria, Cameroons.

48. *Spindasis tavetensis* (Lathy). Rhodesia.

49. *Spindasis trimeni* (Neave). Rhodesia. UP resembles ella.

50. *Spindasis waggae* (E. M. Sharpe). Somaliland.

51. *Stugeta bowkeri* (Trim.). E. and S. Africa.

52. *Stugeta marmorea* (Btlr.). Ghana across Africa to Abyssinia.

PLATE 127: Lycaenidae

1. *Tanutheira timon* (F.). Sierra Leone to Cameroons.

2. *Tarucus thespis* (L.). Cape to Rhodesia. Similar: bowkeri (Trim.).

3. *Tarucus bowkeri* (Trim.). Natal, Transvaal. Similar: thespis (L.).

4. *Tarucus sybaris* (Hpff.). Cape, E. Africa to Abyssinia. UP as thespis.

5. *Tarucus thespis* (see 2).

6. *Telipna acraea* (Dbl. & Hew.). Ghana to Cameroons.

7. *Telipna carnuta* (Hew.). Sierra Leone to Uganda.

8. *Telipna bimacula* (Plotz). Ghana to Congo.

9. *Telipna erica* (Suff.) Cameroons. Similar: acraeoides (Smith & Ky.); sanguinea (Plotz), Angola, Cameroons.

10. *Telipna transverstigma* (Druce). Cameroons.

11. *Teratoneura isabellae* (Dudg.). Sierra Leone.

12. *Teriomima puellaris* (Trim.). Rhodesia, Tanzania. Similar: zuluana (Van Son), more and larger spots UN.

13. *Teriomima subpunctata* (Ky.). Kenya, Tanzania.

14. *Thermoniphas plurilimbata* (Karsch.). Uganda, Congo.

15. *Thestor basuta* (Wallengr.). Cape to Transvaal, Rhodesia.

16. *Thestor brachyara* (Trim.). Cape.

17. *Thestor protumnus* (L.). Cape to Transvaal. Variable.

18. *Thestor obscurus* (Van Son.). Cape.

19. *Thestor strutti* (Van Son.). Cape.

20. *Toxochitona gerda* (Ky.). Cameroons.

21. *Uranothauma poggei* (see 28).

22. *Trichiolaus mermeros* (Mab.). Madagascar. Similar: argentarius (Btlr.), Madagascar, UP duller blue.

23. *Uranothauma antinorii* (Oberth.). E. Africa to Abyssinia, Congo.

24. *Uranothauma crawshayi* (Btlr.). Nyasaland.

25. *Uranothauma falkensteini* (Dew.). Sierra Leone to Kenya.

26. *Uranothauma nubifer* (Trim.). E. Africa to Natal. Similar: cuneatum (Tite), Kavirondo.

27. *Zizina antanossa* (Mab.). Sudan through E. Africa to Natal, Congo, Madagascar.

28. *Uranothauma poggei* (Dew.). Nigeria to Kenya, Rhodesia, Angola.

29. *Virachola bimaculata* (Hew.). Sierra Leone.

30. *Virachola livia* (Klug.). Egypt, Arabia, E. Africa. Lfp: Acacia. Terrain: arid districts. Female UP grey blue. Similar: perse (Hew.), Himalayas to Philippines; dinomenes (Gr.Sm.), Uganda, larger, brighter.

31. *Zeritis neriene* (Bsd.). Ghana, Nigeria, Rhodesia. Similar: amine (Btlr.).

32. *Zeritis sorhageni* (Dew.). Angola.

Nemeobiidae

33. *Abisara gerontes* (F.). Sierra Leone, Congo, Uganda.

34. *Abisara rogersi* (Druce). Congo, Angola. Similar: dewitzi (Auriv.), Congo; delicata (Lathy), Nyasaland.

35. *Abisara rutherfordi* (Hew.). Nigeria, Cameroons, Congo.

36. *Abisara rutherfordi* (see 35).

37. *Abisara talantus* (Auriv.). Nigeria, Cameroons.

38. *LIBYTHEID: Libythea labdaca* (Ww.). Sierra Leone, Congo, Uganda.

39. *Saribia tepahi* (Bsd.). Madagascar.

PLATE 128: Hesperiidae

1. *Abantis bicolor* (Trim.). Cape, Natal.

2. *Abantis bismarcki* (Karsch.). Tanganyika.

3. *Abantis leucogaster* (Mab.). Sierra Leone, Cameroons. Similar: efulensis (Holl.), Cameroons, Congo, larger, brown streaks UPH.

4. *Abantis paradisea* (Btlr.). Natal, Transvaal, Rhodesia.

5. *Abantis zambesiaca* (Ww.). Zambia, Rhodesia.

6. *Abantis tettensis* (Hpffr.). Cape to Angola and River Zambezi.

7. *Abantis venosa* (Trim.). Transvaal to Rhodesia, Angola. Similar: flava (Evans), Uganda, smaller transparencies UPF.

8. *Acada annulifer* (Holl.). Nigeria to Gaboon.

9. *Acada biseriatus* (Mab.). Dar-es-Salaam, E. Africa.

10. *Acleros mackenii* (Trim.). Cape to Angola and Tanzania. Few subspecies. Similar: leucopyga (Mab.), Madagascar, much smaller.

11. *Acleros mackenii* (see 10).

12. *Acleros placidus* (Plotz). Ghana to Cameroons.

13. *Alenia sandaster* (Trim.). Cape.

14. *Andronymus neander* (Plotz). Nigeria, Natal, Transvaal. Similar: gander (Evans), Uganda, darker UN.

15. *Andronymous philander* (Hopff.). W. Africa to Angola, E. Africa. Subspecies of hero (Evans).

16. *Artitropa comus* (Cr.), W. Africa to Congo.

17. *Artitropa erinnys* (Tr.). Cape to Transvaal, E. Africa. Dusk flyer.

18. *Artitropa shelleyi* (E. Sharpe). W. Africa. Similar: hollandi (Oberth.), Madagascar.

19. *Astictopterus anomaeus* (Plotz). Nigeria, Sierra Leone.

20. *Astictopterus inornatus* (Trim.). Cape, Natal.

21. *Astictopterus stellatus* (Trim.). Mozambique, E. Africa.

22. *Borbo borbonica* (Bsd.). Throughout Africa.

23. *Borbo detecta* (Trim.). Natal to Kenya. Similar: chagwa (Evans), Uganda, larger.

24. *Borbo fallax* (Gaede). Cameroons to Nyasaland, Natal to Transvaal.

25. *Borbo fatuellus* (Hpffr.). Sierra Leone to E. and S. Africa.

26. *Borbo gemella* (Mab.). S. Africa.

27. *Borbo holtzii* (Plotz). Transvaal, Angola, to Ethiopia. UNH spotting sometimes absent.

28. *Borbo lugens* (Hpffr.). E. Africa.

29. *Borbo micans* (Holl.). Nigeria through Cameroons to Kenya, Ethiopia.

30. *Borbo perobscura* (H. Druce). Ghana to Uganda.

31. *Borbo ratek* (Bsd.). Madagascar.

32. *Brusa saxicola* (Neave). Congo.

33. *Caenides benga* (Holl.). Cameroons.

34. *Caenides dacena* (Hew.). Sierra Leone to Gaboon.

35. *Caenides hidarioides* (Auriv.). Cameroons, Congo.

36. *Caenides soritia* (Hew.). Senegal to Gaboon.

37. *Calleagris hollandi* (Btlr.). Nyasaland.

38. *Calleagris jamesoni* (E. Sharpe). Rhodesia.

39. *Calleagris kobela* (Trim.). Cape to Transvaal.

40. *Calleagris lacteus* (Mab.). Nigeria to Uganda.

41. *Caprona pillaana* (Wallengr.). Natal to Rhodesia.

42. *Celaenorrhinus atratus* (Mab.). Cameroons. Similar: boadicea (Hew.), Cameroons to Gaboon.

43. *Celaenorrhinus bettoni* (Btlr.). Nigeria to Sudan.

44. *Celaenorrhinus chrysoglossa* (Mab.). Cameroons.

45. *Celaenorrhinus galenus* (F.). Senegambia to Nigeria.

46. *Celaenorrhinus humbloti* (Mab.). Madagascar.

47. *Celaenorrhinus illustris* (Mab.). Cameroons. Similar: beni (Bet. Bak.), Congo, smaller and darker.

48. *Celaenorrhinus meditrina* (Hew.). Cameroons.

49. *Celaenorrhinus mokeezi* (Walleng.). Cape to Rhodesia.

50. *Celaenorrhinus proxima* (Mab.). Sierra Leone to Gaboon.

51. *Celaenorrhinus rutilans* (Mab.). Congo. Female UP paler.

52. *Ceratricia aurea* (H. ·Druce). Congo. Similar: argyrosticta (Plotz), Uganda, black edge to UPH.

53. *Ceratricia flava* (Hew.). Cameroons, Congo, C. Africa. Male UPF mostly yellow, also UPH. Similar: woolastoni (Heron), UNF has solid brown tip.

54. *Ceratricia nothus* (F.). W. Africa. Similar: brunnea (B.B.), Kenya, much larger marginal brown patch UNH.

55. *Ceratricia phocion* (F.). Sierra Leone to Congo. Similar: hollandi (B.B.), Congo, darker, with larger brown patches UNH; semilutea (Mab.), Uganda, small, UPH yellow.

56. *Chondrolepis niveicornis* (Plotz). Angola, Rhodesia to Malawi. Similar: nero (Evans), Cameroons, much darker UN; cynthia (Evans), Kenya, bar across UNH very faint.

57. *Coliades anchises* (Gerst.). E. Africa to Somalia, Natal, Aden. Similar: jucunda (Btlr.), Socotra.

58. *Coliades aeschylus* (Plotz). Senegal. Similar: lucagus (Cram.), Gold Coast, without white fringe.

59. *Coliades chalybe* (Dbl. & Hew.). Togo to Congo. Similar: Pyrrhopyge bixae (L.).

60. *Coliades fervida* (Btlr.). Madagascar. Similar: fidia (Evans) Madagascar, yellow rather than orange UP; arbogastes (Guenee), Madagascar, UPH whitish.

61. *Coliades forestan* (Cr.). Throughout Africa.

62. *Coliades keithloa* (Wallengr.). Cape to Natal.

63. *Coliades libeon* (Dre.). Cameroons to Natal.

64. *Coliades pisistratus* (F.). Sierra Leone to S. Africa. Similar: hanno (Plotz), Sierra Leone to Gaboon.

65. *Coliades ramanatek* (Bsd.). Madagascar.

PLATE 129: Hesperiidae

1. *Eagris decastigma* (Mab.). Cameroons. Similar: tigris (Evans), Uganda.

2. *Eagris denuba* (Plotz). Sierra Leone to Cameroons.

3. *Eagris hereus* (Druce). Angola.

4. *Eagris lucetia* (Hew.). Angola, Uganda.

5. *Eagris nottoana* (Wallengr.). Cape to Rhodesia.

6. *Eagris phyllophila* (Trim.). E. Africa.

7. *Eagris sabadius* (Gray). Madagascar, Mauritius, Comoro. Many subspecies, whose UN sometimes entirely lacks yellow.

8. *Eagris tetrastigma* (Mab.). Rhodesia to Cameroons.

9. *Eretis djaelaelae* (Wallengr.). S. Africa to Angola, Somalia and Abyssinia.

10. *Eretis lugens* (Rog.). E. Africa.

11. *Fulda coroller* (Bsd.). Madagascar.

12. *Fresna netopha* (Hew.); W. Africa to Uganda, south to Angola.

13. *Fresna nyassae* (Hew.). Rhodesia, Mozambique.

14. *Fulda rhadama* (Bsd.). Madagascar. Several similar species, all from Madagascar.

15. *Gegenes hottentota* (Latr.). S. Africa, W. Africa, Yemen.

16. *Gegenes hottentota* (see 15).

17. *Gegenes ursula* (Holl.). E. Africa.

18. *Gamia bucholzi* (Plotz). Ghana.

19. *Gomalia elma* (Trim.). Cape to Angola and Nyasaland.

20. *Gorgyra aburae* (Plotz). Ghana to Gaboon.

21. *Gorgyra afikpo* (H. Druce). Cameroons, Gaboon.

22. *Gorgyra aretina* (Hew.). Togo, Gaboon. Similar: subflavida (Holl.), E. Africa.

23. *Gorgyra johnstoni* (Btlr.). Gaboon to Nyasaland. Several species. Similar: minima (Holl.), smaller, UN less blued.

24. *Gorgyra rubescens* (Holl.). Cameroons.

25. *Gorgyra subnotata* (Holl.). W. Africa.

Similar: Subfacatus (Mab.), Sierra Leone, UN yellow marking diffuse.

26. *Gretna cylinda* (Hew.). Ghana, Togo, Angola. Similar: lacida (Hew.), Gaboon; zaremba (Plotz), Nigeria to Congo, smaller.

27. *Gretna balenge* (Holl.). Sierra Leone.

28. *Gretna waga* (Plotz). Ghana to Nigeria.

29. *Hypoleucis tripunctata* (Mab.). Togo to Gaboon. Similar: ophiusa (Hew.), UNH more broadly marked with brown.

30. *Katreus dimidia* (Holl.). Gaboon.

31. *Katreus johnstoni* (Btlr.). Sierra Leone to Cameroons.

32. *Kedestes barberae* (Trim.). Cape, Natal, Transvaal.

33. *Kedestes callicles* (Hew.). Congo, Natal and E. Africa to Somalia. Similar: malua (Neave), Rhodesia.

34. *Kedestes callicles* (see 33).

35. *Kedestes lepenula* (Wallengr.). Natal, Transvaal, Rhodesia, Mozambique. Several subspecies.

36. *Kedestes mohozutza* (Wallengr.). Cape, Natal, Transvaal. Similar UP: chaca (Trim.).

37. *Kedestes nerva* (F.). Natal, Transvaal.

38. *Kedestes niveostriga* (Trim.). S. Africa.

39. *Kedestes wallengreni* (Trim.). Natal, Transvaal, Kenya.

40. *Leona leonora* (Plotz). Ghana to Congo.

41. *Leona stohri* (Karsch.). Ghana to Cameroons. Similar: lissa (Evans), Uganda, UPF large yellow patches coalesced.

42. *Lepella lepeletier* (Latr.). C. Africa.

43. *Leucochitonea levubu* (Wallengr.). Cape to Transvaal and Rhodesia.

44. *Malaza carmides* (Hew.). Madagascar.

45. *Melphina malthina* (Hew.). Sierra Leone to Gaboon. Similar: tarace (Mab.), Uganda, markings yellowish.

46. *Melphina statirides* (Holl.). Sierra Leone. Subspecies of tarace (Mab.).

47. *Melphina statira* (Mab.). Sierra Leone. Similar: melphis (Holl.), Nigeria, narrower white bar UNH.

48. *Metisella aegipon* (Trim.). S. Africa. Terrain: montane.

49. *Metisella meninx* (Trim.). Natal and Transvaal.

50. *Metisella metis* (L.). S. Africa to Angola and Kenya. Similar: malgacha (Bsd.), Cape to Transvaal, Madagascar, smaller; quadrisignatus (Btlr.), Zomba, fewer orange spots UP.

51. *Metisella perexcellens* (Btlr.). Nyasa.

52. *Metisella syrinx* (Trim.). Cape. Terrain: montane.

53. *Metisella willemi* (Wallengr.). Transvaal, Somalia.

54. *Meza cybeutes* (Holl.). Cameroons, Congo.

55. *Meza mabillei* (Holl.). Cameroons.

56. *Meza meza* (Hew.). Togo to Angola. Similar: larea (Neave), Nyasaland, lighter colour.

57. *Meza indusiata* (Mab.). Cameroons. A few similar species.

58. *Miraja sylvia* (Evans). Madagascar. Several similar species all from Madagascar.

59. *Moltena fiara* (Btlr.). Cape, Natal. Lfp: Banana.

60. *Monza alberti* (Holl.). Cameroons to Gaboon to Nyasaland.

61. *Monza cretacea* (Snell.). Sierra Leone to Congo.

62. *Mopala orma* (Plotz). Togoland.

63. *Netrobalane canopus* (Trim.). Cape to Transvaal and Rhodesia.

64. *Osmodes adon* (Mab.). Sierra Leone to Gaboon.

65. *Osmodes adosus* (Mab.). Sierra Leone to Gaboon. Similar: distinctus (Holl.), Gaboon, UN is darker.

66. *Osmodes costatus* (Auriv.). Cameroons.

67. *Osmodes laronia* (Hew.). Ghana to Gaboon, Nigeria.

68. *Osmodes laronia* (see 50). This is the general female pattern of Osmodes species.

69. *Osmodes lux* (Holl.). Congo.

PLATE 130: Hesperiidae

1. *Osphantes ogawena* (Mab.). Congo.

2. *Osmodes thops* (Holl.). Togo, Gaboon.

3. *Parasmodes morantii* (Trim.). Transvaal, Natal to Zambezi River.

4. *Pardaleodes bule* (Holl.). Cameroons, Congo.

5. *Pardaleodes edipus* (Cr.). Sierra Leone to Cameroons.

6. *Pardaleodes incerta* (Snell.). Nigeria to Congo.

7. *Pardaleodes sator* (Westwood). Congo.

8. *Pardaleodes tibullus* (Fab.). Nigeria.

9. *Parnara monazi* (Trim.). Natal, Transvaal.

10. *Paronymus ligora* (Hew.). Sierra Leone to Angola.

11. *Paronymus xanthias* (Mab.). Nigeria to Gaboon.

12. *Perrotia eximia* (Oberth.). Madagascar.

13. *Platylesches ayresii* (Trim.). S. Africa to Rhodesia.

14. *Platylesches chamaeleon* (Mab.). W. Africa. Similar: affinissima (Strand), Nyasa.

15. *Platylesches galesa* (Hew.). Nyasaland, Transvaal.

16. *Platylesches moritili* (Wallengr.). S. Africa to C. Africa.

17. *Platylesches picanini* (Holl.). Liberia, Congo, Transvaal.

18. *Platylesches robustus* (Neave). E. Africa to Transvaal. A few similar species.

19. *Ploetzia amygdalis* (Mab.). Madagascar.

20. *Prosopalpus duplex* (Mab.). Sierra Leone.

21. *Pteroteinon caenira* (Hew.). Cameroons, Congo. Female has four hyaline spots UPF, no white band.

22. *Pteroteinon capronnieri* (Plotz). Ghana to Congo.

23. *Pteroteinon iricolor* (Holl.). Cameroons to Sierra Leone.

24. *Pteroteinon laufella* (Hew.). Ghana to Congo.

25. *Pteroteinon laufella* (see 24).

26. *Pyrrhochalcia iphis* (Drury). Sierra Leone to Congo. UP black-blue, female UP veined green-gold. Similar: juno (Plotz), Ghana, smaller.

27. *Rhabdomantis galatia* (Hew.). Sierra Leone to Mozambique.

28. *Rhabdomantis sosia* (Mab.). Cameroons to Mozambique. Male UP as galatia, but deeper brown.

29. *Sarangesa astrigera* (Btlr.). Rhodesia. Similar: pandaensis (J. & T.), Rhodesia, marginal spots UP yellow.

30. *Sarangesa exprompta* (Holl.). Ghana, Abyssinia.

31. *Sarangesa grisea* (Hew.). Liberia to Gaboon.

32. *Sarangesa laelius* (Mab.). Togo, Gaboon, E. Africa. Similar: eliminata (Holl.), Sahara, Sudan.

33. *Sarangesa motozi* (Wallengr.). Cape to Angola, Somalia and Abyssinia. Similar: lucidella (Mab.), Zanzibar, Rhodesia, UP marks smaller, UN less yellow.

34. *Sarangesa phidyle* (Walk.). Cape to Rhodesia.

35. *Sarangesa seineri* (Strd.). Natal to Rhodesia.

36. *Sarangesa tricerata* (Mab.). Sierra Leone, Nigeria.

37. *Semalea pulvina* (Plotz). Sierra Leone to Gaboon and Mozambique.

38. *Spialia colotes* (Dre.). Transvaal Rhodesia, Angola, Congo.

39. *Spialia dromus* (Plotz). Natal, E. Africa, Gaboon. Very many subspecies.

40. *Syrichtus abscondita* (Plotz). Natal, Transvaal, Rhodesia.

41. *Syrichtus agylla* (Trim.). Cape to Transvaal and Rhodesia.

42. *Syrichtus asterodia* (Trim.). Cape to Transvaal and Rhodesia.

43. *Syrichtus delagoae* (Trim.). Natal Transvaal, Rhodesia.

44. *Syrichtus diomus* (Hpffr.). Throughout S. Africa, north to Tanzania.

45. *Syrichtus nanus* (Trim.). Cape, Rhodesia.

46. *Syrichtus ploetzi* (Auriv.). Sierra Leone to Congo.

47. *Syrichtus rebeli* (Higgins). Uganda.

48. *Syrichtus ' sataspes* (Trim.). Cape, Rhodesia.

49. *Syrichtus secessus* (Trim.). Transvaal, Rhodesia.

50. *Syrichtus spio* (L.). Cape to Angola and Tanzania.

51. *Teniorrhinus watsoni* (Holl.). Congo. Subspecies niger (Dre.).

52. *Tagiades flesus* (F.). Sierra Leone to E. Africa, south to Natal. Similar: insularis (Mab.), Madagascar.

53. *Tagiades flesus* (see 52).

54. *Teniorrhinus harona* (Westw.). E. Africa.

55. *Teniorrhinus herilus* (Hpffr.). Mozambique.

56. *Teniorrhinus ignita* (Mab.). Sierra Leone to Cameroons.

57. *Tsitana tsita* (Trim.). Cape to Transvaal. UP brown, unmarked. Similar: tulbagha (Evans), Cape.

58. *Tsitana wallacei* (Neave). Rhodesia.

59. *Xanthodisca astrape* (Holl.). Togo Gaboon.

60. *Xanthodisca vibius* (Hew.). Sierra Leone.

61. *Zophopetes cerymica* (Hew.). Senegambia to Congo.

62. *Zophopetes dysmephila* (Trim.). E. Africa to Cape. Lfp: date palms.

63. *Zenonia zeno* (Trim.). S. Africa to Nigeria, E. Africa to Kenya.

Indo-Australasia

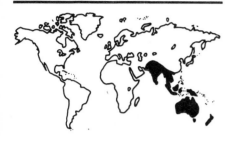

PLATE 131 : Papilionidae

1. *Chilasa paradoxa* (Zink.). Assam to Malaysia. Form niasicus. Very variable with many forms.

2. *Chilasa paradoxa* (Zink.). Malaysia, Indonesia. Form enigma.

3. *Chilasa slateri* (Hew.). N. India to Malaysia, Sumatra.

4. *Graphium empedovana* (F.). Malaysia, Java, Sumatra. Several subspecies. Similar: codrus (Cr.), Philippines, Celebes, Solomon Islands.

5. *Chilasa veiovis* (Hew.). Celebes.

6. *Graphium agetes* (Westw.). Sikkim to Malaya and Sumatra.

7. *Dabasa gyas* (Westw.). Sikkim, Assam, Upper Burma.

8. *Dabasa payeni* (Bsd.). Sikkim to Java and Borneo. A few subspecies.

9. *Graphium androcles* (Bsd.). Celebes. Similar: dorcus (de Haan), Celebes, lacks green stripes on UPF.

10. *Graphium agamemnon* (L.). Indo-Malayan area, N. Australia. Many subspecies. Similar: macfarlanei (Btlr.), Moluccas, New Guinea.

11. *Cressida cressida* (F.). N. Australia, New Guinea. Female with hardly any colour.

12. *Graphium antiphates* (Cr.). Assam through Burma to China and south through Siam to Malaysia, India and Ceylon. Many subspecies. Similar: euphrates (Fldr.), Borneo to Philippines.

13. *Graphium aristeus* (Cr.). N. India through Burma to N. Australia and south through Siam to Malaysia. Several subspecies.

14. *Graphium arycles* (Bsd.). Burma through Siam to Malaysia.

15. *Graphium bathycles* (Zink.). Himalayas to Malaysia.

16. *Graphium cloanthus* (Westw.). Kashmir to China, Sumatra.

17. *Graphium delesserti* (Guer.). Malaysia.

18. *Graphium deucalion* (Bsd.). Moluccas.

19. *Graphium doson* (Fldr.). N. and S. India, Ceylon, Burma, Assam, Malaysia, Philippines. Many subspecies.

20. *Graphium evemon* (Bsd.). Assam to Malaysia, Java. Similar: eurypelus (L.), Philippines, Moluccas, New Guinea.

21. *Graphium macareus* (Godt.). N. India to Philippines, Siam to Malaysia.

22. *Graphium macleayanus* (Leach). E. Australia.

23. *Graphium nomius* (Esp.). S. India, Ceylon, Burma, Siam.

24. *Graphium ramaceus* (Westw.). Malaysia.

PLATE 132 : Papilionidae

1. *Graphium thule* (Wall.). New Guinea. Female extensive white markings UP.

2. *Graphium wallacei* (Hew.). Moluccas, New Guinea. Similar: browni (Grdm. & Salv.).

3. *Graphium weiski* (Ribbe) New Guinea. With a blue subspecies.

4. *Graphium xenocles* (Dbl.). N. India, Burma and Siam.

5. *Lamproptera meges* (Zink.). Philippines, Celebes, Burma, Siam, Malaysia. Similar: curius (F.).

6. *Ornithoptera chimaera* (Rothsch.). New Guinea. Female resembles paradisea female. Similar: tithonus (Deh.).

7. *Pachlioptera aristolochiae* (F.). China, Siam, Burma, Malaysia. Many subspecies and species. Similar: mariae (Semp.), Philippines; phegeus (Hopff.).

8. *Ornithoptera croesus* (Gray). Halmahera. Female resembles victoriae female.

9. *Ornithoptera priamus* (L.). Moluccas, New Guinea, Solomon Islands, N. Australia. Many local forms, with females as Ornithoptera victoriae.

10. *Ornithoptera goliath* (Oberth.). New Guinea.

11. *Pachlioptera atropos* (Stgr.). Palawan.

12. *Pachlioptera jophon* (Gray). S.W. India and Ceylon.

13. *Ornithoptera paradisea* (see 15).

14. *Pachlioptera liris* (Godt.). Timor. Similar: oreon (Doherty); pandiyana (Moore), S. India, paler.

15. *Ornithoptera paradisea* (Stgr.). New Guinea. Similar: meridiorialis (Rothsch.).

PLATE 133 : Papilionidae

1. *Ornithoptera victoriae* (Gray). Solomon Islands.

2. *Ornithoptera urvillianus* (see 3).

3. *Ornithoptera urvillianus* (Guer.). Admiralty Islands, Solomon Islands.

4. *Papilio deiphobus* subspecies *deiphontes* (Fldr.). Sumatra.

5. *Papilio aegeus* (Don.). New Guinea to New South Wales. Several subspecies.

6. *Papilio aegeus* (see 5).

7. *Papilio deiphobus* (L.). Moluccas. Female tailed, UP as Papilio deiphontes.

8. *Papilio ascalaphus* (Bsd.). Celebes.

9. *Papilio deiphobus* (see 7).

10. *Pachlioptera polydorus* (L.). Moluccas to N. Australia. Many local subspecies. Similar: liris (Godt.).

11. *Papilio crino* (F.). Calcutta to Ceylon.

12. *Papilio anactus* (MacLeay). Australia Queensland to New South Wales.

13. *Papilio canopus* (Westw.). Timor, N. Australia. Several subspecies, some tailless.

14. *Papilio castor* (Westw.). Sikkim to Malaya. Female resembles C. clytia.

15. *Papilio ambrax* (Bsd.). New Guinea to Queensland. Several subspecies. Female small white patch UPH, red lunules, brownish.

16. *Papilio demolion* (Cr.). Burma, Siam, Malaysia, Sumatra. Similar: liomedon (Moore), S. India; gigon (Fldr.), Celebes, larger.

PLATE 134: Papilionidae

1. *Ornithoptera victoriae* (Gray). Solomon Islands.

2. *Papilio lorquinianus* (Fldr.). Moluccas, New Guinea.

3. *Papilio gambrisius* (Cr.). Moluccas, Amboina. Male similar, no white UPF.

4. *Papilio elephenor* (Dbl.). Assam. UP as P protenor.

5. *Papilio euchenor* (Guer.). New Guinea. Many subspecies.

6. *Papilio iswara* (White). Burma, Malaysia. Similar: sataspes (Fldr.), Celebes.

7. *Papilio godeffroyi* (Semp.). Samoa.

8. *Papilio hoppo* (Mats.). Formosa.

9. *Papilio ilioneus* (Don.). New Caledonia.

10. *Papilio fuscus* (Goeze). Andamans through Malaysia to Philippines. Extremely variable with many subspecies.

11. *Papilio krishna* (Moore). Himalayas.

12. *Papilio laglaizei* (Depuis.). New Guinea.

13. *Papilio laglaizei* (see 12).

14. *Papilio dravidarum* (Wood-Mas.). S. India.

15. *Papilio memnon* (L.). N. India through Burma to China, south to Malaysia, Java. Very many subspecies and forms.

16. *Papilio memnon* (L.). Female form *butlerianus* (Rothsch.)

17. *Papilio memnon* (L.). Female form *distantianus* (Rothsch.)

PLATE 135: Papilionidae

1. *Papilio nephelus* (Bdv.). Malaysia. Several subspecies and similar species. Similar: helenus (L.); chaon (Westw.).

2. *Papilio palinurus* (F.). Burma to Malaya, Sumatra, Philippines.

3. *Papilio peranthus* (F.). Java, Celebes.

4. *Papilio polymnestor* (Cr.). Calcutta to Ceylon.

5. *Parides hageni* (Regenh.). Sumatra.

6. *Papilio phestus* (Guer.). Solomon Islands, New Britain. Female white veining UPF.

7. *Parides nox* (Swains). Malaysia. Several subspecies.

8. *Papilio hector* (L.). Ceylon to Bengal.

9. *Papilio woodfordi* (Godm. & Salv.). Solomon Islands.

10. *Parides latreillei* (Don.). Himalayas, Burma.

11. *Parides neptunus* (Guer.). Malaysia, Sumatra.

12. *Papilio ulysses* (L.). New Guinea. Many forms and subspecies. Similar: montrouzieri (Bdv.), smaller.

13. *Papilio toboroi* (Ribbe). Bougainville, Solomon Islands.

14. *Parides philoxenus* (Gray). Himalayas to Indo-China.

15. *Parides varuna* (White). Sikkim to Burma and Malaysia. Similar: aidoneces (Dbl.)

16. *Parides priapus* (Bsd.). Burma, Malaysia, Sumatra, Java.

17. *Papilio ulysses* (see 12).

18. *Parnassius simo* (Gray). Ladakh, Tibet. Similar: acco (Gray), Karakorum.

19. *Trogonoptera brookiana* (Wall.). Malaya, Sumatra, Borneo. Similar: trogon (Voll.)

PLATE 136: Papilionidae

1. *Parides coon* (F.). Malaysia. Few subspecies. Similar: rhodifer (Butler).

2. *Papilio rumanzovia* (Eschsch.). Philippines, Celebes.

3. *Trogonoptera brookiana* (Wall.). Malaya, Sumatra, Borneo. Similar: trogon (Voll.)

4. *Troides helena* (L.). India, Malaysia. Many local subspecies.

5. *Troides helena* (see 4).

6. *Troides haliphron* (Bsd.). Timor, Celebes. Similar: socrates (Stgr.); iris (Rob.).

7. *Troides hypolitus* (Cr.). Moluccas, Celebes.

8. *Troides haliphron* (Bsd.). Timor, Celebes. (See 6 also.)

9. *Teinopalpus imperialis* (Hope). Nepal to Burma.

10. *Eurytides xanticles* (Bates). Panama, Colombia. Similar: oberthueri (R. & J.), Honduras; arcesilaus (Luc.), Venezuela, Colombia.

11. *Troides rhadamantus* (see 13).

12. *Teinopalpus imperialis* (see 9).

13. *Troides mirandus* (Btlr.). Borneo, Sumatra. Similar: amphrysus (Cr.), Malaya, Sumatra, Java, Borneo.

PLATE 137: Amathusidae

1. *Aemona amathusia* (Hew.). Assam.

2. *Aemona lena* (Atk.). Burma. Male resembles oberthuri.

3. *Amathusia binghami* (Fruhst.). Malaya, Sumatra.

4. *Amathusia masina* (Fruhst.). Borneo. Similar: virgata (Btlr.), S. Celebes.

5. *Amathusia perakana* (Honr.). Malaya.

6. *Amathusia phidippus* (L.). Siam, Burma, Malaya. Many subspecies.

7. *Amathuxidia amythaon* (Dbl.). Assam, Burma, Malaysia.

8. *Amathuxidia amythaon* (see 7).

9. *Discophora bambusae* (Fldr.). Celebes.

10. *Discophora celinde* (Stoll.). Java. Male resembles tullia, UPF dots very small.

11. *Faunis arcesilaus* (F.). Siam, Assam, Malaysia, Java.

12. *Faunis gracilis* (Btlr.). Malaysia.

13. *Discophora necho* (Fldr.). Borneo to Philippines.

14. *Discophora necho* (see 13).

15. *Discophora timora* (Dbl. & Hew.). India. UP as tullia, but only one row of dots UPF.

16. *Discophora tullia* (Cr.). Burma to S. China. Similar: lepida (Moore), S. India, shorter band of dots UPF.

17. *Enispe cycnus* (Westw.). Assam, Burma.

18. *Enispe euthymius* (Dbl.). Sikkim, Burma, Malaya. UP resembles lunatus.

19. *Faunis faunula* (Westw.). Siam, Burma, Malaysia.

20. *Discophora deo* (Nicer.). Upper Burma to Indo-China.

PLATE 138: Amathusidae

1. *Faunis kirata* (Nicer.). Malaysia, Sumatra.

2. *Faunis menado* (Hew.). Celebes. Subspecies with white band UNF

3. *Faunis phaon* (Ev.). Philippines. UN very variable. UP brown unmarked. Similar: leucis (Fldr.).

4. *Faunis stomphax* (Westw.). Sumatra, Borneo.

5. *Hyantis hodeva* (Hew.). New Guinea.

6. *Morphopsis albertisi* (Oberth.). New Guinea.

7. *Stichopthalma camadeva* (Westw.). Sikkim to Upper Burma.

8. *Stichopthalma louisa* (Wood-Mas.). Burma to Indo-China.

9. *Stichopthalma nourmahal* (Westw.). Sikkim.

10. *Tenaris artemis* (Voll.). New Guinea, N.E. Australia. Several subspecies.

11. *Tenaris artemis* (see 10).

12. *Tenaris bioculatus* (Guer.). New Guinea.

13. *Tenaris chionides* (Godm.). New Guinea.

14. *Tenaris diana* (Btlr.). N. Moluccas.

15. *Tenaris dimona* (Hew.). New Guinea. Few subspecies. UP resembles biocelatus.

16. *Tenaris domitilla* (Hew.). N. Moluccas.

17. *Tenaris gorgo* (Kirsch.). New Guinea. Few subspecies.

18. *Tenaris horsfieldi* (Swains.). Java, Malaya, Sumatra.

19. *Tenaris myops* (Fldr.). New Guinea. Variable. Few subspecies. Similar: dioptrica (Voll.).

20. *Tenaris myops* (see 19).

21. *Tenaris onolaus* (Kirsch.). New Guinea.

22. *Tenaris phorcas* (Westw.). Solomon Islands, Bismarch Archipelago.

PLATE 139: Amathusidae

1. *Tenaris selene* (Westw.). S. Moluccas. Similar: macrops (Fldr.), N. Moluccas; catops (Westw.).

2. *Tenaris schonbergi* (Fruhst.). New Guinea.

3. *Tenaris staudingeri* (Honr.). New Guinea. Variable.

4. *Tenaris urania* (L.). Amboina.

5. *Thaumantis diores* (Dbl.). Sikkim, Assam.

6. *Thaumantis klugius* (Zinken). Malaya, Borneo.

7. *Thaumantis noureddin* (Westw.). Malaya, Borneo.

8. *Thaumantis odana* (Godt.). Malaya, Borneo, Java.

9. *Xanthotaenia busiris* (Westw.). Malaya, Sumatra, Borneo.

10. *Thauria aliris* (Westw.). Burma, Malaysia, Tonkin.

11. *Thauria aliris* (see 10).

12. *Zeuxidia amethystus* (Btlr.). Burma, Malaysia, Philippines.

13. *Zeuxidia amethystus* (see 12).

14. *Zeuxidia aurelius* (Cr.). Borneo, Malaya, Sumatra.

15. *Zeuxidia aurelius* (see 14).

16. *Zeuxidia doubledayi* (Westw.). Malaysia.

PLATE 140: Nymphalidae

1. *Abrota ganga* (Moore). India. Similar: juruna (Moore), rather more orange sheen.

2. *Amnosia decora* (Dbl. & Hew.). Sumatra, Borneo.

3. *Amnosia decora* (see 2).

4. *Apatura ambica* (Koll.). Kashmir to Upper Burma. Similar: garlanda (Fruh.), Upper Burma.

5. *Apatura chevana* (Moore). Sikkim, Assam N. Burma.

6. *Apaturina erminia* (Cr.). Moluccas, New Guinea, Solomon Islands. Female UP is brown.

7. *Apatura parisatis* (Westw.). Himalayas to China, Ceylon through Malaya to Celebes. Several subspecies. Similar: nakula (Moore), Sumatra, Java, Philippines; danae (Fruh.), Mindanao.

8. *Apatura parisatis* (see 7).

9. *Argyreus hyperbius* (Johanns.). India, Ceylon, Burma, China to Japan, Malaya, Australia, Abyssinia. Lfp: Viola.

10. *Apatura rhea* (Fldr.). Philippines.

11. *Ariadne ariadne* (L.). India to Malaysia, Formosa and Celebes. Similar: specularia (Fruhst.).

12. *Ariadne isaeus* (Wall.). Malaysia, Java, Sumatra.

13. *Ariadne merione* (Cr.). India, Ceylon, Malaysia.

14. *Ariadne taeniata* (Fldr.). Philippines.

15. *Byblia ilithyia* (Drury). Throughout Africa, Arabia, India.

16. *Calinaga lhatso* (Oberth). Yunnan.

17. *Cethosia chrysippe* (F.). New Guinea, Solomon Islands, Australia. Lfp: Adenia. Many forms and subspecies. Form alkmene (Fruh.) has female olive UP.

18. *Cethosia cyane* (Drury). India, Burma.

PLATE 141: Nymphalidae

1. *Cethosia hypsea* (Dbd.). Burma, Malaya, Sumatra. Male resembles cyane.

2. *Cethosia myrina* (Fldr.). Celebes. Female has no blue sheen.

3. *Cethosia penthesilea* (Cr.). Java, Malaysia to Australia.

4. *Cethosia nietneri* (Fldr.). S. India, Ceylon. Female is dark blue-grey.

5. *Cethosia obscura* (Guer.). Bismarck Archipelago. The UP spots and brown colour vary in intensity.

6. *Charaxes fabius* (F.). India, Ceylon, Celebes, Philippines. Several subspecies.

7. *Charaxes durnfordi* (Dist.). Malaya, Assam, Burma, Java.

8. *Charaxes eurialus* (Cr.). Amboina.

9. *Charaxes harmodius* (Fldr.). Sumatra. Similar: aristogiton (Fldr.), Sikkim to Burma.

10. *Charaxes marmax* (Ww.). India.

11. *Charaxes nitebis* (Hew.). Celebes. Female UP brown.

12. *Chersonesia peraka* (Dist.). Burma, Malaysia, Java, Bali.

13. *Chersonesia rahria* (Moore). Malaysia, Borneo, to Celebes.

14. *Chersonesia risa* (Dbd.). Himalayas to Tonkin, Malaysia.

15. *Cirrochroa fasciata* (Fldr.). Malaya to Burma.

16. *Cirrochroa aoris* (Dbl.). Assam, Burma. Female UP olive.

17. *Cirrochroa emalea* (Guer.). Malaya, Sumatra, Borneo. Few subspecies. Similar: malaya (Fldr.), UNH silvery band uniform in width.

18. *Cirrochroa imperatrix* (Gr.Sm.). Celebes, New Guinea.

PLATE 142: Nymphalidae

1. *Cirrochroa orissa* (Fldr.). Sumatra, Malaya, Borneo.

2. *Cirrochroa regina* (Fldr.). New Guinea, Moluccas. A few races. Similar: semiramis (Fldr.), Celebes, UP border lines more distinct, UN margins paler.

3. *Cirrochroa tyche* (Fldr.). Sikkim to Hainan and Philippines, Malaysia. Male resembles aoris, but smaller. Similar: surya (Moore), Burma, Malaya, much smaller.

4. *Cyrestis lutea* (Zink-Somm.). Java, Bali. Female ground colour white, resembles nivalis male.

5. *Cupha erymanthis* (Drury). India to China, Malaysia, Ceylon, Java. The yellow band UP varies in shade.

6. *Cupha lampetia* (L.). S. Moluccas. Similar: melichrysops (Math.), Solomon Islands, UPH yellowish; myronides (Fldr.), N. Moluccas, brighter yellow, particularly UPH.

7. *Cupha maeonides* (Hew.). Celebes. Similar: arias (Fldr.), Celebes, narrower orange band UPF.

8. *Cyrestis maenalis* (Erichs.). Philippines, Siam, Malaya.

9. *Cupha prosope* (F.). Australia.

10. *Cyrestis achates* (Btlr.). New Guinea.

11. *Cyrestis acilia* (Godt.). Celebes. Similar: strigata (Fldr.), Celebes.

12. *Cyrestis cocles* (F.). Siam, Sikkim, Burma, Malaya. Female very pale.

13. *Cyrestis nivea* (Zink-Somm.). Malaya, Java, Burma, Assam. Similar: nivalis (Fldr.), Borneo, Malaya, larger and paler.

14. *Cyrestis telamon* (L.). Moluccas.

15. *Cyrestis thyonneus* (Cr.). Celebes. Similar: tabula (Nicer.).

16. *Dichorragia nesimachus* (Bsd.). N. India to Japan and through Malaysia to Philippines. Few subspecies. Female larger and paler. Similar: nesiotes (Fruh.), greenish black UP.

17. *Cyrestis themire* (Honrath). Burma Malaya, Sumatra, Tonkin.

18. *Dilipa morgiana* (Ww.). N. India. Terrain: montane. Female UP is grey-blue. Similar: fenestra (Leech), W. China, UP bright orange-gold, black markings smaller.

19. *Doleschallia bisaltide* (Cr.). India, Malaysia to Philippines, Australia. Many subspecies.

20. *Doleschallia bisaltide* (see 19).

PLATE 143: Nymphalidae

1. *Doleschallia dascon* (G. & S.). New Guinea.

2. *Doleschallia dascylus* (G. & S.). New Guinea. Male UP resembles dascon but blue band broken up.

3. *Doleschallia hexopthalmos* (Gmel.). Moluccas, New Guinea.

4. *Eulaceura osteria* (Ww.). Java, Borneo, Malaya.

5. *Eulaceura osteria* (see 4).

6. *Euripus consimilis* (Ww.). India to Upper Burma and Siam. Female mimics Euploea.

7. *Euripus consimilis* (see 6).

8. *Euripus halitherses* (Dbl.). Assam to Malaya and Indo-China. Great number of local and insular forms; several female forms, mimics of Euploea.

9. *Euripus halitherses* (see 8).

10. *Euthalia aconthea* (Cr.). Malaya, Java, Bali.

11. *Euthalia agnis* (Voll.). Malaya, Java, Sumatra.

12. *Euthalia aeetes* (Hew.). Celebes. A female aberration is yellow brown UP with brown markings.

13. *Euthalia aeropa* (L.). Moluccas, New Guinea. Female bands yellow white. Variable.

14. *Euthalia cyanipardus* (Btlr.). Assam, Siam, Borneo. Female as dirtea female but larger and spots blue.

15. *Euthalia aetion* (Hew.). Moluccas, New Guinea. Female markings UP yellowish. Similar: plateni (Stgr.), Batjan, Halmahira.

16. *Euthalia alpheda* (Godt.). Malaya, Sumatra, Java. Similar: jama (Fldr.), India.

17. *Euthalia anosia* (Moore). Assam, Malaya.

18. *Euthalia cocytus* (F.). Siam, India, Malaya. Similar: godartii (Gray), narrower, pale blue, border UPH.

PLATE 144: Nymphalidae

1. *Euthalia dirtea* (F.). India to Hainan. Malaya to Philippines. Male as cyanipardus but smaller. Very variable with many forms and subspecies.

2. *Euthalia duda* (Stgr.). Sikkim, Assam, Tibet. Similar: durga (Moore), Naga Hills; thibetana (Pouj.), W. and C. China; andosa (Fruh.), W. China; and several others, all from China.

3. *Euthalia dunya* (Dbd.). Burma to Malaya, Java.

4. *Euthalia evelina* (Stoll.). Assam to Malaya, Ceylon to Java and Celebes.

5. *Euthalia monina* (F.). Borneo, Sumatra, Malaya. Very variable. Similar: mahadeva (Moore), Malaya.

6. *Euthalia aconthea* (Cr.). Malaya. Similar: garuda (Moore), India, Ceylon, Andamans.

7. *Euthalia lepidea* (Btlr.). India to Malaya.

8. *Euthalia iapis* (Godt.). Malaya, Java. Similar: telchinia (Moore), India; cocytus (F.), Siam to Malaya, margins UP grey green.

9. *Euthalia iapis* (see 8).

10. *Euthalia jahnu* (Moore). India to Malaya.

11. *Euthalia franciae* (Gray). Nepal to Upper Burma.

12. *Euthalia lubentina* (Cr.). India to S. China, Burma to Malaya. Many subspecies. Similar: adonia (Cr.), Malaya, broad white bands UP.

13. *Euthalia lubentina* (see 12).

14. *Euthalia merta* (Moore). Philippines, Borneo, Sumatra, Malaysia. Variable. Similar: eriphyle (Nicer.), Burma.

15. *Euthalia merta* (see 14).

16. *Euthalia monina* (see 5).

17. *Euthalia nais* (Forst.). India.

18. *Euthalia nara* (Moore). Sikkim to N. Burma. Similar: omeia (Leech), W. China; strephon (G. & S.), China, paler, UP markings clearer.

PLATE 145: Nymphalidae

1. *Euthalia nara* (see 144/18).

2. *Euthalia patala* (Koll.). Himalayas to Assam and S. Burma. Subspecies in W. and C. China.

3. *Euthalia phemius* (see 4).

4. *Euthalia phemius* (Dbd.). Sikkim, Burma, S. China to Hong Kong. Lfp: Litchi tree.

5. *Fabriciana kamala* (Moore). N.W. Himalayas.

6. *Euthalia satrapes* (Fldr.). Philippines.

7. *Euthalia teuta* (Dbd.). Assam to Malaya. Similar: recta (Nicer.), Assam to Malaya; gupta (Nicer.), Burma.

8. *Herona marathus* (Dbl.). Sikkim, Burma Indo-China.

9. *Herona sumatrana* (Moore). Borneo, Java. Similar: djarang (Fruh.), Nias, UP markings tinged violet.

10. *Hestina nama* (Dbl.). Himalayas through Assam, Siam to W. China, Malaya. Mimics Danaus tytia and Danaus melanippus.

11. *Hypolimnas alimena* (L.). Moluccas, New Guinea, Australia. Many subspecies.

12. *Hypolimnas alimena* (see 11).

13. *Hypolimnas antilope* (Cr.). Malaya to Philippines and New Guinea and Australia. Many subspecies, very variable.

14. *Hypolimnas bolina* (L.) 'Common Eggfly'. Mauritius, India, Malaysia to Australia. Lfp: Portulaca, Pseuderanthemum, etc. Extremely variable, very numerous races and subspecies.

PLATE 146: Nymphalidae

1. *Hypolimnas bolina* (see 145/14).

2. *Hypolimnas deois* (Hew.). New Guinea, Moluccas. Female UPH white, broad white band UPF. Similar: panopion (Gr.S.), New Guinea, orange band UPH much broader.

3. *Hypolimnas misippus* (L.). Indo-Malayan region, Australia, Africa, N. America, W. Indies, S. America (North), Syria, Palestine, Hong Kong. Lfp: Portulaca. UP resembles bolina.

4. *Hypolimnas misippus* (see 3).

5. *Hypolimnas diomea* (Hew.). Celebes. Female UP patches are white. Similar: fraterna (Wallace), Macassar.

6. *Hypolimnas octocula* (Btlr.). New Hebrides, Marianas.

7. *Hypolimnas pandarus* (L.). Moluccas. Female UPH no blue, wide orange band and small orange band UPF. Few races.

8. *Hypolimnas panopion* (Gr.S.). New Guinea.

9. *Laringa horsfieldii* (Bsd.). India, Andamans, Java, Sumatra.

10. *Laringa horsfieldii* (see 9).

11. *Kallima paralekta* (Horsf.). Malaya. Female no blue, white band UPF.

12. *Kallima paralekta* (see 11).

13. *Kallima philarchus* (Ww.). India, Ceylon. Similar: alompra (Moore), Naga Hills.

14. *Lebadea martha* (F.). India to Indo-China and Malaya.

15. *Lebadea alankara* (Horsf.). Sumatra, Java, Borneo.

16. *Laringa castelnaui* (Fldr.). Malaysia, Borneo, Philippines, Sumatra. Female brown UP. Similar: niha (Fruh.), Nias, no black edge UP, female brown UP with white patches UPF; ottonis (Fruh.), Palawan.

17. *Limenitis danava* (Moore). Himalayas, Assam, Burma.

PLATE 147: Nymphalidae

1. *Kallima spiridiva* (Sm.). Sumatra.

2. *Limenitis daraxa* (Moore). India to Malaya, Borneo and Indo-China.

3. *Limenitis dudu* (Westw.). India, Burma to Hongkong and Formosa.

4. *Neptis consimilis* (Bsd.). New Guinea, Australia. Several subspecies.

5. *Neptis duryodana* (Moore). Borneo, Malaysia, Sumatra. Similar: magadha (Fldr.), Malaya, no white streak base of UNH; nata (Moore), Malaya to Indo-China, UPF spots not in line.

6. *Neptis cyrilla* (Fldr.), Philippines.

7. *Neptis eblis* (Btlr.). Bismarck Archipelago.

8. *Limenitis imitata* (Btlr.). Nias.

9. *Limenitis lymire* (Hew.). Celebes.

10. *Limenitis lysanias* (Hew.). Celebes. Similar: lymire (Hew.), larger, UP white band narrower.

11. *Limenitis procris* (Cr.). India to Philippines, Malaysia, Java. Several subspecies. Similar: calidosa (Moore), Ceylon, darker.

12. *Limenitis zulema* (Dbl.). Sikkim, Burma.

13. *Mynes geoffroyi* (see 14).

14. *Mynes geoffroyi* (Guer.). New Guinea, Australia.

15. *Mynes woodfordi* (Godm. & Salv.). Solomon Islands.

16. *Neptis ananta* (Moore). Himalayas, Assam, Burma, Malaya. Similar: chinensis (Leech), W. China, browner UP, UPF orange spot round and regular.

17. *Neptis anjana* (Moore). Malaya, Burma, Java.

18. *Polyura dehaani* (Dbl.). Java, Sumatra.

PLATE 148: Nymphalidae

1. *Neptis columella* (Cr.). India, Burma, Siam, Malaya, Java, Celebes, Philippines. Many subspecies.

2. *Neptis ebusa* (Fldr.). Philippines. White dots tip UPF sometimes clear.

3. *Neptis heliodore* (F.). Malaya, Indo-China, Java.

4. *Neptis heliopolis* (Fldr.). N. Moluccas. Similar: amphion (L.), Moluccas.

5. *Neptis hordonia* (Stoll). India to Tonkin, Malaysia, Andamans, Nicobars.

6. *Neptis illigera* (Esch.). Philippines.

7. *Neptis jumbah* (Moore). S. India, Ceylon.

8. *Neptis mahendra* (Moore). India.

9. *Neptis manasa* (Moore). Sikkim, Nepal, N. Burma. UP resembles arachne. Subspecies: narcissina (Oberth.), Tibet.

10. *Neptis miah* (Moore). Sikkim, Assam, Burma. Subspecies: disopa (Swinh.), W. China. Similar: viraja (Moore).

11. *Neptis mysia* (Fldr.). Moluccas. Similar: antara (Moore), Celebes, UPF has marginal thin orange and dull violet band.

12. *Neptis nandina* (Moore). India to Philippines and Formosa, Andamans to Malaysia. Very many forms and subspecies. Similar: soma (Moore), UN dark red-brown, UPF stripe and dash separated.

13. *Neptis nausicaa* (Nicer.). New Guinea.

14. *Neptis nirvana* (Fldr.). Celebes.

15. *Neptis nitetis* (Hew.). Philippines. Similar: vikasi (Horsf.), India, Malaya.

16. *Neptis nycteus* (Nicer.). Sikkim.

17. *Neptis peraka* (Btlr.). Burma, Siam to Indo-China, Malaya. Similar: dindinga (Btlr.), UPF thin marginal lines blue grey.

18. *Neptis praslini* (Bsd.). New Guinea, Australia. Several subspecies. Similar: nausicaa (Nicer.), New Guinea.

19. *Neptis sankara* (Koll.). Kashmir to Nepal. Subspecies: antonia (Oberth.), W. China, markings yellow.

20. *Neptis satina* (Sin.). New Guinea.

21. *Neptis shepherdi* (Moore). Australia, New Guinea.

22. *Neptis shepherdi* (see 21).

23. *Neptis venilia* (L.). Moluccas, New Guinea, Australia. Several subspecies.

24. *Neptis vikasi* (Horsf.). India, Malaya, Java.

25. *Neptis zaida* (Dbl.). Himalayas, Assam, Burma. Several subspecies from China.

26. *Neurosigma doubledayi* (Ww.). India. Female ground colour blue-grey.

27. *Pandita sinope* (Moore). Java, Sumatra, Malaya.

PLATE 149: Nymphalidae

1. *Pantoporia asura* (Moore). E. Himalayas, Assam. Lfp: All Pantoporia feed on Rubiaceae, Euphorbia and Oleaceae. Similar: elwesi (Leech), W. and C. China.

2. *Pantoporia cama* (Moore). C. and E. Himalayas, Assam, Upper Burma.

3. *Pantoporia eulimene* (Godt.). Celebes, Moluccas.

4. *Pantoporia gordia* (Fldr.). Philippines. Similar: bruijni (Oberth.).

5. *Pantoporia karwara* (Frust.). Karnara, W. India.

6. *Pantoporia kasa* (Moore). Philippines. Seasonally variable.

7. *Pantoporia larymna* (Dbd.). Burma, Siam, Malaysia, Java.

8. *Pantoporia nefte* (see 9).

9. *Pantoporia nefte* (Cr.). India, Burma to Malaya and Hong Kong.

10. *Pantoporia opalina* (Koll.). Himalayas, Upper Assam, Upper Burma, Similar: constricta (Alph.), W. and C. China.

11. *Pantoporia perius* (L.). Himalayas, India, Burma, Malaya to S. China.

12. *Pantoporia pravara* (Moore). Malaya, Assam to Indo-China, Sumatra.

13. *Pantoporia ranga* (Moore). N. India to Indo-China, Malaya.

14. *Pantoporia selenophora* (Koll.). Himalayas, Assam, Upper Burma to Hong Kong, S. India.

15. *Pantoporia selenophora* (see 14).

16. *Pantoporia speciosa* (Stgr.). Palawan. Female lacks blue sheen.

17. *Parthenos sylvia* (Cr.). India to China, Malaya, Philippines, New Guinea. Many races and subspecies. Similar: cyaneus (Moore), Ceylon, larger.

18. *Parthenos tigrina* (Voll.). New Guinea.

19. *Parathyma reta* (Moore). Assam, Malaya, Sumatra. Similar: kanwa (Moore), Assam to Malaya.

20. *Pareba vesta* (F.). India, W. and C. China. Lfp: Boehmeria.

21. *Phalanta alcippe* (Cr.). Sikkim to Malaysia, Nicobar, Philippines, Moluccas. Many forms and subspecies.

22. *Phalanta phalantha* (Dru.). India to S. China, Malaya, Ceylon, Japan, Philippines, Australia. Lfp: Flacourtia, viola.

PLATE 150: Nymphalidae

1. *Polyura athamas* (Dru.). N.W. India to S. China, Burma, Siam, Malaya.

2. *Polyura delphis* (Dbl.). Assam to Malaya, Sumatra and Borneo. UP as dolon.

3. *Polyura eudamippus* (Dbl.). India to C. China. Few subspecies.

4. *Polyura jalysus* (Fldr.). Malaya, Borneo. Similar: ephebus (Fruh.), Burma.

5. *Polyura moori* (Dist.). Malaya to Burma. Similar: hebe (Btlr.); athamas (Dru.).

6. *Precis orithya* (L.). Widely distributed from Asia Minor to Japan, through Malaysia to Australia, Africa. Lfp: Acanthaceae. Few local subspecies.

7. *Polyura pyrrhus* (L.). Timor, Moluccas, New Guinea, Australia.

8. *Polyura schreiberi* (Godt.). Assam to Siam and Malaya, Java.

9. *Precis almana* (L.). India, Malaysia, Java, Sumatra, Formosa, Philippines, Hong Kong,

Andaman and Nicobar Islands. Lfp: Acanthaceae. Dry season form; wet season form lacks tails.

10. *Precis atlites* (L.). India to Malaya to Celebes.

11. *Precis evigone* (Cr.). Java to Philippines to New Guinea. Wet season form; dry season form resembles lemonias.

12. *Precis hedonia* (L.). Malaya through New Guinea to Australia. Few subspecies, with brighter markings.

13. *Prothoe calydonia* (See 151/1).

14. *Prothoe australis* (see 18).

15. *Precis villida* (F.). Australia, Tasmania, Samoa, Solomon Islands, New Hebrides.

16. *Precis hierta* (F.). Himalayas, India, Ceylon, Burma through Cambodia to W. and S. China, Andaman and Nicobar Islands. Lfp: Acanthaceae. Similar: celrene (Trim.), Arabia, Socotra, Africa south of Sahara.

17. *Precis iphita* (Cr.). India, Malaya, Ceylon, Sumatra, W. and C. China. Lfp: Acanthaceae. Wet season form; dry season form is much paler.

18. *Prothoe australis* (Guer.). Moluccas, New Guinea. Many forms and subspecies.

PLATE 151 : Nymphalidae

1. *Prothoe calydonia* (Hew.). Malaya, Borneo, Sumatra.

2. *Prothoe franckii* (Godt.). Burma, Malaya, Java, Sumatra, Philippines.

3. *Pyrameis dejeani* (Godt.). Java. Similar: samani (Hagen), Sumatra, UP brown orange.

4. *Symbrenthia hippoclus* (Cr.). Himalayas, Assam, Burma to Malaya, W., C. and S. China. Lfp: Urtica. Several subspecies.

5. *Pyrameis itea* (F.). Australia, New Zealand.

6. *Pyrameis gonarilla* (Fab.). New Zealand.

7. *Pyrameis indica* (Hbst.). Himalayas, India, Ceylon, Burma through China to Japan, Korea. Lfp: Urtica. Similar: Vanessa vulcania (Godt.), Canary Islands.

8. *Rhinopalpa polynice* (Cr.). Assam to Malaya, Sumatra to Philippines and Celebes. Several races and subspecies.

9. *Rhinopalpa polynice* (see 8).

10. *Stibochiona coresia* (Hbn.). Java, Sumatra. Female UP brown.

11. *Stibochiona nicea* (Gray.). Himalayas, Assam, W. China, Malaya.

12. *Symbrenthia hippalus* (Fldr.). Celebes.

13. *Stibochiona schonbergi* (Honrath). Borneo. Male dark brown UP/UN unmarked.

14. *Symbrenthia hypselis* (Godt.). Himalayas, Assam, Burma, Malaya, W. China. Several subspecies.

15. *Symbrenthia hypatia* (Wall.). Malaya. UP resembles hypselis.

16. *Symbrenthia niphanda* (Moore). E. Himalayas, Kashmir. Similar: brabira (Moore); UN paler yellow, markings fewer.

17. *Tanaecia aruna* (Fldr.). Malaya, Borneo Sumatra.

18. *Tanaecia cibaritis* (Hew.). Andaman Islands. Similar: trigerta (Moore), Java.

19. *Tanaecia clathrata* (Voll.). Malaya Borneo. Similar: coclebs (Cbt.), blue edges UP.

20. *Tanaecia julii* (Boug.). Malaya, India Siam.

PLATE 152 : Nymphalidae

1. *Tanaecia lutala* (Moore). Borneo.

2. *Tanaecia munda* (Fruhst.). Malaya, Borneo.

3. *Tanaecia palguna* (Moore). Malaysia, Java.

4. *Tanaecia pelea* (F.). Malaya, Borneo. Similar: vikrama (Fldr.), Sumatra.

5. *Terinos atlita* (F.). Malaya, Sumatra, Borneo.

6. *Terinos clarissa* (Bsd.). Sumatra, Borneo, Malaya. Similar: abisares (Fldr.), Celebes.

7. *Terinos taxiles* (Hew.). Celebes.

8. *Terinos terpander* (Hew.). Malaysia.

9. *Terinos tethys* (Hew.). New Guinea.

10. *Vagrans egista* (Cr.). India, Philippines, Samoa, Malaysia, Australia. Several subspecies. Similar: Smerina manoro (Ward), Madagascar, no tail to HW.

11. *Vanessa canace* (L.). Himalayas to Burma and Malaya. Subspecies through China to Korea and Japan.

12. *Vindula arsinoe* (Cr.). Malaysia to Australia.

13. *Vindula arsinoe* (see 12).

14. *Vindula erota* (F.). Sikkim to Indo-China, Malaysia, Celebes, Philippines. Many races and subspecies.

15. *Yoma sabina* (Cr.). India to Moluccas and Australia.

16. *Cirrochroa thais* (F.). S. India, Ceylon. Dry season form is paler.

PLATE 153 : Acraeidae

1. *Acraea andromacha* (F.). Australia, New Guinea.

2. *Acraea violae* (F.). India, Ceylon.

3. *Miyana moluccana* (Fldr.) Moluccas, Celebes Form nebulosa. (see 4).

4. *Miyana moluccana* (Fldr.). Moluccas, Celebes.

Danaidae

5. *Danaus genutia* (Cr.). India, Malaysia W. and C. China, Australia.

6. *Danaus melaneus* (Cr.). India to W. China. Few races.

7. *Danaus septentrionis* (Btlr.). India, Ceylon to W. China. Similar: limniace (Cr.).

8. *Danaus affinis* (F.). Australia, Malaysia, Philippines. Many races and subspecies.

9. *Danaus affinis* (see 8).

10. *Danaus aglea* (Cr.). India, Ceylon, Burma, Siam, Malaya.

11. *Danaus aspasia* (F.). Burma, Malaysia, Siam. Several subspecies.

12. *Danaus choaspes* (Btlr.). Sula Islands. Form choaspina (Fruh.).

13. *Danaus eryx* (F.). Burma, Siam, Indo-China, Borneo.

14. *Danaus ferruginea* (Btlr.). New Guinea, N. Australia.

15. *Danaus gautama* (Moore). Burma.

16. *Danaus hamata* (Macl.). S. and E. Asia, Australia. Similar: melittula (Herr Schf.), Samoa, much smaller.

17. *Danaus ismare* (Cr.). Moluccas, Celebes.

18. *Danaus juventa* (Cr.). Malaysia to Philippines. Many island races.

19. *Danaus limniace* (Cr.). India, Burma, Ceylon, Hong Kong.

20. *Danaus lotis* (Cr.). Borneo to Philippines.

21. *Danaus melanippus* (Cr.). Indo-China, Malaysia, Celebes.

22. *Danaus melanippus* (Cr.). Subspecies haruhasa (Doh.), Sambawan (see 21).

23. *Danaus philene* (Cr.). Moluccas, New Guinea.

24. *Danaus pumila* (Bsd.). New Caledonia, New Hebrides.

25. *Danaus schenki* (Koch.). New Guinea to Solomon Islands. Male UP ground colour pale yellow.

PLATE 154 : Danaidae

1. *Danaus sita* (Koll.). Himalayas to Japan and Malaya.

2. *Danaus similis* (L.). Ceylon, Malaysia, Hong Kong, Formosa. Many subspecies.

3. *Euploea alcathoe* (Godt.). Moluccas, New Guinea, Australia.

4. *Euploea andamanensis* (Atkins). Andamans. Subspecies of core.

5. *Euploea arisbe* (Feld.). Timor. Many similar species in this area.

6. *Euploea batesi* (Fldr.). New Guinea, Australia.

7. *Euploea callithoe* (Bsd.). New Guinea.

8. *Euploea climena* (Cr.). Nicobars, Java, Moluccas, Australia. Very variable in each locality. This is subspecies euryphon (Hew.), New Guinea.

9. *Euploea climena* (Stoll.). Form nobilis (Strd.), Admiralty Islands (see 8).

10. *Euploea core* (Cr.). India to Australia. Many subspecies.

11. *Euploea coreta* (Godt.). S. India, Ceylon. Resembles core but has two bands UPF.

12. *Euploea corus* (F.). Burma, Ceylon. Form vitrina.

13. *Euploea corus* (see 12).

14. *Euploea crameri* (Luc.). Malaysia to Bali, Burma, Siam.

15. *Euploea darchia* (Macl.). Aru, Key Islands. Subspecies hopfferi (Feld.).

16. *Euploea deheeri* (Doh.). Java. One of several subspecies of modesta.

17. *Euploea deione* (Westw.). India, Siam, Malaysia, Java. Variable, with many subspecies.

18. *Euploea diana* (Btlr.). Celebes.

19. *Euploea diocletianus* (F.). Nepal, Burma to Singapore.

20. *Euploea diocletianus* (see 19).

21. *Euploea doubledayi* (C. & R. Fldr.). India, Burma, Siam, N. Malaya.

22. *Euploea dufresne* (Godt.). Philippines, Formosa. Female resembles mulciber female.

23. *Euploea duponcheli* (Bsd.). Moluccas, Solomon Islands. Similar: algea (Godt.). Moluccas, darker.

24. *Euploea eichhorni* (Stgr.). Australia.

PLATE 155: Danaidae

1. *Euploea eurianassa* (Hew.). New Guinea.

2. *Euploea gloriosa* (Btlr.). Celebes.

3. *Euploea godartii* (Luc.). Siam, Indo-China.

4. *Euploea harrisi* (Fldr.). India, Siam, Indo-China. Many races and subspecies.

5. *Euploea klugi* (Moore). India, Malaya, Ceylon.

6. *Euploea leucostictos* (Gmel.). Nicobars, to Formosa, Celebes, Fiji. Lfp: Ficus hispida. Many subspecies. Similar: klugi erichsonii (C. & R. Feld.), Ceylon and India.

7. *Euploea melanopa* (Rob.). New Guinea.

8. *Euploea midamus* (L.). Himalayas, Malaysia, W. China. Lfp: Strophanthus, Nerium.

9. *Euploea modesta* (Btlr.). Siam, Indo-China, Malaya.

10. *Euploea moorei* (Btlr.). Borneo, Sumatra.

11. *Euploea mulciber* (Cr.) 'The Striped Blue Crow'. India, Malaysia, Java, Philippines. 'Crows' is a common name for the Genus Euploea. Many subspecies.

12. *Euploea mulciber* (see 11).

13. *Euploea nechos* (Math.). Solomon Islands. Form prusias (G. & S.) has broad white edges UP.

14. *Euploea phaenarete* (Schall.). Malaysia.

15. *Euploea pumila* (Btlr.). Papuan region. Very variable.

16. *Euploea redtenbacheri* (Fldr.) 'The Malayan Crow'. Burma, Malaysia, Celebes, Moluccas. Lfp: Strophanthus dichotomus. Very variable in amount of spotting UP.

17. *Euploea salpinxoides* (Fruh.). West New Guinea. Female form amida.

18. *Euploea scherzeri* (Fldr.). Nicobars. Subspecies of core.

19. *Euploea swainson* (Godt.). Philippines, Celebes.

20. *Euploea sylvester* (F.). India, Malaysia, New Guinea, Australia. Lfp: Ichnocarpus.

21. *Euploea treitschkei* (Bsd.). New Guinea, Solomon Islands, Fiji. Several subspecies.

22. *Euploea tulliolus* (F.) 'The Dwarf Crow'. Solomon Islands, Malaysia, Formosa, Australia. Lfp: Malaisa scandens.

23. *Euploea usipetes* (Hew.). New Guinea.

24. *Idea blanchardi* (March) celebes. A few s/species ?

PLATE 156: Danaidae

1. *Idea d'urvillei* (Bsd.). New Guinea.

2. *Idea hypermnestra* (Westw.). Malaysia.

3. *Idea jasonia* (Westw.). Ceylon, S. India, Assam to Malaysia. Lfp: Agonosma.

4. *Idea leuconoe* (Eschsch.). Philippines to Borneo, Formosa. Very variable.

5. *Ideopsis gaura* (Horsf.). Malaya to Hong Kong. Lfp: Melodinus. Variable.

6. *Idea lynceus* (Drury). Malaysia.

7. *Euploea viola* (Btlr.). Celebes.

8. *Ideopsis vitrea* (Blanch.). Celebes, Moluccas, New Guinea.

9. *Euploea vollenhovi* (Fldr.). Celebes.

10. *Tellervo zoilus* (F.). New Guinea, Solomon Islands, Australia.

Pieridae

11. *Anaphaeis java* (Sparrm.). Australia to Fiji, Java, Celebes. Many subspecies.

12. *Aoa affinis* (Vollenh.). Celebes.

13. *Aporia agathon* (Gray). Himalayas.

PLATE 157: Pieridae

1. *Appias ada* (Cr.). Moluccas, New Guinea, Australia.

2. *Aporia soracta* (Moore). N.W. Himalayas.

3. *Aporia leucodyce* (Ev.). Baluchistan, Kashmir. Similar: soracta (Moore); delavayi (Oberth.), W. China. Few subspecies.

4. *Appias albina* (Bsd.). India to Moluccas and Philippines and N. Malaya and N. Australia. Many local races.

5. *Appias cardena* (Hew.). Malaysia.

6. *Appias libythea* (F.). India, Ceylon, Siam Indo-China, Malaysia to Philippines. Female varies in wet and dry seasons.

7. *Appias celestina* (Bsd.). New Guinea, Australia. Variable; there is also a similar female with white ground colour UP. Similar: placidia (Stoll.), Moluccas.

8. *Appias indra* (Moore). Sikkim to Burma, S. India and Ceylon, Indo-China to Formosa, Malaysia. Variable.

9. *Appias ithome* (Fldr.). Celebes.

10. *Appias lalage* (Dbl.). N. India, Assam, Burma, Malaya. Similar: ialassis (Gr.-Sm.), Malaya.

11. *Appias celestina* (see 7).

12. *Appias libythea* (see 6).

13. *Appias lyncida* (Cr.). Bengal, S. India, Ceylon, Nicobars, Malaysia to Philippines. Many subspecies. Similar: ada (Cr.), Moluccas, Solomon Islands, New Guinea.

14. *Appias melania* (F.). Sikkim to W. China and Australia.

15. *Appias nephele* (Hew.). Philippines.

16. *Appias nero* (F.). N. India to Burma and Malaysia and Philippines. Many subspecies.

17. *Appias pandrone* (Hbn.). Malaysia.

18. *Appias placidia* (Stoll.). Philippines.

19. *Appias paulina* (Cr.). Ceylon, Siam, Cambodia to W. China, Australia. Male UP white.

20 *Appias wardii* (Moore). S. India.

21. *Catopsilia scylla* (L.). Siam, Malaysia, Moluccas. Several subspecies.

22. *Catopsilia crocale* (Cr.). Whole Indo-Australasian region. Lfp: Cassia. Similar: pomona (F.), variable, antennae red above.

23 *Catopsilia pomona* (F.). India to Australia.

PLATE 158: Pieridae

1. *Catopsilia scylla* (see 157/21).

2. *Cepora abnormis* (Wall.). New Guinea.

3. *Cepora aspasia* (Stoll.). Philippines and Moluccas. Female rather yellower. Several subspecies.

4. *Cepora lea* (Dbl.). Burma, Siam.

5. *Cepora eperia* (Bsd.). Celebes. Similar celebensis (Roths.), Celebes, shading at tip UPF regular and no clear white streaks.

6. *Cepora judith* (F.). Malaysia.

7. *Cepora perimale* (Don.). Java to Australia. Many races on the different islands.

8. *Cepora lacta* (Hew.). Timor.

9. *Baltia shawii* (Bates). Pamirs, Ladak, N.W. Himalayas. (See Asian Pierids also).

10. *Delias aglaia* (L.). Nepal to Burma and Siam, Malaysia, S. China. Several subspecies.

11. *Cepora nadina* (Luc.). Sikkim to Siam, Ceylon, Malaya.

12 *Cepora temena* (Hew.). Indonesia. Very variable, female UP salmon yellow ground.

13. *Colias eogene* (Fldr.). Kashmir, Ladak, Fergana. Several subspecies.

14. *Colias alpherakii* (Stgr.). Pamirs.

15. *Colias eogene* (see 13).

16. *Delias albertisi* (Oberth.). New Guinea. Variable. Similar: discus (Honr.), New Guinea, UNH large black dot on yellow ground.

17. *Delias agostina* (Hew.). Himalayas to Assam.

18. *Delias aganippe* (Don.). S. and E. Australia.

19. *Cepora nerissa* (F.). India, China, Burma, Siam, Malaya, Java, Sumatra. Variable.

20. *Colias marcopolo* (Gr.-Grsh.). Pamirs.

21. *Colias sieversi* (Gr-Grsh.). Pamirs.

22. *Delias argenthona* (F.). Australia. Female UP ground colour pale yellow.

23. *Delias baracasa* (Semp.). Malaysia.

24. *Delias aruna* (Bsd.). New Guinea, N. Australia.

25. *Delias aruna* (see 24).

26. *Delias bagoe* (Bsd.). Bismarck Archipelago.

27. *Delias belisama* (Cr.). Java. UPF black tip, narrow black margins, otherwise UP creamy-white.

28. *Colotis etrida* (Bsd.). Baluchistan, India. Similar: evippe (L.) W. Africa.

PLATE 159 : Pieridae

1. *Delias bornemanni* (Ribbe). New Guinea. Similar: caroli (Kenr.), New Guinea, red circle UNH complete.

2. *Delias caeneus* (L.). Moluccas.

3. *Delias crithoe* (Bsd.). Java.

4. *Delias candida* (Voll.). Philippines, Moluccas.

5. *Delias candida* (see 4).

6. *Delias descombesi* (Bsd.). Himalayas to Malaysia.

7. *Delias clathrata* (R. & J.). New Guinea.

8. *Delias ennia* (Wall.). New Guinea, Australia.

9. *Delias eucharis* (Drury). India, Ceylon, N. Burma.

10. *Delias cuningputi* (Ribbe). New Guinea. Terrain: montane. Similar: pheres (Jordan), New Guinea, UN paler.

11. *Delias harpalyce* (Don.). S. and E. Australia.

12. *Delias descombesi* (see 6).

13. *Delias gabia* (Bsd.). New Guinea.

14. *Delias kummeri* (Ribbe). New Guinea. Similar: weiskei (Ribbe); ligata (R. & J.), red circle UNH complete.

15 *Delias nigrina* (F.). S. and E. Australia. Flies all the year round. Similar: funerea (Roths.), UN darker, red circle UNH farther from edge.

16. *Delias harpalyce* (Don.). S. and E. Australia.

17. *Delias henningia* (Ersch.). Philippines. Very variable.

18. *Delias itamputi* (Ribbe), New Guinea.

19. *Delias hyparete* (L.). Himalayas, to Formosa, Celebes, Philippines, Malaysia. Female dark blue-grey UP, very variable.

20. *Delias mysis* (F.). New Guinea, Australia. Several local variations.

21. *Delias nysa* (F.). N. and E. Australia. Similar: momea (Bsd.), Java and Australia, UPF solid black tip and UNF more yellow area.

PLATE 160 : Pieridae

1. *Delias periboea* (Godt.). Java.

2. *Delias rosenbergi* (Voll.). Celebes. Similar: eucharis (Drury).

3. *Dercas verhuelli* (Hoev.). N. India, China, Malaya. Similar: enara (Swn.), C. and W. China.

4. *Delias thysbe* (Cr.). Nepal, Burma, Malaysia, S. India. Similar: ninus (Wall.), Malaysia.

5. *Delias totila* (Heller). New Britain.

6. *Dercas lycorias* (Dbl.). Sikkim, Assam, China.

7. *Delias timorensis* (Bsd.). Timor.

8. *Elodina perdita* (Miskin). N. Australia. Several similar subspecies.

9. *Elodina egnatia* (Godt.). Sydney to Cape York. Several similar subspecies.

10. *Eurema andersonii* (Moore). Malaysia.

11. *Eurema blanda* (Bsd.). India to Malaysia, New Guinea and Australia.

12. *Eurema candida* (Cr.). Moluccas, New Guinea. Male UP ground colour yellow.

13. *Eurema laeta* (Bsd.). India, Ceylon, Burma through China to Korea and Japan, Australia. Lfp: Cassia. Seasonal forms. Similar: sana (Btlr.), Australia.

14. *Eurema hecabe* (L.). India, Ceylon, Burma, E. Asia, Australia. Lfp: Cassia, Acacia. Many subspecies. Very variable, seasonal forms. Similar: blanda (Bsd.), 3 dots in cell UNH; venata (Moore).

15. *Eurema libythea* (F.). India, Ceylon, Burma. Similar: herla (Macl.), Australia; venata (Moore), India.

16. *Eurema norbana* (Fruhst.). Celebes Moluccas.

17. *Eurema sari* (Horst.). S. India, Ceylon, Malaysia, Philippines.

18. *Eurema smilax* (Don.). Australia. Similar: herla (Macl.), Australia, larger.

19. *Eurema tilaha* (Horsf.). Malaysia, Java, Sumatra. Many similar subspecies.

20. *Eurema tominia* (Voll.). Celebes. Several subspecies. Similar: celebensis (Wall.), Celebes, much smaller.

21. *Eurema tominia* (see 20).

22. *Gandaca harina* (Horsf.). India, Burma Andamans, Malaysia, Moluccas and New Guinea. Several subspecies.

23. *Hebomoia glaucippe* (L.). China, India, Hong Kong, Okinawa, Ceylon, Malaysia, Celebes, Philippines. Very many races and subspecies.

24. *Gonepteryx zaneka* (Moore). N. India to Burma. Lfp: Rhamnus. Similar: aspasia (Men.), N. and C. China, Turkestan, Korea, Japan, UPH less serrated.

25. *Ixias marianne* (Cr.). India.

26. *Ixias reinwardti* (Voll.). Indonesia.

27. *Ixias pyrene* (L.). Ceylon, India, through Cambodia to China. Several subspecies. Variable.

28. *Hebomoia leucippe* (Cr.). Moluccas.

29. *Leptosia xiphia* (F.). India, Ceylon, Malaysia, Philippines. Several subspecies.

30. *Phrissura aegis* (Fldr.). Philippines, Malaysia.

PLATE 161 : Pieridae

1. *Hebomoia glaucippe* (see 23).

2. *Nepheronia avatar* (Moore). Sikkim, Burma. Female resembles Valeria valeria female.

3. *Phrissura aegis* (see plates 160/30).

4. *Prioneris autothisbe* (Hbn.). Java. Similar: hypsipyle (Weym.), Sumatra.

5. *Pieris canidia* (L.). Pamirs, India through China to Korea.

6. *Prioneris clemanthe* (Dbl.). Burma, Siam, Malaysia.

7. *Saletara cycinna* (Hew.). New Guinea. Similar : liberia (Cr.), Moluccas.

8. *Prioneris sita* (Fldr.). Ceylon, S. India.

9. *Prioneris clemanthe* (see 6).

10. *Prioneris thestylis* (Dbl.). Himalayas, Siam, Malaysia, Formosa.

11. *Saletara cycinna* (see 7).

12. *Saletara panda* (Godt.). Philippines to Celebes. Similar : liberia (Cr.), Malaysia.

13. *Colotis vestalis* (Btlr.). Baluchistan, W. India. UP black and white.

14. *Valeria argolis* (Fldr.). Philippines. Resembles tritaea but smaller.

15. *Valeria jobaea* (Bsd.). Moluccas, New Guinea.

16. *Valeria aviena* (Fruh.). New Guinea.

17. *Valeria ceylanica* (Fldr.). S. India, Ceylon.

18. *Valeria valeria* (Cr.). S. India, Burma, Siam, Malaysia to Philippines. There is a female form with yellow at UP wing bases. Many subspecies.

19. *Valeria valeria* (see 18).

20. *Valeria tritaea* (Fldr.). Philippines, Celebes.

PLATE 162: Satyridae

1. *Acropthalmia artemis* (Fldr.). Philippines.

2. *Argyronympha pulchra* (Math.). Solomon Islands. Similar : ugiensis (Math.), Solomon Islands, more orange UP.

3. *Argyrophenga antipodum* (Dbl.). New Zealand.

4. *Callerebia kalinda* (Moore). Chitral.

5. *Callerebia annada* (Moore). Himalayas to W. China. Similar : scanda (Koll.), Kashmir, UN dark.

6. *Bletogona mycalesis* (Fldr.). Celebes.

7. *Callerebia nirmala* (Moore). Himalayas. Variable. Similar : daksha (Moore), smaller, high altitudes.

8. *Callerebia shallada* (Lang). Kashmir.

9. *Chazara heydenreichii* (Led.). Pamirs, Himalayas. Similar : prieuri (Pier.), Spain, N. Africa.

10. *Dodonidia helmsi* (Btlr.). New Zealand.

11. *Cyllogenes suradeva* (Moore). Sikkim. Similar : janetae (Nicer.), UPF band broad, no purple tinge.

12. *Coelites epiminthia* (Ww.). Malaysia, Sumatra.

13. *Coelites euptychioides* (Fldr.). Malaya, Sumatra.

14. *Coelites nothis* (Bsd.). Siam. UP resembles epiminthia.

PLATE 163: Satyridae

1. *Elymnias agondas* (Bsd.). New Guinea, Australia. Male UP black, edged green, lunule UPH.

2. *Elymnias casiphone* (Hbn.). Malaya, Java, Burma. Female UP grey green with veins outlined in brown, resembles malelas female.

3. *Elymnias caudata* (Btlr.). S. India. Female ground colour UPF is brown orange.

4. *Elymnias ceryx* (Bsd.). Java, Sumatra.

5. *Elymnias cottonis* (Hew.). Burma, Andaman Islands.

6. *Elymnias cumaea* (Fldr.). Celebes.

7. *Elymnias cybele* (Fldr.). N. Moluccas. UP resembles mimalon. Similar : vitellia (Cr.), S. Moluccas.

8. *Elymnias dara* (Dist.). Burma, Malaya, Java, Sumatra.

9. *Elymnias esaca* (Ww.). Malaya, Sumatra, Borneo. Female ground colour blue-grey. Similar : maheswara (Fruhst.), Java, marginal dots UP white ; vasudeva (Moore), Sikkim, Assam, Burma, UPF black stripes more distinct.

PLATE 164: Satyridae

1. *Elymnias hicetas* (Hew.). Celebes. Male UP blue black with blue margin.

2. *Elymnias malelas* (Hew.). Sikkim to Malaysia. Male UP resembles casiphone.

3. *Elymnias hewitsoni* (Wall.). Celebes.

4. *Elymnias hypermnestra* (L.). India, Burma, Ceylon, Siam, Malaysia, Indo-China. Variable.

5. *Elymnias mimalon* (Hew.). Celebes.

6. *Elymnias patna* (Ww.). Assam to Malaya. Similar : beza (Hew.), Philippines.

7. *Elymnias nesaea* (L.). India to Siam, Malaysia, Java. Several subspecies.

8. *Elymnias panthera* (F.). Malaya, Java. Many subspecies.

9. *Elymnias penanga* (Ww.). Malaysia, occurs rarely in Assam.

PLATE 165: Satyridae

1. *Elymnias pealii* (W–Mason). Assam. Male UP dark blue.

2. *Elymnias penanga* (Ww.). Malaysia, occurs rarely in Assam.

3. *Erycinidia gracilis* (R. & J.). New Guinea.

4. *Elymnias singhala* (Fldr.). Ceylon.

5. *Elymnias vasudeva* (Moore). Sikkim, Burma, Malaya.

6. *Geitoneura achanta* (Don.). Australia.

7. *Geitoneura hobartia* (Ww.). Tasmania.

8. *Erites angularis* (Moore). Malaysia.

9. *Erites argentina* (Btlr.). Java, Sumatra, Borneo, Malaya.

10. *Erites elegans* (Btlr.). Malaysia, Sumatra.

11. *Ethope diademoides* (Moore). N. Burma.

12. *Ethope himachala* (Moore). Assam to Upper Burma.

13. *Eumenis mniszechi* (Fldr.). Kaskmir to W. China.

14. *Geitoneura kershawi* (Misk.). S.E. Australia.

15. *Geitoneura lathoniella* (Ww.). Australia and Tasmania. Similar : correae (Olliff), UNH no silver markings, darker UP.

16. *Geitoneura minyas* (W. & L.). W. Australia. Similar : klugi (Guer.), UP/UN more heavily marked.

17. *Geitoneura tasmanica* (Lyell). Tasmania.

PLATE 166: Satyridae

1. *Harsiesis hygea* (Hew.). New Guinea.

2. *Heteronympha merope* (F.). Australia, Tasmania. Similar : banksi (Leech), UP markings darker ; cordace (Hbn.), UNH 2 bluish spots.

3. *Heteronympha merope* (see 2).

4. *Hypocysta adiante* (Hbn.). E. Australia.

5. *Hypocysta antirius* (Btlr.). Queensland.

6. *Hypocysta osyris* (Bsd.). New Guinea. Similar : calypso (Gr.Sm.), Queensland, New Guinea ; haemonia (Hew.), Aru Island, UP brown.

7. *Heteronympha mirifica* (Btlr.). Australia.

8. *Hypocysta aroa* (Beth.-Baker). New Guinea.

9. *Hypocysta euphemia* (Westw.). E. Australia.

10. *Lamprolenis nitida* (Godm. & Salv.). New Guinea. UP brown shot pale green.

11. *Lethe chandica* (Moore). Himalayas, W. and C. China, Malaya. Variable.

12. *Lethe bhairava* (Moore). Assam.

13. *Hypocysta pseudirius* (Btlr.). E. Australia. Similar : metirius (Btlr.), Australia, darker, larger lunule UPH.

14. *Lethe baladeva* (Moore). Himalayas.

15. *Lethe confusa* (Auriv.). India, China, Malaysia.

16. *Lethe confusa* (see 15).

PLATE 167: Satyridae

1. *Lethe darena* (Fldr.). Java, Sumatra, Borneo.

2. *Lethe drypetis* (Hew.). S. India, Ceylon. Similar: daretis (Hew.), Ceylon, UN bands and ocelli more clear-cut.

3. *Lethe europa* (F.). India, China, Malaya.

4. *Lethe elwesi* (Moore). Himalayas to W. China. Similar: gracilis (Oberth), Tibet, UP, UN, ocelli more distinct.

5. *Lethe goalpara* (Moore). Himalayas. UP resembles sura.

6. *Lethe jalaurida* (Nicer.). Himalayas.

7. *Lethe kansa* (Moore). Assam, Sikkim. Similar: vindhya (Fldr.), UN outer areas paler violet.

8. *Lethe latiaris* (Hew.). Sikkim, Assam.

9. *Lethe serbonis* (Hew.). Assam, Burma to W. China. Variable.

10. *Lethe mekara* (Moore). Assam to Tonkin, Malaya.

11. *Lethe minerva* (F.). Java, Malaya. Male UP resembles mekara.

12. *Lethe pulaha* (Moore). Himalayas to W. and C. China.

13. *Lethe rohria* (F.). Ceylon, India, Burma, China. Female white band forewing. Many subspecies.

14. *Lethe scanda* (Moore). E. Himalayas.

15. *Lethe maitrya* (Nicer.). N. India.

PLATE 168: Satyridae

1. *Lethe sidonis* (Hew.). Afghanistan, Himalayas.

2. *Lethe sinorix* (Hew.). Sikkim to Upper Burma, Malaya.

3. *Lethe sura* (Dbl.). Sikkim through Burma to W. China.

4. *Lethe syrcis* (Hew.). Java. Similar: gemina (Leech), W. China, wings more pointed.

5. *Lethe verma* (Koll.). Himalayas to W. China, Malaya.

6. *Maniola lupinus* (Costa). N.W. Himalayas

7. *Melanitis amabilis* (Bsd.). Moluccas, New Guinea. Female band UPF white.

8. *Maniola boisduvalia* (Fldr.). Philippines.

9. *Melanitis atrax* (Fldr.). Philippines. Few forms.

10. *Melanitis constantia* (Cr.). Moluccas, Solomon Islands, New Guinea. Many subspecies. Female resembles boisduvalia, but no hook to UPF.

PLATE 169: Satyridae

1. *Melanitis leda* (L.). India to China, Korea and Japan, Australia, Africa. Very variable.

2. *Melanitis phedima* (Cr.). India, China, Malaysia. Many races and subspecies. UP resembles velutina.

3. *Mycalesis anapita* (Moore). Malaysia, Sumatra. Similar: marginata (Moore).

4. *Mycalesis anaxias* (Hew.). India, Malaya. Similar: siamica (R. & G.), N. Siam, one eye spot UPF.

5. *Melanitis zitenius* (Herbst.). N. India, Malaysia, Sumatra, Java.

6. *Mycalesis discobolus* (Fruhst.). New Guinea.

7. *Melanitis velutina* (Fldr.). Celebes. Female UP ground colour orange brown.

8. *Mycalesis barbara* (Sm.). New Guinea.

9. *Mycalesis dexamenus* (Hew.). Celebes.

10. *Mycalesis duponcheli* (Guer.). New Guinea. Variable.

11. *Mycalesis durga* (Sm.). New Guinea.

12. *Mycalesis fuscum* (Fldr.). Malaysia, Java, Sumatra.

13. *Mycalesis horsfieldi* (Moore). Malaysia, Java, Celebes.

14. *Mycalesis ita* (Fldr.). Philippines. Similar markings: felderi (Btlr.), Philippines, UP dark brown.

15. *Mycalesis janardana* (Moore). Malaysia to Philippines, Celebes, Moluccas. Several subspecies.

16. *Mycalesis lepcha* (Moore). India. Several subspecies.

17. *Mycalesis maianeas* (Hew.). Malaya and Borneo.

18. *Mycalesis lorna* (Gr.-Sm.). New Guinea. Similar: elia (Sm.), New Guinea, male UP lighter brown, female less white UPF.

PLATE 170: Satyridae

1. *Mycalesis malsara* (Moore). India, Burma.

2. *Mycalesis malsarida* (Btlr.). Assam.

3. *Mycalesis mahadeva* (Bsd.). New Guinea. UP resembles messene, but eyespot UPF clear of black margin.

4. *Mycalesis messene* (Hew.). Moluccas.

5. *Mycalesis mestra* (Hew.). India.

6. *Mycalesis mineus* (L.). India, Burma, Malaya to China. Lfp: grasses. Wet and dry season forms, this is wet season form.

7. *Mycalesis mnasicles* (Hew.). Malaysia, Upper Burma, Assam.

8. *Mycalesis mucia* (Hew.). New Guinea. UPF male orange patch, female larger, paler.

9. *Mycalesis oroatis* (Hew.). Malaya, Java.

10. *Mycalesis orseis* (Hew.). Assam, Malaysia, Sumatra.

11. *Mycalesis phidon* (Hew.). New Guinea.

12. *Mycalesis patnia* (Moore). 'The Glad-eye Bush Brown'. Ceylon, S. India. Lfp: rice.

13. *Mycalesis perseus* (F.). S. Asia to Australia. Very variable with season. Many forms, this is wet season form.

14. *Mycalesis sirius* (F.). Australia, New Guinea, Moluccas.

15. *Mycalesis tagala* (Fldr.). Philippines.

16. *Mycalesis subdita* (Moore). S. India and Ceylon.

17. *Mycalesis terminus* (F.). Australia, Moluccas. Many races and subspecies.

18. *Mycalesis visala* (Moore). Assam to Malaya. Dry season form.

19. *Mycalesis sudra* (Fldr.). Java, Bali.

20. *Neope bhadra* (Moore). Sikkim to Upper Burma.

PLATE 171: Satyridae

1. *Neope yama* (Moore). Himalayas. Subspecies: serica (Leech), C. and W. China. Similar: muirheadi (Fldr.), W. and C. China, UN pale stripe top to bottom; bremeri (Fldr.), Tibet to C. China, UP ocelli on bright yellow ground, UN lighter colour.

2. *Neope yama* (see 1).

3. *Platypthima ornata* (R. & J.). New Guinea.

4. *Neorina hilda* (Ww.). India. Subspecies: patria (Leech), W. China.

5. *Neorina krishna* (Ww.). Java.

6. *Neorina lowi* (Dbl.). Malaya, Sumatra.

7. *Pararge schakra* (Koll.). Himalayas. Similar: adrastoides (Bien.), Iran, UP deep black-brown, bright red-yellow band; maerula (Fldr.), Kashmir, UPF orange band broken into streaks; majuscula (Leech), W. China, Tibet, large UPF ocellus double.

8. *Orsotriaena medus* (F.). India, Ceylon, New Guinea, Australia, Malaysia. Similar: jopas (Hew.), Celebes.

9. *Pieridopsis virgo* (R. & J.). New Guinea.

10. *Parantirrhoea marshalli* (W-Mas.). S. India.

11. *Pararge menava* (Moore). Himalayas. Similar: majuscula (Leech), C. China, UPF lunules very large.

12. *Orinoma damaris* (Gray). Assam, Upper Burma.

PLATE 172: Satyridae

1. *Ptychandra lorquini* (Fldr.). Philippines, Moluccas. Female UP resembles schadenbergi female UP.

2. *Ptychandra schadenbergi* (Semp.). Philippines. UP male resembles lorquini male.

3. *Ragadia crisia* (Hbn.). Malaya.

4. *Xois sesara* (Hew.). Fiji.

5. *Ragadia crisilda* (Hew.). Bhutan, Assam, Burma, Malaya, Borneo. Similar: latifasciata (Leech), white stripes UP; aunulata (Sm.), Philippines, Borneo.

6. *Rhaphicera moorei* (Btlr.). W. Himalayas to Sikkim.

7. *Rhaphicera satricus* (Dbl.). N. India to China.

8. *Satyrus brahminus* (Blanch.). Himalayas. Similar: seraha (Koll.), UPF band rosy yellow; padma (Koll.), Himalayas to W. China, UPH band quite straight; saraswati (Koll.), smaller, white band very broad; merlina (Oberth.), W. China, UNF white stripe base of wing; magica (Oberth.), W. China, UN white stripe base both wings.

9. *Satyrus huebneri* (Fldr.). Kashmir, Ladakh.

10. *Ypthima avanta* (Moore). India, Ceylon, Burma.

11. *Satyrus parisatis* (Koll.). N.W. Himalayas. Form shiva.

12. *Ypthima ceylonica* (Hew.). Ceylon.

13. *Ypthima aphnius* (Godt.). Celebes, Timor.

14. *Ypthima chenui* (Guer.). S. India. Terrain: montane.

15. *Ypthima baldus* (F.). India, Malaya, China, Korea, Japan. Similar: avanta (Moore). Variable.

16. *Satyrus pumilus* (Fldr.). Kashmir, Tibet.

17. *Satyrus parisatis* (Koll.). Baluchistan, Himalayas to Chitral. Form parsis.

18. *Tisiphone abeona* (Don.). Australia. Subspecies joanna (Btlr.) has yellow-white bars UPF and UPH.

19. *Tisiphone helena* (Oll.). Australia.

PLATE 173: Satyridae

1. *Ypthima fasciata* (Hew.). Malaysia, Sumatra.

2. *Ypthima huebneri* (Kirby). Himalayas, Burma.

3. *Ypthima methora* (Hew.). Assam, Sikkim, Bhutan. UP resembles savara. Similar: dohertyi (Moore), Burma, 5 clear lunules UPH.

4. *Ypthima nareda* (Koll.). Himalayas to C. China. UN resembles praenubila. Similar: arctous (F.), Australia, UP only, UNH has only one ocellus.

5. *Zethera pimplea* (Er.). Philippines.

6. *Ypthima philomela* (Joh.). India, Java and Sumatra.

7. *Zethera incerta* (Hew.). Philippines.

8. *Ypthima savara* (Gr.-Sm.). Burma, Malaya.

9. *Ypthima sakra* (Moore). Himalayas to Burma. Many subspecies. Similar: methorina (Oberth.), China, UP grey brown, ocelli nearly blind.

10. *Zipoetis saitis* (Hew.). S. India.

11. *Zipoetis scylax* (Hew.). Assam. UP dark brown.

12. *Zethera pimplea* (see 5).

13. *Zethera musa* (Fldr.). Philippines. Female resembles female pimplea.

PLATE 174: Lycaenidae

1. *Albulina omphisa* (Moore). Kashmir.

2. *Allotinus apries* (Fruh.). Malaya, Java, Sumatra, Borneo.

3. *Allotinus drumila* (Moore). Assam. Male UP brown, narrow yellow band UPF.

4. *Allotinus fabius* (Dist.). Burma, Malaya, Sumatra, Borneo.

5. *Allotinus nivalis* (Druce). Malaya to Philippines.

6. *Allotinus fallax* (Fldr.). Philippines, Celebes. Several subspecies.

7. *Allotinus horsfieldi* (Moore). Malaya, Burma, Java, Celebes. Similar: macassariensis (Holl.), S. Celebes.

8. *Allotinus multistrigatus* (Nicer.). E. Himalayas to Upper Burma. Wet season form of drumila.

9. *Allotinus punctatus* (Semp.). Philippines. Subspecies of fabius (Dist.), N. Borneo, etc.

10. *Araotes lapithis* (Moore). Sikkim to Indo-China, Malaya. Similar: perrhaebis (Semp.).

11. *Allotinus subviolaceus* (Fldr.). Malaya, Sumatra, Java.

12. *Allotinus taras* (Doh.). Burma, Malaya, Borneo, Java. Similar: panormis (Elwes), Borneo.

13. *Allotinus unicolor* (Fldr.). Malaya, Borneo, Java, Celebes. Similar: rebilus (Fruh.), W. Borneo.

14. *Anthene emolus* (Godt.). India to Solomon Islands, Malaysia. Similar: licates (Hew.).

15. *Anthene lycaenoides* (Fldr.). Malaya to New Guinea.

16. *Anthene lycaenoides* (see 15).

17. *Araotes perrhaebis* (Semp.). Philippines. Similar: lapithis (Moore), Malaysia, UN.

18. *Arhopala axiothea* (Hew.). New Guinea.

19. *Azanus jesous* (Guer.). India, Burma, Africa.

20. *Aurea aurea* (Hew.). Borneo, Malaya. Similar: trogon (Dist.), Malaya, Sumatra.

Male UPH narrower black border, female UPH broader black border.

21. *Austrozephyrus absolon* (Hew.). Sumatra, Java.

22. *Azanus ubaldus* (Cr.). India and Ceylon, Arabia. Lfp: Acacia.

23. *Bindahara phocides* (see 29).

24. *Candalides absimilis* (Fldr.). Australia. Similar: persimilis (Waterh.); consimilis (Waterh.); margarita (Semp.).

25. *Candalides blackburni* (Tuely). Oahu.

26. *Candalides absimilis* (see 24).

27. *Bothrinia chennellii* (Nic.). Assam. Similar: nebulosa (Leech), W. and C. China.

28. *Candalides subrosea* (Gr.Sm.). New Guinea.

29. *Bindahara phocides* (F.). India to Australia. Subspecies moorei (Fruh.) has blue edge UPH.

30. *Callictita cyara* (B.B.). New Guinea.

31. *Camena blanka* (Nicer.). India, Sumatra.

32. *Camena cleobis* (Godt.). India to Malaya.

33. *Camena cotys* (Hew.). India to Java. Similar: anysis (Hew.), Celebes.

34. *Camena deva* (Moore). India, Malaya, Java.

35. *Candalides cuprea* (Rob.). New Guinea.

36. *Candalides cyprotus* (Oll.). Australia.

37. *Candalides intensa* (Btlr.). Aru Islands. Similar: butleri (Sm. & Ky.); fulgens (Sm. & Ky.).

38. *Candalides erinus* (F.). Australia. Similar: acasta (Cox), Tasmania, Australia.

39. *Candalides griseldis* (Stgr.). Moluccas.

40. *Candalides heathi* (Cox). Australia.

41. *Candalides helenita* (Semp.). Australia. Similar: gilberti (Waterh.).

42. *Candalides pruina* (H. Druce). New Guinea.

43. *Candalides refusa* (Gr.Sm.). New Guinea.

44. *Candalides sublutea* (B.B.). New Guinea.

45. *Candalides tringa* (Gr.Sm.). New Guinea. Similar: margarita (Semp.), New Guinea, not so bright blue.

46. *Candalides xanthospilos* (Hbn.). Australia.

47. *Candalides ziska* (Sm. & Ky.). New Guinea.

48. *Castalius caleta* (Hew.). Ceylon, Philippines, Celebes.

49. *Castalius evena* (Hew.). New Guinea.

50. *Castalius ethion* (Dbl. & Hew.). India to Philippines, Ceylon to Malaya. Very variable. Similar: ilissus (Fldr.), Celebes.

51. *Castalius mindarus* (Fldr.). New Guinea.

52. *Castalius rosimon* (F.). India to Philippines, Ceylon to Malaya.

PLATE 175: Lycaenidae

1. *Castalius roxus* (Godt.). Indo-China to Philippines and Celebes, New Guinea, Malaya. Similar: elna (Hew.), India, Malaya to Bali.

2. *Catapaecilma elegans* (Druce). India, Ceylon, Malaya, Philippines.

3. *Catapaecilma major* (Druce). Malaya, India.

4. *Catapaecilma subochracea* (Elwes). India to Malaya.

5. *Catopyrops ancyra* (Fldr.). Australia, New Guinea. Similar: florinda (Btlr.), Australia.

6. *Catopyrops keiria* (Druce). Solomon Islands.

7. *Catochrysops panormus* (Dist.). India, Ceylon through Malaya to Australia. Similar: strato (F.), India to Moluccas.

8. *Catochrysops strabo* (F.). India to Moluccas.

9. *Celastrina akasa* (Horsf.). S. India, Ceylon, Malaya to Celebes. Terrain: montane.

10. *Celastrina albocaeruleus* (Moore). India, Malaya, Hong Kong.

11. *Celastrina camenae* (Nicer.). Malaya, Borneo to Celebes.

12. *Celastrina carna* (Nicer.). Assam to Malaya and Sumatra.

13. *Celastrina ceyx* (Nicer.). Sumatra, Malaya, Java. Terrain: montane.

14. *Celastrina cossaea* (Nicer.). Malaya, Java, Sumatra, Borneo.

15. *Celastrina dilectus* (Moore). India to W. and C. China, Malaya. Many subspecies.

16. *Celastrina lavendularis* (Moore). Sikkim, Assam to Indo-China, Malaya to Philippines and Celebes.

17. *Celastrina melaena* (Doh.). Sumatra, Malaya, Indo-China.

18. *Celastrina musina* (Snellen). Burma to Malaya, Sumatra, Java. Terrain: montane.

19. *Celastrina nedda* (Smith). Moluccas, Celebes, New Guinea. Subspecies of philippina (Semp.), Philippines.

20. *Celastrina puspa* (Horsf.). India to New Guinea, Philippines, Ceylon, Nicobars. Many races and subspecies.

21. *Celastrina puspa* (see 20).

22. *Celastrina quadriplaga* (Snell.). Malaya, Java.

23. *Celastrina tenella* (Misk.). New Guinea, Australia.

24. *Celastrina transpectus* (Mr.). Sikkim, Burma.

25. *Celastrina vardhana* (Moore). Kashmir to Kumaon in Himalayas. Similar: orcas (Leech), W. China; Bothrinia nebulosa (Leech) W. and C. China.

26. *Charana hypoleuca* (Hew.). Java, Sumatra, Malaya. Similar: martina (Hew.), Borneo.

27. *Charana jalindra* (Horsf.). India, Java, Malaya, Borneo.

28. *Charana jalindra* (see 27).

29. *Cheritra freja* (F.). India to Ceylon, Malaya and Borneo.

30. *Cheritra orpheus* (Fldr.). Philippines.

31. *Chilades lajus* (Stoll.). India, China, S. Asia. Lfp: Aurantiaceae. Variable. Female dark.

32. *Chliaria amabilis* (Nicer.). Malaya, Borneo.

33. *Chliaria kina* (Hew.). Himalayas.

34. *Chliaria othona* (Hew.). Himalayas to Andaman Islands, Malaya. Similar: tora (Kheil), smaller spots UN.

35. *Chrysozephyrus syla* (Koll.). Himalayas. Similar: Favonius orientalis (Murr.), Amurland, C. and N. China, Korea.

36. *Curetis bulis* (Dbl. & Hew.). India, Indo-China, Japan.

37. *Curetis insularis* (Horsf.). Malaya to Philippines and Celebes.

38. *Curetis felderi* (Dist.). Malaya, Sumatra.

39. *Curetis santana* (Moore) Malaysia.

40. *Curetis sperthis* (Fldr.). Malaya. Similar: siva (Evans), S. India, darkened base to UPH.

41. *Cyaniriodes libna* (Hew.). Malaya, Borneo.

42. *Curetis thetis* (Druce). India to Celebes. Female as acuta.

43. *Dacalana vidura* (Horsf.). Assam to Sumatra, Malaya, Java.

44. *Dacalana vidura* (see 43).

45. *Deramas livens* (Dist.). Burma, Malaya, Java. Female UP dull violet, black borders.

46. *Deudorix dohertyi* (Oberth.). New Guinea.

47. *Deudorix epijarbas* (Moore). India, Malaysia, Australia. Similar: diara (Swh.).

48. *Deudorix epirus* (Fldr.). Moluccas, New Guinea, Australia.

49. *Deudorix eryx* (L.). Himalayas to Hong Kong, Malaysia.

50. *Deudorix hypargyria* (Elwes). Burma, Malaya, Java.

51. *Drina discophora* (Fldr.). Philippines.

Similar: wavortia (Hew.), Philippines, male has no sex mark UPF.

52. *Drina maneia* (Hew.). Malaya.

53. *Drupadia estella* (Hew.). Borneo, Malaya, Sumatra.

PLATE 176: Lycaenidae

1. *Drina maneia* (see 175/52).

2. *Drupadia melisa* (Hew.). Burma, Sikkim, Malaya.

3. *Drupadia scaeva* (Hew.). Malaya, Sumatra.

4. *Eooxylides tharis* (Hbn.). Sumatra, Malaya, Java. Similar: meduana (Hew.), Philippines.

5. *Epimastidia pilumna* (H. Druce). New Guinea. Male UP as staudingeri, subspecies of inops (Feld.).

6. *Epimastidia staudingeri* (Rob.). Ceram (Moluccas). UN resembles pilumna.

7. *Everes lacturnus* (Fruh.). India, Ceylon to Malaya, China and Australia.

8. *Euaspa milionia* (Hew.). Kashmir to Nepal.

9. *Euchrysops cnejus* (F.). Himalayas to W. China, India, Malaysia to Australia. Lfp: Cycas, Phaseolus. Similar: pandava (Horsf.), attended by ants.

10. *Euchrysops cnejus* (see 9).

11. *Flos anniella* (Hew.). Philippines, Moluccas, Malaya.

12. *Flos apidanus* (Cr.). Assam to Malaya and Celebes.

13. *Flos diardi* (Hew.). Assam to Malaya and Celebes.

14. *Heliophorus androcles* (Dbl. & Hew.). Himalayas to W. China. Similar: tamu (Koll.).

15. *Heliophorus bakeri* (Evans). India. Similar: oda (Hew.).

16. *Heliophorus bakeri* (see 15).

17. *Heliophorus brahma* (Moore). Himalayas to W. China.

18. *Heliophorus ila* (Nicer.). Malaya, Sumatra. Similar: epicles (Godt.).

19. *Heliophorus moorei* (Hew.).

20. *Horaga amethystus* (Druce). Malaya.

21. *Horaga lefebvrei* (Fldr.). Philippines.

22. *Horaga onyx* (Moore). India, Malaysia. Similar: viola (Moore).

23. *Horaga selina* (Gr.Sm.). Celebes.

24. *Horaga viola* (Moore). India.

25. *Horsfieldia narada* (Horsf.). India through Siam to Malaya, Ceylon.

26. *Hypochlorosis antipha* (Hew.). Aru Islands.

27. *Hypochlorosis danis* (Feld.). Australia, New Guinea.

28. *Hypochlorosis humboldti* (H. Druce). New Guinea. Similar UP: antipha (Hew.), Aru Islands.

29. *Hypochrysops anacletus* (Fldr.). New Guinea.

30. *Hypochrysops apelles* (F.). Thursday Island, Australia.

31. *Hypochrysops apollo* (Misk.). Australia.

32. *Hypochrysops apollo* (see 31).

33. *Hypochrysops architas* (G. Salv.). Solomon Islands.

34. *Hypochrysops arronica* (Fldr.). New Guinea.

35. *Hypochrysops aurigena* (Fruh.). Amboina.

36. *Hypochrysops byzos* (Bsd.). Australia.

37. *Hypochrysops chrysanthis* (Fldr.). Amboina.

38. *Hypochrysops chrysanthis* (see 37).

39. *Hypochrysops delicia* (Hew.). Australia. Similar: regina (Sm. & Ky.), Moluccas.

40. *Hypochrysops doleschallii* (Fldr.). Ceram, Amboina.

41. *Hypochrysops halyaetus* (Hew.). W. Australia.

42. *Hypochrysops ignita* (Leech). Australia. Similar: epicurus (Misk.), Australia.

43. *Hypochrysops meeki* (Roths. & Jordan). New Guinea. Similar: protogenes (Fldr.), Australia.

44. *Hypochrysops narcissus* (F.). Australia.

45. *Hypochrysops crateras* (G. Salv.). Solomon Islands. Similar: architas (G. Salv.).

46. *Hypochrysops pagenstecheri* (Ribbe). New Guinea.

47. *Hypochrysops plotinus* (Gr.Sm.). New Guinea.

48. *Hypochrysops plotinus* (see 47).

49. *Hypochrysops polycletus* (L.). Moluccas to Australia. Similar: rex (Bsd.).

PLATE 177: Lycaenidae

1. *Hypochrysops polycletus* (L.). New Guinea, N. Australia.

2. *Hypochrysops polycletus* (see 1). Subspecies rovena (Druce).

3. *Hypochrysops pythias* (Fldr.). New Guinea, Australia.

4. *Hypochrysops regina* (Sm. & Ky.). Moluccas.

5. *Hypochrysops rex* (Bsd.). New Guinea. Male UP as polycletus.

6. *Hypochrysops scintillans* (Btlr.). New Britain.

7. *Hypochrysops rufinus* (Gr.Sm.). New Guinea.

8. *Hypochrysops taeniata* (Jordan). San Christobal.

9. *Hypochrysops theon* (Fldr.). Australia. Similar: doleschallii (Fldr.).

10. *Hypolycaena cinesia* (Hew.). Borneo.

11. *Hypolycaena erylus* (Godt.). Sikkim to Indo-China, Malaya to Philippines. Several races.

12. *Hypolycaena phorbas* (F.). Australia, New Guinea. Variable.

13. *Hypolycaena phorbas* (see 12).

14. *Hypolycaena sipylus* (Fldr.). Moluccas, Celebes, Philippines.

15. *Hypothecla astyla* (Fldr.). Philippines.

16. *Hypolycaena thecloides* (Fldr.). Malaya to Philippines.

17. *Hypolycaena thecloides* (see 16).

18. *Hypothecla astyla* (Feld.). Philippines.

19. *Iraota distanti* (Stgr.). Malaya, Sumatra, Borneo.

20. *Iraota lazarena* (Fldr.). Philippines. Similar: Thaduka multicaudata (Moore), Burma.

21. *Iraota timoleon* (Stoll.). Himalayas, to China, S. India, Ceylon. Lfp: Banyan, Peepul, Pomegranate. Similar: maccenas (F.); rochana (Horsf.), India. Malaya, Burma.

22. *Iraota timoleon* (see 21).

23. *Jacoona amrita* (Fldr.). Sumatra Malaya, Borneo.

24. *Jacoona anasuja* (Fld.). Borneo, Malaya.

25. *Jacoona irmina* (Fruh.). Nias.

26. *Jacoona scopula* (Druce). Malaya.

27. *Jalmenus evagoras* (Hbn.). Australia.

28. *Jalmenus evagoras* (see 27).

29. *Jalmenus icilius* (Hew.). Australia.

30. *Jalmenus inous* (Hew.). Australia.

31. *Jamides abdul* (Dist.). Malaya, Borneo, Java.

32. *Jamides aleuas* (Fldr.). New Guinea, Australia.

33. *Jamides aratus* (Cr.). Borneo to Celebes. Variable.

34. *Jamides aratus* (see 33).

35. *Jamides bochus* (Cr.). Himalayas to C. China, Malaysia, Formosa and Australia. Lfp: Xylia and Butea.

36. *Jamides caeruleas* (Druce). India, Malaya, Borneo, Java.

37. *Jamides celeno* (Cr.). India, Ceylon, Indo-China, Malaya to Celebes. Numerous forms and subspecies.

38. *Jamides celeno* (see 37).

39. *Jamides cyta* (Bsd.). New Guinea, Australia, Malaya to Solomon Islands.

40. *Jamides cunilda* (Snell.). Malaya, Borneo, Java.

41. *Jamides elpis* (Godt.). Assam to Indo-China, Malaya to Celebes. Many subspecies.

42. *Jamides elpis* (see 41).

43. *Jamides euchylas* (Hbn.). Moluccas, New Guinea. UN as nemophila.

44. *Jamides kankena* (Fldr.). India to Java.

45. *Jamides festivus* (Rob.). Celebes.

46. *Jamides lucide* (Nicer.). Sumatra.

47. *Jamides lugine* (Druce). Burma, Borneo.

48. *Jamides malaccanus* (Rob.). Malaya.

49. *Jamides nemophila* (Btlr.). New Guinea, Australia. UP resembles euchylas (Hbn.).

PLATE 178: Lycaenidae

1. *Jamides philatus* (Snell.). Burma to Malaya to Celebes and Philippines. Many forms.

2. *Jamides pura* (Moore). India to Malaya to Hong Kong. Similar: celeno (Cr.).

3. *Jamides talinga* (Kheil.). Malaysia.

4. *Jamides zebra* (Druce). Malaya.

5. *Logania hampsoni* (Fruh.). New Guinea.

6. *Logania malayica* (Dist.). Malaya to Philippines.

7. *Logania marmorata* (Moore). Burma to Malaya, Java.

8. *Liphyra brassolis* (Ww.). India to Moluccas, Malaya to Australia. The most primitive lycaenid alive today.

9. *Liphyra castnia* (Strand.). New Guinea. Similar: grandis (Weym.), New Guinea, much larger, orange band UPF.

10. *Logania massalia* (Doh.). Assam through Burma, Malaya, Borneo. Similar: drucei (Moulet.).

11. *Logania regina* (Druce). Malaya, Borneo.

12. *Loxura atymnus* (Cr.). India, Burma, Ceylon, Malaya to Philippines. Similar: cassiopeia (Dist.).

13. *Luthrodes cleotas* (Guer.). New Guinea, Solomon Islands, Bismarch Archipelago.

14. *Lucia limbaria* (Swains.). Australia. Several subspecies.

15. *Lycaena feredayi* (Bates). New Zealand.

16. *Lycaena kasyapa* (Moore). India.

17. *Lycaena pavana* (Koll.). Himalayas.

18. *Lycaena salustius* (F.). New Zealand.

19. *Lycaenopsis haraldus* (F.). Sumatra, Malaya, Java.

20. *Lycaenopsis haraldus* (see 19).

21. *Mahathala ameria* (Hew.). India to Tonkin to Malaysia.

22. *Mahathala atkinsoni* (Doh.). Burma.

23. *Marmessus caesarea* (Weym.). Celebes.

24. *Marmessus ravindra* (Horsfield). Malaya, India, Burma. Many races.

25. *Marmessus rufotaenia* (Frus.). Burma, Sumatra, Malaya, Java. Similar: niasicus (Rob.), and several other species.

26. *Marmessus theda* (C. & R. Felder). Malaya to Philippines. Similar: archbaldi (Evans), Burma.

27. *Megisba malaya* (Horsf.). Himalayas to Ceylon, Malaya to New Guinea.

28. *Miletus ancon* (Doh.). Burma, Indo-China, Malaya. Similar: gigantes (Nicer.), Sumatra.

29. *Miletus archilochus* (Fruh.). Malaya, Borneo, Indo-China.

30. *Miletus biggsi* (Dist.). Malaya. Similar: nymphis (Fruh.), Burma to Sumatra, UPF larger white patch.

31. *Miletus boisduvali* (Moore). Sikkim to New Guinea, Malaya, Celebes. Variable. Similar: biggsi (Dist.).

32. *Miletus leos* (Guer.). Moluccas, New Guinea.

33. *Miletus melanion* (Fldr.). Philippines. Similar: celinus (Eliot), S. Celebes.

34. *Miletus symethus* (Cr.). Assam to Philippines, Sumatra, Malaya, Java.

35. *Mota massyla* (Hew.). Assam, Burma.

36. *Nacaduba aluta* (Druce). Malaya, Sumatra to Philippines.

37. *Nacaduba angusta* (Druce). Malaya, Indo-China to Celebes. Similar: kerriana (Dist.).

38. *Nacaduba berenice* (H. Schaff.). India, Ceylon, Malaya to Australia.

39. *Nacaduba beroe* (Fldr.). India, Ceylon, Malaya to Philippines. Many subspecies.

40. *Nacaduba biocellata* (Fldr.). Australia.

41. *Nacaduba helicon* (Moore). Sikkim to Ceylon to Indo-China, Malaysia.

42. *Nacaduba pavana* (Horsf.). Tibet, India, to Burma, Malaysia. UP blue purple.

43. *Nacaduba nora* (Fldr.). India, Ceylon, Burma. Similar: dubiosa, has no tails.

44. *Nacaduba pactolus* (Fldr.). Ceylon to Formosa and Solomon Islands, India to Malaya. Several subspecies.

45. *Narathura abseus* (Hew.). India to Indo-China, Malaysia to Philippines.

46. *Narathura agelastus* (Hew.). Malaya.

47. *Narathura aexone* (Hew.). New Guinea.

48. *Narathura aedias* (Hew.). Malaya, Java.

49. *Narathura alitaeus* (Hew.). Malaya, Borneo, Celebes. Similar: pseudomuta (Stgr.), Malaya, UN much browner.

50. *Narathura bazalus* (Hew.). India through Malaya to Sumatra.

51. *Narathura amantes* (Hew.). India, Malaya to Timor.

52. *Narathura clarissa* (Stgr.). Celebes, Philippines. Similar: argentea (Stgr.).

PLATE 179: Lycaenidae

1. *Narathura camdeo* (Moore). Sikkim to Tonkin. Similar: varro (Fruh.), Burma, smaller.

2. *Narathura cleander* (Feld.). Borneo.

3. *Narathura epimuta* (Moore). Malaya.

4. *Narathura atosia* (Hew.). Indo-China through Malaya to Sumatra.

5. *Narathura atrax* (Hew.). Burma to Malaya. Similar UN: alea (Hew.), India, purple gloss UN.

6. *Narathura centaurus* (F.). India to Ceylon, Malaysia.

7. *Narathura centaurus* (see 6).

8. *Narathura dodonea* (Moore). Himalayas. Similar: ganesa (Moore), N. India, white speck UPF.

9. *Narathura dohertyi* (B.B.). Celebes.

10. *Narathura eumolphus* (Cr.). India, Burma, Malaya, Philippines, New Guinea. Similar: horsfieldi (Pag.), Malaysia, broader black margins UP.

11. *Narathura fulla* (Hew.). Malaya, Andaman Islands.

12. *Narathura horsfieldi* (Pag.). Sumatra, Malaya, Java. Similar: eumolphus female, less bright.

13. *Narathura hercules* (Hew.). New Guinea.

14. *Narathura ijauensis* (B.B.). Malaya.

15. *Narathura madytus* (Fruh.). Australia. Similar: meander (Bsd.).

16. *Narathura major* (Stgr.). Sumatra, Malaya to Philippines.

17. *Narathura moorei* (B.B.). Malaysia, Sumatra, Borneo.

18. *Narathura muta* (Hew.). Malaya, Java.

19. *Narathura phaenops* (Fldr.). Malaya to Philippines. Similar: normani (Eliot), Borneo.

20. *Narathura silhetensis* (Hew.). Burma to Malaya.

21. *Narathura wildei* (Misk.). Australia. Similar: antharita (Gr.Sm.), New Guinea.

22. *Neomyrina nivea* (Godm.). Siam to Indo-China, Malaya.

23. *Neopithecops zalmora* (Btlr.). India, Ceylon, Malaya to Australia.

24. *Niphanda cymbia* (Nicer.). Sikkim to Malaya.

25. *Niphanda tessellata* (Mr.). Malaya.

26. *Ogyris aenone* (Waterh.). Australia. Similar: iphis (W. & L.).

27. *Ogyris abrota* (Westw.). Australia. Male resembles barnardi.

28. *Ogyris amaryllis* (Hew.). Australia. Similar: hewitsoni (Waterh.).

29. *Ogyris barnardi* (Misk.). Australia.

30. *Ogyris genoveva* (Waterh.). Australia. This is zosine female.

31. *Ogyris ianthis* (Waterh.). Australia.

32. *Ogyris ianthis* (see 31).

33. *Ogyris idmo* (Hew.). Australia. UP resembles otanes (Fldr.).

34. *Ogyris otanes* (Fldr.). Australia.

35. *Ogyris olane* (Hew.). Australia. Similar: barnardi (Misk.).

PLATE 180: Lycaenidae

1. *Ogyris oroetes* (Hew.). Australia.

2. *Ogyris zosine* (Hew.). Australia.

3. *Panchala ammon* (Hew.). Burma to Malaya and Sumatra.

4. *Panchala paraganesa* (Nic.). India to Malaya.

5. *Parachrysops bicolor* (B.B.). New Guinea.

6. *Parelodina aroa* (B.B.). New Guinea.

7. *Petrelaea dana* (Nic.). India to Malaya to New Guinea.

8. *Pithecops corvus* (Fruh.). India to Formosa, Malaya.

9. *Pithecops fulgens* (Doh.). Assam and Sumatra.

10. *Pithecops peridesma* (Oberth.). Halmaheira.

11. *Poritia erycinoides* (Fldr.). Malaya, Borneo, Java. Female UP ground colour buff.

12. *Poritia promula* (Hew.). Java, Malaya. Subspecies elegans.

13. *Poritia karennia* (Evans). Karen Hills.

14. *Poritia phalena* (Hew.). India, Malaya, Sumatra. Female UP brown. Similar: pavonica (Nic.), Indo-China; pharyge (Hew.), Malaysia.

15. *Poritia philota* (Hew.). Malaya, Sumatra, Borneo. Similar: erycinoides (Fldr.), India.

16. *Poritia sumatrae* (Fldr.). Sumatra, Malaya.

17. *Poritia sumatrae* (see 16).

18. *Pseudodipsas cephenes* (Hew.). Australia, N.S.W. to Kuranda.

19. *Pseudodipsas digglesii* (Hew.). Australia.

20. *Pseudodipsas eone* (Fldr.). Australia. Male UP dark brown, UPH has blue spots in margin.

21. *Pseudodipsas myrmecophila* (W. & L.). Australia. Female UPF blue edged black. Similar: brisbanensis (Misk.).

22. *Purlisa giganteus* (Dist.). Malaya, Borneo.

23. *Rapala abnormis* (Elw.). Malaya, Java.

24. *Rapala affinis* (Rob.). Celebes.

25. *Rapala drasmos* (Druce). Malaya, Borneo.

26. *Rapala elcia* (Hew.). Malaya, Philippines.

27. *Rapala iarbas* (F.). India to Burma and Malaya, Indo-China and Sunda Islands. Female UP brown.

28. *Rapala kessuma* (Horsf.). Java, Malaya, Borneo.

29. *Rapala manea* (Hew.). India to Moluccas and Celebes, Malaya.

30. *Rapala dioetas* (Hew.). Celebes, Malaya. Similar: melampus (Cr.), Himalayas, Malaysia; sthenas (Fruhst.), Philippines.

31. *Rapala nissa* (Koll.). Himalayas to W. and C. China, Malaysia.

32. *Rapala scintilla* (Nicer.). Assam to Malaya.

33. *Rapala pheretima* (Hew.). India, Malaya, Sumatra, Borneo. Female as female varuna. Similar: buxaria (Nicer.), Sikkim, Bhutan.

34. *Rapala varuna* (Hsf.). India, Ceylon, Malaya to Celebes and Australia. Several subspecies.

35. *Rathinda amor* (F.). India, Ceylon.

36. *Remelana jangala* (Hsf.). Malaya, Assam to Philippines and Hong Kong.

37. *Remelana jangala* (see 36).

38. *Ritra aurea* (Druce). Malaya. Similar: Cheritra orpheus (Fldr.), Philippines, UP veins darkened.

39. *Semanga superba* (Druce). Malaya, Java, Sumatra.

40. *Simiskina phalenà* (Hew.). Assam, Burma.

41. *Simiskina phalia* (Hew.). Burma, Malaya, Borneo.

42. *Simiskina pharyge* (Hew.). Malaya, Borneo.

43. *Simiskina pheretia* (Hew.). Malaya, Borneo.

44. *Simiskina philura* (Druce). Borneo, Malaya.

45. *Simiskina philura* (see 44).

46. *Sinthusa chandrana* (Moore). India.

47. *Sinthusa indrasari* (Snell.). Celebes. Several similar species.

48. *Sinthusa malika* (Hsf.). Sumatra, Malaya, Java. Few subspecies.

49. *Sinthusa nasaka* (Hsr.). India to Malaya. Similar: malika (Hsf.).

50. *Sinthusa peregrinus* (Smfr.). Philippines.

51. *Sinthusa virgo* (Elwes). Sikkim.

52. *Sithon nedymond* (Cr.). Malaya, Java, Sumatra.

53. *Sithon nedymond* (see 52).

54. *Spalgis epius* (Ww.). India, Burma, Andamans to Celebes. Variable.

PLATE 181 : Lycaenidae

1. *Spindasis abnormis* (Moore). India.

2. *Spindasis ictis* (Hew.). Kashmir, India to Ceylon.

3. *Spindasis nipalicus* (Moore). India.

4. *Spindasis lohita* (Hsf.). Himalayas to Malaya, Indo-China. Similar: syama (Hsf.).

5. *Spindasis rukma* (Nicer.). India.

6. *Spindasis syama* (Hsf.). India, C. and W. China, Malaysia, Philippines. Similar: lohita (Hsf.).

7. *Spindasis syama* (see 6).

8. *Spindasis vulcanus* (F.). India, Ceylon.

9. *Suasa lisides* (Hew.). India, Malaya.

10. *Suasa lisides* (see 9).

11. *Surendra florimel* (Doh.). Burma, Malaya, Sumatra, Java.

12. *Surendra vivarna* (Hsf.). Sumatra, Malaya, Java, Celebes. Female UP brown. Similar: florimel (Doh.).

13. *Syntarucus plinius* (F.). India, Australia. Similar: pirithous (L.), Europe; telicanus (Lang.), Africa, Arabia, S. and E. Asia.

14. *Syntarucus plinius* (see 13).

15. *Tajuria cippus* (F.). India, Ceylon, Malaysia, Burma. Lfp: Lantana, Pointsettia.

16. *Tajuria cippus* (see 15).

17. *Tajuria iapyx* (Hew.). Celebes.

18. *Tajuria isaeus* (Hew.). Malaya, Borneo. Similar: Camena cleobis (Godt.), India to Malaya, larger.

19. *Tajuria jalajala* (Fldr.). Malaya, Philippines.

20. *Tajuria maculata* (Hew.). Sikkim to Malaya.

21. *Tajuria mantra* (Fldr.). Burma to Malaya to Celebes. Similar: jalysus (Fldr.), Celebes, darker blue.

22. *Tajuria megistia* (Hew.). Himalayas.

23. *Talicada nyseus* (Guer.). Assam to Ceylon.

24. *Talicada nyseus* (see 23).

25. *Tarucus waterstradti* (H. Druce). Malaya, Assam, S. India. Similar: hazara (Evans), Punjab to Kashmir.

26. *Thamala marciana* (Hew.). Burma, Sumatra, Malaya, Borneo.

27. *Thamala marciana* (see 26).

28. *Thrix gama* (Dist.). Malaya, Sumatra, Borneo.

29. *Thysonotis drucei* (Sm. & Kirby). New Guinea. Similar: regalis (Sm. & Kirby).

30. *Thysonotis regalis* (Sm. & Kirby). New Guinea.

31. *Thysonotis albula* (Gr.Sm.). New Guinea.

32. *Thysonotis apollonius* (Fldr.). New Guinea. Subspecies of danis. Similar: philostratus (Fldr.), Moluccas.

33. *Thysonotis apollonius* (see 32).

34. *Thysonotis aryanus* (Gr.Sm.). Moluccas.

35. *Thysonotis caelius* (Fldr.). Moluccas, New Guinea.

36. *Thysonotis carissima* (Sm. & Ky.). Timor.

37. *Thysonotis cyanea* (Cr.). Australia, New Guinea. Subspecies obiana (Fruh.). Many subspecies.

38. *Thysonotis danis* (Cr.). New Guinea, Australia.

39. *Thysonotis epicoritus* (Bsd.). New Guinea.

40. *Thysonotis esme* (Gr.Sm.). New Britain. UN as schaeffera.

41. *Thysonotis hengis* (Sm. & Ky.). New Guinea. Similar: wallacei (Fldr.).

42. *Thysonotis horsa* (Gr.Sm.). New Guinea.

43. *Thysonotis hymetus* (Fldr.). Moluccas, New Guinea, Australia. Subspecies of caelius.

44. *Thysonotis piepersii* (Snell.). Celébes.

45. *Thysonotis manto* (Sm. & Ky.). New Guinea.

46. *Thysonotis perpheres* (see 47).

47. *Thysonotis perpheres* (Dr. & B.B.). New Guinea.

48. *Thysonotis phroso* (Gr.Sm.). New Guinea. Male resembles horsa, female hengis.

49. *Thysonotis plotinus* (Sm. & Ky.). New Guinea. Subspecies of caelius. Similar: plateni (Sm. & Ky.).

PLATE 182: Lycaenidae

1. *Thysonotis schaeffera* (Esch.). Philippines, Moluccas.

2. *Thysonotis stephani* (Druce). Loyalty Islands.

3. *Una purpurea* (Sm. & Ky.). New Guinea.

4. *Ticherra acte* (Moore). Sikkim to Burma. UP as Cheritra freja.

5. *Una usta* (Dist.). Assam to Malaya, Java, Borneo.

6. *Virachola isocrates* (F.). India to Ceylon, Burma.

7. *Virachola isocrates* (see 7).

8. *Zizina alsulus* (H. Sch.). Australia.

9. *Zizula gaika* (Trim.). Arabia, Iran, Kashmir, S. and E. Africa, Madagascar, E. America. UP as Zizeeria lysimon (Hbn.). Female brown.

10. *Zizina otis* (F.). Tibet, India to Formosa, Australia.

11. *Zizina oxleyi* (Feld.). New Zealand.

12. *Waigeum dinawa* (B.B.). New Guinea. Several similar species.

13. *Waigeum dinawa* (see 12).

14. *Waigeum ribbei* (Rob.). New Guinea.

15. *Waigeum thauma* (Stgr.). New Guinea. Form of miraculum.

16. *Yasoda pita* (Hsf.). Malaya, Java. Similar: tripunctata (Hew.).

17. *Zeltus amasa* (Hew.). India, Burma, Malaysia. Female UP is brown.

Nemeobiidae

18. *Abisara celebica* (Rob.). Philippines, Celebes.

19. *Abisara celebica* (see 1).

20. *Abisara echerius* (Moore), India, Ceylon, China. Several subspecies.

21. *Abisara fylla* (Ww.). Himalayas, W. and C. China. Female white band UPF.

22. *Abisara kausambi* (Fldr.). Malaya, Borneo, Sumatra, Burma, Assam. Similar: geza (Fruhst.), paler patch on UPF.

23. *Abisara kausamboides* (Nlc.). Malaya, Sumatra, Borneo. Similar: saturata (Moore), larger pale patch UPF.

24. *Abisara neophron* (Hew.). Assam to S. China.

25. *Abisara savitri* (Fldr.). Malaya, Sumatra, Borneo.

26. *Dicallaneura decorata* (Hew.). New Guinea.

27. *Dicallaneura decorata* (see 9).

28. *Dicallaneura leucomelas* (R. & J.). New Guinea.

PLATE 183: Nemeobiidae

1. *Dicallaneura ribbei* (Rob.). New Guinea.

2. *Dodona adonira* (Hew.). Nepal to Upper Burma.

3. *Dodona deodata* (Hew.). Assam to Burma.

4. *Dodona dipoea* (Hew.). Himalayas.

5. *Dodona durga* (Koll.). Kashmire, Tibet, W. & C. China.

6. *Dodona dracon* (de Nicer.). N. Burma.

7. *Dodona egeon* (Dbl.). Nepal, Sikkim to Upper Burma.

8. *Dodona eugenes* (Bat.). Himalayas, W. and C. China. Similar: egeon (Dbl.).

9. *Dodona fruhstorferi* (Rob.). Java, Sumatra, Borneo.

10. *Dodona ouida* (Moore). Himalayas to W. China, Burma, Nepal.

11. *Dodona ouida* (see 10).

12. *Dodona windu* (Fruhst.). Java.

13. *Laxita damajanti* (Fldr.). Malaya, Borneo.

14. *Laxita damajanti* (see previous plate/24).

15. *Laxita orphna* (Bsd.). Borneo, Malaya, Sumatra.

16. *Laxita orphna* (see 15).

17. *Laxita teneta* (Hew.). Borneo.

18. *Zemeros flegyas* (see 184/8).

19. *Laxita teneta* (see 17).

20. *Laxita telesia* (Hew.). Malaya, Borneo.

21. *Praetaxila segecia* (Hew.). New Guinea, Australia.

22. *Laxita telesia* (see 20).

23. *Praetaxila weiskei* (Rothsch.). New Guinea.

24. *Praetaxila weiskei* (see 23).

25. *Sospita satraps* (Sm.). New Guinea.

PLATE 184: Nemeobiidae

1. *Sospita statira* (Hew.). New Guinea.

2. *Sospita statira* (see 1).

3. *Stiboges nymphidia* (Btlr.). Malaya, W. China, Burma, Assam.

4. *Taxila haquinus* (F.). Burma, Siam, Malaya, Borneo. Similar: thuisto (Hew.).

5. *Taxila haquinus* (see 4).

6. *Taxila thuisto* (Hew.). Burma, Malaya, Sumatra, Borneo.

7. *Zemeros emesoides* (Fldr.). Malaya, Sumatra, Borneo.

8. *Zemeros flegyas* (Cr.). India through Indonesia, Malaysia, China. Several subspecies.

Libytheidae

9. *Libythea geoffroyi* (Godt.). Siam, Laos, Moluccas, New Guinea, Australia, Solomon Islands.

10. *Libythea geoffroyi* (see 9).

11. *Libythea lepita* (Moore). India to W. China.

12. *Libythea myrrha* (Godt.). India, Ceylon, Siam, W. China, Malaya. Lfp: Celtideae.

13. *Libythea myrrha* s/s rama, Nilgiris.

14. *Libythea narina* (Godt.). Philippines, New Guinea, Sumba.

Hesperiidae

15. *Acerbas anthea* (Hew.). Burma to Malaya and Java. Similar: azona (Hew.), Celebes, larger, white edge to UPH, no brown; martini (Dist.), Philippines, larger markings UP, less white UPH.

16. *Aeromachus dubius* (Elwes & Edwards). India to China, Malaya. Several subspecies.

17. *Aeromachus plumbeola* (Fldr.). Philippines.

18. *Aeromachus stigmata* (Moore). Himalayas. Similar: chineusis (Edw.), W. China; piceus (Leech).

19. *Allora doleschalli* (Fldr.). New Guinea.

20. *Arnetta atkinsoni* (Moore). Sikkim to Burma. Similar: vindhiana (Moore).

21. *Arnetta verones* (Hew.). Siam, Malaya.

22. *Ampittia dioscorides* (F.). India, Malaya, Ceylon, S. China. Many similar species.

PLATE 185: Hesperiidae

1. *Ancistroides armatus* (Druce). Sumatra, Malaya, Borneo, Burma.

2. *Ancistroides gemmifer* (Btlr.). Malaya, Sumatra.

3. *Ancistroides longicornis* (Btlr.). Borneo, Sumatra.

4. *Ancistroides nigrita* (Latreille). Sumatra, Malaya to Philippines.

5. *Anisynta dominula* (Plotz). Australia, Tasmania.

6. *Anisynta sphenosema* (Meyr. & Low). Australia.

7. *Anisynta tillyardi* (Waterh. & Ly.). Australia.

8. *Anisyntoides argenteomata* (Hew.). Australia.

9. *Astictopterus jama* (Fldr.). Sumatra, Malaya, India. Similar: abjecta (Snell), Sierra Leone to Congo.

10. *Baoris oceia* (Hew.). Burma, Malaysia, Philippines. Similar: penicillata (Moore), India, Ceylon, darker.

11. *Badamia exclamationis* (F.). India, Malaysia, to Australia. Lfp: Terminalia.

12. *Baracus vittatus* (Feld.). Assam to China.

13. *Bibasis etelka* (Hew.). Malaya, Borneo. Similar: lusca (Swh.), Celebes; arradi (Nicer.), Sikkim, much smaller.

14. *Baracus vittatus* (Fldr.). S. India, Ceylon, Burma. Similar: Aeromachus plumbeola (Fldr.), Philippines, smaller.

15. *Bibasis gomata* (Moore). China, Malaya to Philippines. Similar: lara (Leech), C. China; kanara (Evans), S. India.

16. *Bibasis harisa* (Moore). Assam, Burma, Malaya.

17. *Bibasis sena* (Moore). India, Ceylon, Malaya to Philippines.

18. *Bibasis jaina* (Moore). India, Siam, Malaya.

19. *Bibasis oedipodea* (Swsn.). Sikkim to Ceylon, Burma, Borneo.

20. *Bibasis vasutana* (Moore). Burma.

21. *Borbo bevani* (Moore). India to Malaya and S. China, Australia. Similar: cinnara (Wallace), larger, UP greenish hairs at wing bases.

22. *Caprona erosula* (Fldr.). Celebes.

23. *Caprona ransonnetti* (Fldr.). S. India, Ceylon, Assam. Many subspecies.

24. *Caprona syrichthus* (Fldr.). Indo-China, Java. Similar: alida (Nicer.), Burma, Siam, smaller.

25. *Caltoris bromus* (Leech). China, Malaya. Similar: nirwana (Plotz), Java to W. China.

26. *Caltoris cahira* (Moore). India, eastwards to China, south to Malaya.

27. *Caltoris cormasa* (Hew.). India to Malaya and Philippines.

28. *Caltoris philippina* (H.Sch.). India, Ceylon, Malaya to New Guinea and Solomon Islands.

29. *Caltoris tulsi* (Nicer.). India to Malaya and China.

30. *Capila phanaeus* (Hew.). Burma, Malaya, Indo-China.

31. *Celaenorrhinus ambareesa* (Moore). India. Similar: consanguinea (Leech), China, darker.

32. *Celaenorrhinus aurivittata* (Moore). Burma, Malaya, Borneo. Similar: dhanada (Moore), Celebes.

33. *Celaenorrhinus asmara* (Btlr.). India,

Burma, Malaysia. Similar: nigricans (Nicer.), Himalayas.

34. *Celaenorrhinus badia* (Hew.). Assam.

35. *Celaenorrhinus putra* (Moore). Burma, Malaya. Similar: nigricans (Nicer.), Sikkim, darker UP, UPF band pearly white.

36. *Celaenorrhinus ladana* (Btlr.). Malaya.

37. *Celaenorrhinus leucocera* (Koll.). Sikkim to Indo-China, Malaya. Several subspecies.

38. *Celaenorrhinus lativittus* (Elwes). Borneo.

39. *Celaenorrhinus spilothyrus* (Fldr.). India, Ceylon. Similar: chamunda (Moore), Burma, Java.

40. *Chaetocneme beata* (Hew.). Australia.

41. *Chaetocneme corvus* (see 42).

42. *Chaetocneme corvus* (Fldr.). New Guinea. Some male subspecies have small orange dots forming a bar UPF.

PLATE 186: Hesperiidae

1. *Chaetocneme critomedia* (Guer.). Australia.

2. *Chaetocneme denitza* (Hew.). Australia.

3. *Chaetocneme editus* (Plotz). New Guinea.

4. *Chaetocneme prophyropis* (Meyr. & Low.). Australia. Similar: callixenus (Hew.) New Guinea, broad yellow band UPF, no blue gloss.

5. *Chamunda chamunda* (Moore). Assam.

6. *Charmion ficulnea* (Hew.). Malaya, Siam, Borneo. Subspecies crona (Hew.) has yellow band, not white. Similar: tola (Hew.), Celebes.

7. *Choaspes benjaminii* (Guer.). Tibet, India, to Japan. Bluish UP. Similar: xanthopogon (Koll.), Sikkim to Burma and Borneo, greenish UP and UN.

8. *Choaspes illuensis* (Rbb.). New Guinea.

9. *Choaspes hemixanthus* (Rothsch.). Malaya to Hong Kong.

10. *Choaspes subcaudata* (Fldr.). Malaya to Java and Celebes. UP resembles illuensis. Similar: plateni (Stgr.), Java, UNH spots smaller, UP darker, more yellow area UPH.

11. *Coladenia dan* (F.). India, Burma, China, Malaysia.

12. *Coladenia igna* (Smpr.). Philippines. Several similar species, including laxmi (Nicer.), Malaya, darker.

13. *Coladenia indrani* (Moore). India, Burma.

14. *Croitana croites* (Hew.). Australia.

15. *Cupitha purreea* (Moore). Sikkim to Malaya to Celebes.

16. *Cyrina cyrina* (Hew.). Brunei.

17. *Daimio bhagava* (Moore). Andaman Islands to Siam.

18. *Daimio corona* (Smpr.). Philippines. Similar: limax (Plotz), Borneo, Sumatra, UP markings white.

19. *Darpa hanria* (Moore). Sikkim, Assam.

20. *Darpa pteria* (Hew.). Malaya to Philippines. Similar: striata (Druce), Siam, Malaysia, black dots on white portion UPH.

21. *Eetion elia* (Hew.). Sumatra, Malaya, Borneo.

22. *Euschemon rafflesia* (McL.). Australia.

23. *Erionota thrax* (L.). India, Manchuria, Malaya. Similar: sybyrita (Hew.), Malaysia; torus (Evans), Malaya, UPF apex rounded, large spot rhomboidal.

24. *Exometoeca nycteris* (Meyr.). Australia.

25. *Gangara thyrsis* (F.). India, Andamans to Philippines.

26. *Gangara lebadea* (Hew.). India, Ceylon, Malaya. Female has three hyaline spots UPF.

27. *Ge geta* (Nicer.). Sumatra, Malaya, Java.

28. *Gomalia albofasciata* (Moore). India and Ceylon.

29. *Halpe homolea* (Hew.). India to Malaya and Java. Several subspecies.

30. *Halpe knyvetti* (Elw.). N. India. Similar: kumara (Nicer.).

31. *Halpe moorei* (Wts.). India to Siam and Indo-China.

32. *Halpe wantona* (Swinhoe). Malaya. Several very similar species in this area.

33. *Halpe zema* (Hew.). India, Malaya, Java. Similar: zola (Evans), Burma, Malaysia, UNH pale band broader.

34. *Hasora badra* (Moore). India, Ceylon, Malaya to Philippines. Male UP plain brown, female with three hyaline spots.

35. *Hasora discolor* (Fldr.). New Guinea, Australia.

36. *Hasora celaenus* (Cr.). Moluccas, New Guinea.

37. *Hasora chromus* (Cr.). S. China, India, Malaya, Australia. Lfp: Pongamia. UP brown black, female with two white spots. Several races and subspecies.

38. *Hasora hurama* (Btlr.). New Guinea, Australia.

39. *Hasora lizetta* (Plotz). Malaya, Java.

40. *Hasora malayana* (Fldr.). Malaya to Indo-China. Subspecies of taminatus (Hubner), S. India.

41. *Hasora mus* (Elwes and Edwards). Malaya. Terrain: montane.

PLATE 187: Hesperiidae

1. *Hasora thridas* (Bsd.). New Guinea.

Similar: leucospila (Mab.), Malaya, Celebes, but UN plain brown as lizetta UP.

2. *Hasora schonherri* (Latr.). Malaya to Java.

3. *Hasora vitta* (Btlr.). Malaya to Philippines.

4. *Hesperilla chrysotricha* (Meyr. & Low.). Australia. Similar: andersoni (Kirby), Victoria, smaller.

5. *Hesperilla crypsargyra* (Meyr.). Australia. Hesperilla lfp: Gahnia.

6. *Hesperilla donnysa* (Hew.). Australia.

7. *Hesperilla idothea* (Misk.). Australia.

8. *Hesperilla picta* (Leech). Australia.

9. *Hesperilla ornata* (Leech). Australia.

10. *Hidari irava* (Moore). Sumatra to Bali.

11. *Hyarotis adrastus* (Stoll.). India to S. China, Malaysia.

12. *Hyarotis microstictum* (Wood-Mas.). India, Malaya. Similar: iadera (Nicer.), UPF no white spots, UNH no spots.

13. *Iambrix obliquans* (Mabille). Sumatra, Malaya, Borneo. Similar: latifascia (E. & E.), Borneo, UPF orange patch large and clear.

14. *Iambrix salsala* (Moore). India to Ceylon, Malaya to Indo-China. Similar: stellifer (Btlr.), more white spots UN; distanti (Shep.), UP dark brown, unmarked.

15. *Ilma irvina* (Plotz). Celebes.

16. *Iton semamora* (Moore). India to Indo-China, Malaya.

17. *Iton watsonii* (Nicer.). Burma.

18. *Isma bonania* (Hew.). Malaya, Borneo. Similar: bononoides (H. Druce), Borneo.

19. *Isma guttulifera* (Elw. & Edw.). Malaya. Similar: miosticta (Nicer.), Malaya, markings very small; umbrosa (Elw. & Edw.), UPF cell spots unequal size.

20. *Isma protoclea* (H.Sch.). Burma, Malaya. Several similar species, including: cronus (Nicer.); miodicta (Nicer.), UPH spots very small.

21. *Isma obscura* (Dist.). Malaya.

22. *Koruthaialos focula* (Plotz). Java, Sumatra. Subspecies kerala resembles sindu but is larger.

23. *Koruthaialos sindu* (Fldr.). Malaya, Assam. Similar: butleri (Nicer.), Assam to Malaya, no markings UP; rubecala (Plotz), UPF band does not reach front edge.

24. *Lobocla bifasciatus* (Br. & Gr.). Himalayas to Indo-China. Similar: simplex (Leech), W. China, UN markings very obscure; proxima (Leech), W. China, Tibet, larger than simplex, more markings UN.

25. *Lobocla liliana* (Atk.). W. Himalayas to Burma.

26. *Lotongus avesta* (Hew.). Malaya, Sumatra, Borneo.

27. *Lotongus calathus* (Hew.). Burma to Malaya.

28. *Lotongus onara* (Btlr.). Java.

29. *Lotongus taprobanus* (Plotz). Celebes. Subspecies of calathus.

30. *Matapa aria* (Moore). India to Ceylon, Malaya to Philippines.

31. *Matapa celsina* (Fldr.). Philippines. Similar: cresta (Evans), Sikkim, smaller yellow end to UPH.

32. *Matapa druna* (Moore). Assam to Malaya. Similar: sasivarna (Moore) Assam, tip of body orange-yellow.

33. *Mesodina aeluropis* (Mayrick). Australia.

34. *Mesodina halyzia* (Hew.). Australia.

35. *Mooreana princeps* (Smpr.). Philippines. Similar: boisduvali (Mab.), Celebes.

36. *Mooreana trichoneara* (Fldr.). India, Malaya to Philippines. Several subspecies.

37. *Motasingha atralba* (Tepp.). Australia.

38. *Motasingha dirphia* (Hew.). Australia.

39. *Neohesperilla xiphiphora* (Low.). Australia.

40. *Netrocoryne thaddeus* (Hew.). Papua. Male and female no white UP.

41. *Netrocoryne repanda* (Fldr.). Australia.

42. *Notocrypta curvifascia* (Fldr.). India to China to Malaya. Similar: paralysos (Wood-Mas. and Nicer.)

43. *Notocrypta clavata* (Stgr.). Malaya, Borneo. Similar: paralysos (Wood-Mas.), UPF white band bent.

44. *Notocrypta feisthamelii* (Bsd.). India to China to Malaysia. Many similar species.

45. *Notocrypta pria* (Druce). Malaya. Similar: Quedara monteithi (Wood-Mason & Nicer.), Malaya, UPF band not smooth edged.

46. *Notocrypta quadrata* (Elw. & Edw.). Malaya.

47. *Notocrypta renardi* (Oberth.). New Guinea.

48. *Notocrypta waigensis* (Plotz). New Guinea, Australia.

49. *Ochus subvittatus* (Fldr.). Khasi Hills, Naga Hills.

50. *Ocybadistes walkeri* (Heron). Australia, Tasmania. Several similar species in Australia.

51. *Odina hieroglyphica* (Btlr.). Assam, Burma, Malaya to Philippines and Celebes.

52. *Odina sulina* (Evans). Celebes.

53. *Odontoptilum angulata* (Fldr.). India to China, Malaya, Java. Similar: helias

(Fldr.), Philippines and Celebes, violet sheen UP.

PLATE 188: Hesperiidae

1. *Odontoptilum pygela* (Hew.). Sumatra, Malaya to Java.

2. *Oerane microthyrsus* (Mab.). Malaya to Philippines.

3. *Oreisplanus perornatus* (Ky.). Australia. UP resembles munionga but larger markings. Similar: munionga (Oll.).

4. *Oreisplanus munionga* (Oll.). Australia. Similar: perornatus (Ky.).

5. *Parnara amalis* (Semper). Queensland.

6. *Parnara guttatus* (Brem.). China, Japan, Malaya, Ceylon, India, Burma. UN as UP, yellowish tinge.

7. *Pasma tasmanicus* (Misk.). Australia, Tasmania.

8. *Pirdana hyela* (Hew.). Burma, Malaya to Celebes. UP resembles distanti. Similar: albicornis (Elw. & Edw.), Borneo, veins not lined, UP more blue.

9. *Pelopidas assamensis* (Wood-Mas. & Nicer.). India to Malaya.

10. *Pelopidas conjuncta* (H.Sch.). India, Ceylon, Malaya to Philippines.

11. *Pelopidas mathias* (F.). S. and C. Asia, Ceylon.

12. *Pelopidas sinensis* (Mab.). Ceylon, S. India, Assam to W. China.

13. *Pirdana distanti* (Stgr.). Sumatra, Malaya, Borneo.

14. *Pintara pinwilli* (Btlr.). Burma to China, Malaya.

15. *Pithauria marsena* (Hew.). Malaysia.

16. *Pithauria stramineipennis* (Wood-Mas. & Nicer.). Sikkim to China, Malaysia.

17. *Plastingia aurantiaca* (Elw. & Edw.). Java, Malaya. Similar: viburnia (Semper), Philippines, UP darker.

18. *Plastingia callineura* (Fldr.). Malaya, Java. Several similar species.

19. *Plastingia corissa* (Hew.). Borneo.

20. *Plastingia pugnans* (Nicer.). Sumatra, Malaya.

21. *Plastingia fuscicornis* (Elw.). Malaya, India, Burma.

22. *Plastingia helena* (Btlr.). Sumatra, Malaya, Borneo. Similar: flavescens (Fldr.), Celebes, less distinct markings UN.

23. *Plastingia latoia* (Hew.). Malaya, Burma.

24. *Plastingia niasana* (Fruh.). Burma to Malaysia.

25. *Plastingia naga* (Nicer.). Malaya, Java, Assam, Burma.

26. *Polytremis eltola* (Hew.). India to Malaya. Similar: discreta (Elw. & Edw.), UN markings greenish, less distinct.

27. *Potanthus dara* (Koll.). Himalayas, India, Indo-China, Malaysia.

28. *Potanthus hetaerus* (Mab.). Burma to Malaya, Philippines, Celebes. Subspecies of serina (Plotz), Java.

29. *Potanthus omaha* (Edw.). Malaysia.

30. *Potanthus trachala* (Mab.). India, Malaysia to China.

31. *Prusiana prusias* (Fldr.). Philippines.

32. *Prusiana kuhni* (Plotz). Celebes.

33. *Psolos fuscula* (Snell.). Celebes. Subspecies of fuligo (Mab.), which is usually paler.

34. *Pudicitia pholus* (Nicer.). Assam.

35. *Sabera caesina* (Hew.). New Guinea, Australia.

36. *Sabera fuliginosa* (Misk.). Australia.

37. *Satarupa gopala* (Moore). India, Malaya. Similar: Daimio diversa (Leech), C. China; Daimio sinica (Fldr.), W. and C. China.

38. *Sarangesa dasahara* (Moore). India, Ceylon to Malaya. UNH sometimes has whitening.

39. *Scobura isota* (Swh.). Sikkim to Malaya. Several very similar species, including: coniata (Hering), China, much larger, UN veins lined; phiditia (Hew.), Burma, Assam.

40. *Seseria affinis* (Druce). Sumatra, Malaya.

41. *Signeta flammeata* (Btlr.). Australia.

42. *Spialia galba* (F.). India, Burma.

43. *Suada albinus* (Semp.). Philippines. Similar: cataleneos (Stgr.).

44. *Suada swerga* (Nicer.). Ceylon, Malaya, Java.

45. *Suastus everyx* (Mab.). Malaya, Java to Bali.

46. *Suastus gremius* (F.). India, China, Ceylon.

47. *Suastus migreus* (Semp.). Philippines.

48. *Suastus minuta* (Moore). Ceylon, Malaya.

49. *Suniana sunias* (Waterh.). Australia. Several similar species in Australia.

50. *Suniana tanus* (Plotz). New Guinea. Subspecies of sunias. Similar: marnas (Fldr.), Moluccas, New Guinea.

51. *Tagiades gana* (Moore). India to Malaya and Philippines.

52. *Tagiades japetus* (Cr.). Siam, Malaya to Indo-China and Australia.

53. *Tagiades lavata* (Btlr.). Malaya, Borneo.

54. *Tagiades menaka* (Moore). Malaya, Sikkim, Borneo. Similar: cohaerens (Mab.), Malaysia, smaller, no dots UPF; waterstradti (Elw.), Borneo, one large black dot at apex of UPH white area; litigiosa (Mschlr.), large black dots at base of UPH white area.

55. *Tagiades toba* (Nicer.). Assam to Malaya.

PLATE 189: Hesperiidae

1. *Tagiades sivoa* (Swh.). New Guinea. Subspecies of nestius (Fldr.).

2. *Tapena thwaitesi* (Moore). Sumatra, Malaya, Borneo, Indo-China. UP colour variable.

3. *Taractrocera archias* (Fldr.). Malaya to Philippines.

4. *Taractrocera ardonia* (see 5).

5. *Taractrocera ardonia* (Hew.). Malaya, Borneo, Celebes.

6. *Taractrocera danna* (Moore). N.E. India.

7. *Taractrocera maevius* (F.). India, Burma, Ceylon.

8. *Taractrocera papyria* (Bsd.). Australia, Tasmania. Several very similar species in Australia.

9. *Telicota augias* (L.). S. Burma and China, Malaya to Australia. Similar: linna (Evans), UPF more rounded, markings yellow.

10. *Telicota kezia* (Evans). New Britain. Few similar species.

11. *Telicota linna* (Evans). S. Burma, Indo-China, Malaysia. Similar: ancilla (H.Sch.), Queensland; ohara (Evans), Himalayas to Formosa, New Guinea, darker, UPF orange band shorter.

12. *Thoressa decorata* (Moore). Ceylon. Similar: masoni (Moore), Burma, UPH yellow patch clearly defined.

13. *Thoressa honorei* (Nicer.). S. India.

14. *Toxidia doubledayi* (Fldr.). Australia. Lfp: grasses. Several similar species.

15. *Toxidia parvulus* (Plotz). Australia.

16. *Toxidia peron* (Latreille). N.S. Wales.

17. *Toxidia thyrrus* (Mab.). Australia. Similar: vietmanni (Semper), Sydney, much darker.

18. *Trapezites eliena* (Hew.). Australia. Lfp: Lomandra.

19. *Trapezites iacchus* (F.). Australia.

20. *Trapezites phigalia* (Hew.). S. Australia.

21. *Trapezites maheta* (Hew.). Australia.

22. *Trapezites lutea* (Tepp.). Australia. Similar: petalia (Hew.), Australia, all markings larger.

23. *Trapezites symmomus* (Hub.). Australia.

24. *Udaspes folus* (Cr.). Himalayas, India, Indo-China, Malaysia.

25. *Unkana ambasa* (Moore). Sumatra, Malaya to Java to Philippines.

26. *Unkana mytheca* (Hew.). Malaya.

27. *Zela zenon* (Nicer.). Borneo.

28. *Zela zeus* (Nicer.). Assam to Malaya to Philippines.

29. *Zographetus ogygia* (Hew.). Malaya, Borneo.

30. *Zographetus satwa* (Nicer.). Sikkim, Malaya, Indo-China.

31. *Zographetus sewa* (Plotz). Celebes.

Asia

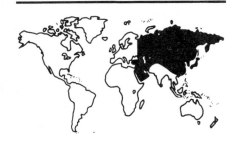

PLATE 190: Papilionidae

1. *Bhutanitis lidderdalei* (Atkinson). Bhutan, Assam to W. China. Lfp: Aristolochiae. Similar: thaidina (Blanchard), W. China.

2. *Chilasa clytia* (L.). India, China, Siam, Burma, Malaya. Form dissimilis. Lfp: Aurantiaceae.

3. *Chilasa clytia* (L.). China, Siam. Form clytia.

4. *Dabasa hercules* (Blanch.). W. China. Similar: gyas (Ww.), Assam to W. China.

5. *Graphium clymenus* (Leech). C. and W. China. Similar: cloanthus (Westw.), India, smaller, lighter colouring.

6. *Graphium eurous* (Leech). Sikkim to C. China. Lfp: Anonaceae. Similar: alebion (Gray), E. China; mandarinus (Oberth), W. China.

7. *Graphium glycerion* (Gray). Nepal, Burma to W. China. Similar: alebion (Gray), E. China; mandarinus (Oberth), W. China; cashmirensis (Rothsch.), N. India to Tibet.

8. *Graphium sarpedon* (L.). Indo-Malayan region, China, Japan, N. Australia. Lfp: Aurantiaceae.

9. *Hypermnestra helios* (Nick.). Persia, Turkestan, Lfp: Zygophyllum.

10. *Leuhdorfia puziloi* (Ersch.). C. China to Japan. Lfp: Asarum. A few subspecies. Similar: japonica (Leech), larger, darker.

11. *Papilio bianor* (Cram.). E. Siberia to S. China. Lfp: Aurantiaceae, Phellodendron. Very variable seasonally and geographically.

12. *Papilio demoleus* (L.). Persia to S. China, all Indo-Malayan region, N. Australia. Lfp: Citrus, especially Orange.

13. *Papilio elwesi* (Leech). Interior of China, Formosa. Female has no white UPH.

14. *Papilio polytes* (L.). Entire Indo-Malayan region, China. Lfp: Aurantiaceae.

15. *Papilio helenus* (L.). India, Burma, Malaya, S. China to Hong Kong. Lfp: Aurantiaceae. Variable, with many subspecies.

16. *Papilio janaka* (Moore). Himalayas to W. China. Similar: bootes (Westw.), male only two white spots UPH.

17. *Papilio maacki* (Men.). Korea and Amurland.

18. *Papilio macilentus* (Jans.). China, Japan. Lfp: Citrus. Similar: demetrius (Cramer), China, Japan, Formosa, N. India.

19. *Papilio paris* (L.). N.W. India to China and Malaya. Lfp: Aurantiaceae. Similar: arcturus (Ww.), China, N. India.

PLATE 191: Papilionidae

1. *Papilio polyctor* (Bsd.). W. China, Himalayas to Afghanistan. Similar: ganesa (Dbl.), N. India.

2. *Papilio polytes* (L.). Form stichius (see 190/14).

3. *Papilio protenor* (Cram.). N. India to Formosa, W. China to Hong Kong. Lfp: Xanthoxylum.

4. *Papilio rhetenor* (Westw.). North India and China.

5. *Papilio rhetenor* (see 4).

6. *Papilio xuthus* (L.). E. China, Formosa, Korea, Japan. Lfp: Sallows. Similar: xuthulus (Brem.).

7. *Parides alcinous* (Klug.). E. China, Japan. Female light grey.

8. *Parides dasarada* (Moore). Himalayas. Similar: nevilli (W. Mason), S.W. China.

9. *Parides dasarada* (see 8).

10. *Parides plutonius* (Oberth.). E. Himalayas, China, Tibet. Lfp: Cocculus. Similar: mencius (Fldr.); confusus (Rothsch.).

11. *Parnassius actius* (Eversm.). Turkestan, E. Pamir. Few subspecies.

12. *Parnassius bremeri* (Fldr.). E. Russia, Lower Amurland. Lfp: Sedum. Similar: felderi (Brem.), Amurland. Few subspecies.

13. *Parnassius charltonius* (Gray). N.W. Himalayas, Pamirs.

14. *Parnassius clarius* (Eversm.). Altai Mountains. Similar: clodius (Men.), N. America.

15. *Parnassius delphius* (Eversm.). Fergana, Samarkand, Turkestan, Himalayas, Kashmir, Tibet, W. China. Many subspecies.

16. *Parnassius discobolus* (Alph.). Tianshon Mountains, Afghanistan, Pamirs. Lfp: Astragalus. Several subspecies. Similar: nomion (Fisch.).

17. *Parnassius epaphus* (Oberth.). N.W. Himalayas, Pamirs, W. China. Many subspecies. Similar: sikkimensis (Elwes).

18. *Parnassius eversmanni* (Men.). Altai Mountains, E. Russia to Alaska.

19. *Parnassius eversmanni* (see 18).

20. *Parnassius glacialis* (Btlr.). E. Asia, Japan. Similar: stubbendorfi (Men.).

21. *Parnassius hardwickii* (Gray). Himalayas. Few subspecies.

22. *Parnassius honrathi* (Stgr.). Samarkand, Darvaz Mountains, Pamirs. Similar: apollonius (Eversm.), Lfp: Scabiosa.

23. *Parnassius imperator* (Oberth.). W. China, Amdo, Naushan, Sikkim, Tibet. A few subspecies.

24. *Parnassius jacquemonti* (Bsd.). N.W. Himalayas, Karakorum, Tibet. Several subspecies.

25. *Parnassius nordmanni* (Men.). E. Armenia and Caucasus.

26. *Parnassius orleans* (Oberth.). W. China. Subspecies groumi (Cramer), Amdo.

PLATE 192 : Papilionidae

1. *Parnassius szechenyi* (Friv.). N.E. Tibet, W. China.

2. *Parnassius tenedius* (Ev.). E. Turkestan, S. Siberia. Similar: acco (Gray), Karakorum, Sikkim; simo (Gray), Ladak, S. Tibet, a few subspecies.

3. *Sericinus telamon* (see 4).

4. *Sericinus telamon* (Don.). Vladivostok to Shanghai. Lfp: Aristolochia. Several subspecies. Similar: montela (Gray), China.

5. *Troides aeacus* (Fldr.). Himalayas, Burma, Malaya to Central China. Lfp: Aristolochia.

6. *Troides aeacus* (see 5).

Amathusidae

7. *Aemona oberthueri* (Stich.). W. China. Female resembles lena.

8. *Enispe lunatus* (Leech). W. China, E. Tibet.

9. *Faunis aerope* (Leech). China.

10. *Faunis aerope* (see 9).

11. *Faunis eumeus* (Drury). China, Burma, Assam.

12. *Stichopthalma howqua* (Westw.). N. and C. China, Formosa. UN similar: neumogeni (Leech), W. China, smaller.

13. *Stichopthalma neumogeni* (Leech). W. China.

PLATE 193 : Nymphalidae

1. *Abrota pratti* (Leech). W. China.

2. *Abrota pratti* (see 1).

3. *Aldania raddei* (Brem.). Amurland. Similar: imitans (Oberth.), Yunnan, blue grey, with orange edge to UPH.

4. *Apatura bieti* (Oberth.). Tibet, W. and C. China. Similar: serarum (Oberth.), UP bands whitish.

5. *Apatura fasciola* (Leech). W. and C. China.

6. *Apatura ulupi* (Doh.). W. China. Similar: subcoerulea, male (Leech).

7. *Apatura laverna* (Leech). W. China.

8. *Apatura leechii* (Moore). W. and C. China. Similar: chevana (Moore), India, UP paler brown, no blue gloss.

9. *Apatura subcoerulea* (Leech). W. China. Similar: lacta (Oberth.).

10. *Apatura schrenki* (Men.). Amurland to Korea.

11. *Argyronome ruslana* (Motsch.). E. China, Korea, Amurland.

12. *Araschnia burejana* (Brem.). C. and W. China, Korea, Japan. Summer brood = fallax (Jans.). Similar: doris (Leech), C. and W. China, wings rounder.

13. *Araschnia oreas* (Leech). E. Tibet, W. China. Similar: davidis (Pouj.), smaller, paler.

14. *Apatura nycteis* (Men.). Amurland to Korea. Lfp: Elm.

15. *Argynnis anadyomene* (Fldr.). Tibet, Amurland, China, Korea and Japan.

16. *Apatura subalba* (Pouj.). W. and C. China.

PLATE 194 : Nymphalidae

1. *Araschnia prorsoides* (Blanch.). N.E. India to W. China.

2. *Calinaga buddha* (Moore). Himalayas, Sikkim to N. Burma. Similar: davidis (Oberth.), W. China, E. Tibet.

3. *Cethosia biblis* (Druce). Nepal through Assam to Burma and Malaya, W. and C. China. Lfp: Passiflora. Female ground colour grey-blue.

4. *Charaxes polyxena* (see 5).

5. *Charaxes polyxena* (Cr.). China, Hong Kong. Subspecies sinensis (Rothsch.), no white band, India to China, Malaya.

6. *Childrena childreni* (Gray). Himalayas, Chitral to Assam, N. Burma, C. and W. China.

7. *Childrena childreni* (see 6).

8. *Childrena zenobia* (Leech). N. and W. China, Tibet. Female olive-green UP.

9. *Calinaga lhatso* (Oberth.). E. Tibet. Similar: Fabriciana funebris (Oberth.), Yunnan, very dark.

10. *Clossiana angarensis* (Ersch.). Amurland. Similar: perryi (Btlr.).

11. *Clossiana gong* (Oberth.). W. China, Tibet. Terrain: montane.

12. *Clossiana hegemone* (Stgr.). Turkestan.

13. *Clossiana jerdoni* (Lang.). Kashmir, Chitral.

14. *Clossiana oscarus* (Ev.). Altai to Amur.

15. *Clossiana selenis* (Ev.). Ural Mountains, S. Siberia to Amurland. Similar: hegemone (Stgr.), Pamirs, Turkestan, lighter colour, smaller spots.

16. *Fabriciana nerippe* (Fldr.). E. Tibet to Korea and Japan. Few subspecies, some large.

17. *Cyrestis thyodamas* (Bsd.). Himalayas through S. China, S. Japan, Liu-Kiu Islands. Lfp: Ficus. Several subspecies. Similar: andamanensis (Stgr.), UP markings tinged with orange.

18. *Damora sagana* (see 19).

19. *Damora sagana* (Dbl. & Hew.). Amurland, China, Korea. Japan species is liane (Fruhst.).

20. *Euphydryas sareptana* (Stgr.). South Russia, Black Sea. Similar: hibernica (Birch), Ireland.

21. *Issoria gemmata* (Btlr.). Sikkim, Tibet. Similar: Clossiana eugenia (Ev.), S. Siberia, W. China.

PLATE 195 : Nymphalidae

1. *Euthalia confucius* (Westw.). W. and C. China.

2. *Euthalia kardama* (Moore). W. and C. China.

3. *Hestina subviridis* (Leech). W. Himalayas to W. China, Japan. Similar: persimilis (Westw.), E. Himalayas.

4. *Melitaea acraeina* (Stgr.). U.S.S.R. Ferghana.

5. *Euthalia sahadeva* (Moore). Sikkim, Assam, N. Burma. Female larger, lighter green, whitish band UPF. Similar: pyrrha (Leech), W. China; khama (Alph.), W. China.

6. *Melitaea phoebe* (Schiff.). Europe and N. Africa through C. Asia to N. China. Lfp: Centaurea. Many subspecies. Similar: aetherie (Hbn.), Spain, Sicily, N. Africa. Very variable.

7. *Melitaea sindura* (Moore). Kashmir, Chitral, Tibet.

8. *Euthalia teutoides* (Moore). Andaman Islands. Male resembles male teuta but UPH band is confluent.

9. *Hestina mena* (Moore). China to Upper Burma.

10. *Kallima inachus* (Bsd.). Himalayas to C. China. Lfp: Acanthus.

11. *Hestina assimilis* (L.). E. Tibet, China to Hong Kong, Korea.

12. *Limenitis albomaculata* (Leech). E. Tibet, W. China. UP has orange markings as Neptis species.

13. *Limenitis cottini* (Oberth.). W. China.

14. *Limenitis albomaculata* (see 12).

15. *Limenitis ciocolatina* (Pouj.). W. China.

16. *Limenitis elwesi* (Oberth.). Tibet.

17. *Limenitis homeyeri* (Taucre). Amurland, S.E. and W. China. UP black and white as Neptis species. Similar: doerriesi (Stgr.), Amurland; amphyssa (Men.), Amurland, C. China, Korea.

18. *Limenitis mimica* (Pouj.). W. and C. China.

19. *Limenitis sinensium* (Oberth.). N. and W. China.

20. *Lelex limenitoides* (Oberth.). C. and W. China.

PLATE 196 : Nymphalidae

1. *Limenitis zayla* (Dbl.). Assam, Sikkim.

2. *Melitaea agar* (Oberth.). W. China.

3. *Melitaea bellona* (Leech). W. China.

4. *Melitaea lutko* (Evans). Altai Mountains, Tibet. Similar: romanovi (Gr.Grsch.).

5. *Melitaea arcesia* (Brem.). C. Asia, Altai Mountains, Amurland.

6. *Melitaea pallas* (Stgr.). Pamirs, C. Asia.

7. *Melitaea saxatilis* (Christ.). Persia. Several subspecies. Similar: persea (Koll.), Afghanistan.

8. *Melitaea sibina* (Alph.). Pamirs, C. Asia.

9. *Melitaea yuenty* (Oberth.). W. China.

10. *Mesoacidalia claudia* (Fawcett). Himalayas.

11. *Neptis arachne* (Leech). S. and W. China. Few subspecies.

12. *Neptis dejeani* (Oberth.). Mongolia, W. China, Japan.

13. *Neptis aspasia* (Leech). W. and C. China. UP resembles arachne.

14. *Neptis breti* (Oberth.). W. China.

15. *Neptis cydippe* (Leech). W. and C. China. UP resembles radha.

16. *Neptis armandia* (Oberth.). C. and W. China. Similar: antilope (Leech), C., W. and S. China.

17. *Neptis narayana* (Moore). Assam. Subspecies sylvia (Oberth.), W. China, markings yellow.

18. *Neptis pryeri* (Btlr.). Amurland, Shanghai, Korea, Japan.

19. *Neptis radha* (Moore). Sikkim. Subspecies sinensis (Oberth.), W. China, orange markings less vivid.

20. *Neptis speyeri* (Stgr.). Amurland. Similar: philyra (Men.), Japan; philyroides (Stgr.), Amurland, Korea.

21. *Neptis themis* (Leech). W. China. Similar: nycteus (Nicer.), Sikkim, white spots; yunnana (Oberth.), W. China. Few subspecies.

22. *Neptis thisbe* (Men.). Amurland to Korea. Several subspecies.

23. *Neptis thisbe* (see 22).

24. *Neptis yerburyi* (Btlr.). Himalayas to W. China. Several subspecies.

25. *Pantoporia disjuncta* (Leech). W. and C. China. Similar: recurva (Leech), W. China; sulpitia (Cr.).

26. *Pantoporia fortuna* (Leech). C. China. Similar: jinoides (Moore), W. and C. China.

27. *Pantoporia punctata* (Leech)(see 197/1)

PLATE 197: Nymphalidae

1. *Pantaporia punctata* (Leech). W. and C. China.

2. *Pantaporia sulpitia* (Cr.). S.E. China, Hong Kong. Similar: disjuncta (Leech), W. and C. China; recurva (Leech), W. China.

3. *Polygonia c-aureum* (L.). China, Japan. Lfp: Cannabis, Humulus.

4. *Polygonia gigantea* (Leech). W. and C. China.

5. *Penthema adelma* (Fldr.). China.

6. *Polygonia l-album* (Esp.). S. Russia, Siberia to Amurland, Chitral, Kashmir, Labrador, Alaska. Lfp: Betula, Ulmus, Salix, Ribes. Subspecies: samurai (Fruhst.),Japan. Similar: j-album (Bsd.), northern part of N. America.

7. *Penthema lisarda* (Dbl.). E. Himalayas to W. China.

8. *Penthema formosanum* (Rothsch.). Formosa.

9. *Polyura dolon* (Westw.). Himalayas.

10. *Polyura narcaea* (Hew.). China. Wet season form like posidonius. Similar: lissanei (Tytler), Naga Hills, UPH lacks broad black border.

11. *Polyura posidonius* (Leech). W. China.

12. *Precis lemonias* (L.). Himalayas to China to Malaya. A favourite food of lizards.

13. *Pseudergolis wedah* (Koll.). Himalayas to C. China. Lfp: Debregeasia.

14. *Sephisa dichroa* (Koll.). W. Himalayas through Siam, China to Korea. Lfp: Quercus. Several subspecies.

15. *Sasakia charonda* (Hew.). Japan. Subspecies: coreana (Leech), W. and C. China, Korea.

16. *Sasakia funebris* (Leech), W. China. Very rare.

17. *Thaleropis ionia* (Eversm.). Asia Minor to Armenia. Lfp: Celtis.

18. *Timelaea albescens* (Oberth.). W. China.

PLATE 198: Nymphalidae

1. *Timelaea maculata* (Brem. and Gray). China. Similar: nana (Leech), W. China, smaller.

2. *Sephisa chandra* (Moore). Sikkim to N. Siam. Female is variable, but always has orange spot UPF; male UP resembles dichroa but with white spots UPF.

3. *Limenitis sydyi* (Led.). C. and W. China. Subspecies: latifasciata (Men.). Amurland, Korea, Japan.

4. *Limenitis trivena* (Moore). Kashmir, Pamirs, Turkestan. Lfp: Quercus. Few subspecies, width of white band varies considerably.

5. *Mesoacidalia alexandra* (Men.). Armenia and Persia. UP as aglaia.

6. *Helcyra superba* (Leech). W. China. Similar: hemiria (Hew.), India, smaller, more black dots UP.

Danaidae

7. *Danaus chrysippus* (L.). Canary Islands, N. Africa, Egypt, Syria, Asia Minor, Arabia, Iran, Tibet, W. and C. China, Japan, S. Asia, N. Australia, India, Malaysia. Lfp: Asclepiadeas. Few subspecies with whitened hindwing.

Pieridae

8. *Anthocharis bambusarum* (Oberth.). China.

9. *Anthocharis bieti* (Oberth.). W. China.

10. *Anthocharis scolymus* (Btlr.). W. and C. China, Japan, Lfp: cress.

11. *Aporia bieti* (Oberth.). C., W. and S. China.

12. *Baltia butleri* (Oberth.). W. China.

13. *Aporia davidis* (Oberth.). W. and C. China. Terrain: montane.

14. *Aporia goutellei* (Moore). Sikkim, Tibet. Similar: sikkima (Fruhst.) Ladak, smaller.

15. *Aporia hippia* (Brem.). S.E. Siberia, Mongolia, N. and W. China. Few subspecies.

PLATE 199: Pieridae

1. *Aporia largeteaui* (Oberth.). Ichang to Tibet. Similar: phryxe (Bsd.), N.W. India, darker; caphusa (Moore). W. Himalayas, Tibet, very dark; oberthuri (Leech), C. and W. China.

2. *Colias christophi* (Gr.-Gr.), Ferghana.

3. *Colias cocandica* (Ersch.), Mongolia.

4. *Aporia lotis* (Leech), W. China.

5. *Aporia nabellica* (Bsd.), Tibet, Himalayas. Similar: llamo (Oberth). W. China, UP more streaky.

6. *Catopsilia florella* (F.), Persia to China, India, Ceylon.

7. *Colias sagartia* (Led.). Iran.

8. *Colias regia* (Gr.-Gr.). Turkestan.

9. *Colias aurora* (Esp.). Altai Mountains, S.E. Siberia to Amurland. A few subspecies. Female form chloe has grey ground colour UP.

10. *Colias sifanica* (Gr.-Gr.). Amdo.

11. *Pieris deota* (Nicev.). Pamirs, Ladak.

12. *Baltia shawii* (Bates). Himalayas. Similar: butleri (Moore), Kashmir, Mongolia, S.W. China. (See Indo-Australasia also).

13. *Colias staudingeri* (Alph.). Ferghana. Terrain: montane.

14. *Colias stoliczkana* (Moore). Ladak, S. Tibet.

15. *Colias wiskotti* (Stgr.). Pamirs, Gergana. Very variable, colour to bright red. Several subspecies.

16. *Colotis calais* (Cr.). S. Iran, Arabia, E. Africa, India and Ceylon. Lfp: Salvadoraceae.

17. *Colotis chrysonome* (Klug.). S. Palestine, E. Africa.

18. *Colotis fausta* (Olivier) 'The Salmon Arab'. Syria through Iran to India and Ceylon.

19. *Colotis liagore* (Klug.). Yemen, Arabia.

20. *Colotis phisadia* (Godt.). Arabia, Palestine to N.E. Africa. Lfp: Salvadora. Female UP ground colour yellow. Similar: rothschildi (E. Sharpe), E. Africa; protractus (Btlr.), W. India.

21. *Microzegris pyrothoe* (Ev.). S.E. Russia, C. Asia.

22. *Mesapia peloria* (Hew.). N.E. Tibet.

23. *Colotis pleione* (Klug.). Arabia, Aden, Ethiopia, Somaliland. Lfp: Capparis. Female UP white.

24. *Delias belladonna* (F.). N. India to W. China, Malaya. Similar: sanaea (Moore), India and Tibet; subnubila (Leech), W. and C. China; patrua (Leech), W. and C. China.

25. *Gonepteryx amintha* (Blanch.). China, Formosa.

26. *Leptidia gigantea* (Leech). C. and W. China.

27. *Pieris dubernardi* (Oberth.). W. China. Similar: chumbiensis (Nicev.).

PLATE 200 : Satyridae

1. *Acropolis thalia* (Leech). W. China.

2. *Coenonympha saadi* (Koll.). Iran, Iraq.

3. *Aphantopus arvensis* (Oberth.). W. China.

4. *Callarge sagitta* (Leech). Yang-tse-kiang.

5. *Coenonympha amaryllis* (Cr.). C. and E. Asia, N. China and Korea. Similar: tyderes (Leech), Tibet.

6. *Coenonympha semenori* (Alph.). Tibet and W. China.

7. *Coenonympha sunbecca* (Ev.). Ferghana, Turkestan.

8. *Erebia alcmena* (Gr.-Gr.). W. China to Japan. Similar: vidleri (Edw.), British Columbia.

9. *Coenonympha nolckeni* (Ersch.). Ferghana.

10. *Coenonympha mongolica* (Alph.). Mongolia.

11. *Erebia edda* (Men.). E. Siberia. Similar: cyclopius (Ev.), Amurland, UP grey brown, not coffee brown as edda; tristis (Brem.), Amurland, UPF row of pale yellow spots; rurigena (Oberth.), Mongolia, very large ocellus UNF.

12. *Erebia herse* (Gr.-Gr.). Tibet, W. China.

13. *Erebia hyagriva* (Moore). Kashmir to Sikkim.

14. *Erebia kalmuka* (Alph.). W. China. UN silver washed.

15. *Erebia meta* (Stgr.). Turkestan, Samar-kand, Alexander Mountains. Several sub-species.

16. *Erebia maurisius* (Esp.). Altai Mountains. Similar: pawlowskyi (Men.), E. Mongolia, UN bright brown; haberhaueri (Stgr.), Altai Mountains, very small spots UPH.

17. *Loxerebia phyllis* (Leech). W. China, Mongolia. Similar: hades (Stgr.), Altai Mountains, two small white spots tip UPF; albipuncta (Leech), UPH has a tiny eye-spot.

18. *Erebia parmenio* (Boeb.). Mongolia, Manchuria to Amurland. Few subspecies.

19. *Erebia maracandica* (Ersch.). Altai Mountains, Pamirs, Samarkand, Turkestan.

20. *Erebia turanica* (Ersch.). Tian-shan.

21. *Erebia radians* (Stgr.). Pamirs, Turkestan. Similar: ocnus (Eversman), Pamirs, UNH faintly marked stripe, UPF faint eye-spots.

PLATE 201 : Satyridae

1. *Eumenis autonoe* (Esp.). S. Russia, Tibet, N.W. China. Similar: hippolyte (Esp.), Spain.

2. *Eumenis persephone* (Hbn.). Armenia, Asia Minor, Afghanistan, Iran.

3. *Eumenis telephassa* (Hbn.). Syria, Asia Minor, Armenia through Iran to Baluchistan. Similar: mnszechii (H-Sch.), UP orange band narrower and more distinct; pelopea (Klug.), UP orange band broken; beroe (Frr.), Asia Minor.

4. *Hyponephele capella* (Christ.). Pamirs, Turkestan, Iran.

5. *Hyponephele davendra* (see 6).

6. *Hyponephele davendra* (Moore). Hima-layas, Baluchistan. Similar: comara (Led.), Turkestan, Iran.

7. *Lethe albolineata* (Pouj.). Yang-tse-kiang basin. Similar: andersoni (Atkins), Upper Burma, S. and C. China; argentata (Leech), W. China, smaller, more silver bands UN, orange marginal lines UN.

8. *Lethe baucis* (see 9).

9. *Lethe baucis* (Leech). W. and C. China.

10. *Lethe christophi* (Leech). C. and W. China.

11. *Lethe diana* (Btlr.). W. China to Korea, Japan. Similar: sicelis (Hew.), UN paler; hecate (Leech), UN very pale, ocelli stand out.

12. *Lethe insularis* (Fruhst.). China, Formosa.

13. *Lethe dura* (Marsh). Himalayas to China and Formosa.

14. *Lethe helle* (Leech). W. China. Similar: armanderia (Oberth.), UN ocelli more distinct.

15. *Lethe labyrinthea* (Leech). W. and C. China.

PLATE 202 : Satyridae

1. *Lethe lanaris* (Btlr.). China. Similar: helena (Leech), China, paler.

2. *Lethe isana* (Koll.). Himalayas to W. China, Formosa.

3. *Lethe manzorum* (Pouj.). W. and C. China.

4. *Lethe marginalis* (Motsch.). W. China, Korea, Japan.

5. *Lethe mataja* (Fruhst.). Formosa.

6. *Lethe nigrifascia* (Leech). China.

7. *Lethe oculatissima* (Pouj.). China.

8. *Loxerebia phyllis* (Leech). W. China, Mongolia. Similar: hades (Stgr.), Altai Mountains, two small white spots tip UPF; albipuncta (Leech), W. and C. China, UPH has a tiny eye-spot.

9. *Lethe proxima* (Leech). W. China. Similar: trimacula (Leech), C. China, UN paler, larger lunules UP.

10. *Lethe satyrina* (Btlr.). Tibet to Shanghai. Similar: butleri (Leech), UN ochreish, no line down centre of UNH.

11. *Lethe titania* (Leech). W. China.

12. *Loxerebia phyllis* (see 8).

13. *Mandarinia regalis* (Leech). W. and C. China, Burma. Female has narrower band UPF.

14. *Loxerebia sylvicola* (Oberth). Se-chuen.

15. *Loxerebia polyphemus* (Oberth.). W. China.

PLATE 203 : Satyridae

1. *Maniola cadusia* (Led.). Iran, Turkestan. UP resembles kirghisa. Similar: hilaris (Stgr.), Turkestan, UP brighter, UPF eye-spot larger.

2. *Maniola kirghisa* (Alph.). Turkestan, Pamirs, Alexander Mountains. Several sub-species.

3. *Maniola narica* (Hbn.). S. Russia, Turkestan.

4. *Mycalesis francisca* (Cr.). Sikkim, China, Korea, Japan. Subspecies: sanatana (Moore), W. to Kashmir, UNH line of ocelli complete.

5. *Maniola pulchra* (Fldr.). Turkestan, Hindu Kush, Kashmir. Similar: pulchella (Fldr.), UPF very light colour.

6. *Maniola wagneri* (H.-Sch.). Armenia Persia, Iraq. Similar: mandane (Koll.), Mesopotamia, darker UP.

7. *Melanargia halimede* (Men.). Mongolia, N. China. Similar: epimede (Stgr.), UNH ocelli very large; montana (Leech), Yang-tse-kiang, large, black markings reduced.

8. *Melanargia titea* (Klug.). Syria, Palestine, Armenia, Iran. Several subspecies.

9. *Maniola naubidensis* (Ersch.). Pamirs, Turkestan.

10. *Mycalesis gotama* (Moore). China,

Korea, Japan.

11. *Minois dryas* (Scop.). N. Spain through C. Europe and Asia to Japan. Several subspecies.

12. *Neope armandii* (Oberth.). W. China, Assam, Burma.

13. *Neope goschkeritschii* (Men.). Japan.

14. *Oeneis dubia* (Elw.). Altai Mountains. Similar: mulla (Stgr.), UP paler marginal bands, larger ocelli.

15. *Neope christi* (Oberth.). W. China. Similar: obertheuri (Leech), W. China, smaller, UP markings less vivid; simulans (Leech), W. China.

16. *Oeneis mongolica* (Oberth.). E. Mongolia.

17. *Oeneis sculda* (Ev.). Amurland. Similar: pumila (Stgr.), smaller and paler.

18. *Oeneis nanna* (Men.). Altai Mountains, Amurland, Korea.

19. *Oeneis urda* (Ev.). Amurland.

PLATE 204: Satyridae

1. *Oeneis tarpeja* (Pall.). S. Russia, Mongolia. Similar: buddha (Gr.-Gr.), Tibet, UP dots very faint.

2. *Palaeonympha opalina* (Btlr.). Yang-tse-kiang.

3. *Pararge climene* (Esp.). S. Russia, Turkey, Asia Minor, Armenia.

4. *Pararge deidamia* (Ev.). Urals through Siberia to China and Japan, Tibet. Similar: dumetorum (Oberth.), W. China, UPF light white dashes, female deidamia has rather broader dashes UPF.

5. *Pararge episcopalis* (Oberth.). Tibet, W. China. Similar: proeusta (Leech), W. China, UPF band reddish yellow.

6. *Pararge eversmanni* (Ev.). C. Asia, Turkestan, Pamirs.

7. *Pararge felix* (Warnecke). Arabia.

8. *Pseudochazara anthelia* (Hbn.). Asia Minor, Balkans.

9. *Pseudochazara regeli* (Alph.). Pamirs, Turkestan. Few subspecies.

10. *Pseudochazara regeli* (see 9).

11. *Rhaphicera dumicola* (Oberth.). W. China.

12. *Satyrus bischoffi* (H.-Sch.). Asia Minor, Armenia, Turkestan. Several subspecies.

13. *Satyrus palaearcticus* (Stgr.). Tibet, W. China.

14. *Pararge schrenckii* (Men.). Tibet to Amurland. Similar: epimenides (Men.), Korea, Japan, W. and C. China, smaller.

15. *Satyrus sybillina* (Oberth.). W. China.

16. *Satyrus thibetana* (Oberth.). Tibet, W. China.

17. *Triphysa phryne* (Pall.). S.E. Russia, Armenia, W. Siberia. Few subspecies.

18. *Ypthima asterope* (Klug.). Syria, Arabia, Africa, India to China. Similar: huebneri (Kirby), Kashmir, UNH ocelli arranged one and three.

19. *Triphysa phryne* (see 17).

PLATE 205: Satyridae

1. *Ypthima conjuncta* (Leech). W. and C. China. Similar: sakra (Moore), Assam, UN ocelli of different sizes.

2. *Ypthima praenubila* (Leech). W. and C. China.

3. *Ypthima iris* (Leech). W. China. Similar: ciris (Leech), W. China, UNH more than three ocelli.

4. *Ypthima insolita* (Leech). W. China. Similar: megalomma (Btlr.), larger, one UPF ocellus circular not oval ringed; beautei (Oberth.), smaller, darker, UPF ocelli large and prominent.

5. *Ypthima lisandra* (Cr.). Hong Kong, Tonkin.

6. *Ypthima motschulskyi* (Brem. & Grey.). W. and C. China, Korea, Formosa, Hong Kong. Several subspecies.

Lycaenidae

7. *Agrodiaetus erschoffi* (Led.). Iran. Similar: alcedo (Christ.), Bokhara, larger.

8. *Agrodiaetus poseidon* (Led.). Pamir, Asia Minor.

9. *Apharitis acamas* (Klug.). Turkestan to Arabia, Iran, N.W. India, N.E. Africa. Similar: epargyros (Eversm.); cilissa (Led.), Syria; Cigaritis zohra (Doug.), Algeria; Cigaritis siphax (Luc.), Algeria.

10. *Apharitis acamas* (see 9).

11. *Antigius butleri* (Fent.). Amurland, Japan. Similar: attilia (Brem.), C. and N. China, Japan; euthea (Jans.), W. China, Amurland, Japan.

12. *Antigius butleri* (see 11).

13. *Artopoetes pryeri* (Murr.). Amurland, Japan. Lfp: Syringa.

14. *Camena ctesia* (Hew.). Himalayas to W. China. Similar: icetas (Hew.).

15. *Camena icetas* (Hew.). Himalayas to W. China.

16. *Chaetoprocta odata* (Hew.). Himalayas.

17. *Chrysozephyrus ataxus* (Dbl. & Hew.). N.W. Himalayas, Tibet, W. China.

18. *Chrysozephyrus ataxus* (see 17).

19. *Chrysozephyrus duma* (Hew.). Sikkim. Male resembles syla, but broader black borders UP.

20. *Cordelia comes* (Leech). W. and C. China.

21. *Curetis acuta* (Moore). China, Japan.

Lfp: Pongamia.

22. *Curetis acuta* (see 21).

23. *Deudorix arata* (Brem.). Amurland, China, Korea, Japan.

24. *Epamera jordanus* (Stgr.). Jordan valley, Arabia.

25. *Esakiozephyrus bieti* (Oberth.). Tibet. UP purple.

26. *Esakiozephyrus icana* (Moore). Himalayas to W. China.

27. *Euaspa forsteri* (Esaki & Shirozu). Formosa.

28. *Everes fischeri* (Ev.). Siberia to Korea.

29. *Everes potanini* (Alph.). China to E. India. Similar: davidi (Pouj.), W. China; filicaudis (Pryer), N. and W. China.

30. *Favonius orientalis* (Murray). Japan. Similar: suffusa (Leech).

31. *Favonius saphirinus* (Stgr.). Similar: cognatus (Staud), Japan.

32. *Glaucopsyche lycormas* (Btlr.). E. Asia, Amurland, N. China, Japan.

33. *Heliophorus moorei* (Koll.). Tibet, W. and C. China, N. India. Similar: epicles (Godt.), India, Malaysia; sena (Koll.), Kashmir.

34. *Heodes ochimus* (H.Sch.). Pamirs, Iran. Male as solskyi (Ersch.).

35. *Heodes solskyi* (Ersch.). Kashmir, Samarkand. Similar: ochimus (H.Sch.); lampon (Led.), Iran, sometimes tailed.

PLATE 206: Lycaenidae

1. *Heodes solskyi* (see 205/35).

2. *Japonica saepestriata* (see 3).

3. *Japonica saepestriata* (Hew.). Amurland, Japan.

4. *Lycaena caspius* (Stgr.). Turkestan, Pamirs. Similar: sultan (Stgr.); sarthus (Stgr.).

5. *Lycaena li* (see 6).

6. *Lycaena li* (Oberth.). W. China.

7. *Lycaena splendens* (Stgr.). Mongolia, Amurland.

8. *Lycaena standfussi* (Gr.Grsh.). Tibet to W. China.

9. *Lycaena pang* (Oberth.). Sze-chuen.

10. *Lycaena tseng* (Oberth.). W. China.

11. *Lycaeides christophi* (Stgr.). Iran, Turkestan, Chitral, Himalayas. Subspecies samudra (Moore).

12. *Lycaeides cleobis* (Brem.). E. Asia to Korea and Japan.

13. *Lycaeides cleobis* (see 12).

14. *Maculinea arionides* (Stgr.). Amurland.

15. *Narathura japonica* (Murr.). Korea, Japan.

16. *Neolycaena tengstroemi* (Ersch.). C. Asia, Pamirs, N. China, Mongolia. Similar: rhymnus (Ev.), S. Russia, S. Siberia, UN markings white dots; sinensis (Alph.), Turkestan, smaller, white-spotted edge UPH.

17. *Neozephyrus taxila* (Brem.). Amurland, Korea, Japan.

18. *Niphanda fusca* (Brem. & Grey.). China to Korea and Japan, Amurland. Similar: cymbia (Nicer.), Sikkim to Burma.

19. *Orthomiella pontis* (Elw.). India, China. Similar: Chilades laius (Stoll.).

20. *Praephilotes anthracias* (Christoph.). Turkestan. UP male and female black-brown as Palaeophilotes triphysina (Stgr.).

21. *Panchala ganesa* (Moore). Kashmir, W. and C. China, Japan.

22. *Phengaris atroguttata* (Oberth.). Naga Hills to W. China.

23. *Plebejus eversmanni* (Stgr.). Pamir, Turkestan. Similar: lucifera (Stgr.), Tibet, Mongolia, UN markings more distinct; euripilus (Frr.), Asia Minor, Iraq, Iran.

24. *Polyommatus alcedo* (Christ.). Iran.

25. *Polyommatus devanica* (Moore). Kashmir.

26. *Polyommatus loewii* (see 27).

27. *Polyommatus loewii* (Z.). Asia Minor, Armenia, Iran, to Chitral.

28. *Polyommatus sieversii* (Christ.). Pamir, Iran, Turkestan. Similar: Vacciniina hyrcana (Led.).

29. *Rapala micans* (Brem. & Grey.). China. Form cismona (Fruh.) has orange patch UPF.

30. *Rapala selira* (Moore). Himalayas, Tibet.

31. *Satsuma pluto* (Leech). W. and C. China.

32. *Satsuma pratti* (Leech). W. and C. China. Similar: nicevillei (Leech), UN markings diffuse; circe (Leech).

33. *Shirozua melpomene* (Leech). China. Similar: lutea (Hew.), Amurland, Japan; Cordelia comes (Leech), W. and C. China.

34. *Spiridasis takanonis* (Mats.). Japan.

35. *Strymon herzi* (Fixs.). Amurland, Korea. Similar: thalia (Leech), C. China.

36. *Strymon ledereri* (Bsd.). Asia Minor, Armenia. Similar: lunulata (Ersch.), Asia Minor, N. Iran, Pamirs, no orange lunules UPH.

37. *Strymon v-album* (Leech). C. China. Similar: ornata (Leech).

38. *Strymon sassanides* (Koll.). Turkestan and Iran to Baluchistan and Kashmir.

39. *Turanana anisopthalma* (Koll.). N. Iran. Similar: Palaeophilotes triphysima

(Stgr.); Praephilotes anthracias (Christ.), Turkestan. UP male and female black-brown.

40. *Turanana cytis* (Christ.). Syria, Asia Minor, Iran, Turkestan.

41. *Teratozephyrus hecale* (Leech). W. China. Similar: Favonius saphirinus (Stgr.), Amurland, Korea, Japan.

42. *Teratozephyrus tsangkii* (Ob.). Szechwan.

43. *Tomares callimachus* (Ev.). Asia Minor, Iran, Iraq.

44. *Tomares fedtschenkoi* (Ersch.). Turkestan, Pamir.

45. *Tomares nogelii* (H.Sch.). Turkey to Armenia. Few subspecies.

46. *Tomares romanovi* (Christ.). Armenia.

47. *Taraka hamada* (Druce). Japan, Formosa.

48. *Ussuriana michaelis* (Oberth.). Amurland.

49. *Vacciniina hyrcana* (Led.). Iran. Similar: Polyommatus sieversi (Christ.), Pamirs, Iran.

50. *Vacciniina iris* (Stgr.). Turkestan. Female brown.

51. *Wagimo signata* (Btlr.). C. and W. China, Amurland, Japan.

52. *Zizeeria maha* (Koll.). Iran, Tibet, India, China, Japan, Burma. Lfp: Oxalis. Many subspecies.

53. *Zizeeria maha* (see 52).

PLATE 207: Nemeobiidae

1. *Dodona henrici* (Holl.). Hainan.

2. *Polycaena lua* (Grum.). Amdo.

3. *Polycaena tamerlana* (Stgr.). Tibet, Turkestan.

Libytheidae

4. *Libythea celtis* (Esp.). Spain to the Tyrol, N. Africa, Asia Minor, C. Asia. Similar: lepita (Moore), India to Japan.

Hesperiidae

5. *Abraximorpha davidii* (Mab.). Sze-chuen.

6. *Actinor radians* (Moore). N.W. Himalayas.

7. *Achalarus simplex* (Leech). W. China. Similar: bifasciatus (Brem.).

8. *Aeromachus inachus* (Men.). Amurland, Japan.

9. *Ampittia dalailama* (Mab.). Tibet, W. China.

10. *Ampittia trimacula* (Leech). W. China.

11. *Ampittia virgata* (Leech). China.

12. *Astictopterus henrici* (Holl.). W. China. UP black.

13. *Astictopterus olivascens* (Moore). C. and S. China. UP black-brown.

14. *Baoris leechii* (Elw.). W. and C. China.

15. *Barca bicolor* (Oberth.). Tibet.

16. *Bibasis aquilina* (Spr.). Amurland, Japan. Female has row of yellowish dots UPF.

17. *Bibasis septentrionis* (Fldr.). China, Sikkim.

18. *Borbo zelleri* (Led.). Syria, N. Africa.

19. *Capila jayadeva* (Moore). Sikkim. Female has hyaline band UPF. Similar: hainana (Crowley), Hainan, paler, male UP brown with one hyaline dot; zennara (Moore), Sikkim, larger, paler.

20. *Capila pennicillatum* (Nicer.). Khasi Hills to Canton.

21. *Capila pieridoides* (Moore). W. China. Female UP brown, resembles phanaeus male.

22. *Capila omeia* (Leech). W. China.

23. *Carterocephalus argyrostigma* (Ev.). China.

24. *Carterocephalus avanti* (Nicer.). Tibet, W. China.

25. *Carterocephalus houangty* (Oberth.). W. China. Female is much darker.

26. *Carterocephalus micio* (Oberth.). China.

27. *Carterocephalus pulchra* (Leech). Tibet, W. China.

28. *Carterocephalus niveomaculatus* (Oberth.). Tibet, W. and S. China. Similar: christophi (Gr.Grsh.), Tibet, larger white patch UPH; dieckmanni (Graes.), Amurland, W. China, more white spots UPF; flavo-maculatus (Oberth.), W. China, Tibet, brownish UP with yellow markings.

29. *Celaenorrhinus pulomaya* (Moore). Himalayas, W. China. Similar: maculosa (Fldr.), W. and C. China; aspersa (Leech), W. China; sumita (Moore), China; leucocera (Koll.), Himalayas to C. China.

PLATE 208: Hesperiidae

1. *Celaenorrhinus tibetana* (Mab.). W. China, Tibet.

2. *Coladenia sheila* (Evans). China. Similar: maeniata (Oberth.), Yannan, much paler, UPH hyaline patch smaller.

3. *Ctenoptilon vasava* (Moore). N. India to China.

4. *Daimio diversa* (Leech). C. China. Similar: sinica (Fldr.), W. and C. China to Malaya.

5. *Daimio phisara* (Moore). Hong Kong to N. India, Assam, S. Burma.

6. *Daimio tethys* (Men.). Amurland, N. China, Japan.

7. *Eogenes alcides* (H.Sch.). Kurdistan to Chitral. Similar: lesliei (Evans), Chitral, darker.

8. *Erionota grandis* (Leech). W. China.

9. *Erynnis montanus* (Brem.). Amurland, China, Japan.

10. *Hasora anura* (Nicer.). China. Female has three large white spots UP. Similar: salanga (Plotz), Malaya, greenish UN; danda (Evans), Karen Hills, bluish sheen UN.

11. *Halpe nephele* (Leech). W. China.

12. *Halpe porus* (Mab.). W. China, Hong Kong.

13. *Isoteinon lamprospilus* (Fldr.). China, Japan.

14. *Leptalina unicolor* (Brem.). Amurland, C. China, Japan. UP black.

15. *Lobocla nepos* (Oberth.). W. China. Similar: germanus (Oberth.), China.

16. *Lotongus sarala* (Nicer.). Assam to W. China.

17. *Ochlodes bouddha* (Mab.). China. Similar: crateis (Leech).

18. *Ochlodes subhyalina* (Brem. & Grey.). Assam, China, Korea, Japan.

19. *Odina decoratus* (Hew.). Tonkin, China, Assam, Burma.

20. *Onryza maga* (Leech). China.

21. *Pedesta baileyi* (South). W. China. Terrain: high altitudes.

22. *Pedesta blanchardi* (Mab.). W. and C. China.

23. *Pedesta masunerisis* (Moore). Himalayas to Assam. Subspecies tail (Swinhoe) has yellow markings.

24. *Pelopidas jansonis* (Btlr.). Japan.

25. *Polytremis caerulescens* (Mab.). W. China.

26. *Polytremis pellucida* (Murr.). Amurland, C. China, Japan. Similar: Pelopidas jansonis (Btlr.), Japan, lighter colour; lubricans (Matsumara), Malaysia to Japan, UNH markings very faint.

27. *Potanthus flava* (Murray). China, Japan, Philippines. Similar: pseudomaesa (Moore), Ceylon.

28. *Pyrgus breti* (Oberth.). W. China, Tibet. Similar: oberthueri (Leech), W. and S. China, paler UN.

29. *Pyrgus thibetanus* (Oberth.). W. China. Similar: maculata (Brem. & Grey), Amurland, N. and C. China.

30. *Satarupa nymphalis* (Spr.). Amurland, N. and C. China.

31. *Scobura cephaloides* (Nicer.). Burma, Assam, Tonkin.

32. *Sebastonyma dolopia* (Hew.). Himalayas, Assam.

33. *Seseria formosana* (Fruh.). Formosa.

34. *Seseria sambara* (Moore). Assam to Indo-China. A few similar species.

35. *Sovia albipectus* (Nicer.). Burma, Indo-China.

36. *Sovia subflava* (Leech). W. China, Assam. Similar: grahami (Evans), Assam, no dark area UNF; hyrtacus (Nicer.), S. India, large whitened areas UN.

37. *Taractrocera flavoides* (Leech). W. China.

38. *Thoressa bivitta* (Oberth.). W. China.

39. *Thoressa bivitta* (see 38).

40. *Thoressa varia* (Murr.). Japan.

41. *Thymelicus sylvatica* (Brem.). Amurland and Japan. Similar: nervulata (Mab.), W. China; leonina (Btlr.), Amurland, Japan, brighter, paler UP.

42. *Udaspes stellata* (Oberth.). China.

Index

Numerical references in italic figures refer to text only

nigrina Delias, 159/15
nigripennis Phyciodes, 40/35
nigrita Ancistroides, 185/4
niha Laringa, 146/16
nimbice Catasticta, 49/1
nina Mesosemia, 75/17
ninias Nymphidium, 76/24
ninonia Hypothiris, 46/28
niobe Acraea, 108/54
– Catasticta, 49/4
– Fabriciana, 2/16, 2/18
– Lepidochrysops, 124/11
nipalicus Spindasis, 181/3
Niphanda, 179, 206
– Symbrenthia, 151/16
niphon Incisalia, 19/30
nireus Papilio, 90/17
nirmala Callerebia, 162/7
nirvana Neptis, 148/14
nirwana Caltoris, 185/25
nisa Eurema, 17/33
nise Ceratinia, 45/17, 45/18
– Eurema, 50/26
nissa Rapala, 180/31
nitebis Charaxes, 141/11
nitetis Neptis, 148/15
nitida Epitola, 122/25
– Lamprolenis, 166/10
– Menander, 75/9
nitocris Hyalothyrus, 83/16
– Speyeria, 16/7
– Speyeria, 16/8
nitra Papilio, 12/14
nivalis Allotinus, 174/5
nivalis Cyrestis, 142/13
nivaria Bebearia, 93/12
nivea Cyrestis, 142/13
– Lymanopoda, 59/3
– Neomyrina, 179/22
niveicornis Chondrolepis, 128/56
nivella Heliopetes, 83/14
niveomaculatus Carterocephalus, 207/28
niveonotis Phyciodes, 41/26
niveostriga Kedestes, 129/38
niveus Colotis, 112/28
– Lachnocnema, 123/39
nobilis Charaxes, 96/17
– Euryphura, 102/23
– Mycalesis, 117/13, 118/2
– Papilio, 90/18
Noctuana, 84
noctula Hades, 74/2
nogelii Tomares, 206/45
nohara Acraea, 108/55
nokomis Speyeria, 16/8
nolckeni Coenonympha, 200/9
nomenia Hypomyrina, 123/21
nomion Parnassius, 191/16
nomius Graphium, 131/23
noquasa Harpendyreus, 123/5
nora Nacaduba, 178/43
norbana Eurema, 160/16
nordmanni Parnassius, 191/25
Nordmannia, 10
norica Eunica, 37/12
– Marpesia, 38/16
norina Symmachia, 79/2
normani Narathura, 179/19
norna Oeneis, 8/8
northbrundii Phyciodes, 41/27
nortia Calycopis, 67/7
– Magneuptychia, 60/3
noseda Carystoides, 81/28
Nosphistia, 84

nossima Amauris, 110/21
nostrodamus Gegenes, 11/16, 11/17
nota Thecla, 68/6
notha Catasticta, 49/2
Notheme, 76
nothis Coelites, 162/14
Notocrypta, 187
nortia Euptychia, 58/2
nossis Euptychoides, 58/18
nothus Ceratricia, 128/54
notilla Pteronymia, 47/39
notoba Scolitantides, 126/37
nottoana Eagris, 129/5
nourmahal Stichopthalma, 138/9
noureddin Thaumantis, 139/7
novatus Heliconius, 44/22
nox Parides, 135/7
nubifer Uranothauma, 127/26
nubifera Liptena, 124/41
nubigena Euphydryas, 13/27
nubila Calisto, 55/10
– Mylothris, 114/4
nugar Thecla, 68/33
numata Heliconius, 44/23
numen Thecla, 68/16
numenes Charaxes, 96/16, 97/1
numidia Anetia, 43/24
numilia Catonephele, 34/12, 34/13
numitor Ancyloxipha, 21/9
nurscia Mimoniades, 83/42
nursei Epamera, 122/4
nussia Phyciodes, 41/8
nyassae Alaena, 119/10
– Fresna, 129/13
nycteis Apatura, 193/14
– Chlosyne, 13/15, 13/16
– Parnes, 77/21
Nyctelius, 84
– Nyctelius, 84/18
nycteris Exometoeca, 186/24
nycteus Neptis, 148/16
– Nymula, 76/30
nyctimene Perisama, 40/12
nyctimus Catonephele, 34/14, 34/15
nympha Phulia, 52/23
nymphaea Phulia, 52/23
Nymphalis, 2, 14
nymphalis Satarupa, 208/30
nymphidia Stiboges, 184/3
Nymphidium, 76
nymphidioides Nymula, 76/30
Nymula, 76, 77
nysa Amblyscirites, 21/10
– Delias, 159/21
nyseus Talicada, 181/23, 181/24
nysiades Neptis, 105/13
nysias Pierocolias, 53/16, 53/17

O
Oarisma, 22
obeira Acraea, 109/2
– Acraea, 109/24
oberthueri Aemona, 192/7
obertheuri Neope, 203/15
oberthuri Acraea, 109/3
– Alaena, 119/8
– Aporia, 199/1
oberthueri Eurytides, 24/7
– Pyrgus, 208/28
obliquans Iambrix, 187/13
Oboronia, 125
obscura Cethosia, 141/5
– Isma, 187/21

– Mycalesis, 116/15
– Pachyneuria, 84/37
obscurus Anastrus, 80/21
– Thestor, 127/18
obsoleta Lymanopoda, 59/6
obvinus Nessaea, 39/18, 39/19
ocalea Corbulis, 45/20
occidentalis Argyrogramma, 70/27
occidentalium Asterope, 92/15
– Pentila, 126/2
occitanica Melanargia, 8/1
oceia Baoris, 185/10
Ocella, 84
ocelloides Euptychia, 18/16, 58/12
ochimus Heodes, 205/34, 205/35
ochlea Amauris, 110/21
Ochlodes, 11, 22, 208
ochracea Coenonympha, 6/6
– Henotesia, 115/9
– Mylothris, 114/14
– Neptis, 105/2
ochrotaenia Pedaliodes, 62/4
Ochus, 187
ochus Eutychide, 82/58
– Panthiades, 67/22
ocna Hypothiris, 46/29
ocnus Erebia, 200/21
– Magneuptychia, 60/4, 60/5
ocola Panoquina, 22/22
ocrinus Paraides, 80/17
ocrisia Thecla, 68/50
octavia Precis, 105/29, 105/30
octavius Anaea, 32/6
octocula Hypolimnas, 146/6
octogramma Bebearia, 93/13
octomaculata Polythrix, 85/24
oculatissima Lethe, 202/7
ocyalus Mimoniades, 83/40
Ocyba, 84
Ocybadistes, 187
ocypete Argyreuptychia, 54/11
ocypore Emesis, 72/21
oda Heliophorus, 176/15
odana Deudorix, 121/34
– Thaumantis, 139/8
odata Chaetoprocta, 205/16
odice Mesosemia, 75/30
odila Pheraeus, 85/11
odin Graphium, 89/10
Odina, 187, 208
Odontoptilum, 187, 188
oedipodea Bibasis, 185/19
oedippus Coenonympha, 6/4
oeme Erebia, 6/17
oemilius Cymothoe, 99/12
oenanthe Ithomia, 46/41
Oeneis, 8, 18, 19, 203, 204
oenomais Anaea, 32/8
Oenomaus, 67
Oeonus, 84
Oerane, 188
ofella Phyciodes, 40/38
ogawena Osphantes, 130/1
ognes Epamera, 121/51
ogygia Zographetus, 189/29
Ogyris, 179, 180
ohara Telicota, 189/11
oileus Caligo, 29/3
– Lasaia, 74/16
olbia Thecla, 68/11
olane Ogyris, 179/35
olena Aeria, 45/9
Oleria, 47
oleris Thecla, 68/20
Oligoria, 22
olinda Nymphidium, 76/22
olivascens Astictopterus, 207/13

olivencia Mesosemia, 75/31
– Phyciodes, 40/34
olympia Euchloe, 17/21
olympias Eunica, 37/1
olympia Eutychide, 82/59
– Leptophobia, 51/22
– Leptophobia, 53/6
olynthia Adelpha, 30/19
Olyras, 47
omaha Potanthus, 188/29
omeia Capila, 207/22
– Euthalia, 144/18
omois Nymphidium, 76/23
omphale Colotis, 112/29
– Porphyrogenes, 85/32
omphisa Albulina, 174/1
omrina Heliopetes, 83/15
onaeum Nymphidium, 76/25
onara Lotongus, 187/28
oncaea Acraea, 109/4, 109/5
oncidia Corbulis, 45/22
onolaus Tenaris, 138/21
Onophas, 84
onophis Anaea, 32/7
onopordi Pyrgus, 11/28
Onryza, 208
ontario Strymon, 20/33
onyx Horaga, 176/22
oodes Ogyris, 180/1
orolina Corbulis, 45/22
oopaca Liptena, 124/42
opalescens Euselasia, 73/23
opalina Palaeonympha, 204/2
– Pantoporia, 149/10
opalinus Cheimas, 55/14
ophelia Thecla, 68/51
ophidicephalus Papilio, 90/19
ophione Neptidopsis, 104/17
ophites Wallengrenia, 88/10
ophiusa Hypoleucis, 129/29
opigena Thespieus, 87/33
opis Cynandra, 100/3
– Speyeria, 15/12
Opoptera, 29
oppelii Perisama, 40/10
Opsiphanes, 29
optilete Vacciniina, 11/7
optima Callithea, 34/9
orabilis Eurytides, 23/24
– Parides, 26/4
Oraidium, 125
orbifera Lasiophila, 59/5
orbis Phoebis, 52/12, 52/20
orbitulus Albulina, 9/6, 9/7
orbona Mesosemia, 75/32
orcas Aphnaeus, 120/24, 120/25
– Celastrina, 175/25
– Polygonia, 14/25
orchamus Xeniades, 88/31
orcidia Calycopis, 67/14
orcilla Thecla, 69/37
orcus Pronophila, 64/8
orcynia Thecla, 68/52
ordinata Euptychia, 64/13
ordys Phyciodes, 14/16
– Hypocysta, 166/6
orea Epiphile, 36/29
oreala Thecla, 68/53
oreas Acraea, 109/6
– Araschnia, 193/13
– Corbulis, 45/21
oreides Phocides, 85/15
Oreisplanus, 188
orellana Parides, 26/18
Oressinoma, 61
orestes Nymula, 76/31
orestia Acraea, 109/8

orestilla Oleria, 47/28
orfita Euselasia, 73/29
orgia Thecla, 69/1, 69/2
oriana Corbulis, 45/21
oriander Drephalys, 82/31
oribazus Papilio, 89/24, 90/11
orientalis Favonius, 175/35, 205/30
Orimba, 77
orina Acraea, 109/7
Orinoma, 171
orion Historis, 38/10
– Scolitantides, 10/28, 10/29
– Typhedanus, 87/50
orise Dismorphia, 50/4
orissa Cirrochroa, 142/1
orites Catonephele, 34/14
orithya Precis, 150/6
orleans Parnassius, 191/26
orma Mopala, 129/62
ornata Hesperilla, 187/9
– Platypthima, 171/3
– Strymon, 206/37
ornatrix Theritas, 69/45
Orneates, 84
Ornipholidotos, 125
Ornithoptera, 132, 133, 134
ornychion Papilio, 12/5
oroatis Mycalesis, 170/9
orobis Thecla, 69/3
oroetes Ogyris, 180/1
orolina Corbulis, 45/22
oropa Metron, 83/36
orphana Dinoptotis, 72/2, 72/19
orphna Laxita, 183/15, 183/16
Orphe, 84
orpheus Cheritra, 175/30, 180/38
orphise Eunica, 37/14
orsedice Proboscis, 64/7
Orses, 84
orseis Mycalesis, 170/10
– Phyciodes, 14/13
orsilochus Marpesia, 39/1
orsina Thecla, 68/32
orsis Myscelia, 39/13, 39/14
Orsotriaena, 171
orthia Phyciodes, 41/9
orthodice Tatochila, 53/15
Orthomiella, 206
Orthos, 84
– Orthos, 84/28
ortygia Hypoleria, 46/12
– Lepidochrysops, 124/16
ortygnus Oenomaus, 67/20
o–rubrum Liptena, 124/43, 124/44
orus Lycaena, 125/9
oryx Cacropterus, 81/32
oscari Acraea, 109/9
oscarus Clossiana, 194/14
osiris Euchrysops, 122/44
osiris Theritas, 69/45
ossuna Ithomia, 46/37
osteria Eulaceura, 143/4, 143/5
osuna Napeogenes, 47/19
osyris Ebrietas, 82/38
– Hypocysta, 166/6
otacilia Anthene, 120/7
othna Thespieus, 87/34
otho Wallengrenia, 22/47
othoe Dismorphia, 49/30
othona Chliaria, 175/34
otis Zizina, 182/10
otlauga Liptena, 124/47

oto Hypoleria, 46/13
otolais Pyrrhogyra, 42/6
otraeda Hypokopelates, 123/13
otriades Chrysoplectrum, 81/45
ottoe Hesperia, 22/5
ottomana Erebia, 6/20
ottomanus Heodes, 9/29
ottonis Laringa, 146/16
ouida Dodona, 183/10, 183/11
Ouleus, 84
oulita Hypothiris, 46/30
Ourochnemis, 77
outis Cogia, 81/52
ovinia Atrytonopsis, 81/2
Oxeoschistus, 61
oxida Thecla, 68/45
oxione Bebearia, 92/20
oxleyi Zizina, 182/11
Oxylides, 125
oxylus Leptoneura, 116/15
Oxynetra, 84
oxynius Papilio, 25/7
Oxynthes, 84
ozema Mylon, 83/59
ozias Lychnuchoides, 83/32
ozomene Actinote, 43/16

P
Paches, 84
Pachlioptera, 132, 133
Pachyneuria, 84
Pachythone, 77
pacifica Callicore, 33/17
– Pierella, 63/5
pactolus Nacaduba, 178/44
pactyes Pedaliodes, 62/1
pacuvius Erynnis, 21/33
padma Satyrus, 172/8
paeania Mygona, 60/14
paeon Euptychia, 58/13
– Papilio, 12/5
pagenstecheri Ariadne, 92/7
– Hypochrysops, 176/46
pais Themone, 79/10
palades Lasiophila, 59/5
– Pachythone, 77/16
palaearcticus Satyrus, 204/13
palaemon Carterocephalus, 11/12
palaeno Colias, 4/7
Palaeochrysophanus, 10
Palaeonympha, 204
palamedes Papilio, 12/12
palegon Thecla, 69/9
palemon Cacyreus, 120/54
pales Boloria, 1/17, 1/23
palguna Tanaecia, 152/3
palia Phyciodes, 41/25
palinurus Papilio, 135/2
Palla, 105, 107
palla Chlosyne, 13/9
palladia Argyreuptychia, 58/17
pallas Melitaea, 196/6
– Siseme, 78/27
pallene Aphniolaus, 120/28
– Colotis, 113/5
pallida Achlyodes, 80/5
– Cnodontes, 121/16
pallidula Dismorphia, 49/30
palmeii Apodemia, 20/39
palmus Poecilmitis, 126/25
pammenes Pedaliodes, 62/2
– Potamanaxas, 84/50
Pampasatyrus, 61
pamphanis Penetes, 29/21
pamphilus Coenonympha, 6/5

306   INDEX